*New Beaco

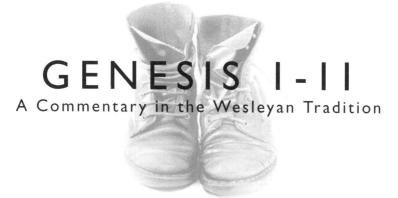

GENESIS 1-11

A Commentary in the Wesleyan Tradition

Joseph Coleson

BEACON HILL PRESS
OF KANSAS CITY

Copyright 2012
by Beacon Hill Press of Kansas City

ISBN 978-0-8341-2403-5

Printed in the United States of America

Cover Design: J.R. Caines
Interior Design: Sharon Page

Library of Congress Cataloging-in-Publication Data

Coleson, Joseph E., 1947-
    Genesis 1-11 / Joseph Coleson.
        pages cm. — (New Beacon Bible commentary)
    Includes bibliographical references.
    ISBN 978-0-8341-2403-5 (pbk.)
    1. Bible. O.T. Genesis I-XI—Commentaries. I. Title.
    BS1235.53.C64 2012
    222'.1107—dc23

                                                                                      2012035652

10 9 8 7 6 5 4 3 2 1

DEDICATION

To Charlotte
In whom my heart safely trusts

COMMENTARY EDITORS

CONTENTS

GENERAL EDITORS' PREFACE

The purpose of the New Beacon Bible Commentary is to make available to pastors and students in the twenty-first century a biblical commentary that reflects the best scholarship in the Wesleyan theological tradition. The commentary project aims to make this scholarship accessible to a wider audience to assist them in their understanding and proclamation of Scripture as God's Word.

Writers of the volumes in this series not only are scholars within the Wesleyan theological tradition and experts in their field but also have special interest in the books assigned to them. Their task is to communicate clearly the critical consensus and the full range of other credible voices who have commented on the Scriptures. Though scholarship and scholarly contribution to the understanding of the Scriptures are key concerns of this series, it is not intended as an academic dialogue within the scholarly community. Commentators of this series constantly aim to demonstrate in their work the significance of the Bible as the church's book and the contemporary relevance and application of the biblical message. The project's overall goal is to make available to the church and for her service the fruits of the labors of scholars who are committed to their Christian faith.

The *New International Version* (NIV) is the reference version of the Bible used in this series; however, the focus of exegetical study and comments is the biblical text in its original language. When the commentary uses the NIV, it is printed in bold. The text printed in bold italics is the translation of the author. Commentators also refer to other translations where the text may be difficult or ambiguous.

The structure and organization of the commentaries in this series seeks to facilitate the study of the biblical text in a systematic and methodical way. Study of each biblical book begins with an **Introduction** section that gives an overview of authorship, date, provenance, audience, occasion, purpose, sociological/cultural issues, textual history, literary features, hermeneutical issues, and theological themes necessary to understand the book. This section also includes a brief outline of the book and a list of general works and standard commentaries.

The commentary section for each biblical book follows the outline of the book presented in the introduction. In some volumes, readers will find section **overviews** of large portions of scripture with general comments on their overall literary structure and other literary features. A consistent feature of the commentary is the paragraph-by-paragraph study of biblical texts. This section has three parts: **Behind the Text**, **In the Text**, and **From the Text**.

The goal of the **Behind the Text** section is to provide the reader with all the relevant information necessary to understand the text. This includes specific historical situations reflected in the text, the literary context of the text, sociological and cultural issues, and literary features of the text.

In the Text explores what the text says, following its verse-by-verse structure. This section includes a discussion of grammatical details, word studies, and the connectedness of the text to other biblical books/passages or other parts of the book being studied (the canonical relationship). This section provides transliterations of key words in Hebrew and Greek and their literal meanings. The goal here is to explain what the author would have meant and/ or what the audience would have understood as the meaning of the text. This is the largest section of the commentary.

The **From the Text** section examines the text in relation to the following areas: theological significance, intertextuality, the history of interpretation, use of the Old Testament scriptures in the New Testament, interpretation in later church history, actualization, and application.

The commentary provides **sidebars** on topics of interest that are important but not necessarily part of an explanation of the biblical text. These topics are informational items and may cover archaeological, historical, literary, cultural, and theological matters that have relevance to the biblical text. Occasionally, longer detailed discussions of special topics are included as **excurses.**

We offer this series with our hope and prayer that readers will find it a valuable resource for their understanding of God's Word and an indispensable tool for their critical engagement with the biblical texts.

Roger Hahn, Centennial Initiative General Editor
Alex Varughese, General Editor (Old Testament)
George Lyons, General Editor (New Testament)

ACKNOWLEDGMENTS

One great joy of a lifetime in biblical scholarship is discovery of the continual unfolding of God's story, of God's passion for creation—including God's beloved human daughters and sons. To be invited to put into the hands of our brothers and sisters a small portion of this treasure with which God has gifted us is a rare privilege and honor. Together with my fellow contributors, I am delighted to express my thanks to NPH for publishing this new commentary series "in the Wesleyan tradition." I pray it will be useful for many years. Thanks to the director of Beacon Hill Press, Bonnie Perry, and her stellar editorial team, for making the vision a reality.

I have studied, taught, and written on Genesis for thirty-five years, now. Through successive drafts of what I had thought to say, OT editor Alex Varughese advised on what to emphasize and what to lay aside for *this* volume. Without his scholarship and editorial wisdom, the work would be much diminished, and I would be much abashed. Thank you, Alex. (Of course, remaining errors and other shortcomings are mine, not his.)

Along the way, many have helped equip me for this venture. Some of my mentors have passed on: Leo Cox and Duane Thompson of Marion College (now IWU); Wilbur Dayton of Asbury Seminary; Anson Rainey and Douglas Young of the IHLS (now JUC); Benjamin Mazar and Abraham Malamat of the Hebrew University, Jerusalem; Nahum Sarna of Brandeis University. May they rest in God's peace.

If I could name only one mentor, of course it would be my doctor-father and dear friend, Dwight W. Young; he is without peer. Professor and Mrs. Young, may God continue to bless you.

I am glad to extend special thanks to the Board of Trustees and the administrative team of Nazarene Theological Seminary: President Ron Benefiel, Dean Roger Hahn, and Dean Marty Butler. The seminary's generous sabbatical policy has enabled me to work on this volume across two sabbatical leaves.

Countless others I must leave unnamed: student colleagues; teachers/professors, and other mentors; faculty colleagues and students at institutions of higher learning on four continents; scholars whose writing has informed and inspired me—many I count as friends, while others I have not met; members/friends of the congregations I have been privileged to serve as pastor.

Perhaps it is only a lame excuse for one whose stock-in-trade is words, but I think not. Words truly are inadequate to acknowledge and thank those nearest and dearest: first, my wife, Charlotte, for her unfailing love, support, and encouragement. Our children and their families have been inconvenienced by Dad's need to write; they have borne it with patience and grace. Charlotte's parents, Rev. and Mrs. H. B. West, have been generous hosts on numerous occasions, creating space for intensive concentration.

Our seven-year-old grandchildren, Madelyn and Joseph, have had a part. Many times, they resigned themselves to Grandpa's going off to his office when, at that moment, we would rather have been on some other adventure together. Their presence has made me mindful always of writing for them and their generation. And so I come around again to where I began: grateful humility is the only proper response to the privilege of opening for others a small window into the awesome reality of God's passionate love and care for all God's "very good" creation—including, of course, you and me. May God bless your study, as God has blessed mine, of the beginning of God's story upon this earth.

ABBREVIATIONS

With a few exceptions, these abbreviations follow those in *The SBL Handbook of Style* (Alexander 1999).

General

*	unattested form
A.D.	anno Domini (precedes date) (equivalent to C.E.)
B.C.	before Christ (follows date) (equivalent to B.C.E.)
B.C.E.	before the Common Era
C.E.	Common Era
cf.	compare
ch	chapter
chs	chapters
e.g.	*exempli gratia*, for example
esp.	especially
etc.	*et cetera*, and the rest
f(f).	and the following one(s)
fem.	feminine
Gk.	Greek
Heb.	Hebrew
i.e.	*id est.*, that is
ktl	*kai ta loipa* (Gk.: etc.)
lit.	literally
LXX	Septuagint
masc.	masculine
MS	manuscript
MSS	manuscripts
MT	Masoretic Text (of the OT)
n.	note
n.d.	no date
n.p.	no place; no publisher; no page
nn.	notes
NT	New Testament
OT	Old Testament
passim	here and there
pl.	plural
Q	Qumran
ref.	reference
Repr.	Reprint(ed)
sg.	singular
s.v.	*sub verbo*, under the word
v	verse
vs.	versus
vv	verses

Modern Edition of the Bible

BHS	*Biblia Hebraica Stuttgartensia*

Modern English Versions of the Bible

ESV	English Standard Version
JPS	Hebrew-Jewish Tanakh
KJV	King James Version
NASB	New American Standard Bible
NIV	New International Version (1984 ed.)
NKJV	New King James Version
NLT	New Living Translation
NRSV	New Revised Standard Version

Print Conventions for Translations

Bold font   NIV (bold without quotation marks in the text under study; elsewhere in the regular font, with quotation marks and no further identification)

Bold italic font   Author's translation (without quotation marks)

Behind the Text: Literary or historical background information average readers might not know from reading the biblical text alone

In the Text: Comments on the biblical text, words, phrases, grammar, and so forth

From the Text: The use of the text by later interpreters, contemporary relevance, theological and ethical implications of the text, with particular emphasis on Wesleyan concerns

Old Testament

Gen	Genesis
Exod	Exodus
Lev	Leviticus
Num	Numbers
Deut	Deuteronomy
Josh	Joshua
Judg	Judges
Ruth	Ruth
1—2 Sam	1—2 Samuel
1—2 Kgs	1—2 Kings
1—2 Chr	1—2 Chronicles
Ezra	Ezra
Neh	Nehemiah
Esth	Esther
Job	Job
Ps/Pss	Psalm/Psalms
Prov	Proverbs
Eccl	Ecclesiastes
Song	Song of Songs / Song of Solomon
Isa	Isaiah
Jer	Jeremiah
Lam	Lamentations
Ezek	Ezekiel

Dan	Daniel
Hos	Hosea
Joel	Joel
Amos	Amos
Obad	Obadiah
Jonah	Jonah
Mic	Micah
Nah	Nahum
Hab	Habakkuk
Zeph	Zephaniah
Hag	Haggai
Zech	Zechariah
Mal	Malachi

(Note: Chapter and verse numbering in the MT and LXX often differ compared to those in English Bibles. To avoid confusion, all biblical references follow the chapter and verse numbering in English translations, even when the text in the MT and LXX is under discussion.)

New Testament

Matt	Matthew
Mark	Mark
Luke	Luke
John	John
Acts	Acts
Rom	Romans
1—2 Cor	1—2 Corinthians
Gal	Galatians
Eph	Ephesians
Phil	Philippians
Col	Colossians
1—2 Thess	1—2 Thessalonians
1—2 Tim	1—2 Timothy
Titus	Titus
Phlm	Philemon
Heb	Hebrews
Jas	James
1—2 Pet	1—2 Peter
1—2—3 John	1—2—3 John
Jude	Jude
Rev	Revelation

Apocrypha

APOT	*The Apocrypha and Pseudepigrapha of the Old Testament.* Edited by R. H. Charles. 2 vols. Oxford, 1913.
Bar	Baruch
Add Dan	Additions to Daniel
Pr Azar	Prayer of Azariah
Bel	Bel and the Dragon
Sg Three	Song of the Three Young Men
Sus	Susanna
1—2 Esd	1—2 Esdras
Add Esth	Additions to Esther
Ep Jer	Epistle of Jeremiah
Jdt	Judith
1—2 Macc	1—2 Maccabees
3—4 Macc	3—4 Maccabees
Pr Man	Prayer of Manasseh
Ps 151	Psalm 151
Sir	Sirach/Ecclesiasticus
Tob	Tobit
Wis	Wisdom of Solomon

OT Pseudepigrapha

Apoc. Ab.	*Apocalypse of Abraham*
2 Bar.	*2 Baruch* (*Syriac Apocalypse*)

1 En.	1 Enoch (Ethiopic Apocalypse)
2 En.	2 Enoch (Slavonic Apocalypse)
3 En.	3 Enoch (Hebrew Apocalypse)
4 Ezra	4 Ezra
Jub.	Jubilees
Pss. Sol.	Psalms of Solomon
Sib. Or.	Sibylline Oracles

Greek and Latin Works

| Geogr. | Strabo, Geographica (Geography) |

Other Rabbinic Works

| Gen. Rab. | Genesis Rabbah |

Greek Transliteration

Greek	Letter	English
α	alpha	a
β	bēta	b
γ	gamma	g
γ	gamma nasal	n (before γ, κ, ξ, χ)
δ	delta	d
ε	epsilon	e
ζ	zēta	z
η	ēta	ē
θ	thēta	th
ι	iōta	i
κ	kappa	k
λ	lambda	l
μ	mu	m
ν	nu	n
ξ	xi	x
ο	omicron	o
π	pi	p
ρ	rhō	r
ρ	initial rhō	rh
σ/ς	sigma	s
τ	tau	t
υ	upsilon	y
υ	upsilon	u (in diphthongs: au, eu, ēu, ou, ui)
φ	phi	ph
χ	chi	ch
ψ	psi	ps
ω	ōmega	ō
'	rough breathing	h (before initial vowels or diphthongs)

Hebrew Consonant Transliteration

Hebrew/ Aramaic	Letter	English
א	alef	ʾ
ב	bet	b
ג	gimel	g
ד	dalet	d
ה	he	h
ו	vav	v or w
ז	zayin	z
ח	khet	ḥ
ט	tet	ṭ
י	yod	y
כ/ך	kaf	k
ל	lamed	l
מ/ם	mem	m
נ/ן	nun	n
ס	samek	s
ע	ayin	ʿ
פ/ף	pe	p; f (spirant)
צ/ץ	tsade	ṣ
ק	qof	q
ר	resh	r
ש	sin	ś
ש	shin	š
ת	tav	t; th (spirant)

BIBLIOGRAPHY

Albright, W. F. 1920-21. "A Colony of Cretan Mercenaries on the Coast of the Negeb." *Journal of the Palestine Oriental Society* 1:187-94.

_____. 1922. "The Location of the Garden of Eden." *American Journal of Semitic Languages and Literatures* 39:15-31.

Alter, Robert. 1981. *The Art of Biblical Narrative.* New York: Basic Books.

Arnold, Bill T. 2009. *Genesis.* The New Cambridge Bible Commentary 1. New York: Cambridge University Press.

Astour, Michael C. 1965. "Sabtah and Sabteca: Egyptian Pharaoh Names in Genesis 10." *Journal of Biblical Literature* 84:422-25.

Bird, Phyllis. 1981. "'Male and Female He Created Them': Gen 1:27b in the Context of the Priestly Account of Creation." *Harvard Theological Review* 74:129-51.

Botterweck, G. J., and Ringgren, H., eds. 1977-2006. *Theological Dictionary of the Old Testament.* Grand Rapids: Eerdmans.

Brueggemann, Walter. 1982. *Genesis.* Interpretation: A Bible Commentary for Teaching and Preaching. Atlanta: John Knox.

Bush, Frederic Wm. 1996. Ruth 4:17: A Semantic Wordplay. Pages 3-14 in *Go to the Land I Will Show You: Studies in Honor of Dwight W. Young.* Edited by Joseph E. Coleson and Victor H. Matthews. Winona Lake, Ind.: Eisenbrauns.

Cassuto, Umberto. 1961. *A Commentary on the Book of Genesis: Part One: From Adam to Noah, Genesis I—VI 8.* Jerusalem: Magnes.

_____. 1964. *A Commentary on the Book of Genesis: Part Two: From Noah to Abraham, Genesis VI 9—XI 32.* Jerusalem: Magnes.

Clarke, Adam. n.d. *The Holy Bible . . . with A Commentary and Critical Notes: The Old Testament, Volume I—Genesis to Deuteronomy.* New York: Abingdon-Cokesbury.

Cross, Frank Moore. 1973. *Canaanite Myth and Hebrew Epic.* Cambridge: Harvard University Press.

Dahood, Mitchell. 1979. "Ebla, Ugarit, and the Old Testament." *Theology Digest* 27:129.

Dorsey, David A. 1999. *The Literary Structure of the Old Testament: A Commentary on Genesis-Malachi.* Grand Rapids: Baker Academic.

Freedman, R. David. 1983. "Woman, a Power Equal to Man." *Biblical Archaeology Review* 9:56-58.

Fretheim, Terence E. 1994. Genesis. *New Interpreter's Bible,* Vol. 1. Nashville: Abingdon.

_____. 2005. *God and World in the Old Testament: A Relational Theology of Creation.* Nashville: Abingdon.

Gordon, Cyrus H. 1971. *Before Columbus.* New York: Crown.

_____. 1978. "The Wine Dark Sea." *Journal of Near Eastern Studies* 37:51-52.

Greathouse, William M. 1998. *Wholeness in Christ: Toward a Biblical Theology of Holiness.* Kansas City: Beacon Hill Press of Kansas City.

Hamilton, Victor P. 1990. *The Book of Genesis, Chapters 1-17.* New International Commentary on the Old Testament. Grand Rapids: Eerdmans.

Harrison, R. K. 1969. *Introduction to the Old Testament.* Grand Rapids: Eerdmans.

Heidel, Alexander. 1951. *The Babylonian Genesis.* Chicago: University of Chicago Press.

_____. 1963. *The Gilgamesh Epic and Old Testament Parallels.* Chicago: University of Chicago Press.

Hess, Richard S. 2009. *Studies in the Personal Names of Genesis 1—11.* Winona Lake, Ind.: Eisenbrauns.

Hess, Richard S., and David Toshio Tsumura, eds. 1994. *I Studied Inscriptions from Before the Flood: Ancient Near Eastern, Literary, and Linguistic Approaches to Genesis 1—11.* Winona Lake, Ind.: Eisenbrauns.

Hoenig, S. B. 1979. "Tarshish." *Jewish Quarterly Review* 9:181-82.

Kaiser, Walter C., Jr. 1988. *Hard Sayings of the Old Testament.* Downers Grove, Ill.: InterVarsity Press.

Kidner, Derek. 1967. *Genesis: An Introduction and Commentary.* Tyndale Old Testament Commentaries. Downers Grove, Ill.: InterVarsity.

Kroeger, Catherine Clark, and Richard Clark Kroeger. 1992. *I Suffer Not a Woman: Rethinking 1 Timothy 2:11-15 in Light of Ancient Evidence.* Grand Rapids: Baker.

LaSor, William Sanford. 1987. "Biblical Creationism," *Asbury Theological Journal* 42:7-20.

Lewis, C. S. 1962a. *The Problem of Pain.* New York: Macmillan.

_____. 1962b. The Weight of Glory: A Sermon. Pages 197-211 in *They Asked for a Paper.* London: Geoffrey Bles.

Louth, Andrew, ed. 2001. *Genesis 1-11.* Ancient Christian Commentary on Scripture: Old Testament I. Downers Grove, Ill.: InterVarsity.

Mazar, Benjamin. 1986. *The Early Biblical Period: Historical Essays.* Jerusalem: Israel Exploration Society.

Mendenhall, George E. 1974. The "Vengeance" of Yahweh. Pages 69-104 in *The Tenth Generation: The Origins of the Biblical Tradition.* Baltimore: Johns Hopkins University Press.

Oswalt, John N. 1988. Golden Calves and the "Bull of Jacob": The Impact on Israel of Its Religious Environment. Pages 9-18 in *Israel's Apostasy and Restoration: Essays in Honor of Roland K. Harrison.* Edited by Avraham Gileadi. Grand Rapids: Baker.

Pritchard, James B., ed. 1950. *Ancient Near Eastern Texts Relating to the Old Testament.* Princeton: Princeton University Press.

Rad, Gerhard von. 1961. *Genesis: A Commentary.* Philadelphia: Westminster.

_____. 1972. *Genesis.* 2d ed. Old Testament Library 1. Translated by J. H. Marks. Philadelphia: Westminster.

Rainey, Anson F. 1996. "Who Is a Canaanite? A Review of the Textual Evidence." *Bulletin of the American Schools of Oriental Research* 304:1-15.

Rainey, Anson F., and R. Steven Notley. 2006. *The Sacred Bridge.* Jerusalem: Carta.

Rendsburg, Gary A. 1986. *The Redaction of Genesis.* Winona Lake, Ind.: Eisenbrauns.

Richardson, Don. 1984. *Eternity in Their Hearts.* Ventura, Calif.: Regal.

Sasson, J. M. 1980. The "Tower of Babel" as a Clue to the Redactional Structuring of the Primeval History (Gen. 1—11:9). Pages 211-19 in *The Bible World: Essays in Honor of Cyrus H. Gordon.* Edited by Gary Rendsburg et al. New York: KTAV.

Skinner, John. 1930. *A Critical and Exegetical Commentary on Genesis.* 2d ed. The International Critical Commentary 1. Edinburgh: T&T Clark.

Speiser, E. A. 1964. *Genesis: A New Translation with Introduction and Commentary.* Anchor Bible [1]. Garden City, N.Y.: Doubleday.

Trible, Phyllis. 1978. *God and the Rhetoric of Sexuality.* Philadelphia: Fortress Press.

Tsumura, David Toshio. 1994. The Earth in Genesis 1. Pages 310-28 in *I Studied Inscriptions from Before the Flood: Ancient Near Eastern, Literary, and Linguistic Approaches to Genesis 1—11.* Edited by Richard S. Hess and David Toshio Tsumura. Winona Lake, Ind.: Eisenbrauns.

Walton, John H. 2001. *Genesis.* The NIV Application Commentary. Grand Rapids: Zondervan.

_____. 2009. *The Lost World of Genesis One: Ancient Cosmology and the Origins Debate.* Downers Grove, Ill.: InterVarsity.

Wenham, Gordon J. 1987. *Genesis 1-15.* Word Biblical Commentary, Vol. 1. Waco, Tex.: Word.

Wesley, John. 1975. *Explanatory Notes upon the Old Testament.* Salem, Ohio: Schmul.

Westermann, Claus. 1984. *Genesis 1-11: A Commentary.* Minneapolis: Augsburg.

Wiseman, P. J. 1985. *Ancient Records and the Structure of Genesis.* Repr. ed. Nashville: Abingdon.

York, Anthony. 1996. The Maturation Theme in the Adam and Eve Story. Pages 393-410 in *Go to the Land I Will Show You: Studies in Honor of Dwight W. Young.* Edited by Joseph E. Coleson and Victor H. Matthews. Winona Lake, Ind.: Eisenbrauns.

Young, Dwight Wayne. 2004. "The Sexagesimal Basis for the Total Years of the Antediluvian and Postdiluvian Epochs." *Zeitschrift fur die Alttestamentliche Wissenschaft* 116:502-27.

INTRODUCTION

A. The Content and Structure of Genesis 1—11

The English title of the book, "Genesis," comes from its title in Jerome's Latin Vulgate Bible, a transliteration from the title of its first translation, the Greek (LXX) version of the third century B.C. The Hebrew title is *Bereshit*, the first word of the book in the Hebrew text. The Hebrew title is best translated, "In the beginning." As a common noun, "genesis" conveys very well the meaning of Greek/Latin/English "Genesis." Other accurate renderings of the word and the concept, as used in Gen 1:1, include "origin," "inception," "establishment."

Genesis 1—11 often is called the "Primeval Prologue," because most of its chapters deal with the so-called primeval world before the flood. The content of this biblical "Prologue" is quite straightforward. Genesis 1:1—2:3 is an overview summary of God's creation, dealing mostly with creation upon the earth, and from the point of view of the earth's surface. Genesis 2:4-25 is another account, complementary rather than contradictory, centered on God's two major creative actions in the formation of humans. Chapter 3 is the narrative of the first humans turning from God and the consequent expulsion from their garden home. Genesis 4 narrates the birth of the first two children, and the murder of the younger by the elder, followed by the seven-generation genealogy of Cain, the elder son, and concluding with a notice of the birth of Seth, the new hope for the continuation of the human line.

Genesis 5 is the genealogical record of Seth's line, brought forward to the birth of Noah's three sons, who would survive the flood along with their father and mother. Genesis 6:1-8, with its short summary of human wickedness in that early day, sets the stage for God's judgment in the flood.

Genesis 6:9—9:29 is the narrative of preparation for the flood, the rising, prevailing, and decrease of the floodwaters, the exit of the surviving human family from the ark, and the immediate aftermath. Chapter 10, often titled "The Table of Nations," is a genealogical record, in three uneven parts, of the families of Noah's three sons. Genesis 11:1-10 narrates the building of the city and the Tower of Babel, the immediate cause of God's dispersal of the human family upon the earth. The Primeval Prologue concludes with a fourth genealogical record, the ten generations from Shem to Abram/Abraham, through whom God would begin to fulfill the promise of redemption and renewal—hinted at already, if not fully stated, in Gen 3.

Because Genesis 1—11 is so important, and has been closely studied over many centuries, scholars have put forward a number of descriptions of its structure, both in the whole and in its various parts. While some may be mutually exclusive, many are not, and may be seen as complementary, rather than contradictory, each adding helpful insights without detracting from the usefulness of others.

Three "nonstandard" proposals will illustrate. Rendsburg (1986, 8), following Sasson (1980, 218), outlines the Primeval Prologue in a pattern of five units (A, B, C, D, E) in 1:1—6:8, followed by five parallel units in 6:9—11:26 (A', B', C', E', D'), with the last two units reversed. The narrative subjects (not the persons and events) of each of the five pairs (A, A', etc.) are identical, by Rendsburg's and Sasson's analysis.

Dorsey (1999, 48-55) outlines Genesis 1—11 in two sets of *seven* "main units," in the order: a, b, c, a', b', c', d. However, Dorsey also presents a second outline of these chapters in two sets of *fourteen* "main units," in the order: Section 1: a, b, c, d, e, f, g; Section 2: a', b', c', d', e', f', g'. Again, Dorsey's two outlines of the same material are not contradictory, but complementary. Moreover, they also complement Rendsburg's and Sasson's outline, rather than contradicting it.

In the commentary below, we have noted (with Cassuto 1961, 91; see also Dorsey 1999, 49) that the final referent of the brief introductory paragraph of 1:1, "the earth," becomes the main subject of the seven paragraphs narrating the creation week. Similarly, *ʾādām*, the climactic subject of the sixth and final day of creation (1:26-28), becomes the main subject of the more detailed account of the human creation in 2:4-25. Finally (though we could go further), using a Hebrew pun, the narrator moves from the climactic statement of 2:25 that the humans were *naked* but unashamed, to the introduction of the *cunning* serpent as the agent of temptation (3:1). This is another structural device employed by the narrator/redactor but, again, it does not contradict other outlines; it complements them.

To say all that could be said concerning the structure of Gen 1—11 would occupy the entire volume. We will be content here with observing that our outline of this section of Genesis, below, and our various comments on structural units within the body of the commentary, will (we hope) suggest to the reader further lines of productive inquiry.

B. The Literary Forms of Genesis 1—11

Considering the (relatively) short length of the Primeval Prologue, it contains a significant number of literary forms. The most obvious descriptor is "narrative prose." Much of it is of an exalted quality; we even could call Gen 1 a "prose poem," without exaggeration. Most of Gen 1—11 is narrative, however, and terms that encompass nearly everything are of limited usefulness in advancing understanding.

1. Genealogies

After narrative, genealogies occupy the most lines of Gen 1—11. The first, a linear genealogy with relatively little added detail, lists the seven generations of Cain's line (Gen 4:16-22); with this genealogy and its addendum of Lamech's boastful poem (4:23-24), the biblical account of Cain closes. A sort of preamble to Adam's genealogy through Seth is Gen 4:25-26. That genealogy proper, Gen 5:1-32 (and concluded with 9:28-29), is also linear, but the life of each of its ten subjects is divided into two segments, the patriarch's age at the birth of his first son, followed by the number of years he lived following that event, with the total years of his lifespan recorded before the final statement, "and he died."

Following the note of Noah's lifespan and his death (9:28-29) that is the real conclusion of Adam's genealogy through Seth, Gen 10 ("The Table of Nations") is a different kind of genealogy. It is segmented; that is, it follows the lines of all three of Noah's sons, Japheth first, then Ham, then Shem. Moreover, it contains considerable horizontal spread, the inclusion of more than one name per generation. Many of these, though, are gentilics, referencing peoples, rather than personal names. These include both plural forms (e.g., *miṣrayim*/Egypt, v 6) and singular forms (e.g., *hayĕbûsî*/the Jebusite, v 16).

The final genealogy is that of Shem alone. On the basis of the phrase *ʾēlleh tôledōt* ("these are the records of . . ."), it comprises Gen 11:10-26, with the same kind of addendum at 11:32 that we see at 9:28-29 for Noah. Alternatively, this genealogy may comprise 11:10-32; vv 28-31, then, are the details necessary to introduce the narrative of Abram's call (12:1).

2. "These Are the *Toledot*"

Certainly, the phrase mentioned above, *ʾēlleh tôledōt*, is an important literary and theological feature of all of Genesis. It occurs ten times, dividing the book into eleven sections of uneven lengths: 2:4; 5:1; 6:9; 10:1; 11:10; 11:27; 25:12; 25:19; 36:1; 37:2. Any discussion of the sources (written and/or oral) behind the present text of Genesis that does not take this phrase and its divisions of the book into account cannot be said to have solved the issue. With Hamilton, we take the phrase as an introduction to what follows (1990, 151). Five times, what follows is primarily genealogical and related information (5:1; 10:1; 11:10; 25:2; 36:1). The other five occurrences introduce narrative accounts, one quite short (11:27), the other four running from two or three chapters, to (perhaps) the entire final quarter of Genesis for the last one (37:2). Both of these types of material support the translation "these are the records" or "these are the reports" of the one whose name is attached to them. As the word *tôledōt* is from *yālad*, meaning "he begat/sired" (fem., "she bore"), translating "these are the generations of . . ." is not "wrong." It does fit some of the occurrences, just not all of them.

3. The Mathematics of the Patriarchal Life Spans

Connected with two of the linear genealogies is the issue of life spans—first, of the line of Adam through Seth to Noah (ch 5), then, of the line of Shem to Terah, the father of Abram/Abraham (11:10-32). Young (2004) has shown that both the segments and the sums of the patriarchal life spans represent sums and products based primarily on the sexagesimal (base 6) system of ancient Mesopotamian mathematics. Every age at the birth of the first son, every number of years lived afterward, and every total life span for the individual patriarchs in both genealogies is either a sum or a product (or both), or the sum of a set of sums and/or products.

For the antediluvian genealogy of Seth (ch 5), the most important number is nine hundred (900), or thirty squared (30^2). The numbers twenty (20) and ten (10) as well as their squares four hundred (400, or 20^2) and one hundred (100, or 10^2) also figure heavily into these spans. For the ages of the postdiluvian patriarchs of the genealogy of Shem (ch 11), the latter two sets of numbers are the key, as no postdiluvian patriarch even began to approach the nine-hundred-some-year life span of most of the antediluvians. From a beginning of around four hundred years, their life spans decreased until they were less than two hundred years in length.

Every number in both genealogies has a basis in the Mesopotamian sexagesimal system, or in the decimal (base 10) system that most use today, or even in both together, since the ancient Mesopotamian scribes and mathematicians used both systems. Every number has the characteristic of a mathematical "problem" set for student scribes as part of their education. Some are Pythagorean, the kind of geometry and algebra problems most of us encountered in high school math classes. Some of them even are recognizable as quadratic equations, or as derived from the math of quadratic equations. In this, these life spans exhibit the same mathematical foundations as do the life spans recorded in, most famously, the Sumerian king list from about 2000 B.C. The reigns of the antediluvian Sumerian kings are impossibly long; the shortest is 18,600 years. Many say the biblical figures also are impossible, but they are much closer to our present ideas of what is reasonable than are the Sumerian numbers. The important point here, however, is that the biblical figures in these genealogies are mathematically based, unquestionably derived from the Mesopotamian mathematical heritage of the biblical narrator/redactor.

The historical/cultural/theological question, then, is why? The answers on both "extremes" are equally unsatisfying. The skeptical reader easily can conclude that these genealogies have no basis in historical reality, since all the numbers are the "answers" to mathematical problems devised to educate scribal students. The nonsatisfying, nonexplanatory answer from the other side could be that God "adjusted" the ages of all these patriarchs. But for what reason? To show that God is good at mathematics? To give the credence of mathematical "coincidence" to these life segments and total life spans? Something else? For the present, at least, we must be content with recognizing the fascinating mathematical foundations of these two genealogies with little hope of discerning the "why."

4. Poetic Passages and Fragments

Another important set of literary forms in these chapters is its various poetic passages, more numerous than usually recognized. Semitic poetry (and other literature) often exhibits rhyme, alliteration, assonance, vivid figurative language, and such other markers as also occur in Western poetry in its many genres. However, none of these defines Semitic poetry. That is done by the "parallelism of the members." Most simply, the second line repeats, echoes, and/or advances the thought of the first line. Many variations on and added complexities to this pattern are possible, but parallelism is the foundational characteristic of virtually all Semitic poetry.

We will discuss some of the poetic characteristics of some of these poetic passages and fragments in the body of the commentary below. Here, we must content ourselves with a mere listing, noting also that not all scholars will agree with some of our inclusions on this list:

2:23	The man's exclamation at seeing the woman
3:14-15	God's pronouncement upon the serpent
3:16	God's pronouncement upon the woman
3:17b-19	God's pronouncement upon the man and the ground
4:23-24	Lamech's boast to his two wives
8:22	God's promise of the perpetual cycle of seasons
9:6-7	God's instruction: murder; human fruitfulness
9:25-27	Noah's curse; Noah's blessings

All these poetic passages and fragments comprise spoken words. Additionally, these chapters also contain a number of other speech forms: God's word spoken in divine council; God's spoken instruction on several occasions—comprising not only command but also warning, blessing, and even comfort; dialogues between the woman and the serpent, between God and the man, and between God and Cain. At several points, it is obvious that someone spoke, but the words are not reported.

C. Ancient Near Eastern Parallels with Genesis 1—11

We have noted already the mathematical foundations of both the Sumerian king list and the genealogies of Seth and of Shem. We will discuss at some length in the body of the commentary the similarities and the differences in form and in theology between the creation account of Gen 1 and the Babylonian account usually known as the *Enuma Elish*. Similarly, we will compare and contrast the flood account of Gen 6—9 with the account of the flood as reported by its Mesopotamian hero, Utnapishtim, and preserved in Tablet XI of the Epic of Gilgamesh. Because of space limitations, we will deal very little or not at all with many other points of comparison and/or contrast that have the power to expand our understanding of these chapters. These include the reasons for, and the materials and processes used in the making of, the human species; the putative presence of both serpent and "tree of life" motifs in several Mesopotamian literary productions, and in glyptic and other art; the symbiotic but sometimes conflicted relationships between pastoral nomads and settled agricultural folk—perhaps reflected in the Cain and Abel story, and certainly well documented in Mesopotamian sources; the presence of several ziggurats in lower Mesopotamia, and the urbanized city-state culture and politics they reflect. If space permitted, we could go on at length; we also could mention additional resources from the Hittite, Egyptian, Canaanite, and other eastern Mediterranean cultural spheres. The interested reader will have much fascinating exploration ahead!

D. Recent Developments in Genesis 1—11 Scholarship

Many have observed over the years that Gen 1—11 is more intensively studied and more extensively written about than any other unit in all of world literature, ancient or modern. Among the more exhaustive commentaries on these chapters is that of Claus Westermann, first published in German; Augsburg published the English edition, *Genesis 1-11*, in 1984. Comparable are the two Hebrew volumes Umberto Cassuto completed before his death, *From Adam to Noah* and *From Noah to Abraham;* Magnes published them in English in 1961 and 1964, respectively. Another important commentary translated from German is Gerhard von Rad's one-volume *Genesis*, published in English by Westminster in 1961. E. A. Speiser's Anchor Bible *Genesis* (1964; second ed., 1978) is less detailed than either Westermann's or Cassuto's works but is another important commentary from the period. A bit later are Gordon Wenham's *Genesis 1-15* in the Word Biblical Commentary series (Word, 1987) and Victor Hamilton's *The Book of Genesis, Chapters 1-17* in NICOT (Eerdmans, 1990). All these are what we could call "standard" critical commentaries; in biblical commentaries, "critical" means only that they are based on the Hebrew text (in the case of the OT), not on any translation into another language. Each of these authors interacted with current scholarship on Gen 1—11 to the point of his own publication; the reader of any of them will grasp most of the important issues in understanding and interpreting the Primeval Prologue of Genesis.

Another important commentary is Walter Brueggemann's *Genesis* in the Interpretation series (John Knox, 1982). It focuses less on verse-by-verse exegesis than do the commentaries mentioned above. Brueggemann dwells more self-consciously on theological issues, and on the ways the structures and movement within the text advance its theological agendas. This is Brueggemann's forte; a masterful example in this volume is his "excursus" (my term) on the "Brother Theme" (61-64).

Terence Fretheim's "The Book of Genesis" in *The New Interpreter's Bible* (Abingdon, 1994) is another theologically oriented commentary. Fretheim's book *God and World in the Old Testament: A Relational Theology of Creation* (Abingdon, 2005) is not a commentary. However, as its subtitle intimates, it draws heavily on Genesis, and its treatments will prove helpful to Wesleyan readers. The reader soon will discover that the writer of this commentary champions a relational understanding of what God is about, in Gen 1—11 and throughout Scripture. Both Fretheim and Brueggemann have been inspirational guides on that path.

We have mentioned already Gary Rendsburg's *The Redaction of Genesis* as a helpful approach to the structures and divisions of Genesis. Another important volume is an anthology, *I Studied Inscriptions from Before the Flood*, edited by Richard Hess and David Tsumura (Eisenbrauns, 1994). Its subtitle reveals its range: *Ancient Near Eastern, Literary, and Linguistic Approaches to Genesis 1—11*. More recently, Richard Hess has authored *Studies in the Personal Names of Genesis 1—11* (Eisenbrauns, 2009). These represent some of the approaches this author believes will lead to deeper, more developed understandings of these marvelous opening chapters of Genesis.

A very helpful recent approach is represented in John Walton's *The Lost World of Genesis One* (InterVarsity, 2009). Walton (with others) takes seriously, as we should, the cultural and intellectual world of which Israel was an integral part, and in which Genesis was written. (This is true whether we date the origin and composition of Genesis relatively early or relatively late.) Walton takes Gen 1 for what it originally and truly is, an example of ancient Near Eastern cosmogony. Genesis 1 serves to correct many points of the (polytheistic) theology of other cosmologies from the ancient Near East, but it also is a Near Eastern cosmology in its own right. We should read and interpret it as such.

When we do, the key discovery is that Gen 1 was written and intended as a *functional* ontology of the earth's origin, not as a *material* ontology. That is, Gen 1 does not summarize the processes by which God created the earth, materially. Rather, the narrator of Gen 1 portrayed God's bringing of the myriad creation entities into the various *functions* God intended them to perform. Another way to say it is that Gen 1 does not focus on God's bringing material entities upon the earth into their respective physical existences. Rather, it focuses on bringing already existing physical entities into the systems and relationships by which they would carry out the functions God intended them to do. Walton says, "I propose that people in the ancient world believed that something existed not by virtue of its material properties, *but by virtue of its having a function in an ordered system*" (26, emphasis original). This commentary writer believes Walton's premise is sound; if we take it seriously, it bids fair to cut the Gordian knot of the creation-evolution controversy.

In this all-too-brief survey, we have left aside entire approaches to these chapters. We have not mentioned even one of the myriads of articles and other notices that constantly appear, dealing with their larger themes, their minutiae, and everything in between. To put it positively, for the interested reader much fascinating discovery still lies ahead!

E. The Relation of Genesis 1—11 to Genesis 12—50

We have said that Gen 1—11 fulfills the function of a "prologue." It gives a theologically oriented account of the origin/inception/establishment of this earth, and of its human and other inhabitants. It gives a theological perspective on the beginnings of human alienation from God, from each other, from ourselves individually and internally, and from the rest of creation. It assures us God did not give up on humans then, nor will God do so now. This prologue summarizes a tremendous collapse into wickedness, so great that God was compelled to **wipe the earth clean** (6:7; 7:4, 23) and start over with just one human family. It chronicles the beginnings of the spread of that family, noting the geographical relationships of western Asia and the eastern Mediterranean—the geographical focus of almost all the succeeding biblical record.

The final verses of the genealogy of Gen 11 make explicit the connection between this prologue and the rest of the book of Genesis. Terah, the last of the Shemite patriarchs treated in this genealogy, is presented primarily as the father of Abram and his brothers; the final paragraph (11:27-32) says more about Abram than it does about Terah. Following the notice of Terah's death (v 32), Gen 12:1 proceeds immediately to God's calling of Abram. The adventures of Abram (Abraham) and his family in following God take the reader to the end of Genesis. The second quarter of Genesis focuses mainly on

Abraham; the third quarter, on his grandson Jacob; the fourth quarter, on his great-grandson Joseph. Isaac functions as a transitional figure between Abraham and Jacob; only in Gen 26 is Isaac the protagonist.

Additionally, Gen 1—11 is the necessary "back story" to explain the Mesopotamian origins and connections of Abraham and his immediate descendants. Not only did Abraham travel to Canaan (probably from lower Mesopotamia) by way of upper Mesopotamia. To find a wife for his son Isaac, Abraham sent to his relatives who had remained in upper Mesopotamia when Abraham left to follow God's call. Jacob went back, in his turn, to escape his brother Esau's threatened vengeance. Domiciled with his uncle Laban in Haran, Jacob acquired two wives, two concubines, eleven of his twelve sons, at least one daughter, and the beginnings of his vast wealth. Only in the final quarter of the book, with Joseph as the central character, does the scene shift from Mesopotamia to Egypt.

F. Genesis 1—11 in the Biblical Canon

The first paragraph, especially, of the previous section is pertinent here, also. Without question, Gen 1—11 is foundational for biblical theology. Consider: the dignified assumption and assertion of God's being; the majestic outline of God's work and purposes in creation; God's delight in and care for all creation; God's passionate valuing and love of the human creation; the grievous harm inflicted by the human breaking of relationship with God; God's grief at that human choice; God's prior decision to redeem, restore, and renew; the escalation of harms when evil goes unchecked and unabated; disaster and death as the unavoidable consequence of total immersion in evil; the breathtaking gift (and gifts) of God's grace. All these and more are introduced and highlighted in these first chapters. It is not too much to say that any theological inquiry, of any and every kind, will visit them, or it will come up short.

Another way of saying this may not be intuitive, but in the broadest reach of theological inquiry, it is true. Within God's construct of "time," our confidence in the realization of God's good ends is based in the revelation of God's good purposes in creation. Creation and eschatology are not separate theological topics; from Gen 1—2 to Rev 21—22, it is the same divine story.

G. The Composition of Genesis

Everything has led us, directly or indirectly, to questions of authorship, composition, and editorial working and reworking—and, thus, also to the dating—of the book of Genesis, including, of course, chapters 1—11. We note, first, that Wesleyans, with most other Christians, affirm a divine/human authorship for the biblical canon. Wesleyans (with others) speak of a partnership, a synergy, of authorship, rather than of a divine initiative imposed upon a passive human receptivity. Inspired and prompted by God, the human partners were active authors, compilers, and editors, actively carrying out whatever tasks the finished canonical products suggest were necessary to bring them to their literary completion. The Bible is a divine library, to be sure; just as surely, it also is a human library.

The questions of authorial/editorial process by which Gen 1—11 came to its present form fall on the human side of the equation. For centuries, Jewish and Christian traditions hardly questioned the assumption of Mosaic authorship of Genesis, along with the rest of the Pentateuch, though nowhere in Genesis itself is Moses declared to be its author.

Following a long development prompted by Enlightenment philosophy and theology, a new paradigm came to the fore and held sway, with little successful challenge, for nearly one hundred years; it is popularly known as the Documentary Hypothesis, or sometimes simply as JEDP. Most simply, J stands for the Yahwist/Jahwist, whose material is earliest, perhaps from about 950 B.C. The Elohist (E) material is from about 850 B.C.; J and E were combined about 750 B.C. (The Deuteronomistic school, about 650 B.C., does not figure into the composition of Genesis.) The Priestly writer or school (P) edited the JE document(s) and added material, probably from about 550-450 B.C., giving us the Genesis we know today. This summary is oversimplified, and few (if any) OT scholars today accept the Documentary Hypothesis in this "classic" form. Still, though the model is much modified—particularly over the last half-century—the vocabulary of JEDP remains as the vocabulary of much of the discussion of the authorial/redactional history of Genesis.

The reader of the commentary will find ample evidence that the writer of this volume is not convinced of the essential soundness of the Documentary Hypothesis. Yet, the text of Genesis does abundantly exhibit the existence of sources upon which its authors/editors drew. Prominent among these are the *toledot*, briefly discussed above. Genesis exhibits a long transmission history, as well. In the body of the commentary, we will discuss both sources and transmission history, as their importance warrants and space allows. Put briefly, I believe the evidence leads to two conclusions: (1) Much of the material of Genesis is very old indeed; (2) The editorial process for Genesis was active (or intermittently so) through the exilic period, or perhaps the beginning of the postexilic period. This final period of editorial focus on Genesis, just before the "fixing" of its canonical form, may have been especially active. As Varughese has cogently expressed it, "[There is] validity in seeing the book reaching its final form in the exilic period. . . . In the hope-filled words of Joseph (see Gen 50:24), did the exiles in Babylon find hope for their own return to the land of promise? Abraham's own migration [from Mesopotamia] would have provided hope to his children in exile in Babylon" (private email correspondence on August 15, 2011).

H. Major Theological Themes of Genesis 1—11

It cannot hurt to say it again; it would be difficult to think of a biblical theological theme *not* introduced, or at least implied, in Gen 1—11.

1. The God Who Is; the God Who Does

The first theological theme of Genesis, of course, is God. In fact, within the first three words (Hebrew) of Genesis, *In the beginning God created*, three important understandings about God are introduced: (1) God exists; (2) God is uncreated and separate from creation; (3) God creates/makes.

Other understandings about God also begin to unfold within these chapters. The transcendent God exists outside the bounds of matter, energy, space, and time, because God created all these. The immanent God can and does enter into relationship with God's creation within God's created universe of matter/energy/space/time. God created the universe to be inherently regular and stable—if not totally along Newtonian lines, then along the lines proposed by Einstein, assuming current scientific knowledge points us aright.

2. The One, the Only, God

These things being so—and Genesis simply asserts they are—God has no rivals in the realm of, or for the position of, deity. The "gods" of ancient Israel's neighbors did not make themselves—not even their own theogonies assert they did. Since the "gods" are created, and not self-existent, they are not transcendent and cannot be "gods." In reality, they are the servants of the God who created them. The Shema (Deut 6:4, usually translated "Hear, O Israel: The LORD our God, the LORD is one") is Israel's later creedal affirmation of the truth already expressed in the narrative of Gen 1.

The issue of the divine name, introduced in Gen 1—11, can help us get our minds around God's oneness and uniqueness. Many opinions are accessible; this commentator understands the biblical text itself as presenting the key in Exod 3:14; 6:2-3. In these revelations to Moses, God gave him to understand that Yahweh is God's personal name, in Hebrew. Its form is third masculine singular imperfect, from *hayah*, "be [he was]." The verb *hayah* is doubly (or triply) irregular; thus, it is best to take "Yahweh" as meaning both "He is" and "He causes (to be)." If we take Yahweh as a Qal form (as it is, or may be), it means, "He is/was/will be." Yahweh is self-existent, nonoriginated, self-sufficient, noncontingent, without beginning and without end. None of Israel's neighbors claimed this for their gods. Oswalt has shown that Israel did not invent or discover this concept on its own; God revealed it (1988, 15-16).

At the same time, Yahweh may be a causative (Hiph'il) form, meaning, "He causes to be," i.e., he makes, creates. Since the form may be either Qal or Hiph'il, we may take it as intended to be both. God's Hebrew name, Yahweh, thus reveals God both as the eternally self-existent ("transcendent") One and, at the same time, as the Creator and Sustainer of all else that is. Strong evidence in support of this understanding that "Yahweh" is the personal name by which God wanted to be known in Israel is the fact that "Yahweh" occurs about 6,600 times in the Hebrew Bible (OT), for an average of seven times per chapter.

"Elohim," God's designation in Gen 1, is a title; it belongs to a cluster of titles from a common root (or related roots), including also El, Elim, Eloah, and (El) Elyon. All these titles represent the one so designated as "the mighty one(s)"; they are applied to prominent humans, as well as to God and the "gods" of Israel's neighbors. In Gen 1, "Elohim" is used of God as the Mighty One par excellence, the true Creator, as distinct from Marduk and the other "creator gods" depicted in the cosmogonies of Israel's neighbors. Elohim ("The Mighty One") is sufficient to bring into being and appoint to their various functions all the entities of creation, both the heavenly and the earthly. In Gen 2—3, the coupling of the divine personal name with this title, in the "new" title "Yahweh Elohim," teaches the hearer/reader that this "Mighty One," Elohim, is, in fact, Yahweh, the God of Israel.

3. Creation for Relationship

We do not know all God's reasons for creation, but Genesis, together with the rest of Scripture, reveals that God created for relationship. God created this universe as a habitation for creatures with whom God could have fellowship. Drawing on his knowledge of the Hebrew Scriptures, as well as his personal acquaintance with Jesus, John affirmed that God is love (1 John 4:16); love requires an object. At least some creatures in the realms we usually call "the supernatural" are the recipients and reciprocators of God's love. As far as we can know now, however, God created this world and placed ʾādām (humankind) in it as the supreme expression of God's love. This includes, of course, the redemption of humankind after our first parents fractured the relationship of love they had enjoyed with God in the garden of Eden. Not only is the estrangement recorded, but also at least the inference of the coming redemption (Gen 3).

Those who consider covenant an important biblical theme find three covenants in Genesis: the Adamic, the Noahic, and the Abrahamic; the first two, of course, are found in Gen 1—11. In phrasing it thus, we are not discounting covenant as an important theological category; covenant *is* important. However, it also is important to remember that covenant in the ancient Near East, the cultural milieu in which the Bible originated, was primarily a political/legal and, secondarily, a commercial category. A covenant was (and still is) a binding agreement between two (or more) parties. Each party had/has obligations under the terms of the covenant; penalties apply in cases of nonfulfillment. In the Noahic covenant, for example, Noah and his descendants were/are to avoid eating blood and to refrain from shedding human blood. The penalty for the latter was to be the shedding of the transgressor's blood, by human agency (Gen 9:4-6). Usually, this is interpreted as a sanction against murder, and as providing for the (usually governmental) execution of the murderer.

Of course, this is important, as are the covenants that follow it in the biblical record. We believe, however, that the usual Protestant emphasis on covenant has obscured the more important category, *relationship*. Relationship is the prior and primary category; covenant is subsequent and secondary. Covenant is essentially a political/legal focus; relationship goes almost infinitely beyond that scope. If covenant is the prism of a drop of water, the relationship(s) God created us for are the oceans of God's love for us and for the rest of creation, including also its manifold reciprocations within and by God's creation. The drop of water is important, but it neither contains nor describes the whole of the ocean. To image this another way, we may ask: Would we rather be limited to a covenant (whose terms we already have violated) or be beloved daughters and sons—welcomed, embraced, and valued within God's own family? Important as covenant is, our *relationship* with God and with each other is infinitely more far-reaching and precious.

4. Stewardship Dominion

Genesis 1 and 2 give a remarkable picture of God's gift of trust in granting to the human race stewardship dominion over this beautiful and productive earth. The terms of the mandate are expressed near the end of ch 1. A small but very important characterization of how and why this charter of dominion means stewardship, and not rapacity, occurs at the point of God's placing the man in the garden of Eden. The text records that God's intention was for the ʾādām "to work [serve] it and to keep [guard, protect] it" (2:15 ESV). Despite the relational fracturings resulting from the human choice to turn from God (3:6 ff.), God never rescinded, modified, or limited that assignment. Responsible creation care is the continuing divine mandate upon the human species.

5. Human Gender Equality

Arising directly from the text of Gen 1—3 are the issues of God's creation intention of equality between the genders of the human species, and of how that creation intention became subverted as a result of the first humans' transgression. Both the broader creation account (Gen 1:27) and the more detailed account of God's creation of humans in two separate actions (Gen 2:7, 22) are clear that God intended male and female as equal partners from the beginning. Genesis 3 records the first couple turning their backs on their relationship with God, and the consequent breaking of their relationship with each other. Genesis 3:16 is God's announcement of this tragic fracturing: the man's grabbing for himself the power of the stewardship dominion mandate, and his exercise of it upon and against the woman. The text presents this as one of the more heartrending results of the human turning away, for them and for their descendants.

The question that remains in biblical, systematic, and pastoral theology is whether this result is permanent or reversible. Genesis itself begins to hint at what the rest of Scripture reveals: God purposed and acted to reverse the alienation, bringing humans and the rest of creation back into our God-intended integrity of relationship(s). With Wesley, we may anticipate that God intends the eschatological resolution to usher in a creation even better than the original.

When may we expect to see this realized? The New Testament teaches that the believer lives in an "already, but not yet" tension. Christ finished the work; with all earthly creation, we already enjoy many of its benefits, but they are not yet fully realized. One of the strongest themes of a Wesleyan approach to Scripture is that the fruits of our redemption in Christ begin already to be realized here on this earth. If that can be true anywhere, surely it can be true in the home of the man and woman committed to living as believers in Christ, and within the gatherings of the body of believers called the church. With other Christians, Wesleyans should live intentionally, and in every way possible, the "already" of creation's restoration in Christ, even as we anticipate the "not yet" of his return. Genesis 1—2 presents the first picture of what such living entails.

6. Reality *Is* Consequence

Perhaps each of us has thought, at one time or another, "If only Adam and Eve had not eaten of that tree! Why didn't God stop them?!" Genesis 3 is but the first of the many scriptural evidences teaching God's total commitment to the "project" of creating a race of true moral agents, beings who can choose to act either with or counter to God's instruction. C. S. Lewis has suggested, "Perhaps this is not the 'best of all possible' universes, but the only possible one" (1962a, 35). If God had created us without the capacity to choose other than God's instructions/prescriptions, this would not be a "world" as we know and experience it; at most, it would be a giant Star Trek Holodeck (my illustration, not Lewis's).

To be real, choices must carry consequences. A rock with the properties of mass and density suitable for its use in building a wall (normally a good thing) of necessity also can become a weapon capable of crushing a skull (obviously a bad thing). In theory, God could change every rock into a mass of feathers or foam just before the fatal impact, but if God did that routinely, God would not have created a universe. We would have the Holodeck again, for God's amusement, and perhaps even for ours, but whatever it was, it would be without meaning.

The expulsion of the first pair from the garden, the ebbing of Abel's blood into the protesting ground, God's decision to wipe clean the earth the antediluvians had soiled by their wickedness, the dispersal of the generation of Babel—all these are primeval attestations that actions have consequences, whether for good or for ill. Moreover, they are early evidences that in God's economy, consequences are not arbitrary.

7. God's Passionate Love of Humanity

This idea does not often enough rank among the great theological themes. Yet it belongs among them and is as clear and unmistakable in Genesis as in any other book of the Bible. We can go further and say that the ubiquitous evidence of Gen 1—11 for God's passionate love of the human race is one of many reasons this book belongs first in the scriptural canon.

As a preparatory aside, we know many people do not believe this. Some flat-out reject it, and even many Christians and Jews, for whom the Scriptures should be sufficient evidence, cannot bring themselves to believe God really loves *them*. "God may love all the worthy people; God even may love everyone else, but God knows me too well ever to love *me*" is the depths-of-the-heart belief or disabling suspicion of far too many who ought to have been taught better. They would be free to live as God designed us to live, if only they could accept God's love for them, embracing their true identity as beloved daughters and sons in God's eternal family, by creation *and* by redemption.

Genesis 1—11 already begins to show in many ways that God created us precisely because God wanted a race to love and individuals to love. The movement of Gen 1 is toward the creation of the human race (vv 26-28). Both literarily and theologically, everything that comes before prepares for and leads to that climactic act. This does not mean God could have had no other purposes in creating the universe, or even this world. However, Gen 1 is designed to emphasize the creation of 'ādām as God's central and crowning purpose in this narrative.

Because of the grandeur of the entire chapter, the reader may miss or undervalue this climactic purpose in Gen 1. This is part of the reason for following Gen 1 with Gen 2 and its primary focus on God's two separate and definitive actions in the creation of the first human pair. Loving, attentive, and passionate care are the hallmarks of God's creative work, in forming the first and building the second, and in providing for them a perfect home.

Genesis 3 records the loss of that home. That part of the story had to be told, too, with the silly posturing of the guilty pair, and the pathos of their eviction from paradise itself. Yet, even here, God's love shines through brightly in the telling. Rather than allowing them to die immediately, God expelled them from the garden and allowed them to live and have children born to them, the sign of a future for the human race. The text is clear that God's love, grace, and mercy prevailed over the world of judgment in which the first human couple lived. In revealing a little of what the future now held, God included a veiled promise of reversal and redemption, of death working backward (to borrow Lewis's Narnian phrase).

In many other ways, Gen 1—11 shows God's love for each individual, as well as for humanity as a whole. Perhaps more poignantly than anywhere else, we see God's grief (even with foreknowledge) in God's first approach to the human pair following their decision to eat of the forbidden fruit. The depth and intensity of the divine sorrow expressed in God's anguished cry, *"Where are you?"* (3:9, emphasis added), will soften the hardest of human hearts, if only we pause to hear it.

8. Holiness

A key tenet of the Wesleyan/Holiness tradition is that holiness is a central concern of Scripture from beginning to end. The major Hebrew root denoting holiness and the holy, *qadash*, occurs first in Gen 2:3, where the narrator stated, "God blessed the seventh day [the Sabbath], and sanctified it [set it apart]" (KJV). In all the Semitic languages where it occurs, *qadash* carried an original and basic meaning of "[to] separate, set apart."

As we move through both the OT and NT of the Christian Scripture, we note, most importantly, that God is characterized as holy, the Holy One. First, this means God is not the same as, nor is God a part of, God's creation, as nonmonotheistic theologies usually teach. God is transcendent, *other than* the creation. That God can enter and interact with God's creation must follow, rather than precede, the understanding that the creation is not to be identified *as* God. What also follows, with respect to moral and ethical categories, is that God's character defines, describes, and illustrates what it means to "be" holy.

This leads to a final observation, here; humans (and other created entities) are, or become, holy (separated) *to* God, rather than *from* other created entities. Separation *to* God is biblical holiness; the mere separation *from* other persons, places, things, and/or actions is not. We shall see that this idea and definition of holiness, together with much else that Wesleyans believe belongs to the doctrines and themes of holiness, is present already in Gen 1—11, sometimes explicitly, sometimes implicitly.

PRIMEVAL PROLOGUE: GENESIS 1:1—11:32

COMMENTARY

I. CREATION AND ALIENATION (GENESIS 1—3)

Overview

None of us ever will read three chapters together—not in the Bible, and certainly not in any other literary work—more important than Gen 1—3. No other three-chapter section of the Bible (and certainly not of any other literary work) evokes the interest, nor elicits the blizzard of written response, that Gen 1—3 evokes and elicits. Yet no other three-chapter section of the Bible has been subjected to as much under-informed, misinformed, ill-informed—and at the extreme end of the spectrum, hostile—commentary as has Gen 1—3. Genesis 1—3 is intensely interesting, and its proper understanding is foundational to Christian faith and life. Yet, its proper understanding is beset with difficulties as small as the meaning of a single noun and as large as the imposition upon it of comprehensive paradigms completely alien to it.

A proper understanding of Gen 1—3 is critical, if for no other reason than its primacy in the canon of Christian Scripture. An accurate understanding of Gen 1—3 should shape our understanding of all else that follows in the biblical and postbiblical records of God's people. Together, Gen 1 and 2 comprise the only extended biblical narrative of God's creation of this earth and of its living entities, culminating in the humans created in the image of God. Genesis 3 narrates the human choice of estrangement from God, from each other, and from the rest of the created order. These chapters separately or together provide the foundation for the biblical theology of creation, estrangement, redemption, and restoration—separately or together. Thus, what these chapters teach us of God's creation intentions, and of the consequences of our turning from God, is of the *utmost* importance. *All* Christian teaching about God, humanity, and God's relationship to the world should conform to the *intended* teachings of these chapters. *None* of our thinking about God, about the earth and the universe we live in, about our human relationships at every level—in short, about anything—should contradict the *intended* teachings of these chapters.

Genesis 1:1—2:3 is the opening literary unit of both the Jewish and the Christian Scriptures. Unlike creation stories from other parts of the world, including those of ancient Israel's pagan neighbors, the opening sentence of this literary unit goes back to the very beginning of all that is, except for God: "In the beginning God created the heavens and the earth" (1:1). Thus, the preceding context, both literarily within the book of Genesis, and theologically in the creation of the cosmos, is nothing—nothing, that is, except God.

Ancient Israel, however, did not exist in a vacuum. For much of their existence as a nation in their own land, Israel had more powerful neighbors, Egypt to their southwest and the empires of Mesopotamia—first Assyria, then Babylonia, then Persia—to their north and east. Moreover, Israel counted the beginnings of their cultural heritage from Mesopotamia, and significant influence came from Egypt early on, as well. Israel's immediate neighbors, also, largely Canaanite/Phoenician in their culture, exercised considerable influence on Israel over the centuries of their existence as a people in their own land. All these neighbors of Israel possessed creation stories, some of them quite elaborate and extended. It is reasonable to assume that educated Israelites would have known the creation stories of their neighbors. It is also possible that Israelites who wavered in their devotion to Yahweh would have been attracted to their neighbors' creation theologies.

Yet, at least a minority in Israel and in Judah always remained faithful to Yahweh and faithfully preserved the historical and theological traditions of the nation. The placement of Israel's creation stories at the beginning of Israel's sacred writings indicates its primary place in Israel's theology. The creation stories in Genesis give Yahweh Elohim his proper place as the transcendent Creator and Maker of all that is in heaven and on earth. The creation stories in Genesis also critique and challenge the religious ideas and claims of the creation stories of their neighbors. Genesis 1:1—2:3 is the great summary of creation, and it takes special care to establish that the natural phenomena worshipped by Israel's neighbors as the pantheon of the great gods are, in fact, not gods themselves, but God's creations.

Genesis 2:4-25 relates God's intimate care in the making of the first humans. Much of modern scholarship views 1:1—2:3 (or, 2:4*a*) and 2:4*b*-25 as two separate accounts, the first from a priestly writer and the second from a Yahwist writer. (The issues of 2:4 are particularly knotty, as discussed in the commentary below.) Moreover, many scholars understand the second account as the earliest version of Israel's creation faith (perhaps from around the eighth century B.C.), and the first account as a later theological reflection of God's creation of the world, from the period of the Babylonian exile or later (sixth or fifth century B.C.). Others, including the writer of this commentary, are less confident in our ability to reconstruct the prehistory of the present text. Whichever perspective one maintains regarding the nature of the relationship between these two accounts, one thing remains clear. In their present canonical form, these two narratives belong together, and together they convey the initial biblical understandings of God as Creator, of creation, of humanity, and of God's creation intentions for the relationships among them.

Genesis 3 paints the vivid picture of the origin of human beings' estrangement from God and others. The narrative depicts the first humans, created in God's own image, listening to a creature (and a stranger, to boot), rather than to their Creator. The consequence was the tragic fracturing of the wholesome relationships that had existed between and among God, humans, and the rest of God's earthly creation.

The various narrative segments in Gen 1—3 reveal a beautiful example of the simultaneous patterning, or the presence of more than one literary patterning or sequencing, often found in great literary works. In Gen 1—3 as a whole, we note the following repeated pattern of bringing a discussion of one subject to a climax, then focusing on the subject of that unit's climax in greater detail in the following discussion, or unit.

> **First Unit:** *Subject*—creation of the heavens and the earth (1:1); *Climax*—the earth (1:1)
>
> **Second Unit:** *Subject*—creation upon the earth (1:2—2:3); *Climax*—creation of the first humans (1:26-31)
>
> **Third Unit:** *Subject*—making of the first human pair (2:4-25); *Climax*—both naked and not ashamed (2:25)
>
> **Fourth Unit:** *Subject*—how humans learned shame (3:1-24); *Climax*—expulsion from the garden (3:23-24)

A. Creation upon the Earth (1:1—2:3)

BEHIND THE TEXT

The seven paragraphs of the creation week

The artistry of literary sequencing found in chs 1—3, as a whole, also is evident in the first longer unit, 1:1—2:3. Following the short introductory paragraph (1:1-2), the narrative of creation is organized into seven successive paragraphs, the seven successive days of the creation week. The seven paragraphs exhibit a number of features in common. Each of the first six paragraphs, narrating the six days of God's actual creative work, begins, "And God [*Elohim*] said, 'Let there be . . .' [or the logical and necessary variant, 'Let X bring forth . . .']." Other recurring features include the report "it was so," and God's assessment or evaluation, "it was good." Each of these paragraphs also ends, "And there was evening, and there was morning—the X day." This feature, of course, is the source of the common titles, "day one" (or "first day"), "second day" (or "day two"), etc., for the successive days of the creation week.

Within these seven paragraphs, however, other common features vary in their presence within or absence from any given paragraph, another sign of the author's literary skill. Moreover, and partly as a sign of its unique subject—the account of the seventh/Sabbath day—the seventh paragraph does not follow the pattern of the first six either at its beginning or at its end, though it does show other commonalities with some of the preceding six paragraphs.

The pairing of the six creation days

Another sign of the skilled literary crafting of this account is the symmetrical pairing of the six days of God's creation work, as follows:

Day 1—Light	**Day 4**—Light-bearers
Day 2—Skies and seas	**Day 5**—Sky creatures and sea creatures
Day 3—Dry land	**Day 6**—Land creatures, including the ʾādām

The importance of these pairings will become evident as we discuss them in the commentary, below.

The number seven

Another literary feature of Gen 1:1—2:3 is its use of the number seven—a number of perfection in many cultures—and its multiples. Besides the obvious seven paragraphs of the seven days of the creation week, we may observe immediately that v 1 comprises seven words (Hebrew), and v 2 comprises fourteen. Cassuto notes these, among others (1961, 13-15): "God" [*Elohim*] occurs thirty-five times; "earth," twenty-one times; "heavens" (together with "expanse/firmament"), twenty-one times; "light" and "day" occur seven times in the first paragraph (day one); "water(s)" occurs seven times in paragraphs two and three; "light" occurs seven times in paragraph four; references to "living creatures" occur seven times in paragraphs six and seven; God's evaluation that "it was good" occurs seven times; the middle three sentences of the seventh paragraph dealing with the seventh day comprise seven words each; in the middle of these three sentences occurs the phrase "the seventh day"; the seventh paragraph contains thirty-five words altogether. As Cassuto comments, "To suppose that all this is a mere coincidence is not possible" (1961, 15).

The lengthening of successive paragraphs

Another literary feature that has to do with word count is the lengthening of the paragraphs as the narrative of the creation days progresses. Paragraph/day one is thirty-one words (Hebrew text); paragraph/day two is thirty-eight words. Paragraphs three, four, and five are approximately double the first two. Paragraph/day three and paragraph/day four are sixty-nine words each; paragraph/day five is fifty-seven words. Paragraph/day six is one hundred forty-nine words, a little more than double the paragraph lengths for each of the previous three days. Dorsey is correct in observing, "This structuring technique conveys the impression of ever-increasing variety and profusion" (1999, 49).

A phenomenological telling

Finally, we never shall understand Gen 1:1—2:3, especially, unless we understand its phenomenological approach. That is, this text is written from the point of view of the earth's surface, and presents its subjects as they present themselves to humans here (cf. LaSor 1987, 7-8). It does not contradict science in any particular, and could not, since it is a very general and generalized, short account. But neither is it intended as a scientific treatise—again, because it is a short and very generalized account, and its interests lie elsewhere than in modern astronomy, geology, biological taxonomy, and cellular biology, including the recent more sensational findings of DNA research.

Thus, Gen 1:6-8 pictures the "expanse," "firmament," or "sky" (*rāqîaʿ*) as a giant bowl resting upside-down upon the surface of the earth. Indeed, when one sees the daytime sky unobstructed through the complete circle of the horizon, it does appear as a bowl resting on the earth at the horizon, all around the circle. On an unclouded night, with views to the horizon all around, it is easy to experience the sky as a giant inverted colander!

Similarly, the account of day four says nothing about the nature, or the celestial positioning and movement, of the light-bearers. For theological reasons it does not even name them, but simply states that God placed them where they are, *with respect to how we see and experience them*, to perform the tasks God appointed them, *with respect to this earth*. Nothing else is said about them, by way of affirmation or of denial, because nothing else is of concern in this account.

The author presents the text in such a way that all humans of all ages could understand the narrative and its purposes and intentions. Science has been important in a number of ages and cultures, but this text deals in what humans can observe with the naked eye, meaning that its observation of the world is quite limited by our standards, and thus difficult for us to recognize as science. (To call this limitation prescientific, though, seems to this writer unnecessarily elitist and prejudicial.) Thus, as noted above, the text references a bowl-like sky. As another example, this text is easy to read as presenting a three-storied view of the universe, with a watery heaven above, subterranean waters beneath, and dry-land-with-water in the middle. (This reading, while common, is not necessarily convincing, as it ignores one of the two meanings of šāmayim within the text.) Moreover, this text deals only summarily with seed-producing plants, with different kinds of fruit-producing trees, with different kinds of animals and birds, etc. The presence of such (to us) rudimentary observations of the world in this text and the integration of that data with the author's theology of creation means this account of creation is not *anti*scientific. However, its focus on God as Creator indicates that its primary purposes are theological, not scientific. Advances in the physical sciences in recent centuries reveal a universe far more complex than this text could have portrayed, even had that been its purpose. Therefore, to read this text as a treatise on science is to misread it almost totally. (For an important nuancing here, see Fretheim 2005, 27-28 and, esp., note 116, 303-4.) This is not so much a tragedy of reading modern science into the text. The real tragedy is that, in focusing on the kind of science that is *not* intended in this text, one inevitably misses the foundational truths about God and God's creation, including especially God's human creation, that *are* intended. It is not too much to say that in missing these truths, God's people also have missed our way at many crucial points along our historical/theological journey, causing much unnecessary skepticism, hostility, and suffering both within and outside our ranks.

The functional ontology of Gen 1

In *The Lost World of Genesis One*, John Walton (2009) sets out the case for viewing Gen 1 as presenting not a *material* but a *functional* ontology of the origins of the earth and the cosmos. These are not literary categories; rather, they are philosophical and theological. The central feature of Walton's thesis is that Gen 1 is not intended to present a summary of the *material* origins of the earth, or of any of the rest of the cosmos: *What* all did God make? *How* did God make it? *When* did God make it? Rather, the purpose of Gen 1 is to report the *functional* beginnings of the earth, its systems, and its creatures, as God's cosmic temple. That is, Gen 1 reports the inauguration of the earth as God's dwelling place, from which God directs and superintends the *functions* of the various entities and systems God has created and set in motion. Walton does not deny a material ontology; God is Creator of the universe in its material as well as its functional origins. He simply says Gen 1 is not the place to find a discussion of *material* origins. Walton argues that to read Gen

1 as though it presents a *material* ontology, when it is intended to present a *functional* ontology, is to read Gen 1 *non*literally, rather than literally.

1. The Heavens and the Earth (1:1-2)

BEHIND THE TEXT

The Genesis creation account is set against the backdrop of and is intended (among other purposes) to correct Egyptian, Canaanite, and Mesopotamian notions of multiple gods and goddesses, each possessing his or her own sphere of power and responsibility. The proclamation of *this* account could not be more vivid in its contrast: Israel's creator God is before all else, and is the Creator of all else. In the stories with the greatest influence on Israel, even the mightiest creator gods could not begin with nothing. In these stories, matter existed even before the gods themselves. As Oswalt has noted, knowledge of the transcendent God, shown first here in Gen 1:1, cannot be deduced; rather, God revealed it to Israel (1988, 16-17).

We have chosen to discuss vv 1 and 2 together, because together they set the scene for the sequence of the six creation days as the narrative presents them: **In the beginning God created the heavens and the earth. Now *as for* the earth . . .** ; then the days are narrated in order, with the creative activities specific to each one. Verse 2 sets up the sequence with its brief description of the earth's state at the *beginning* of the creative process upon it.

IN THE TEXT

■ 1 If one begins reading the Bible at the first line, as we do with most books, one reads, **In the beginning God created the heavens and the earth**—the simple, yet sublime, beginning of the greatest story ever told. **In the beginning** (*bĕrēʾšît*) is not the beginning of God, but of **the heavens and the earth.** Also, this verse does not state anything about the time of this beginning, whether it was billions of years ago, or only thousands. It only says God began it all.

With respect to God, v 1 affirms one God, and one God only. The divine title *ʾĕlōhîm* (plural noun form, **God**) denotes divine majesty and power. The author uses the plural form *ʾĕlōhîm* here in a singular sense, which is the case in most instances of its occurrence in the Hebrew Scripture. The plural form conveys the plural of majesty, the idea that Israel's God is the God of all gods, the only true God, the God of majesty and power, and the Lord of the universe, history, and nature. The text thus begins with an emphatic claim of God's rightful title (God's personal name *Yahweh* is introduced in Gen 2) and the acknowledgment of Israel's God as the Creator of all else that is.

God (*ʾĕlōhîm*)

In the ancient Semitic world, El (*ʾēl*, noun, masc. sg.) was the basic word for "God"; this title most likely denotes power and strength. In the Canaanite

39

religion depicted in the Ugaritic epics, El is the name of the supreme deity, father of all the gods and goddesses, and lord of heaven. In the Hebrew Bible, the noun *ʾēl* can be linked with other nouns (e.g., "The God of Israel," Ps 68:35), and with adjectives (e.g., "the faithful God," Deut 7:9). Though in some instances the plural form (*ʾĕlōhîm*) is applied to gods of other nations (e.g., Judg 11:24; 1 Kgs 11:5; 2 Kgs 1:2), in most cases the plural form refers to Israel's God.

Another important implication of v 1 is that only God is eternal. This verse, rightly read, does not leave room for the coexistence with God of the energy/matter, or of the space/time, continuums. Rather, it affirms God's creation of all else: of energy and matter, of space and time. Nothing is coeternal with God. This first sentence in the Bible, this first logical and theological assertion with all its implications, precludes any and all forms of Gnosticism and dualism and their claims.

The Hebrew Verb *bārāʾ*

The Hebrew verb *bārāʾ*, "he created," occurs about fifty times in the Hebrew Bible; seven of those occurrences are in this chapter. When *bārāʾ* occurs in the Qal (basic) stem, as it does here in its first six occurrences, God always is its subject, i.e., God is the Creator.

The verb *bārāʾ* does not, in and of itself, mean *creatio ex nihilo*, creation from nothing. It does, however, signify an extraordinary creative work, something greater and/or more special than even God usually does—if that is possible! In this account, it is used once to introduce God's extraordinary creative activity, altogether (1:1). Once it introduces the beginning of sentient life on this earth (1:21). It is used twice in the summary of God's creative action (2:3, 4). In the middle three occurrences of *bārāʾ*, all in 1:27, the object is humans (*ʾādām*). This is the clearest and most emphatic statement possible of the unique and extraordinary value God placed, and places, upon humans (*ʾādām*).

Furthermore, God (*Elohim*) created **the heavens and the earth.** This phrase is not the ancient Hebrew equivalent of "the universe"; ancient Israel conceived of the heavens as one entity, and the earth as another. The universe, of which the earth is a small part, is a later (Greek, astronomical) understanding. Though we comprehend the universe conceptually as the Greeks discovered it to be, we still *experience* it in two parts as this verse names it—the heavens we see "above" us, and the earth (including the seas) "beneath," upon which we dwell.

The Hebrew noun *šāmayim* is rightly translated here **heavens,** the place of the heavenly bodies beyond the firmament/expanse. A few verses later, in the account of the second day (v 8), God named the firmament (*rāqîaʿ*) itself *šāmayim;* there the context requires the translation "firmament," "expanse," or, more commonly today, "sky," or even "atmosphere."

Similarly, the noun ʾereṣ is translated correctly here **earth**, meaning the planet we inhabit. Depending on the context, ʾereṣ may be translated "land" in the sense of a district, a region, or a nation or even "earth" in the sense of the ground or the soil. The immediate context of v 1 is v 2; as we shall see, v 2 confirms the translation here, **the heavens and the earth.**

Genesis 1:1

The traditional translation of v 1 as an independent clause (sentence) is correct, though some modern scholars (preeminently Speiser 1964, 11-13), and some English versions, translate it as a subordinate clause, "When God began to create . . . ," or the like. Cassuto has demonstrated that the syntax of v 2 requires v 1 to be an independent sentence (1961, 19-20). Hamilton, using different theological and syntactical arguments, reaches the same conclusion that v 1 is an introductory sentence to the entire seven-day creation account (1990, 105-8). As an independent sentence, v 1 stands both as an introduction to and a summary statement of this creation narrative.

■ **2** Verse 2 confirms the reading of v 1 as an independent clause. The subject of discussion in the first short unit (v 1) is God's creation of the heavens and the earth. Immediately in v 2, **the earth,** the climactic entity of the first unit (v 1), becomes the main subject of the next unit; we translate věhāʾāreṣ, **Now as for the earth.** That this was the author's literary intent is clear from two facts: (1) the earth and its inhabitants are the predominant interest of 1:2—2:3, the second literary unit by this analysis; (2) the heavens are discussed from here on only from the perspective of the earth. As Westermann has noted, "Any attempt . . . which leaves the first two or three verses in isolation and does not enquire into the function of these verses as part of a whole neglects a very important methodological approach" (1984, 93).

We believe the following is an accurate (though a bit stilted) translation of the whole of v 2: **Now as for the earth, it was a desert and a vacancy, and darkness was upon the face of the deep; and the Spirit of God [Elohim] was hovering/brooding over the face of the waters.**

In this verse we find the writer describing the condition of the earth when God brought it into existence. Though often translated as two adjectives, the Hebrew phrase tōhû vāvōhû actually comprises two nouns, joined by the Hebrew conjunction vav/waw, usually translated "and." David Tsumura has shown conclusively that no idea of a hostile or violent chaos inheres in either of these nouns separately, nor in both when used together (1994, 310-28). The basic meaning of tōhû is "desert, a desert place." Here, it refers to the earth that is present, but covered by the primeval waters. It depicts the earth as yet unproductive, as desert wastelands are unproductive (from the ancient point of view). The second noun bōhû, Tsumura explains (albeit tentatively) as "a Semitic term based on the root *bhw and possibly a cognate of Arabic bahiya 'to be empty,'" as a tent or a house bare of furnishings and other contents is empty (1994, 315-16).

This makes a vivid picture and excellent sense, as well. This phrase (*tōhû vāvōhû*) pictures the earth, when God had brought it into existence but had not yet begun to act creatively in and upon it, as an unproductive **desert** and, moreover, as **a vacancy,** or **empty.** (Fretheim translates *tōhû vāvōhû* "desolate and unproductive"; 1994, 342.) Jeremiah's use of *tōhû vāvōhû* (4:23-26; see esp. v 26) also conveys the image of the nonproductive desert. Here in Gen 1:2, the earth was *not yet* the earth as it would be when God had finished the work of the initial creation week, nor even as we experience it now, after its extensive ruination because of human unfaithfulness. Walton takes a slightly different perspective, proposing that *tōhû* and *bōhû* together conveys the idea of nonexistence (in their functional ontology); i.e., the earth was not yet functioning in an ordered system. (Functional) creation had not yet taken place; therefore, there was only (functional) nonexistence (2009, 49).

The next part of v 2 indicates that **darkness was upon the face of the deep. Darkness** here is only the absence of light (see more discussion on darkness below). Verse 2 implies the presence of the raw materials for the creative processes that would bring the earth to its fullness. The text does *not* imply the raw materials always existed; on the basis of v 1, we may conclude that God the Creator brought even these into existence. The accounts of the successive creation days in the rest of this chapter describe God's activity in bringing content and productivity—the fertility both of the earth and of the multiplicity of created entities upon it. This would begin with God's creation of the light, which set the limits to the darkness on day one.

The deep (*tĕhôm*) in v 2 refers to the primeval waters covering the earth. Heidel has shown that Hebrew *tĕhôm* derives from the same Semitic root as does the divine name Tiamat, the goddess of the saltwater oceans in the Mesopotamian creation accounts (1951, 98-101). (This is not to say Hebrew *tĕhôm* is derived from Babylonian Tiamat.) However, these waters of Gen 1:2 were *not* the raging monster goddess whom the creator god Marduk had to defeat and slay before he could set to work creating the earth from her dead body. If anything, the author's choice of the noun *tĕhôm* here seems to be deliberate; the author could have described this primeval condition using different vocabulary. This was an opportunity to deny the deity of the goddess without naming her directly, as well as to deny either the power or the desire (could they have experienced desire) of the primeval waters to resist the will of their creator.

Verse 2 ends with a final description of the primeval condition, **and the Spirit of God** [*Elohim*] **was hovering/brooding over the face of the waters.** Hebrew *rûaḥ* may mean "Spirit," "spirit," "wind," or "breath." We may rule out "wind" as a translation here; "the wind of God" would imply a great windstorm, gale force or beyond. This is not the picture provided by the rest of the clause, of a peaceful **hovering** or **brooding** (*mĕraḥepet*), like a bird watching over and protecting its young. It is difficult, too, to imagine "breath" **brooding over the waters** (*māyim* here, not *tĕhôm*). The phrase **the Spirit of God** (*rûaḥ ʾĕlōhîm*) is the appropriate translation here; in this first context, **the Spirit of God** is the pensive, creative, nurturing, soon-to-be-acting presence of God.

Partly because chaotic waters feature in some other biblical texts, many have argued that the waters of this verse, also, identified by the use of two different nouns (*tĕhôm, māyim*), *were* chaotic and rebellious, needing God's strong hand to bring them into submission before beginning God's creative work. Tsumura's work on the phrase *tōhû vāvōhû* (see above) proves this was not the case with the primeval waters. Rather, this earth, as God was about to begin God's creative action upon it, wheeled in space—dark, unproductive, and vacant, as a stripped and deserted tent or house is vacant. Far from being an unruly or a hostile primeval nature in rebellion, the earth and its mantle of covering waters were still, motionless, receptive, waiting quietly in the darkness for the Creator's next step.

Ephrem the Syrian on Gen 1:2

It was appropriate to reveal here that the Spirit hovered in order for us to learn that the work of creation was held in common by the Spirit with the Father and the Son. The Father spoke. The Son created. And so it was also right that the Spirit offer its work, clearly shown through its hovering, in order to demonstrate its unity with the other persons. Thus we learn that all was brought to perfection and accomplished by the Trinity. (Louth 2001, 6)

FROM THE TEXT

The first line of the traditional version of the Apostles' Creed is, "I believe in God the Father Almighty, maker of heaven and earth." The Hebrew/Israelite/Jewish faith, and the Christian faith that descended from it, always have affirmed God as Creator. Today, some Jews and many Christians believe God created by a process they have recently labeled creation science or, sometimes, intelligent design. However, most Jews and many Christians, still affirming God as Creator, believe God created by means of one of the several evolutionary models advanced in the century-and-a-half since Darwin published *On the Origin of Species*. Some of these folks refer to themselves as theistic evolutionists. As we have noted already, and hope to show in more detail below, Gen 1—2 addresses the *what* of God's creation only in the most general of terms, not in any way resembling a modern scientifically descriptive manner. Similarly, it does not address the timeline of creation, the *when*, in a manner that would allow us to draw modern scientific conclusions from the text. Finally, it does not address the multiple *hows* of creation in a way that answers the modern concerns of, e.g., geomorphology or biological taxonomy.

43

Occupied with greater concerns, the text does not (partly because it could not adequately, for our day) address any of these.

This is not to say that believers in God (Jewish or Christian) are forbidden to pursue scientific answers to the *what, when,* and *how* questions of creation—far from it. It is to say, however, that those who find one set of answers currently more persuasive—and acting by love's constraints—ought not to denigrate or condemn others who find another set of answers more persuasive, since all are agreed in affirming their belief in "God the Father Almighty, maker of heaven and earth." (Atheistic evolutionary hypotheses are another issue, of course.) Science has its multiple, valuable places, but Gen 1—2 is a theological, not a scientific, narrative. "I believe in God . . ." is the tenet binding us together as brothers and sisters in *God's* creation. Disagreeing, with love, on the science of origins, is both the privilege and the responsibility of Christian brothers and sisters who find themselves on opposite sides in these matters, while affirming together, "I believe in God . . . , maker of heaven and earth."

One can find various attempts to reconcile geological and other data that seem to indicate the age of the earth as in the billions of years with a common young earth understanding of Gen 1—2. One such attempt is the so-called gap theory, which begins by positing a perfect creation in v 1. Something happened to make the earth *a desert and a vacancy,* as we have translated the description of its state at the beginning of v 2. In the gap theory, that *something* is said to have been the casting of Lucifer to the earth following his unsuccessful rebellion against God in heaven. Proponents of this theory interpret Isaiah's oracle against the king of Babylon to have a broader secondary application to Satan's fall (Isa 14:12-15). To be fair, these gap theory proponents base this interpretation of Isaiah on Jesus' words in Luke 10:18, *I watched Satan falling from heaven like lightning.* However, this line of interpretation produces far too small a gap into which to stuff the entire geological column, the astrophysical evidences, and the other assorted data that must be disposed of between Gen 1:1 and 1:2 to make the gap theory tenable.

More importantly, Gen 1:2 cannot be made to support such an understanding. The gap theory requires translating the beginning of v 2, "Now as for the earth, it *had become* a desert and a waste" (as a result of some here-unspecified catastrophe). The grammatical structure and the positioning of the verb and the noun in this verse do not support this translation. The verb would have to be imperfect (with *vav* consecutive) and come first in the clause to translate, "the earth had become." However, the *vav* conjunction is attached to the noun, the noun precedes the verb, and the aspect of the verb is perfect (*hāyĕtâ*). The only translation that makes grammatical and syntactical sense is, *Now as for the earth, it* was *a desert and a vacancy* (in keeping with our discussion above). The gap theory is a fanciful, too-clever-by-half attempt to reconcile competing *scientific* hypotheses, but ultimately is capable only of inflicting damage upon a *theological* text, if taken seriously.

On another matter, no reader before the first century (and possibly not even then) would have placed a Trinitarian interpretation upon Gen 1:2. However, reminding ourselves that the earliest readers would not have seen the Trinity in v 2 is not the same as denying the cooperative presence and work of all three persons of the Trinity in creation. John asserted, "Through [the Word, i.e., Jesus Christ] all things were made" (John 1:3). Paul agreed, "For by [the Son] all things were created" (Col. 1:16). If God the Father and God the Son partnered in creation, Christians are justified in believing that God the Holy Spirit was also an equal partner. We may think of Gen 1:2, then, as referencing the Holy Spirit in a foreshadowing kind of way, though it does not prove the Trinity. That would be too great a burden for this verse to bear by itself.

Though the verb *bārā'* is not used extensively through the rest of the Hebrew Scripture, its later uses link creation with God's redemption first, of Israel, then of all God's earthly creation. We see this in Isa 40—45, both in Isaiah's multiple uses of *bārā'* (nearly one-third of its total occurrences are in these six chapters), and in the internal reciprocity of Isaiah's comprehensive argument through this section: God will rescue/redeem Israel because God as Creator is wise enough and powerful enough to do it; God will demonstrate to unfaithful Israel that God is the only God and Creator by rescuing/redeeming Israel from its foreign exile.

In Rom 4:16-17, Paul commended the faith of Abraham in **God, the one giving life to the dead, and calling [into existence] the things which do not exist, as existing.** Abraham, Paul declared, believed God's promise that God was not finished creating; as a result, Abraham became "the father of us all" in faith.

If we had the space, we could discuss many other ramifications of God's ongoing creative/redemptive work in the world. The creative power of God reversed the hold of death and raised Jesus from the dead on the third day. That same creative power God continues to exercise against the day when the eschaton shall be fully realized and, as John the Revelator heard from the mouth of the One sitting on the throne, "Behold, I make [am making] all things new" (Rev 21:5 KJV). The first verses of Genesis open the Bible as the end of Revelation closes it, with the great hope anchored in the Alpha and Omega, the One who creates and re-creates—from the individual believer to all creation.

2. Days of Preparation (1:3-13)

a. Let There Be Light (1:3-5)

BEHIND THE TEXT

On the narrative structure of the creation week, see "The pairing of the six creation days" in the first Behind the Text section, above.

Genesis 1 has been called poetic prose, exalted prose, and other, similar admiring descriptors. Its literary artistry is evident even in the verbs of this short section. Its three verses contain nine verb forms. Four of these are forms of the verb *hāyâ* ("to be"), with one pair of occurrences near the beginning in v 3, another pair as the last two verbs of the section (v 5). The first of these "to be" verbs is God's fiat command (**let there be**); the other three, statements of existence resulting from God's fiat (**and there was**). The other five verb forms all have God as their subject: **and God said** [*ʾāmar*]; **and God saw/evaluated** [*rāʾâ*]; **and God separated** [*bādāl*]; **and God called/named** (*qārāʾ*). The last of these occurs twice, but with a fine sense of artistic variation (*yiqrāʾ* and *qārāʾ*). The divine title itself is not actually repeated in the second occurrence of *qārāʾ*; it occurs four times altogether in the section. The last four verb forms are two pairs of two different verbs, **he called/named** (*qārāʾ*) twice, then **and it was** (*vayyĕhî*) twice.

IN THE TEXT

■ **3** God's first act in shaping and filling the earth was a spoken command: **Let there be light** (v 3). Its breathtaking brevity and simplicity serve to accent God's sovereignty. The Hebrew text is even shorter, more spare: *yĕhî ʾôr*; two words; three syllables; six letters. As often, in the accounts of royal commands in ancient Near Eastern narratives, the fulfillment of this command is recorded immediately, in identical language (**and there was light,** *vayyĕhî ʾôr*). Even more to the point for Israel's faith (and ours), this immediacy of fulfillment was/is striking evidence of God's sovereignty—that even that ubiquitous and mysterious entity, light, should have made its first appearance merely at this briefest of directives.

The ancients did not conceive of light as an entity and, with all our vaunted advances in the disciplines of physics, we, too, still cannot fully grasp the dual nature of light as both matter and energy. Despite (or perhaps because of) the continuing gaps in our knowledge, this report that the primordial light simply appeared at God's bidding is entirely in character for light as we experience it, even as it was for the ancients.

Having initiated creation upon the earth in this way, however, God did not act exactly the same way twice. Each creative act God fitted to the nature of its object. The text reports, **And God said,** eight more times (vv 6, 9, 11, 14, 20, 24, 26, 29). However, only here is that report *not* followed up by action of some kind, such as "God made" (see v 7), or the action of some previously created entity.

■ **4** Verse 4 begins with God's evaluation of the light that came into existence at his command. ***And God saw the light, that it was good*** is the first of seven such positive assessments in this creation narrative (vv 10, 12, 18, 21, 25, 31). **Good** (*tôb*) in this context is not in the middle of a scale from totally bad to most excellent; it is itself a superlative assessment, completely positive in the highest degree, as far from bad or evil as it is possible to get. When God pronounces something (or someone) **good,** God is judging it as being, and functioning, as God intended—by creation or, as often is necessary now, by redemption and restoration.

Verse 4 concludes with the report of another divine activity. ***And God caused a separation between the light and the darkness.*** We see the significance of this in v 5; this is not an everywhere-and-for-all-time separation of light and darkness, but the separation we experience upon the earth as the alternating of day and night. If light were not assigned its own times and timing, we would not experience darkness at all.

The question well may occur to the reader, "If 'the light' was 'good,' what was 'the darkness'?" The answer is, "Nothing." First, we must stipulate that this is not a text on the physics of light. Nevertheless, we are allowed to recognize that what we experience and name as "light" is the same substance/energy studied and explained by the physicist whose specialty is light. Thus, in the physics of light, the Hebrew word ʾôr and the English word "light" denote the existence/presence of the almost infinitesimal mass/energy particles to which we give those names in our respective languages. The Hebrew word ḥōšek and the English word "darkness" signify the nonexistence/nonpresence of such particles in the place being described as "dark." The words ʾôr and "light" are real words, apart from what they symbolize and, physically, "light" is "something." The words ḥōšek and "darkness" are real words, apart from what they symbolize, but what they symbolize does not, in fact, exist, except as an abstract concept. "Darkness," the absence of light, is "nothing." The statement, for example, "The darkness was so deep I could feel it," is merely a literary device called hyperbole (exaggeration for effect); it cannot *give* substantive existence to that which has no substantive existence apart from the literary figure.

Later, in Hebrew as in other languages, "darkness" acquired metaphorical significance as designating and describing "evil." Since this text deals with our world before the "presence" of evil within it, it is best not to import that metaphorical use of "darkness" into it.

■ **5** God's separation of light and darkness was followed by God's naming of light and darkness. ***And God called the light, day; and the darkness he called, night.*** The common noun šēm (name), which would be necessary to make this a formal naming, is not present in either clause here (Bush 1996, 7-8). This may be because **light** is an inanimate entity, and **darkness** is not an entity at all, but only the *absence* of light. Rather than giving them proper names, then, God designated the common nouns by which these two states (as we experience them on the earth's surface) would be called henceforth: **the light** [ʾôr] **day** (yôm); its absence, **the darkness** (ḥōšek), **night** (lāyĕlâ).

> "And God divided the light and the darkness, and God called the light day and [God] called the darkness night." It did not say here "God made the darkness," because darkness is merely the absence of light. Yet God made a division between light and darkness. . . . "He called the light day, and he called the darkness night" was said in the sense that he made them to be called, because he separated and ordered all things so that they could be distinguished and receive names. (Louth 2001, 8)

Verse 5 concludes with the placement of God's creative work in a temporal framework, a recurring feature of this creation narrative. **And it was evening, and it was morning.** It is common for people to quote this phrase as the reason the Jewish faith reckons the day from sunset to sunset. That may be so, at least in part, but such a reckoning of the day's beginning and ending is a misunderstanding of these statements. Their natural import is, "So the day went along until it was evening, then the night went along until it was morning, and then one full day had elapsed." Thus, when on day four the sun and the moon began their appointed tasks of regulating for the earth its hours of day and night, respectively, the day began and ended with sunrise.

In biblical narrative the day after a specified night is called "tomorrow," i.e., the day begins at sunrise (e.g., Gen 19:33-34; 1 Sam 28:19). Even the laws that prescribe the beginning of the *observance* of a holy day at sundown reckon the holy day itself as beginning with the following sunrise (e.g., Exod 12:18; Lev 23:32). Cassuto summarizes, "It will thus be seen that throughout the Bible there obtains only one system of *computing time:* the day is considered to begin in the morning; but in regard to the festivals and appointed times, the Torah ordains that they shall be observed also on the night of the *preceding day*" (1961, 29, emphases original; see his entire discussion, 28-30). Our Western custom of reckoning the day as beginning at midnight is a part of our heritage from Rome.

The last two Hebrew words we should render, **one day;** "day one" is grammatically acceptable but could be conceptually misleading. We definitely should *not* translate, **the first day,** even though this was the first day of the creation week. Logically, there was no first day yet, because a second day had not yet come into existence for a first day to be prior to. So far, there had been only **one day.** This day, at this point in the creation narrative, stands alone. The reader soon will know this day is only a beginning. *Within the narrative,* however, we do not yet know that, and that fact invites us to evaluate it without comparisons. God pronounced this day **good;** in and of itself, and on its own merits, it was good because God had made it good.

Westermann on the Creation of Light

The first thing that God created was light. . . . It is only possible to describe the work of creation as a whole because of the creation of light at the beginning. And so those exegetes are correct who understand vv. 3-5 as a process which makes creation possible rather than as a single work of creation. But the point should not be pressed. . . . The separation of light from darkness is temporal, not spatial. (1984, 112)

FROM THE TEXT

Beginnings are necessary to all that follows; it does not follow that beginnings are only means to subsequent ends. If any given beginning is to be worthy of evaluation as "good," it probably will be because its initiator regarded it as a worthy end, *before* considering its value as a means to further ends. Even here, already in the **one day,** we may learn about creating from the Creator in whose image we are created. We, too, may evaluate our work as good, and take joy for its own sake in work only begun, if only it is well begun.

A sevenfold repetition of God's appraisal of all God's creative work as **good,** in the very first, and only sustained, biblical narrative account of creation stands as a powerful theological statement. The physical, material universe is *not* intrinsically evil. Matter and energy, space and time, the universe and this earth—all are *essentially* good, because God created them so. *All* forms of gnostic thought, ancient and modern, are ruled out of consideration from the beginning, in the judgment and the positive word of the God who made all that is, both the physical/material and the spiritual. The equations, "physical is evil" and "spiritual is holy," are shown already to be false—in effect, blasphemy against the good and holy God who delights in *all* God's creation, material *and* spiritual. Human faithlessness, though making necessary Christ's redemptive, restorative work, could not and cannot negate the initial and essential goodness of all God's creation, material or otherwise.

b. Let There Be an Expanse (1:6-8)

BEHIND THE TEXT

We noted briefly above (v 2) that many of Israel's neighbors regarded the seas as gods, or as goddesses. Actually, almost any source, movement, or body of water was deified in antiquity, from oceans and seas to lakes and rivers, from clouds and mists to springs and wells.

Here we see another learning unit of this text's teaching that the waters are not gods in any shape, form, or fashion. Like all else in creation, they are God's servants, doing God's bidding. If they could experience and express thought and feeling, they would exude joy that God created them and found them worthy of God's calling to the being and the tasks God appointed them. This paragraph records the next step in God's working upon all the waters, assigning them their respective places and functions. This was a two-stage process, the first stage accomplished on the second creative day, the second stage on the third day.

IN THE TEXT

■ **6** The account of the second creative day begins with another command of God, **Let there be.** The fulfillment of this command, however, was a creative *act* of God, as we see in v 7, "So God made." We often visualize God as speaking everything into existence during the creative process. The narrative of Gen 1, however, records only the light of day one as coming into existence solely at God's spoken word. Everything else, though always mandated at the beginning of its narrative by God's spoken word, is a product of God's making or arranging, or of the ground or seas producing. This is not to deny the power of God's spoken word, only to say that God apparently delights in *making*, perhaps more than in *merely* speaking entities into existence. As we are made in God's creative image, we may see here the ultimate source of human delight in the myriad things we make in imitation of our Creator's good work, and of our joy in that making, following upon God's own joy in God's making.

God commanded that there should be **an expanse *in the midst of* the waters to separate water from water** (v 6). To this point, the narrative has pictured the waters as covering the whole surface of the earth. Now something would change, but it would have to do entirely with the primeval waters. Since the *expanse* would be *in the midst of the waters,* we must look for the change as having to do with the form, the characteristics, and/or the functions of the waters.

■ **7** Verse 7 reports that God fulfilled his command by his own creative act. **So God made the expanse.** Hebrew *rāqîaʿ* (expanse) refers to something shaped by beating out its malleable substance, as the smith formed a gold, silver, or bronze bowl by beating it into the desired shape with a hammer. Indeed, when one has an unobstructed view of the entire three-hundred-sixty-degree circle of the horizon, the sky looks like a bowl set upside-down upon the edge of the earth. We even have a saying, "The heavens are brass," reflecting this sometime appearance and feel of the atmosphere.

It is the atmosphere that **expanse/***rāqîaʿ* names, as we discover now, for God caused the *rāqîaʿ* to divide (separate) *between the waters which were under the expanse and the waters which were above the expanse.* This was not a new entity, but a second division, this one within a single entity already in existence, namely, the primeval waters. (The first division was the separation between light, a created entity, and darkness, merely the absence of light, v 4.)

This is not to say the atmosphere consists entirely of water, nor that ancient Israel thought it does. It reflects the fact that rain, snow, and other forms of precipitation—all of which are water—come from the atmosphere, the sky. Job 38:22-41 largely reflects, in exquisite poetic language, this imagery of the sky as the immediate source of snow, water, ice, frost, hailstorm, etc. ***The waters . . . above the expanse,*** both in their suspension within the atmosphere and in their falling upon the earth in myriad forms, sustain the life upon the earth's surface.

This is the beginning of the hydrological cycle (briefly outlined also in Eccl 1:6-7), upon which all life upon the land, at least, depends. The ability of the sun to evaporate moisture from the waters on the earth's surface, and of the atmosphere to absorb it, then to relinquish it again in the form of precipitation is a critical function of the ***expanse.***

A *Phenomenological* Telling

It is important not to slight the *phenomenological* approach of this broad, sweeping, very limited description of God's initial creative activity. Genesis 1 is not intended as a detailed scientific description. If it had been, all humans except the educated minority of the last two or three hundred years would have been excluded from understanding and learning from it.

Rather, Gen 1 describes the sky above us *phenomenologically*. That is, it describes it only as we see it and as we experience it—most vividly, as a bowl (*rāqîaʿ*) inverted above us. On a clear, moonless night, with an unobstructed view to the horizon in all directions, and the several thousand stars visible to the naked eye shining down upon us, we experience the night sky as a colander, a bowl pierced through with many holes, and a light source beyond it. We know this is not a scientific description of the daytime sky or of the nighttime sky; moreover, this description has nothing to do with the science of the sky, but only with how we see and experience it. Because it *does* record that God called the expanse "sky" (v 8), we can identify it as the earth's atmosphere, comprising air, water vapor, etc. More than that we ought not ask of this text, for on other issues it simply is silent.

Similarly, this narrative presents "the greater light" and "the lesser light" (v 16) of day four only from the perspective of their appearance from this earth's surface, and only mentions their functions related to the earth and its inhabitants. It says nothing else, nothing about the solar system, or of our place in our galaxy, or of our galaxy's place among the galaxies. How could it, and mean anything, since none of this was known to ancient Israel? Again, this is not a negation of science. Science as we practice it today, the detailed investigation and description of entities and their processes and interactions over time, simply is not a part of this discussion.

■ **8 God called the expanse "sky."** The Hebrew word for **sky** is *šāmāyim*, the same word translated "heavens" in v 1. Here, it means the atmosphere above us. In v 1, it means "everything above" the earth and our atmosphere, i.e., what

English, also, means by "the heavens" (what C. S. Lewis in his space trilogy called "deep heaven").

The final phrase of v 8, **the second day,** leads the readers of this text to anticipate the ongoing creative activity of God. Now that two days had come and gone, not just a single day, it was appropriate for the author to speak of "second," using the ordinal, an adjectival form, rather than the cardinal, as at the end of day one (v 5).

FROM THE TEXT

Perhaps the average ancient Israelite did not, could not, make the distinction between "the heavens" and the "sky." As we see and experience them—i.e., as we know them phenomenologically—the two are not easily distinguishable. Unaided observation and experience from the earth's surface will not give most of us an idea of "the heavens" *beyond* "the sky." We cannot know whether the narrator had a hint of "the heavens" as far more complex and far-reaching, or whether he even acknowledged a distinction between "the heavens" and "the sky." Perhaps he did. However, it is easy to read this text as intending to depict the ancient model of a three-storied universe, with heaven above, the earth's flat surface in the middle, and the place of the dead (*sheol*) below, the common cosmology of the ordinary ancient observer of the heavens and the earth. Whatever this narrator's understanding, he spoke phenomenologically, to be understood by the readers of his day, whose knowledge could not have been based on anything other than what they experienced and observed in their own everyday lives. Of course, today's reader can understand "the heavens" with the tools of modern astronomy, which continue to reveal the mysteries of "the heavens" in all their depth, variety, and marvelous complexity, unknown and unknowable to human beings of any past age. What we may not do is patronize our bygone elders, merely because we have been privileged to live in a different era.

c. Let the Dry Land Appear (1:9-13)

BEHIND THE TEXT

We see in this section another corrective to ancient pagan ideas of the creation of the earth. The Mesopotamian creation theologies, specifically the *Enuma Elish*, spoke of the creator god Marduk as killing the hostile ocean goddess Tiamat in hand-to-hand combat. Here in the biblical text there is not even a hint of force. On the contrary, God invited the waters and the dry land to participate in this stage of God's creative action, calling the waters to **gather themselves to one place,** and the dry land to **show itself.**

In an even more radical correction of ancient pagan theologies, God commanded/invited the earth to **vegetate vegetation.** All Israel's neighbors (and, too often, many Israelites themselves) believed the earth itself was a goddess whose active, willing (and sexual) participation they needed to secure if their fields, vineyards, orchards, and gardens were to be fruitful. This magisterial, and totally irenic, correction proclaims the earth, too, as God's good creation, willing servant, and glad partner in God's design for abundant and joyful life upon its surface.

The phrase *according to its kind* occurs ten times altogether (another number of completion in the decimal system, which ancient Israel also used) in the accounts of days three (vv 11-12), five (vv 20-23), and six (vv 24-31). It occurs once in v 11, twice in v 12 (thus a total of three for day three), twice in v 21 (two for day five), twice in v 24, and three times in v 25 (five for day six). This can be read as $3 + 2 = 5$, followed by $2 + 3 = 5$, two pairs of fives achieved by simple addition. The significance is that the first cluster of three occurrences pertains to plant life upon the land, the second cluster of two occurrences pertains to animal life in the seas and the skies, while an equal total of five in two successive verses (vv 24-25) pertains to the making of animal life upon the land. This concentrated and equal repetition signals movement toward the climax of the creative process.

IN THE TEXT

■ **9** The third creative day featured another mode of creation; the Creator is not limited in means or methods of creation, except as one choice may preclude other choices, at that or other points in the entire creative enterprise. Here, the method is rearrangement, rather than introduction of new entities. Both verbs are Hebrew *Niph'al*, the passive/reflexive stem. We may translate either *Let the waters under the heavens be gathered to one place, and let the dry ground appear/be seen* or *Let the waters under the heavens gather themselves to one place, and let the dry ground show itself.* Given both the explicit and the implicit notices of God's invitation to the creation to partner with God in the creative/procreative process at other points in the text of Gen 1, one may take the latter understanding to be the intent of the writer. Even at this early stage, though God retained sovereignty, God invited responsive participation. The command and its fulfillment in v 9 reflect what humans observe and experience. The earth's ocean waters cover the earth's great surface depressions, and all are connected—albeit sometimes by narrow straits—and the dry land rises above the oceans' various depressions.

John of Damascus on Gen 1:9

Now, the fact that Scripture speaks of one gathering does not mean that they were gathered together into one place, for notice that after this it says: "And the gathering together of the waters he called seas." Actually, the account meant that the waters were segregated by themselves apart from the earth. And so the waters were brought together into their gathering places and the dry land appeared. (Louth 2001, 12)

The phrase **to one place,** as the words of John of Damascus show, illustrates the dangers of reading the *details* of any current science (observation and/or experimentation, with explanatory analysis) back into any Scripture as its original and intended meaning. John of Damascus apparently followed the LXX reading of v 9, "And the waters under the heavens [*ouranou*] were gathered together into their gathering places, and the dry land appeared." Knowing various large and small bodies of water, John apparently assumed that the earth's surface always had been marked by these features in this kind of arrangement, and visualized many original large and small gatherings of waters as God's direction reported in v 9.

All modern geologists—whether theists and others espousing old earth uniformitarian geology or young earth creationists espousing a major geological upheaval as part of the processes of Noah's flood—agree that today's continents originally were a single land mass, usually called Pangaea/Pangea. The Hebrew reading of v 9 can be marshaled as "evidence" on either side. Both sides may agree that the original gathering of the waters into **one place** covering a greater part of the earth's surface resulted in the "dry land," i.e., a supercontinent. For old earth proponents, continental drift explains its breakup. For young earth proponents, the geological cataclysm of the deluge explains it. Thus, the existence of a primeval Pangaea really is evidence for neither side in the debate, nor is the minimal statement of v 9 (from the perspective of any modern science).

■ **10** As recorded in v 10, God named **the dry ground "land," and the gathered waters . . . "seas."** Hebrew *ʾ ereṣ* is the same word translated "earth" in vv 1 and 2. There, *ʾ ereṣ* refers to the planet as a whole; here it refers to the dry land of the earth as a whole, in its original appearance as the supercontinent Pangaea. Later, *ʾ ereṣ* designates regions, such as Canaan and Mesopotamia; the lands populated by ethnic groups; the territories of nation-states; the smaller territories of city-states; and even the ground or soil of the earth's dry land surfaces. This semantic range of *ʾ ereṣ* is important; later, it bears on the variety of interpretations of the narrative of Noah's flood.

The Hebrew word for **seas** (*yammîm*) is the plural of *yām*. In Canaanite mythology, Yam was god of the sea, a dangerous enemy of Baal; Baal was the most prominent, popular, and seductive of the Canaanite gods for ancient Israel. Here, as so many places in Gen 1, the pagan god is *not* a god, but God's creation, ever attentive and responsive to God's invitational instruction for the good ordering of the earth.

Verse 10 concludes with the report of God's evaluation: **And God saw that it was good.** We may have expected this affirmation at the end of day two. However, on the earth's surface, we experience and observe three great vistas: earth, sky, and sea. Only at this point in the third creation day did all three become evident. Thus, the evaluation expected at the end of day two occurs here (Cassuto 1961, 40), the real conclusion of this step in God's creative process.

■ **11-12** The next stage follows the now-established pattern: God gave a command; the author reported the fulfillment of the command. God called on **the land** to **produce vegetation;** we could translate *vegetate vegetation,* since the verb and the noun are from the same root. The earth responded by bringing forth vegetation. The text is clear that the earth produced at the command/invitation of God the Creator. Contrary to the earth-goddess theology of most of ancient Israel's neighbors, the earth does not produce anything of its own volition; it does not possess the independent power to do so. The text mentions only two categories of vegetation: the ***green plant seeding seed according to its kind and the tree making fruit, which its seed is in it, according to its kind*** (v 12).

With only two broad botanical categories listed, we cannot press this statement too far. Some nonwoody plants produce fruits; some trees produce fruits that are neither large nor edible. In this creation narrative, the big picture is only and always in mind, never its minutiae. Nevertheless, the stability of life on this earth requires the order and normal predictability reflected in the phrase ***according to its kind.*** The fertility, and thus the endurance, of species normally depend on their offspring being of the same species as the parents.

Here again, we see a corrective to the pagan belief in the erratic unpredictability of nature, with its consequent need to appease, placate, or bribe the gods, if the fields, orchards, and gardens were to produce the food necessary for human and animal life. The true God, truly responsible for all the earth's goodness, said, ***Let the earth bring forth vegetation*** (v 11), and ***the earth brought forth vegetation*** (v 12). Neither bribery nor wheedling nor sympathetic magic is necessary; none of these is effective. The earth is not a goddess, but another of God's good creations. A lushly productive earth was and is God's intention from the beginning. Even here, what is diminished by humankind's turning our back upon God shall one day be restored.

Verse 12 concludes with the typical report of God's evaluation: **And God saw that it was good.**

Basil the Great on Gen 1:11

> For the voice that was then heard and the first command became, as it were, a law of nature and remained in the earth, giving it the power to produce and bear fruit for all succeeding time. (Louth 2001, 14)

■ **13** The refrain **And there was evening, and there was morning** concludes each of the six "work" days of the creation week, marking them off with elegant literary cadence as separate paragraphs in the narrative. For days three, four, and five—the middle three of the *seven* days of the complete creation week account—the refrain is given verse numbers all to itself (vv 13, 19, 23). Though this creates a certain symmetry, it is an accident of the much later versification of the text, rather than an original intent of the narrator.

Some poetic passages in the Hebrew Scripture do speak of God control-ling the rebellious seas by force. Some of these reassure us of God's present control of nature, even when violent storms seem to show the seas as rebellious (e.g., Ps 89:9-10; Nah 1:4). Others depict foreign empires metaphorically as the sea, or a monstrous sea creature, rebelling against the Creator (e.g., Ps 65:7). Still others depict the sea as unruly at the time of Israel's exodus, either as a metaphor for Egypt or simply as uneasy in the presence of God's awesome acts on Israel's behalf (e.g., Ps 74:13-14; Hab 3:8-10, 15).

That this passage, however, is a scene of the primeval ocean's peaceful response to God's further creative instruction is clear from the several other passages referring to the sea at the time of creation. The foremost example is Job 38:8-11, where the sea is depicted, not as a raging monster, but as a new-born infant. There, God, as the sea's divine "Parent," simply marked off the play area of the energetic child so it could hurt neither itself nor God's other valued creations. Ocean storms are not rebellious temper tantrums, but a joy-ous indulgence of the oceans' God-given powers, powers of immense benefit (though now of too-frequent destructive force, also) to the dry land and its creatures, as modern meteorological and other sciences have discovered.

It is not legitimate exegesis to press the phrase *according to its kind* into service as evidence against the hypothesis of evolution. First, evolutionists do not claim parents of one species produce offspring of another species; rather (they say), most evolutionary transitions occur in countless tiny steps. Second, individuals of two different species (both of plants and of animals) occasion-ally do mate and produce viable offspring; sometimes, such offspring even are fertile and produce another—we may call it a hybrid—species.

This phrase is repeated ten times in Gen 1 for the purposes both of praising God's wisdom and of thanking God for God's great goodness, in cre-ating and superintending this marvelous, orderly, and dependable creation. As a statement of biological science, it says "only" that, all things being equal, like begets like. That is a very large "only"; we should be content with it as it is.

3. Days of Population (1:14-31)

a. Stationing the Luminaries (1:14-19)

BEHIND THE TEXT

Perhaps more than with any other paragraph in this creation account, an accurate understanding of *this* paragraph hinges on an understanding that Gen 1 was written with two original purposes in mind. One purpose is obvious— glorifying Yahweh (whose name appears for the first time in Gen 2) as the only God, and as sole Creator. The second purpose is not so obvious to Christians with a millennium or more of monotheistic belief and understanding as our heritage. This second purpose is the correction of the dominant pagan theologies of Israel's neighbors, including their faulty views of creation, and of the purposes and mechanisms of creation upon this earth.

All ancient Israel's pagan neighbors regarded the sun, the moon, the five visible planets, the twelve signs of the zodiac, other major constellations, and several individual stars, as deities—as gods and goddesses. Many Israelites themselves, at various times in their history, abandoned their worship of Yahweh or added to it the worship of one or more of these heavenly bodies as gods (see, e.g., Jer 44:15-19; Ezek 8:16). In this paragraph, especially, the narrator of Genesis marshaled vocabulary choice, syntax, and the order of the paragraph as a whole to combat this diminished theology. We hasten to agree with Westermann, however, that his intention was "not to degrade [the heavenly bodies], but to set their limits" (1984, 129).

IN THE TEXT

■ **14-15** As we have seen, day one of the creation week narrative records God's calling light into existence. Day four, its partner in the pairing of the days of God's creative work, records God's making of the luminaries, the light-bearers. God's command, **Let there be lights in the expanse of the sky** (v 14), is the most obvious example of the author's phenomenological approach in this narrative. The author already has defined **the expanse** as what we call today, scientifically, the atmosphere. Yet, here, God proposed and placed the **lights** in the atmosphere, **in the expanse.** Phenomenologically, that is true; that is how we see and experience the sun, the moon, and the stars. Similarly, further into the paragraph, these **lights** are discussed in terms of their time-keeping functions on this earth, without denying their other characteristics and other functions, because these are the ways the vast majority have experienced them throughout human history.

The author structured this account very carefully for an important theological reason. First, note that all the heavenly bodies are subsumed under the single noun, **lights,** *then* the three ordained tasks of these lights with respect to the earth are enumerated: (1) **to separate the day from the night;** (2) one task with four aspects, marking the progression of time as we measure time by various lengths: **to serve as signs; to mark seasons;** [to mark] **days;** [to mark] **years;** (3) **to give light on the earth.**

Cyril of Jerusalem on Gen 1:14-15

Men ought to have been astonished and amazed not only at the arrangement of the sun and moon but also at the well-ordered movements of the stars and their unfettered courses and the timely rising of each of them; how some are signs of summer, others of winter; how some indicate the time for sowing, others the times of navigation. (Louth 2001, 17)

And it was so is proleptic (as also in vv 11*b*, 24*b*). God's spoken word of command/instruction was sufficient guarantee of the appearance of the entities and processes commanded. Yet the text continues in all three places, reporting that "the land produced" (v 12), and "God made" (vv 16, 25). God spoke *and* God acted. Word and action, action and word; stated purpose and ensuing fulfillment—the seamless narrative reflects the sure wisdom of the God who does not misstep or flounder between resolve and act but carries God's purposes forward, unhesitatingly and unerringly. The emphasis is not on the timing or the duration but on the certainty of God's flawless completion; the text also suggests God's joy and satisfaction both in the proposing and in the doing.

■ **16** Second, only after enumerating their functions for the benefit of the earth did the author refer to these **lights** separately; then, only to the two most obvious ones separately; and finally, to these two not by name, but only by circumlocution—**the greater light** and **the lesser light**! All the rest of the majestic and multitudinous heavenly host are subsumed in a single common noun: *and* **the stars.** (**He also made** is not in the Hebrew text of v 16.) The functions of **the greater light** and **the lesser light** are to ***rule*** (*māšal*, "to have dominion," "rule," "reign") **the day** and **the night,** respectively. The text is clear that God not only **made** these lights but also delegated to these created entities the task of regulating the cycle of day and night.

The purposely omitted Hebrew names include *šemeš* (the sun) and *yārēaḥ* (the moon). Of the unnamed stars and planets, the planet Venus was the most prominent as a goddess among Israel's neighbors, variously known as Inanna, Ishtar, and Astarte. Even in Judah's final days as a vassal state under Babylon, Judean women were worshipping her (as "The Queen of Heaven"), and her paramour Tammuz, with their husbands' knowledge and consent (Jer 44:15-30; Ezek 8:14).

Enuma Elish and Gen 1

That Gen 1 was written with the Sumerian/Babylonian account we now know as the *Enuma Elish* especially in mind is disputed by hardly any today. The best-known version is Babylonian, with Marduk, Babylon's patron god, as its hero. Earlier versions and fragments demonstrate that this story originated in Sumer, south of Babylon at the head of what usually we call today the Persian Gulf. It is a safe assumption that (at least) educated ancient Israelites knew of this polytheistic cosmogony by oral account, if not in one of its written versions.

In the Babylonian version of creation, Apsu was the god of the fresh waters, the rivers and streams, lakes and springs. Tiamat, the goddess of the primeval saltwater oceans, mainly the Persian Gulf for the Sumerians, was his consort. Apsu and Tiamat were the parents and grandparents of the younger gods. Some of these killed Apsu, in circumstances that are less than clear.

Obviously, Tiamat did not take kindly the murder of her husband and threatened the gods with annihilation. As the goddess of the primeval oceans, she easily could have swept in and inundated everything in the marshy Sumerian homeland. The gods cowered together in fear, not knowing what to do. In the Babylonian version, Marduk, a strapping young god, stood up and volunteered to meet Tiamat in mortal combat. He demanded a price, however. Before he would fight Tiamat, the other gods had to make Marduk king. Not seeing an alternative, they agreed and Marduk became king of the gods.

Marduk did defeat and kill Tiamat in battle. Following a brief celebration, he split her carcass into two halves. From one half, he formed the earth; from the other, the skies. Translators even have translated "the firmament" at that point in this story. Marduk placed others of the gods as "great gods" in the firmament— sun, moon, planets, constellations, etc.

The gods who had sided with Tiamat in her "rebellion" Marduk forced into servitude, to wait on him and the gods who had sided with him. When the servant-gods became tired of their service, they came to Marduk, asking for relief. Ea, the wise counselor of the gods, gave Marduk a plan. They executed Kingu, Tiamat's closest confidant in her battle against Marduk. From Kingu's blood, mixed with mud, Ea [or Marduk in some texts] formed "man" to serve the gods, replacing the lesser gods who had been on the "wrong" side in the divine battle.

■ **17-19** Verse 17 begins with the author's categorical statement, **God set them**—all these lights—**in the expanse of the sky**. Verses 17 and 18 then comprise a second listing of their three functions (see the first list in vv 14-15), in chiastic (reverse) order, and in similar but not identical language: (1) **to give light;** (2) **to govern,** i.e., to regulate time; (3) **to separate light from darkness.** The heavenly bodies emphatically are *not* gods, as claimed in the *Enuma Elish*. They are God's creations and servants, established in their places and in their movements by God, for God's purposes. These include, but are not limited to, their services to God's smaller creations upon this earth.

Augustine on Gen 1:17-18

Everyone understands that there is a great difference between astrological prediction and observing the stars as natural phenomena, in the way that farmers and sailors do, either to verify geographical areas or to steer their course somewhere . . . There is a great difference between these practical customs and the superstitions of men who study the stars . . . in an effort to peer into the predestined outcome of events. (Louth 2001, 18-19)

Finally, in the paragraph as a whole, the author recorded that "God said" (v 14), "God made" (v 16), **God set/*placed*** (v 17), and **God saw** [evaluated] (v 18)—four verbs with God explicitly the subject of each, the only four indicative action verbs in the paragraph. Nothing could be more explicit, or more clear: Elohim (Yahweh Elohim in Gen 2), *not* Marduk, is the God who creates and sustains all else that is. The Babylonian creation account, the *Enuma Elish*, does not even claim that Marduk created everything, but what it does claim for Marduk, Gen 1 denies and corrects. For our day, the claim is equally forceful, partly because the text does *not* divert attention with details: nothing and no one except God is eternally existent; nothing arose spontaneously. God created all that exists. Verse 18 ends with the typical report of God's evaluation of what God had made, followed by the refrain, **and there was evening, and there was morning—the fourth day** (v 19).

FROM THE TEXT

All this day four description together—extremely sketchy as it is from the standpoint of astronomical science, yet so vividly extraordinary even with its economy of words—compels the reader to ask, Why?

The author of Genesis, in this account, was at pains to establish that these heavenly bodies, powerful and impressive to every human being though they are, are not gods. So far are they from being gods that in this account, celebrating the wisdom and power of God's creative work, they are not even named, lest their names remind Israelite hearers/readers that their neighbors worshiped them as gods. Nameless here, they reflect God their Creator's glory the more brightly.

The luminaries are, in fact, God's creations and God's servants, with specific tasks to perform at God's behest, for the benefit of God's tiny creation—measured in astronomical distances—upon this minuscule sphere in the middle of this smallish solar system, itself at the edge of our medium-sized galaxy. But size does not measure importance; by itself, dominance does not merit worship. The dominion of the sun and the moon in the heavens, a real dominion only from our vantage point, is appointed them by their Creator, just as our dominion upon the earth is appointed by that same Creator. They cannot forsake their appointed tasks until God releases them. We ought not forsake ours.

The Inca Pachacuti on the Sun as God's Servant

The name Inca refers properly to the ruler of the Andean Quechua Empire before Pizzaro's arrival. The Inca Pachacuti, ruling about 1438-71, built temples to Inti (the sun) in various Quechua centers, in what now is Peru. Upon further reflection, he realized the sun could not be the supreme deity. Acting like a laborer and a servant, Inti always follows the same path and keeps the same hours—Pachacuti's capital, Cuzco, is fewer than fourteen degrees south of the equator—and even a passing cloud can dim its light. Pachacuti redirected worship among the Quechuan upper classes from Inti, the servant, to Viracocha, "the Lord, the omnipotent Creator of all things," at that time nearly lost to Quechuan memory. All this more than fifty years before the European conquest of Pachacuti's Andean empire! (Adapted from Don Richardson, *Eternity in Their Hearts* [Ventura, Calif.: Regal Books, 1984], 33-39)

b. Populating Seas and Skies (1:20-23)

BEHIND THE TEXT

In this paragraph, the author used the phrase *nepeš hayyâ* ("living creatures") for the first time (v 20). Next, he employed the verb *bārā'* ("he created") for only the second time in the creation account (v 21). Finally, the first blessing of anything by anyone occurs here (v 22), with God's blessing (*bārak;* "he blessed") of the first animate, sensate life, the creatures of the seas and the skies. These three significant vocabulary choices, brought together in this short paragraph, are the author's tip-off to the reader that this day's activity marked a signal advance in God's creative design for and work upon the earth.

IN THE TEXT

■ **20** As day two marked the separation of *the waters . . . above* (the firmament, or sky) from *the waters . . . below* (the seas), now day five marked God's command to the seas and skies to **teem** with the first animate life on the planet—largely speaking, the fishes and the fowls. A full translation is instructive, *Let the waters swarm with swarms of living creatures, and let birds [or winged creatures] fly above the earth, against the face of the firmament of the heavens.*

God's command, *Let the waters swarm,* is parallel to the previous command, *Let the earth bring forth* (vv 11-12). Here again, God invited what God already had created to participate as responsive partners in further acts of creation.

Here, the category **living creatures** corresponds to the animal kingdom of modern biological taxonomy. These are the first representatives of animal life on the earth, as contrasted with plant life. As we have noted earlier with respect to the gathering of the seas (v 9), neither can this part of the account be used either for or against the young earth or the old earth positions on origins. In fact, it agrees with both these positions that animal life originated in the seas.

The Hebrew category *'ôp* refers to birds, but also goes beyond to include all flying or *winged creatures.* Again, the objective is not biological precision, but inclusiveness. The two prepositional phrases (both with Hebrew *'al*) are further examples of the phenomenological approach of this narrative. As seen by humans from the earth's surface, winged creatures fly **above the earth** and *against the face of the firmament,* i.e., the "surface" of the sky, as we see and experience it from "below."

■ **21** As before (vv 9, 11-12, 14-16), the command is followed by its implementation.

The choice of the verb *bārā'* (**So God created**) is fitting because the focus here is on God's creation of the first animate life on the earth, the fishes of the sea and the fowl of the air. Nothing created in days one to three moves of its own volition. The author took great pains in reporting God's work of day four to emphasize that the luminaries move, but at God's will and in God's paths, and on God's errands, not their own. Here, for the first time, are creatures that move as they will, though much more by instinct than by reason.

Biblical writers, elsewhere in the OT, metaphorically present **the great creatures of the sea** as creatures that rebel against God, or as creatures that may try to resist God (see Job 7:12; Ps 74:13-14). Here, as with the waters of the primeval deep (Gen 1:2), there is no hint of that. Every creature in the sea, both great and small, and every bird of every kind in the sky, received its life from God. Again the phrase, ***according to their/its kind,*** reflects the writer's understanding and observation of various kinds (or, in our scientific term, "species") of sea creatures and flying creatures in the sky.

Verse 21 concludes with the typical evaluation: **And God saw that it was good.** This report conveys God's assessment that the animals of the seas and the skies exist and function as God planned and created them to be and do.

1:21-23

■ **22** Verse 22 reports the first blessing recorded in Scripture, **God blessed them.** The first animate life upon the earth, the sea creatures and birds of the sky, received God's blessing in the form of the power of sexual reproduction. In this way, the writer introduces blessing as an essential part of God's creational activity. We shall encounter a blessing fulfilling this purpose again, in the account of the creation of humankind on day six (1:28). Even the verbs of blessing/command here are those we shall see again in the blessing of humankind ('ādām): "be fruitful and multiply, and fill" (NRSV). The slightly different wording, **and let the birds *multiply upon* the earth,** credits the fact that, while birds fly in the skies, they nest upon, or close to, the earth. God's original creation intention was and still is that all creatures, great and small, multiply and fill their natural habitats to their natural healthy capacities. Scarcity in all its manifestations is a result and condition of the marring, scarring, and depletion caused by the breaking of relational harmony introduced into God's good creation by human sin.

John Wesley on Gen 1:22

Observe, 2, The *blessing* of them in order to their continuance. Life is a wasting thing, its strength is not the strength of stones; therefore the wise Creator not only made the individuals, but provided for the propagating of the several species, . . . Fruitfulness is the effect of God's blessing, and must be ascribed to it; the multiplying of the fish and fowl from year to year, is still the fruit of this blessing here. (Wesley 1975, 6)

■ **23** Verse 23 assigns God's creation of the sea creatures and the birds in the sky to the fifth day with the typical refrain, **and there was evening, and there was morning.**

FROM THE TEXT

We would not *need* any other biblical text than this paragraph to understand the value God places on the earth and its life forms, which God delighted in creating, then entrusted to our care as God's stewards. This text invites the people of God to be at the forefront with others who act out of concern for the earth and all its inhabitants. It is true that some approach these causes from a secular, or from other religious, perspectives, some even from a belief in the earth as a mother goddess. However, this is not a warrant for the community of Judeo-Christian faith to neglect God's stewardship mandate. After all, God has given us a proper historical and theological foundation for a biblical stewardship, rooted here and elsewhere in the biblical narrative. As humans created by God in the image of God, as stewards appointed by God upon this earth, we are to care for, bless, and enjoy what God created, blessed, and enjoys. We are to regard and value God's creation as God regards and values it.

c. Populating the Land (1:24-25)

BEHIND THE TEXT

This short section presents the third of God's command/instructions for an already existent entity to bring forth life (see vv 11, 20, above), to respond to God's invitation and become a kind of junior partner in creation. This third time the instruction was for the earth/land to *spring forth living creatures.* This time, however, the narrative records that God **made** rather than "created," *ʿāśâ* rather than *bārāʾ*. The use of *bārāʾ* in v 21 emphasizes the magnitude of the step from inanimate to animate life, in God's initial creation of sensate life in the seas and the skies. Using *ʿāśâ* here conveys the (now) "normal" continuance of God's bringing forth animal life, but now upon the land.

Moreover, as the dry land appeared on day three, so now the land animals were created on day six. Thus, the third of the three pairings of creation days and their works is introduced, and the symmetry is complete.

IN THE TEXT

■ **24 Let the land produce living creatures; produce** (*yāṣâ*, "to go out," "to come out," "to go forth"; see also v 12) we may understand as "send forth." This corresponds to its occurrence in v 12, where the narrator used the same verb to describe the land causing vegetation to spring forth on day three. Certainly this was a conscious choice, the writer acknowledging the earth as God's appointed bearer and nurturer of all life, inanimate and animate alike. Moreover, in a number of important respects, and on the level of the cell, life's basic building block, all life is more alike than different.

Verse 24 presents the living creatures of the sixth day in three groups (see v 21). While the modern reader may see these as "prescientific" categories for classifying land animals, they make perfect sense in an agrarian subsistence culture, such as ancient Israel's. First listed are the **livestock,** the domesticated animals; cattle, sheep, goats, and the donkey would have been important species within this first group.

Second to be listed are the **creatures that move along the ground,** including many smaller (and undomesticated) mammals, reptiles, and amphibians, among others. Not all these creatures *crawl* on the ground as, e.g., KJV's "creeping thing" could imply. However, from the vantage point of human height looking down—i.e., phenomenologically, once again—many of them appear to creep or crawl even when they are moving on four legs. Walton tentatively suggests this group comprises mostly the wild animals that move about in herds and later were permitted for food (9:2-3), as distinct from the larger (also wild) predators—which he then would place in the third group, below (2001, 341-43).

The third group includes the larger **wild animals,** or the *living creatures of the land,* those that do not belong to the domesticated group of the farmstead and/or the courtyard stable of the house. Though many of the animals in this group are dangerous to humans at close range, we see here a glimpse of the marvelous variety of God's creation from the beginning.

Fretheim on Human and Nonhuman Vocation

We have suggested that it is a mistake to consider creation as an activity that moves in only one direction: from God to creature. Creatures are also involved in creative activity—*for God's sake.* It is also a mistake to think that vocation moves only in one direction: from the human to the nonhuman. . . . I want to claim that vocation also moves from the nonhuman to the human. Thus I speak of *a mutuality of vocation;* both humans and nonhumans are called to a vocation on behalf of each other in the furtherance of God's purposes for the creation. (2005, 273, emphases original)

■**25** Again, what God proposed and commanded, God caused to come to pass. Again, the completion of this part of the creation is reported, so the reader/hearer can know it was, in fact, accomplished. And again, the wording of the report is slightly different from the proposal, this time with a different order of the three major groupings (the **wild animals** first, then the **livestock,** and finally **the creatures that move along the ground**). Again, the repetition of the phrase, *according to its kind,* with each animal group in vv 24-25, shows the significance of God not only creating, organizing, and ordering various types of animal life out of the disorder of inanimate life but also establishing a process for the continuation of life.

Verse 25 ends with the typical evaluation, **And God saw that it was good,** though the report of God's work on day six continues in vv 26-31. The evaluation here pertains to the land creatures. We find another evaluation at the end of the activities on day six, there with respect to the whole of creation, following its culmination in the creation of humankind (v 31; compare the two evaluations of vv 10, 12, both pertaining to day three).

FROM THE TEXT

Once again, the multiple repetition—five times in these two verses—of the notation *according to its kind,* stands as an emphatic reminder that, while God is sovereign, God is not totalitarian in God's rule, even toward those creatures who are not said to reflect God's image as humans do. God designed, formed, and gave life to myriad species, but endowed them with procreative powers, bringing them into partnership with God in the ongoing existence of God's good creation. As Hamilton succinctly states it, "The Creator makes creators" (1990, 132).

The repeated phrase *according to its kind* also emphasizes the importance of the reasoned and reasonable order God established in and for the creation. One may see here a foundation for subsequent biblical teaching on the order of godly relationship(s) inherent in the reality and the experience of holiness. While we may characterize this idea as a "typological" interpretation, the repetition of the phrase indicates that this was a legitimate concern of the narrator. We note this emphasis without asking it to bear more theological weight than the writer may have intended; it is a reflection, not a dogma.

d. Creating the ʾādām as Male and Female (1:26-28)

BEHIND THE TEXT

"What's past is prologue"; in the literary ordering of this creation chapter, we have reached the climactic act. The author signals this in several ways: (1) this is the last act of creation in the creation week; (2) v 26 implies a heavenly "council"—**Let us make** ʾādām; this was not done previously; (3) the verb bārāʾ (**he created**) used only seven times in the entire account, occurs three times in v 27.

Once again, we will understand this climactic act of God's earthly creation better if we understand its literary precursor, the *Enuma Elish,* and that text's profoundly pessimistic account of the formation of humankind, and the gods' reasons for it. As noted above, in that account Marduk executed Kingu, Tiamat's chief ally, and formed man from his blood.

Marduk's Speech and the Forming of Humankind in *Enuma Elish*

"Blood will I form and cause bone to be;

65

Then will I set up *lullu*, 'Man' shall be his name!

Yes, I will create *lullu*: Man!

(Upon him) shall the services of the gods be imposed that they may be at rest."

. . . .

They bound him [Kingu] and held him before Ea;

Punishment they inflicted upon him by cutting (the arteries of) his blood.

With his blood they created mankind;

He [Ea] imposed the services of the gods (upon them) and set the gods free.

(Heidel 1951, 46-47)

At another place, the text speaks of Ea "nipping" bits of clay from a large lump and forming each bit into a "man," as part of this process. Thus, we are to understand that human beings were formed from the blood of a rebellious, executed minor deity, mixed with clay—i.e., we were formed from bloody mud, tainted by the gravest guilt and shame, from our creation.

Israel's creation theology critiques and corrects this (and other) inadequate versions of human origins.

The verb, **Let us make** (a single verb in Hebrew), naturally raises the question of to whom God was speaking. Commentators have proposed a number of answers to this question. Early on, many of the church fathers read this as the first OT reference to the Trinity.

A second view is that the first person plural in this phrase is a plural of divine majesty; God was speaking of himself in the first person plural form. Perhaps more common today is a third explanation, that God was speaking to the "heavenly council" of angels and other created beings in attendance around God's heavenly throne. These two views are not mutually exclusive, and even could stand, conceivably, with the fourth view discussed below. In potential support of the third, we have hints of such a heavenly council in other OT passages, perhaps most notably Job 1:6; 2:1.

Cassuto (1961, 55-56), Westermann (1984, 145), and others adopt, and Hamilton (1990, 133-34) treats as plausible, a fourth view, interpreting this verb as a plural of self-exhortation, as when a person says to himself or herself, "Let's go!"; "Let's get on with it!" This view, too, may not be incompatible with one or more of the others and encourages us to see God as passionate about God's creation. Indeed, we know from all of Scripture that God loves and delights in creation. Why should not God have been keen to get on with the crown of God's earthly creation, *ʾādām*, since all else now was ready?

IN THE TEXT

■ **26** Verse 26 introduces a significant transition in the narrative. The shift from the more impersonal jussives, "let there be . . . ," "let the waters . . . ," and "let the land . . . ," to the emphatically personal cohortative **let us make . . .** , indicates that God's creation of humankind was to be a new and different order of action. Though we may not be able to define with complete confidence the full range of meaning of **us** in this text (see above), what is clear is that God involved himself fully and without the direct participation of other entities already created. The verb **make** (*ʿāśâ*, "do," "make"), with God as subject, often conveys the idea of God creating something (e.g., vv 7, 16). The psalmists confessed that humans are made by God (Ps 100:3), even that we are made by the *hands* of God (Ps 119:73; see also Job 31:15).

Gregory of Nyssa on Gen 1:26*a*

> This same language was not used for (the creation) of other things. The command was simple when light was created; God said, "let there be light." Heaven was also made without deliberation. . . . These, though, were before (the creation of) humans. For humans, there was deliberation. He did not say, as he did when creating other things, "Let there be a human." See how worthy you are! Your origins are not in an imperative. Instead, God deliberated about the best way to bring to life a creation worthy of honor. (Louth 2001, 28)

The focus of vv 26 and 27 is on God making/creating the *ʾādām*, or humankind. The subsequent context (vv 28-31) confirms that both *ʾādām* in v 26 (*without* the definite article) and *hāʾādām* in v 27 (*with* the definite article) refer to human beings in a generic sense. In our discussion of Gen 2 (below), we will treat in greater detail the use of *ʾādām* in the larger narrative of Gen 1—5.

The two prepositional phrases together, **in our image, in our likeness,** constitute a brief example of the well-known Semitic device called parallelism, a literary usage in which the second line (here, phrase) repeats the idea of the first, but not in identical language. Thus, **image** (*ṣelem*) and **likeness** (*dĕmût*) are essentially synonyms in Hebrew, as in English. Both terms mean that God created the *ʾādām* like God, or reflecting God, as a mirror reflects the image of the one looking into it, as a fine sculpture is the likeness of the one it was made to represent or, even better, perhaps, as a child is the likeness of the parent.

The clear teaching of Christian Scripture, though, is that God became human only in the incarnation of Jesus, the Second Person of the Trinity. Thus, the creation of *ʾādām* in the **image** of God cannot mean here, "in God's physical image." Rather, we are in God's image as spiritual beings, as possessing the powers of love, reason, and wisdom, of imagination and creativity, and real emotions, among other attributes or characteristics.

The divine speech, ***And let them exercise stewardship dominion/oversight,*** prefigures the task(s) God would assign to the *ʾādām*. This rendering is appropriate in light of the more specific naming of the tasks, ***to serve it and to guard it,*** given to the first human when God placed him in the garden (2:15). As we shall see in 1:27, "them" refers to male and female together, thus to humankind collectively.

All three realms of life upon the earth (see comments on vv 9-10, above) are included within the sphere of humankind's stewardship dominion—seas, skies, and dry land. God's creation purpose in this regard is that the whole earth and all its creatures should benefit from humankind's wise, caring, and conscientious stewardship, arising from our love, honor, and respect for God, and from our identification with our fellow creatures *as* fellow creatures in our common home, God's good earth.

■ **27** The first noteworthy feature of v 27, reporting the completion of God's purpose to create ʾādām, is the use of *bārāʾ* three times in three lines. As noted above (see sidebar, 1:1), *bārāʾ* is used fewer than fifty times in the entire Hebrew text of the OT, seven times in this chapter. That three of these seven occurrences are in one verse, three consecutive lines, is extremely significant. The creation of the ʾādām is very special, indeed! God intended and regards ʾādām as the goal and crown of God's earthly creation.

So what, or who, is ʾādām? ʾādām is the one creature on this earth created **in the image of God.** This is the first "theological" understanding the author wished the reader/hearer to gain from this verse, so he said it twice. Furthermore, the second line is *more* emphatic than the first; **in the image of God** comes before the verb. (In the normal Hebrew sentence order, the verb is first.) As though this were not emphasis enough, the author used the noun rather than the pronoun in the second line—**in the image of God**, rather than "merely" **in his own image**—to build a crescendo of emphasis from the first to the second line.

The third and the really climactic line of v 27 reveals that **male and female** are the two genders of ʾādām. Written in a patriarchal society, and intended for the instruction of patriarchal cultures of every time and place, this final climactic line is a real blockbuster. **Female,** too, is specially created; **female,** too, is ʾādām; **female,** too, is **in the image of God**! This line can mean nothing less than that God's creation intention is human gender equality.

Also important here is to note use of the singular pronoun in the second line, **he created him**, and the plural pronoun in the third line, **he created them**. As Brueggemann has stated, "Humankind is a single entity. All human persons stand in solidarity before God. But on the other hand, humankind is a community, male and female. And none is the full image of God alone. . . . God is . . . not mirrored as an individual but as a community" (1982, 34).

■ **28** What just had been clearly and unequivocally stated, now could be assumed: **God blessed them** [male *and* female] **and said to them** [male *and* female]. Moreover, the five imperative verbs constituting God's blessing of the first pair all are plural; the humans were partners in receiving God's blessing, as well as in fulfilling the commission of the fivefold instruction.

Another indicator of human physical kinship with the rest of God's earthly animate creation is that the first three imperatives are the same as the three by which God instructed the sea creatures at the end of day five. The first of the three was, **Be fruitful.** Since human reproduction (as with most earthly life) requires sexual congress, it follows that sexual activity, in and of itself, cannot be sinful. Sustained bringing forth of children, then, would lead to the fulfillment of the second and third of these five commands, **increase in number** and **fill the earth.** The ordinary meaning of the verb *miló'û,* and the necessary meaning here, is **fill,** "populate," or some synonym. The KJV translation "replenish" the earth is wrong and misleading. This mistranslation of the KJV is partly responsible for the rise of the erroneous gap theory we discussed (and dismissed) in our commentary on 1:2.

Subdue and **rule over,** together, do constitute God's mandate for human governance of our fellow creatures upon the earth. This is clear especially since the creatures of all three already prepared and filled habitats of the earth are mentioned here—**fish, birds,** and **every living creature** of the sea, the air, and the ground, respectively. However, as noted already with our translation of v 26, we must establish the meaning of these two verbs, not in isolation from, but within, their literary and theological context. The narrative of 2:5-17 (v 15, particularly) stipulates the intended meaning of the verbs **subdue** and **rule over.** In 2:15, the mandate to the human was to "serve" and to "guard/watch over/keep/protect" the garden. By logical inference, this vocation included not just the trees and other plant life in the garden but also its animals. The human vocation is to care for, protect, and preserve the earth and its plant and animal life—not to exploit, destroy, or abuse God's creation.

Gregory of Nyssa on the Image of God

1:28

God creates man for no other reason than that God is good; . . . the perfect form of goodness is here to be seen by his both bringing man into being from nothing and fully supplying him with all good gifts. . . . The language of Scripture therefore expresses it concisely by a comprehensive phrase, in saying that man was made "in the image of God," for this is the same as to say that he made human nature participant in all good; for if the Deity is the fullness of good . . . then the image finds its resemblance to the archetype in being filled with all good. (Louth 2001, 34)

Brueggemann on Humans in the Image of God

There is one way in which God is imaged in the world and only one: humanness! This is the only creature, the only part of creation, which discloses to us something about the reality of God. . . . God is known peculiarly through this creature who exists in the realm of free history, where power is received, decisions are made, and commitments are honored. . . . The image of God in the human person is a mandate of power and responsibility. But it is power exercised as God exercises power. The image images the creative use of power which invites, evokes, and permits. There is nothing here of coercive or tyrannical power, either for God or for humankind. (1982, 32)

These three verses comprise the introduction of human beings, the first scriptural mention of ʾādām, here in the primal account of the planet's origins. As such, they constitute a paradigmatic text, against which other, subsequent texts must be measured. This text and the considerably more detailed account of ch 2, together, comprise the biblical record of God's intentions for humans—our being and our place—in the original design of creation, before our turning from God fractured relationships at every level. Because of its narrative primacy in the creation accounts, and because of its canonical primacy with respect to all other texts, this announcement of God's creation of humans, with all the meaning it conveys, shapes our understanding of every subsequent text, and not the other way around. Other texts do not interpret this text, though they may illumine it. *This* text interprets every *other* text. This is true even for several points in our understanding of the more detailed account of ch 2, as we shall see below.

So what *do* these three verses tell us about ʾādām, the human being? Already in v 26, when God declared the divine intention of making ʾādām in God's own image and likeness, God's declared purpose for doing so, in this statement, was to let **them** exercise stewardship dominion over the rest of God's earthly creation. This, before the reader even is told who **them** may be!

Verse 27 reveals the identity of the plural ʾādām; it is male and female. *Only* male and female, *both*, created in God's image—that is, *neither* the one *nor* the other, *alone*. In v 28, God blessed both male and female and gave the word of blessing/command to both male and female. This means that to be female is to be in God's image; to be male is to be in God's image. Not even a hint of the possibility of subordination of one to the other—whether female to male or male to female—ever would occur to the reader, from this text. That has to be imported from elsewhere, and thus is illegitimate here. Moreover, if we were to make such an ill-advised interpretive decision on this text, it would support subordination of the male to the female equally as well as subordination of the female to the male.

In fact, female subordination to the male as God's creation intention usually has been "discovered" in the more detailed account of ch 2, then imported back into this account. But the influence must go the other way. Since this text does not hint at subordination of either to the other, we ought to look again at our understanding of the male/female relationship as presented in ch 2. This we shall do below.

John Wesley's "Analogy of Faith"—the principle that we must interpret unclear passages of Scripture by those passages that are clear—is essential to our hermeneutical practice here. Interpreters (and critics of faith) often make some such claim as, "The Bible is patriarchal." As the first and clearest declaration of God's original creation intention, this text governs our understanding of all other texts. This report clearly does not represent God's intention for humans as either patriarchal or matriarchal. Therefore, the appropriate response to the false charge that the Bible is inherently and intentionally patriarchal is to affirm that this text *precludes* patriarchalism. As we shall see below in ch 3, our first parents' choice to break relationship with God resulted in the broken human relationships of patriarchalism, matriarchalism, and all other unethical power relationships of some humans over other humans.

That this is God's intention also in the grand plan of redemption/restoration is clear from the paradigmatic NT text on the matter, Paul's statement, ***There is neither Jew nor Greek, there is neither slave nor free, there is not male and female, for you are all one in Christ Jesus*** (Gal 3:28). ***Neither Jew nor Greek*** invalidates "spiritual" or ethnic privilege falsely perceived as God-ordained. ***Neither slave nor free*** invalidates social and economic privilege falsely perceived as God-ordained. ***There is not male and female*** means that gender is not abolished in Christ, as the other categories ultimately are. However, in most of first-century Greco-Roman-Jewish culture, adult females usually found their standing, and sometimes even their hope of salvation, only in and through their married state, which is to say, in and through their husbands. Our text, and Paul, both invalidate gender privilege falsely perceived as God-ordained. Woman does not need man to experience relationship with God; God extends that to her on her own, just as God does to man. That our understanding of Gen 1:26-27 is correct is affirmed by Paul's grounding his radical evangelistic ("Good News") egalitarianism in his affirmation that all this is so "in Christ." If it is "in Christ" in redemption/restoration, then it also is "in Christ" by God's original creation intention.

The use of the plural verb, **let us make,** and the two plural pronouns, **in our image, in our likeness,** has led to much discussion. Almost all Jewish, and many Christian, exegetes have taken these as plurals of divine majesty, following on the fact that the title for God used throughout this chapter also is a plural form, *Elohim*, and certainly is used as a plural of divine majesty for the one, the only, transcendent God.

Some Christian writers have read this verse as saying more, pointing to it as the first explicitly Trinitarian reference in the Bible. Exegetically, this is going too far. We cannot press this verse to be, in and of its own intent, a Trinitarian declaration, and then use it as a proof text for the Christian doctrine of the Trinity. The most we may do with integrity, as Christian interpreters who accept that God is the Three-in-One, is to include this as the first (or second, cf. 1:2) of a number of OT hints, prefigurings, or foreshadowings of the Trinitarian nature of God. We come to this understanding of God in Gen 1 only because we already believe, from the NT and the early church's Spirit-led understanding, that God is Trinity. (See, however, Hamilton 1990, 134, for a spirited and plausible defense of going a bit further than we have gone here.)

Augustine on the Prefiguring of the Trinity in Gen 1:26-27

> For God said, "Let us make man in our image and likeness": a little later, however, it is said "And God made man in the image of God." It would certainly not be correct to say "our," because the number is plural, if man were made in the image of one person, whether Father, Son or Holy Spirit. But because he is made in the image of the Trinity, consequently it was said "in our image." Again, lest we choose to believe in three gods in the Trinity, since the same Trinity is one God, he said, "And God made man in his image," as if he were to say "in his [own triune] image." (Louth 2001, 30)

Finally, wise, compassionate stewardship as the standard of human care for the earth and for our fellow creatures upon it is implicit in the record of God's exquisite care in the creation of it all, to this point in the text. God would not throw away all God had so carefully and joyously made, by handing it over to humans with the *instruction* to be careless, destructive stewards. Our translation, **exercise stewardship dominion,** reminds us that stewards are charged with promoting the welfare of all things and all creatures entrusted to their supervision. Collectively and individually, humankind will render to God an accounting of and for our stewardship of the planet God has entrusted to our care.

Genesis 1 (along with many others) helps us understand love as God's true nature and character. John Wesley regarded the love God shows, and the love God engenders in us, as the touchstone of Christian faith and practice. Whatever does not arise from love, whatever does not exhibit love, is less than whole. Though the word "love" does not occur in Gen 1, we may conclude with confidence that God did everything this chapter reports from the motivation of the love that is God's nature, God's essential characteristic.

If "God is love" (1 John 4:8), then the human species whom God created in God's image also was characterized by love, originally. We may think of the first humans as God's agents in representing God's love to all earthly creation; this was part of the exercise of their stewardship/dominion upon and for the earth and its inhabitants. Of course, we do not have a lengthy account of their exercise of that stewardship; they forsook that agency relatively early in their tenure upon the earth. But as God's "image" and "likeness," while they displayed it in the perfection of their original creation, certainly they comported themselves, and acted toward all creation, in love.

In the person and work of Jesus Christ, the second Adam (1 Cor 15:45-47), God restored the possibility and the reality of humans once again becoming and acting in the image and likeness of God, as God's agents of love in and for all this earthly creation. As Wesley rightly understood, this is our calling both individually and together, as the body of Christ (John 17:22-26; 1 Cor 12:12-27).

e. Provision and Benison (1:29-31)

■ **29-30** God's direct speech to the newly created ʾādām continues in v 29. Here, the idea of stewardship dominion over, of care for and protection of the earth and its resources, is carried further in at least two ways. First, God assigned the plants and trees—much of the vegetation created on day three—as food for the humans and for the rest of the animal kingdom. Second, the implication of giving plants as food is the withholding, at least in the beginning, of permission to eat flesh. Of course, we may not press this too far; the silence of a text on a matter is not proof. Taking this paragraph as a whole, however, we at least may wonder whether it would have occurred to the first humans to look at their fellow creatures as a source of food. (See, also, Walton 2001, 341-43; his alternative approach to this issue is worth serious consideration.)

God's opening words, ***Behold, I have given to you,*** are further evidence of God's goodness and of God's goodwill toward humans and the others of God's animal creation on the earth. ***Upon the face of all the earth*** is a reminder of God's creation mandate to "fill the earth" (v 28). Wherever the ʾādām would go in fulfillment of this mandate, there they would find plants for food, at least in the beginning, before sin disrupted the earth, as well as the humans upon it.

God's instruction to the humans let them know that God's provision also extended to the other creatures with whom they shared the earth. We should read v 30 as mentioning only the two broadest categories of creatures that do not live in the waters, ***And also to every living creature of the earth—even to every flying creature of the heavens, and to every creature that moves about upon the earth, which in it [them] is sensate life—[I have given] every green plant for food.*** This instruction functions syntactically as the conclusion of the sentence begun in v 29 with the verb ***I have given.*** As indicated, the verb is not actually repeated in the Hebrew text of this verse. Even the syntax of this lengthy sentence revealed to the first couple their common animate life with their fellow creatures. From a very basic and generalized perspective, we eat the same food. Humans are *more* than "animal," but we are not *less.*

And it was so; this is now the sixth occurrence of this refrain. It occurs once in the account of the second day (v 7), and twice in the account of the third day (vv 9, 11); it occurs once in the account of the fourth day (v 15), and now twice in the account of the sixth day (vv 24, 30). Cassuto's comment makes clear the narrator's intent, "So it came to pass, and so it has remained for all time" (1961, 34).

■ **31** This is God's concluding evaluation of **all that [God] had made,** as distinct from the previous (usually daily) partial evaluations. Now that all was finished, God declared it, not just **good** in its several parts and systems, but

very good as a whole. This final word functions as a summative, overall evaluation of *all* God's good creation upon this good earth, as it came unspoiled from the mind, heart, and hand of the Creator. With this positive evaluation, the six days of creative work were finished.

Gregory of Nazianzus on the Goodness of God's Creation

He made a first day, a second, a third, and so forth until the seventh day which was a rest from work. According to these days, everything created was subdivided, brought into an order by inexpressible laws. So creation was not an instantaneous act by the all-powerful Word; for him to think or to speak is to accomplish a task. If humans were last to enter the world—and in such a way as to honor God's handiwork with God's image—is this not marvelous? It is like saying that as a king he prepared the palace, and then, as king, when everything was already prepared, led in the procession. (Louth 2001, 44-45)

FROM THE TEXT

God not only created the humans and the animals but also provided for their existence. The provisions in vv 29-30 are God's gift, at God's initiative. Even after the human turning from God became universal, God's provision continued, though human sin has made both our work and our enjoyment of God's provision more difficult. Today, human shortsightedness and outright wickedness cause many to suffer privation and death. The bondage under which the earth finds itself now causes famine and other disasters. Nevertheless, God remains well-intentioned toward us in the provision of the physical and other needs with which, after all, God created us.

God's evaluation, **very good,** is a strong refutation of Gnosticism in all its forms. Matter is not evil, but very good. God is not an inferior demiurge, unimportant or even evil, a half-god (as Marcion taught), but the transcendent Maker and, therefore, the Sovereign Lord of all else that is. This distinction is at the heart of the difference between God's revelation—the basis of the comprehensive theology and philosophy generally known today as the Judeo-Christian heritage—and all other religious and philosophical (as distinct from moral and ethical) systems.

John Wesley on Gen 1:31

It was *good* . . . for it is all agreeable to the mind of the creator. Good, for it answers the end of its creation. Good, for it is serviceable to man, whom God had appointed lord of the visible creation. Good, for it is all for God's glory; there is that in the whole visible creation which is a demonstration of God's being and perfections, . . . Now *All* was made, every part was *good*, but all together *very good*. (Wesley 1975, 9)

Many fascinating questions must remain unanswered for now. Everything we currently know from prehistoric anthropology indicates that our ancestors were flesh-eaters from the beginning. Yet Gen 1:29-30 seems to imply, though it does not state, that the first humans were vegetarian. Either Genesis does not mean what it seems to imply or the anthropological record is incomplete or some other explanation awaits discovery. For the present, we must be content to hold a question with no satisfactory answer.

4. Day of Rest (2:1-3)

BEHIND THE TEXT

This paragraph also serves to correct the seductive cosmogony of Israel's neighbors, as represented in the Sumerian/Babylonian *Enuma Elish*. There, too, we are told the "gods" rested, both the victorious gods, Marduk and his allies, and the defeated gods, allies of the slain Tiamat and Kingu. But in that falsification of the earth's beginnings in the *Enuma Elish*, the gods gained their rest at the expense of human beings, who were created to take over the defeated gods' wearisome toil. Here, God (*Elohim*) rested because God's initial creative work was finished. The work appointed to humans was not (in the beginning) drudgery, nor was it excessively arduous or onerous. Finally, as the Fourth Commandment of the Decalogue makes abundantly clear (Exod 20:11), humans are invited to join God in a weekly Sabbath rest, *because* God rested on this seventh day of the creation week, the first Sabbath.

We treat Gen 2:1-3 as a unit. The summative statement of completion (v 1) also functions as a transition statement to the record of God's institution of the Sabbath (vv 2-3). Transition statements in the Bible (and in other Semitic literature), however, are not trivial. They function also as important statements of positive (or negative) evaluation, and of completion. A text without such a conclusion/transition often would have been regarded as incomplete. This short statement also serves another important purpose, however. It is the first line of a five-line, semi-poetic paragraph relating God's institution of the Sabbath from the very beginning.

IN THE TEXT

■ **1-3** The five-line poem we may translate and set out, for clarity:
Thus, the heavens and the earth were completed, and all their hosts.
Now, God [Elohim] had completed by the seventh day his work which he had made.
So he ceased on the seventh day from all his work which he had made.
Therefore, God [Elohim] blessed the seventh day and sanctified it [set it apart].
Because in it he ceased from all his work which God [Elohim] had creatively made.

As "the heavens and the earth" were the focus of the short introductory paragraph (1:1), so they begin the summary of this concluding paragraph; the narrator has begun to bring the reader full circle. The myriad works of the creative project are summarized here in the phrase, **and all their hosts,** i.e., everything that is a part of them or pertains to them. What once (v 2) was *a desert [or emptiness] and a vacancy* (tōhû vāvōhû), now is filled with **hosts,** all the created entities the author has presented in the intervening narrative.

All these **were completed** (passive voice), but the narrator also was at pains once again to remind the reader that **God** [*Elohim*] was the one who *had completed* them (active voice; v 2). Neither Marduk nor Ptah (for the ancients) nor unaided chance and time (for modern readers) had anything to do with bringing this marvelous creation into being.

The middle three lines of this paragraph contain seven words each in the Hebrew text, and in each, the words **the seventh day** conclude the first half-line (Cassuto 1961, 61). *Elohim*, God's most important and frequently used title of majesty, occurs three times in this paragraph. Finally, a crescendo of reference to God's work goes as follows: *his work which he had made* (v 2*a*); *from all his work which he had made* (v 2*b*); *from all his work which God* [*Elohim*] *had created to make [creatively made]* (v 3*b*). Such is the exalted setting of the first announcement of Sabbath day and Sabbath rest.

The primary meaning of *vayyĭšbōt* (from *šābat*, meaning "cease," "rest," "desist") is "he [God] ceased" from the work God had done in the previous six days, not because God was tired, but because the work was completed. The heavens and the earth were the way God wanted them to be. Just as we may sit back, reflect on, and enjoy a project we have completed to our own satisfaction, so God did with this six-day project of creation, the heavens and the earth.

Chrysostom on Gen 2:2

You see, in saying at this point that God rested from his works, Scripture teaches us that he ceased creating and bringing from nonbeing into being on the seventh day, whereas Christ, in saying that "my father is at work up until now and I am at work," reveals his unceasing care for us: he calls "work" the maintenance of created things, bestowal of permanence on them and governance of them through all time. If this wasn't so, after all, how would everything have subsisted, without the guiding hand above directing all visible things and the human race as well? (Louth 2001, 46)

God blessed the seventh day (v 3); this is the third time the narrative reports that **God blessed** something. God had blessed the first animate life, in the seas and the skies (1:22), and by implication the land creatures that followed; animate life represents a major step in the forms of life upon the planet. God had blessed the humans (1:28); humans represent a major step from the rest of animate life, in that we are created in God's image. Now God blessed a day, the seventh day, upon which God ceased from the major creative labor of establishing the earth and its inhabitants in their respective functions; having completed something also is a major step. Moreover, as with any threefold repetition, the three blessings within this account signal a major emphasis on blessing.

God's blessing is affirmation of God's positive intention toward the object of the blessing, to establish it in shalom, i.e., in wholeness and overall well-being. With respect to the Sabbath day, this blessing celebrates, first, the completion of God's major creative work upon the earth. Second, it marks the beginning of God's occupancy of this special place prepared for God's own pleasure—a large part of which is regular communion with humankind (3:8). In light of the later development of Sabbath theology, we may say also that God's blessing of the Sabbath day here anticipates God's intention to provide for a regular time of positive encounter in the process of (and toward) redemption/restoration, even in the vastly changed conditions beyond Eden.

God **sanctified** (*yiqadēš* from *qādaš*, meaning "consecrate," "set apart," "sanctify," etc.) the seventh day, that is, set it apart as a joy-filled memorial of the **very good** completion of the initial creation, to be celebrated each week by all God's human creation. However, little more is made of Sabbath in the biblical text until its inclusion as the Fourth Commandment of the Decalogue given at Sinai (Exod 20:8-11). Modern observance of a seven-day week, and also of an every-seventh-day Sabbath and Lord's Day observance by Jews and (most) Christians, respectively, is rooted in this account of God's ceasing from new creative work on the seventh day of the creation week.

The Hebrew clause in which the author used the verb *bārā'* for the sixth time in this creation narrative could be rendered as follows: **Which God** [*Elohim*] **had creatively made** (v 3). A more literal rendering, but clumsy in English, would be **which God** [*Elohim*] **had created, to make**. This difficult syntax is a reminder that to create (*bārā'*) is not a unique *manner* of making, but the special character or quality of that which is said to be created; one could say, in this narrative, even a step up, as it were, from what had come before. *How* God created (in very general terms, not in anything like what we would call "scientific" detail today) is reported by a fairly wide variety of verbs, as we see in both Gen 1 and 2.

Walton on the Earth as God's Residence/Temple

In the "after" picture the cosmos is now not only the handiwork of God . . . but it also becomes God's residence—the place he has chosen and prepared for his presence to rest. People have been granted the image of God and now serve him as vice regents in the world that has been made for them. Again it is instructive to invoke the analogy of the temple before and after its inauguration.

77

After priests have been installed and God has entered, it is finally a fully functioning temple—it exists only by virtue of those aspects. (2009, 98)

As many readers will be aware, scholars do not agree on whether Gen
2:4 closes this creation account (1:1—2:4), opens the second (2:4-25), or both
(e.g., dividing as v 4a and v 4b). We have chosen to treat 2:4 as primarily intended to begin the second account, but with major qualifications; that discussion leads the commentary on 2:4-25, below.

FROM THE TEXT

This final paragraph tells us God ceased from the work of initial creation, because this creative project was completed to God's satisfaction at that
time. This does not mean God never created again, nor that God does not
intend to create again in the future. Neither does this mean God ceased from
all work of every kind on this first Sabbath. The rest of the biblical witness is
that God continues to create, both in ways we can know and understand now,
and in ways we will not know until all is revealed. This includes God's re-cre-
ative activity in the redemption and restoration of all things—accomplished
in Christ's life, death, and resurrection (though not all is as yet revealed), and
announced in the proclamation of Rev 21:5, "I am making everything new!"
Moreover, God continued and continues the work of sustaining creation (Col
1:17), if we may call that "work" (a small task for the Infinite One!). God did
not become legalistic and obsessive about avoiding all that possibly could be
called work, whether by cultural definition, by some more precise and minute
definition from the realms of physics, or by any other measure. God finished
the project of this creation; God ceased from the work of substantially new
creation; God enjoyed the creation God had completed.

This is emphasized by Jesus' *midrashim* (commentaries) on the Sabbath
in several of his confrontations with his legalistic opponents during his earthly
teaching ministry. Establishing a moral authority to heal on the Sabbath, Jesus
compared his healing to his opponents' rescue of a sheep, should they discover it fallen into a pit on the Sabbath (Matt 12:11-12). An even larger principle resides in Jesus' dictum, ***The Sabbath was made for the human being***
[*anthropon*], ***not the human being*** [*anthropos*] ***for the Sabbath*** (Mark 2:27).
Humans rest in reflection of God's Sabbath rest, and extend Sabbath rest to
their livestock (Exod 20:10; Deut 5:14) in reflection of God's beneficent care
for all creation. When Sabbath regulations become onerous, rather than restful, they no longer are in the liberating spirit of God's initial rest from God's
creative work.

Exodus 20:11 cites this report of God's seventh-day rest as warrant for
the Fourth Commandment, the instruction that humans need a weekly Sabbath. The privilege of Sabbath rest *within* creation is conferred, theologically,
by the Creator's rest *from* creative work on this first Sabbath. The second Pen-

tateuchal version of the Decalogue varies from the first most dramatically at this point, yet a second look shows not so much variation, as supplementation. Deuteronomy 5:15 places Sabbath rest as a perpetual memorial of Israel's Egyptian servitude, when they did not have the privilege of rest on any day at their own initiative. Thus, Sabbath rest also functions as a solemn *and* joyful reminder that no one has the arbitrary right to another's labor at any time, under any circumstances. The Creator rested; the Creator's gift of Sabbath rest cannot be violated with impunity. The Creator labored freely; every human's labor, and the fruit of it, is his or hers alone to use or to assign to another. Sabbath rest is a perpetual reminder that the Creator alone is sovereign.

This is true in another way also, as much in rabbinic tradition teaches. By taking our hands off the wheel, so to speak, one day in every seven, we acknowledge that we are not in control. Our Sabbath rest reminds us of our finitude, of our dependence upon God and even upon each other. God created the universe and this earth without our help; God can sustain it without our help. Much as we are welcomed into, and valued in, partnership with God and with God's people, we are not indispensable. This weekly dose of reality and appropriate humility is good for us. If we take it to heart in the right spirit, it also makes our presence and our contributions all the more valuable and welcome. A renewed Sabbath/Lord's Day theology can guide us in accepting and observing the Sabbath as the good gift God intended it to be.

Brueggemann on Sabbath

Sabbath is the end of grasping and therefore the end of exploitation. Sabbath is a day of revolutionary equality in society. On that day all rest equally, regardless of wealth or power or need. . . . [T]he keeping of sabbath, in heaven and on earth, is a foretaste and anticipation of how the creation will be when God's way is fully established. Sabbath is an unspoken prayer for the coming of a new sanity shaped by the power and graciousness of God. (1982, 35-36)

Finally, the question of which day of the week we should observe as the Sabbath cannot be determined from this paragraph. No one on earth could calculate back to this first Sabbath—if such a chronology is (or were) the intent of this text—and assert with confidence that it was our Saturday, our Sunday, or any other day of our modern week. Nor has God revealed this information to anyone past or present. Because of Christ, most Christians traditionally have observed Sunday, the day of his resurrection, as our Sabbath, but as Paul instructed the Colossian church, *which* day we set aside for rest and worship ultimately is of little import. *That* we worship and follow Christ is what counts (Col 2:16-17).

B. The Making of the Humans (2:4-25)

1. God's Creation of the Humans: Stage One (2:4-7)

BEHIND THE TEXT

In our discussion of Gen 2:4, we will present the case for considering this verse as *both* the necessary conclusion of the first creation account (Gen 1:1—2:4), *and* the necessary introduction to the second creation account (Gen 2:4-25). The reader may think of a two-part episode in a television drama; to begin the second part, the director/editor usually includes snippets of scenes from the first part, refreshing the viewer's memory and setting up the action to come. Similarly, Gen 2:4 summarizes Gen 1:1—2:3 and also introduces Gen 2:5-25.

Most scholars today recognize these as two creation traditions, each of which had some kind of independent existence early in Israel's history. (The *toledot* formula of 2:4*a* is one of many lines of evidence for this view; see the section "These Are the Toledot" in the Introduction.) The canonical form of these two chapters (the text as we have it), then, is the work of a skilled narrator, using two different sources (as authors often do) and weaving them into a coherent literary artistry of his own. The completed work is the most important statement we have of Israel's creation theology—though much else in Scripture supplements and illumines the first account.

The focus of the second creation narrative is on the creation of the ʾādām, the climax of the first creation narrative. In Gen 1, the notice of the creation of the ʾādām, majestic and important as it is, is but the barest of summaries, well-proportioned to the rest of that account. Here, we find a more detailed account of the creation of ʾādām, which in many ways amplifies the themes of 1:26-31.

Genesis 2 contains elements that have led to much disagreement in their interpretation. As an example, vv 5-6 sometimes are taken as representing the condition of the earth before the creative events of day three, in 1:11-12. More importantly, many interpreters see in 2:19 a contradiction of the order of 1:24-27, in God's supposed creation of the land animals and birds after the creation of the first human. We will discuss these and other issues as we encounter them in the text.

Throughout this chapter, we will transliterate Hebrew ʾādām rather than translate it. Most commentators and translations hold the view that ʾādām has at least two or perhaps three connotations in ch 2 (the human community, the first human—a male, the personal name Adam). English versions differ on where in the text the narrator first intended ʾādām as a proper name. The NIV translates ʾādām as "Adam" for the first time in 2:20 [where the noun appears twice, first as hāʾādām ("the man"), then as ʾādām ("Adam")]. The NIV consistently translates hāʾādām as "the man," except in 3:20 and 4:1, where it translates "Adam," despite the presence of the definite article. The NRSV translates *ʾādām* as the proper name "Adam" for the first time in 4:25 (however, see NRSV footnotes that read "Adam" in 2:20; 3:17; 3:21). The noun appears twice in 5:1 without the definite article; the context makes it clear that the writer intended its first use as a proper name (Adam), the second as a reference to the first human couple. The noun also appears without the definite article on 5:2 as the name God gave to the human race. (**Male and female** [God] **created them, and he blessed them, and he called their name** *ʾādām* **in the day of their creation.**) In a formal naming (see on 2:19, below), God named *both* male and female *ʾādām*.

In a few places, the back-and-forth use of the noun—i.e., with (*hāʾādām*) or without the definite article (*ʾādām*)—has made it difficult for interpreters to determine whether the first human being, human beings in a generic sense, or the proper name "Adam" is intended. This is one reason for our preference for transliterating the noun as *ʾādām* or as *the ʾādām* when the noun appears in the text with a definite article. If we were to insist on a translation at this point, it would be better to render "the human," rather than "the man"—in part, because in our era most people normally think "male" when they see or hear "man." A better translation would be "earthling," if we can detach other connotations suggested by popular culture. The predominant use of the noun with the definite article in chs 1—5 (see sidebar) suggests that the focus of the narrative is on the human beings as a whole, suggesting (among other things) what we know to be true, that the human story is in every way exemplified by the story of the first human couple.

ʾādām in Gen 1—5

The noun *ʾādām* occurs a total of thirty-three times in Gen 1—5. Twelve times it occurs without the definite article (*ʾādām*, meaning either "human being" in a generic sense or the proper name, "Adam"). Twenty-one times the definite article is attached (*hāʾādām*, meaning "the man" or "the human being[s]" in a generic sense). In some of these, one could argue for a different pointing from the MT, either adding or removing the definite article. (As a later Masoretic addition, the system of vowel pointing is not regarded as inspired.)

ʾādām	*hāʾādām*
1:26	1:27
2:5	2:7, 8, 15, 16, 18, 19 (2x), 20, 21, 22 (2x), 23, 25
2:20	
3:17	3:8, 9, 12, 20, 22, 24
3:21	
4:25	4:1
5:1 (2x)	
5:2	
5:3	
5:4	
5:5	

■ 4 *These are the accounts of the heavens and the earth, when they were created, in the day of Yahweh Elohim making the earth and the heavens.* This is awkward in English, of course, but is true to the Hebrew syntax of the verse. Our translation also reflects the double chiasm contained within the verse:

> A *the heavens and the earth*
> B *when they were created*
> B' *in the day of Yahweh Elohim making*
> A' *the earth and the heavens*

Besides this primary chiasm of the verse as a whole, one of the elements contains a chiastic arrangement between its two repetitions:

> *the heavens and the earth :: the earth and the heavens*

The MT itself divides this verse, treating the first half as the end of the account of the creation week, and the second half as the beginning of the more detailed account of the creation of the human being, which occupies most of ch 2. Many modern scholars, and several of the newer English versions (e.g., NRSV, NLT, JPS), also divide v 4. It is a very difficult question, but with Cassuto (1961, 96-100), Harrison (1969, 548), Hamilton (1990, 150-53), and others—and against von Rad (1961, 74), Speiser (1964, 5, 14), Westermann (1984, 197-99), and many others—we take the verse as a unit. The double chiastic structure strongly indicates a unity of content in this verse intended by the narrator (or editor). Almost as important is the fact that the second half of the verse cannot stand alone as a complete Hebrew sentence, and attempts to connect it as a subordinate clause to vv 5 and 6—or to vv 5, 6, and 7—end in a complex and cumbersome sentence, contrary to the usual spirit of Hebrew grammar and syntax.

Having chosen to treat v 4 as a unit, the next decision is whether it concludes the creation narrative that begins in Gen 1:1 or begins the following one. Compelling evidence for placing it as the conclusion of 1:1—2:3 is that *běhibbār'ām* (**when they were created**) is the seventh, final, and absolutely necessary occurrence (in literary terms) of the verb *bārā'* in this account. It is inconceivable that our author would be satisfied with only six occurrences of this vital verb in the account of the creation week; this occurrence is the seventh, climactic one, and absolutely essential to the literary artistry of this account.

And yet, at least two other considerations also weigh heavily in our decision. First, the clause which begins the verse, **These are the accounts of the heavens and the earth,** occurs ten times in Genesis. This is the first occurrence; the last is 37:2a. P. J. Wiseman (1985) saw this clause as evidence that the sections it marks off were originally separate documents written on clay tablets, and that the clause itself marks the end of each of the ten documents, in the common manner of the ancient Mesopotamian scribe. Hamilton (citing Cross 1973 and Skinner 1930) takes the verse as the introduction to the narrative of Gen 2 that follows. Hamilton's most important point (acknowledging Skinner) is that the genitive (*the generations of*) in this clause always is "the genitive of the progenitor, never of the progeny" (1990, 151). Here, then, Hamilton takes the clause as introducing the "progeny" of (the heavens) and the earth, namely, the human pair whose making is the narrator's concern in ch 2. Hamilton's line of reasoning is persuasive.

A second vital issue is that v 4 introduces the compound name-with-title, *Yahweh Elohim*, perhaps best translated (if we must translate), "Yahweh, the Supreme God." This designation for God does not occur at all in ch 1, and only one other time in the Pentateuch (Exod 9:30), after chs 2—3. This first occurrence of the title in v *4b* is the evidence usually adduced in support of splitting v 4 in the middle. However, other explanations for introducing this title just here are both available and plausible. First, the narrator's move from exclusive use of *Elohim* to the compound *Yahweh Elohim* was for the purpose of identifying *Yahweh* as the God who creates (as opposed to Marduk, Ptah, or others). Additionally, it was appropriate now to introduce the name, Yahweh, because the narrative of ch 2 reports the up-close-and-personal details of the creation of the first humans in two stages, each stage a work of amazing care and intimacy. In this climactic act of creation upon this earth, God was (a) Person(s) creating persons. (See Cassuto 1961, 87; Hamilton 1990, 153.)

We may summarize:

1. Because of the double chiasm of v 4, because the second half of v 4 is a lengthy (for Hebrew) prepositional phrase that cannot stand alone, and because this prepositional phrase is very awkward if attached to the following verses, splitting between paragraphs in the middle of v 4 is not a realistic option in the Hebrew text.

2. Because v 4 contains the seventh occurrence of the verb *bārā'* in the initial creation account, v 4 belongs with that account; we cannot detach it from v 3.

3. Because v 4 introduces the divine name-with-title, *Yahweh Elohim*, used by the narrator throughout chs 2—3, it belongs with ch 2; we cannot detach it from v 5.

The narrator (or editor) has presented us with a very neat conundrum, for a specific important purpose. Verse 4 is so tightly tied with what comes before it, and also with what comes after it, that we dare not detach it from either. The narrator/editor invites (almost, we should say, compels) the reader to treat Gen 1 and 2 as mutually complementary sections of the same account. An accurate reflection of this intention includes v 4 in *both* outline sections:

A. Creation upon the Earth (1:1—2:4)

B. Creation of the *'ādām*/Earthling (2:4-25)

The opening phrase, **these are the accounts of** (*ʾēlleh tôlĕdôt*), is essential to the structure and the understanding of Genesis as a whole. It occurs another nine times in Genesis (5:1*a;* 6:9*a;* 10:1*a;* 11:10*a;* 11:27*a;* 25:12; 25:19*a;* 36:1; 36:9; 37:2*a*), thus dividing Genesis into eleven sections.

The phrase **in the day of** is singular, though this is the conclusion of a creation account that describes *six* days of creation. Here, the phrase means "when," or "at the time of." It also functions as a caution that we may not insist that "day" (*yôm*) in this account *must* mean a twenty-four-hour day, and nothing else. Hebrew usage of *yôm* is as wide-ranging as our English usage of "day." Context, and context alone, must determine which meaning is appropriate in a given place. Context here, including this occurrence, precludes "twenty-four hours" as the only possible meaning of the term in this account. (This is evidence neither for nor against either a young earth or an old earth view of creation. That must be decided on other grounds; this noun, in this account, cannot help us.)

The divine name **Yahweh Elohim** occurs for the first time in this compound form in Gen 2:4. The author uses this name throughout the more detailed account of the creation of *ʾādām* that follows. This is to inform and reassure the reader that *Elohim*, whom Gen 1 insists is sole Creator, is one and the same as *Yahweh*, the God of Israel. Though the multitude of pagan deities are also known by the common noun *ʾelohim* ("gods" in plural), the author of the Genesis account of creation clearly denies their status as "gods" by affirming *Yahweh Elohim* as the One who made the heavens and the earth. Thus, this identification of *Elohim* in this account with *Yahweh* (the personal name of God that occurs about 6,600 times through the Hebrew Bible) is necessary here. This compound name/title also serves as another transition device between the two accounts of chs 1 and 2.

■ **5** We view vv 5-7 each as an independent sentence, though v 5 and v 6 could be connected loosely by a semicolon in translation, without doing violence to the Hebrew syntax. Thus, we will translate each verse completely (to avoid the confusion of comparing our discussion with a translation that takes them as a single compound sentence, beginning with 2:4*b*).

> *Now no shrub of the field was yet on the earth [or: the land]*
> *And no plant of the field had yet sprung up;*
> *For Yahweh Elohim had not caused it to rain upon the earth [or: the land]*
> *And there was no ʾādām to work the ground.*

Verse 5 begins with a picture of an unproductive earth/land. The lack of vegetation (**no shrub, no plant**) indicates a desert-like condition and the lack of life on the earth/land (perhaps intended as an echo of the description of the earth as "formless and empty" in 1:2). This introductory statement is followed by two reasons for the barren condition of the earth/land: (1) **Yahweh Elohim had not caused it to rain upon the earth/land;** (2) **There was no ʾādām to**

work the ground. From the outset, this narrative is clear that the ʾādām was to be a partner with God in the productivity of the ground. The negligence either of God or of humans would lead to unproductive ground. The narrator thus affirmed Israel's faith that the land produces only because of the cooperative work both of God and of humans. In Israel's ancient context, this bold affirmation constituted strong repudiation of the Canaanite cult, which traced both rain and productivity to Baal and his consort.

Fretheim on Gen 2:5

The absence of a human being to "till" (ʿābad, "serve") the ground is considered crucial for the becoming of the creation that God intended. . . . Responsible human beings are said to be as important to the development of the creation as is rain! . . . The tasks outlined in these two texts [2:5, 15] give to the human a responsibility not only for the maintenance and preservation of the creation but also for intracreational development. This human activity stands in the *service* of the nonhuman world, moving it toward its fullest possible potential; at the same time, no precise future is suggested; the future is open-ended to some degree. (2005, 53, emphasis original)

It often is assumed from this statement that no rain fell anywhere upon the earth until the heavens opened to release the deluge, once Noah and his family were safely in the ark (7:11). Neither this text nor the flood story explicitly makes that assertion. Hebrew ʾereṣ, used twice in this verse, can mean "[the] earth," as we have seen in Gen 1, but it also often means "land" or "region" and even occasionally "ground" or "soil." That is to say, Hebrew ʾereṣ has about the same semantic range as English "earth" or "land." Though ʾereṣ could designate the entire earth here, it seems more likely that it refers to the region or district this text calls "Eden," in which God was about to plant a garden.

■ **6** Verse 6 suggests what *Yahweh Elohim* began to do to turn the unproductive earth/land to productivity, beginning with this initiative of watering it (strictly speaking, this is implied here, not stated directly). In the account that follows, the narrative does relate, explicitly, seven distinct activities of *Yahweh Elohim* (see vv 7, 8, 9, 15, 19, 21, 22). The noun ʿēd, with which v 6 begins, occurs only here and in Job 36:27, where it seems to convey the same meaning as it does here. However, neither context helps us determine the precise meaning of ʿēd. English versions have translated **streams,** "mist" (KJV, NASB), "a stream" (NRSV), and "springs" (NLT); Hamilton translates "groundwater" (1990, 150).

With most others, we take ʿēd as a collective noun (a singular form with singular or plural/collective meaning, depending on context), and translate: ***However, springs used to spring up from the earth and water all the surface of the ground.*** The text thus implies water below the earth as the source of springs that watered the surface of the ground. The author's choices of the two verb forms (***used to spring up . . . and water***) here do not require us to assume these springs no longer flowed, only that when the time under discussion had passed, they no longer were sole sources of water for the earth/land. In vv 10-14 the narrative describes a river, with four branches, serving as the main water source for the area of greater Eden.

■ **7** Verse 7 records the first of the seven direct activities of *Yahweh Elohim* mentioned above. The goal of God's work was to remedy the unproductive condition of the earth/land. With at least an initial water source provided for the growth of plants, God formed the ʾādām to till the ground. If we render the initial *vav* consecutive as "so," in the sense of "all this being the case," we may translate v 7 as follows: **So the Lord God [Yahweh Elohim] formed the** ʾādām, **dust from the ground, and breathed into his nostrils the breath of life, and the** ʾādām **became a living creature**.

It would be impossible to overestimate the importance of this single verse to our understanding of what makes a human, human—theologically, psychologically, physically, and in a number of other ways. The verb **formed** (*vayyîṣer*, "and he formed") comes from the root *yāṣar*, which means to "form," "shape," or "fashion," as the potter forms a vessel on the potter's wheel or a sculptor shapes a figure from a lump of clay.

We have seen already, in the summary report from day six (1:26-27), that *the* ʾādām is the human race; we now learn that the creation of *the* ʾādām, the human race, began with an individual human being, also referred to as *the* ʾādām. The noun occurs thirteen times in ch 2 with the definite article [*hāʾādām*; 2:7, 8, 15, 16, 18, 19 (2x), 20, 21, 22 (2x), 23, 25]; in ch 2, ʾādām occurs only twice without the article (2:5, 20). This clearly implies that the narrator intended this text as a narrative of the human race. The creation of the human race that began with an individual ʾādām was not completed until the making of the woman (vv 21-22).

As the physical material for this "sculpture," God used ʿāpār, usually translated **dust**. Some scholars and versions translate "clay," partly because ʿāpār occurs as a synonym for *ḥomer* ("clay"); e.g., Job 10:9. We may regard ʿāpār as a more general term and translate, **dust,** "dirt," or sometimes even "earth"; ʿāpār includes, but is not limited to, clay; *ḥomer* is the more specific term for "clay." Cassuto notes that another term for "clay" is used in various Egyptian and Mesopotamian accounts of gods forming humans; the author of Genesis used the more general Hebrew term ʿāpār because he did not want to suggest too close an association with these pagan ideas (1961, 104-5). Finally, ʿāpār provides a literary and theological link to God's final statement to the man at the end of this section (3:19). For these reasons, we may conclude (though perhaps not insist) that God formed the first human from the specific kind of ʿāpār, **dust** or earth, that we would call clay. Another important noun here is **ground** (ʾădāmâ). The text thus makes clear that *Yahweh Elohim* formed ʾādām from ʾădāmâ, an "earthling" from the "earth/ground," an intentional play on words in the Hebrew text.

Gregory of Nyssa on Gen 2:7

"God took of the dust of the earth and fashioned man." In this world I have discovered the two affirmations that man is nothing and that man is great. If you consider nature alone, he is nothing and has no value; but if you regard the honor with which he has been treated, man is something great. (Louth 2001, 51)

Verse *7b* is climactic, as God did what no other artist could do; **And [God] breathed into his nostrils the breath of life.** The figure sculpted by the hands, the fingers, of God lay before God life-size and lifelike, but so far lifeless. God bent over, as it were, breathed God's own breath into it, and the life of the human race began. Fretheim correctly describes this as "God's own breath of life" (2005, 39). It is not too big a stretch to say, even, that all humans since have carried the breath of God, as a part of our bearing the image of God.

And the ʾādām *became a living creature*; *living creature* translates Hebrew *nepeš ḥayyâ*, the same phrase used in ch 1 to designate the creatures of the seas, the skies, and the dry land (1:20, 24). A key question, then, is what sets humans apart from the rest of the biological animal kingdom, as both are called *nepeš ḥayyâ* in the creation texts? The answer will have many aspects, but with respect to God's *actions*, this text is clear. God's breathing God's own life-giving breath into the nostrils of the first human was the action that constitutes humans (the *ʾādām*) in the image of God.

The KJV translates "living soul" and the NASB has "Lit., *soul*" as a marginal note. However, "soul" is not a literal translation of Hebrew *nepeš*, except in a very specialized sense having nothing in common with the popular meaning of English "soul." It is also important to note that the "soul" of later Greek philosophical thought is alien to the Hebrew understanding of *nepeš*. A human is a *nepeš ḥayyâ* in the same way almost any other member of the earthly animal kingdom is a *nepeš ḥayyâ*; most are sensate, animate, mobile creatures, endowed with breath in some manner. A literal translation of *nepeš* is "throat"; close off the throat of any human, or of any animal or bird known to ancient Israel, and that individual creature's life ends. We live by the breath that passes through our throat, not to our esophagus, but to our lungs.

Many, including scholars, have speculated on the sexual identity of the *ʾādām* in 2:7. This noun is masculine gender, which most have taken as implying a "male" being. A few, both ancients and moderns, have suggested this original, single *ʾādām* was androgynous (hermaphroditic), combining the physical characteristics of both male and female in one individual. This text does not support that view.

A biblical theology of the human creation begins in Gen 1:26-27, with God's creation of the ʾādām, both male and female, in the image of God. It continues here in the account of the first human individual formed with infinite skill, love, and grace by the hand of God, then brought to life by the breath of God. We acknowledge God tacitly with every breath we take, twelve times a minute, on average. Parents, siblings, spouse, children, sisters and brothers in the Christian faith, neighbors, coworkers, fellow citizens, "enemies"—all share God's breath, all are living images of God by creation, all are shaped as each of us is, because all were shaped in our first parent by the very finger of God.

Though this text does not say God has "hands," we are invited to think of God as coaxing a human figure from the dust or clay scooped up by hand from the ground—carefully, patiently, intimately molding it inch by inch, bottom to top or top to bottom, by the loving touch of God's own fingers. The language of the Hebrew text does not allow us either to insist or to deny it happened this way, *physically*. We are, however, invited by this language to *picture* it this way, in our minds and even in our emotions, as a way of impressing upon us the nearly infinite value God places upon the crown of God's creation upon this earth. Excellent sculptors care about their masterpieces as they sculpt them, and afterward when they are completed. Just so, God cares about humankind (the ʾādām), all the more because we are not a lifeless, but a living, "sculpture."

"The Weight of Glory"

In a sermon preached in the Church of St. Mary, Oxford, June 8, 1941, C. S. Lewis defined one aspect of the glory in and for which humans were created and to which, in redemption, we are recalled as, "what may happen when the redeemed soul, beyond all hope and nearly beyond belief, learns at last that she has pleased Him whom she was created to please." In light of this passion of God for God's human creation, Lewis went on to say, "There are no *ordinary* people. You have never talked to a mere mortal. . . . Next to the Blessed Sacrament itself, your neighbor is the holiest object presented to your senses" (1962b, 205, 210-11).

Here are the beginnings of human worth and dignity. Because every human is a representation/image/icon of God, we are privileged every day to meet and treat each other as such. These are the gifts of God by creation to every woman and man, every girl and boy. No social construct, much less any government, possesses a legitimate right to grant or to withhold them from any individual or group.

Implications abound everywhere. If all our fellow humans carry the image of God, if they represent God to us by virtue of their existence, then racism is wrong; sexism is wrong; class, wealth, and educational distinctions as ways of judging human worth are wrong. In our economic decisions, whether individual, communal, corporate, or governmental, we must take account of their impact on persons bearing the image of God. Human trafficking for sex, labor, or other "reasons" is wrong. We cannot steal another's time—hours and days of another's life—for such a trivial reason as adding to our own temporary wealth in our brief span upon the earth; how could we face the God whose icon (image) we have insulted, wronged, and caused to suffer? This holds true, too, for governments that waste or unjustly transfer the tax money (i.e., the portions of lives spent earning it) of those they tax using the coercive powers of government.

Sex for money or any other transactional consideration is wrong; how could we hire or coerce the body of a sister (or brother) created in God's image merely to relieve a biological itch? Theft is wrong, because possessions represent (at the least) time, dignity, and a measure of security. Murder is wrong, because God gave each of us life—it is not ours to take. We could go on, but it all begins here. If it is only a Hebrew romantic notion, why should we bother with anything? If, however, all this is true, it is of staggering importance. Each of us should ask ourselves, "Have I contemplated, have I greeted, have I treated, each of my human brothers and sisters as the image and representation of God to me today?"

In addition to the way we treat others individually, living as the image of God also calls for a communal responsibility to each other. Socially, culturally, politically, every human being is worthy of life, and of the opportunity for health, for education, and for dignified gainful occupation, at a minimum. Christians, even more than others, are called to assist those who have been excluded. We can do this individually; we can work together as the body of Christ; we even may challenge our governments to greater effectiveness in putting these opportunities within the reach of those who cannot afford them, unaided.

On a related subject, each of us is a ***living creature*** of the animal kingdom, sharing structural and systemic likenesses with many of them to an astonishing degree. With the closest of our animal "cousins" we share a genome that is identical by a ratio of up to 96 percent, differing only in the "final" 4 percent or so. That we are animal, animate, sensate creatures is not a disputed point between "evolution" and "special creation." It is a given, known in different ways and to varying degrees throughout human history and cultures, clearly affirmed and even celebrated by this text, and lately discovered anew by scientific researches impossible to conduct even a decade ago. Yet at the same time, we are unique: created in the image of God, formed by the hand of God, and animated by the breath of God, bequeathed to each of us, from generation to generation.

All this appears to some as overanthropomorphizing God. On the other end of the interpretive spectrum, some have noted the partnership in creation of the three persons of the Trinity and have taken the creation of the humans as a preincarnate appearance of the Son. While this second position appears to go beyond the available evidence, this text definitely emphasizes God's personal, intimate, even passionate, care in forming the first human pair. However we should visualize the process, God created the human race for fellowship and for love, with God and with each other.

Jesus affirmed this understanding when he made the Good Samaritan the hero of his story answering the lawyer's question about his neighbor (Luke 10:25-37). Paul affirmed it when he declared to the Athenians on Mars Hill that "from one man" God had "made every nation of men" (Acts 17:26), and when he urged Philemon to restore Onesimus to his household and charge any loss he had suffered to Paul's account (Phlm 12-18). The "new song" of eternity affirms it in its praise of the Lamb who has **purchased [people] for God, by your blood, from every tribe and language and people and ethnicity . . . and they will reign upon the earth** (Rev 5:9-10).

2. The Garden and Its Rivers (2:8-14)

BEHIND THE TEXT

Scholars have looked for Eden in the area of Sumer in the southern part of ancient Mesopotamia, through which flow even today two of the rivers of Eden, the Tigris and the Euphrates. Some scholars have attempted to trace the name Eden itself back through Akkadian *edinu* to Sumerian *eden*. The Akkadian word means "steppe-land, wilderness," which does not agree with the biblical description of Eden as a well-watered area. Others have sought the meaning of "Eden" in another root found both in Ugaritic and in Hebrew, "a place well watered throughout"; this etymology seems plausible (see Cassuto 1961, 107-8).

The description of Eden in ch 2 is from the point of view of the garden looking upstream, northward, to the lands outside the garden, and even beyond the region of Eden, to the separation of the river into its four tributaries, and ultimately to their individual headwaters. These headwaters were probably located in the north, the northeast, and possibly to the east of central and lower Mesopotamia. The four streams flowed separately in their courses near or through northern and central Mesopotamia. Before they reached the garden of Eden in southern Mesopotamia, they had joined together to form a single river, as two of them, the Tigris and the Euphrates, still do today—or perhaps we should say, do again today.

All this is predicated on the assumption that we still could locate the region of Eden if only we possessed a bit more of the right kinds of data. Hamilton points out that the descriptions of the four tributaries in vv 11-14 sound as though the author thought of them as still flowing in the region in his day (1990, 168). That the Tigris and the Euphrates are two of the four rivers named could be taken as evidence for this understanding.

IN THE TEXT

■ **8** Verse 8 reports a second creative work; ***Yahweh Elohim had planted.*** **Had planted** is an appropriate translation of *vayyiṭṭaʿ*; the Hebrew verb form traditionally called *vav* consecutive with imperfect may be translated either with English perfect or past perfect, depending on context. This translation, using the English past perfect, advances the position that God did not form the *ʾādām*, then realize the need for a home; rather, **God** already **had planted a garden** as a home for the *ʾādām*. Hamilton's remark that the trees of the garden "do not appear *ex nihilo* or grow overnight from saplings to towering trees" can be seen as supporting this understanding, though Hamilton himself translates this verb as a perfect, "planted" (1990, 160, 162).

Hamilton is not alone; KJV, NRSV, NASB, NLT, Cassuto (1961, 106-7), and others also translate "planted"; this translation, too, is grammatically and syntactically plausible. In either case, God planted the garden **in Eden, eastward**, i.e., east of the land of Israel, which lay along the Mediterranean. The preposition **in** before **Eden** indicates **Eden** was a region or district. That is, Eden was larger than just **the garden.**

And there [*God*] put the *ʾādām* ***whom*** **he had formed**; whether God planted the garden before or after making the *ʾādām*, the narrator here revealed one reason for the (relatively) detailed description of the garden and its region. God prepared it as the home of the *ʾādām*. A few verses later (v 15), the narrative records that God also assigned the garden as the place of work for the *ʾādām*.

■ **9** This third report of yet another creative work of *Yahweh Elohim* once again features **the ground** (*ʾădāmâ*) from which *Yahweh Elohim* had formed *the ʾādām* as the context of his work. (Alternatively, one could view this verse as an expansion upon the statement of v 8. What did it mean for God to plant a garden? Well, "From the ground, God caused to sprout. . . .") *Yahweh Elohim* caused to sprout (*ṣāmaḥ*) **all kinds of trees** (*kol-ʿēṣ*) in the garden; the emphasis of the Hebrew *kol-ʿēṣ* is not on God planting all the species of trees in the garden. Rather, every tree God now placed in the garden was **pleasing to the eye and good for food.** Thus, the garden was not simply an address for the *ʾādām*; God designed it as a real home, a place of delight and joy.

Two trees receive special attention in v 9. We may translate, ***Now the tree of life was in the midst of the garden; also, the tree of the knowledge of good and evil. In the midst*** means not just "among the rest of the trees, generally," but **in the middle,** though not necessarily with mathematical precision. By the end of the account, these two trees will be at the center of the action. Their placement in the center of the garden, then, here at the beginning, is an artistically pleasing hint to the reader, "Remember these trees." If the author intended us to take this account literally in a physical sense, the fruit of the tree of life was the immediate means by which the first human pair maintained their immortality. At least, that is the implication of God's decision to deny further access to it after the first pair had sinned.

■ **10** Hamilton's observation of vv 10-14 is sound. "These verses should be seen as an extension of v. 9, the two component parts of the garden being trees (v. 9) and rivers (vv. 10-14)" (1990, 167). The following, somewhat expanded, translation is an attempt to make clear the meaning of v 10: ***Now, a river used to arise in Eden*** [or: ***Eden-ward***] ***to water the garden, and from there*** [i.e., outside the garden] ***it*** [i.e., the river] ***was divided and became four tributary streams*** [lit., "heads," i.e., sources].

The traditional reading of v 10 implies that a river flowing from Eden watered the garden, then divided and became four rivers watering the larger surrounding lands. The river originating in Eden would have been the source of productivity and beauty, not only within the garden, but also in the lands outside the garden. Theologically attractive as this scenario may seem at first blush, it founders on the impossibilities of riverine geography. Rivers do not rise at their headwaters as single streams, then branch into four rivers downstream, except in delta regions built up at or near a river's mouth, and no one has suggested that this text describes a delta region.

The translation proposed here (following Speiser 1964, 14-20; Hamilton 1990, 166-68) treats the Hebrew text with great care and also takes into account the geography and physical features of the earth's river systems. As is normal with rivers having multiple tributaries, this river's four major tributaries combined into one river *before* it entered the region of Eden. Alternatively, since we do not know the extent of the *region* of Eden, after the four tributaries entered Eden separately they combined into one river before entering the *garden*.

Ultimately, the emphasis of the narrative is on the presence of a river in the garden. As a result, the garden was a well-watered place, sustaining life abundantly. Later biblical writers, no doubt with this passage in mind, used similar river imagery to describe the vitality of life in the presence of God (e.g., Ps 46:4; Isa 33:21; Ezek 47:1-12; Zech 14:8; Rev 22:1-2).

■ **11-12** Verses 11-14 contain the names and descriptions of the four rivers. The name of the first river, **Pishon,** means something like "Gusher." It corresponds to no known river name, either from antiquity or from modern times. However, it was said that it **winds through the . . . land of Havilah.** The translations of the KJV ("compasseth") and of the NASB and NRSV ("flows around") represent another understanding of the Hebrew participle *sōbēb,* because in other contexts it often does mean "surrounds/surrounding." However, this river did not encircle an entire land or region; rather, it meandered (looped) through it, as many rivers do in many regions. Havilah, associated with Cush in Gen 10:7, is listed there as Cush's second son; since the land of Cush also occurs in our text (2:13), we will discuss this identification below.

Mentioning gold (v 11) is one thing; why an editorial comment, **the gold of that land is good** (v 12), should follow is a bit mysterious. Gold is gold. Cassuto has suggested this is an indirect rebuttal of the legends of the garden of Eden from Mesopotamia, which pictured gold and other precious metals and gemstones growing as fruits upon the Tree of Life. No, the Torah says, these are natural products of the ground, available for human use, wherever they may be found (1961, 119).

Suggestions abound for the identification of *bĕdōlaḥ* (bdellium) and onyx (*šōham*) in the land of Havilah. The Septuagint translates "ruby"; "pearls" (NIV n.) is another suggestion. **Aromatic resin** is a possibility; these resins were the dried sap of various Near Eastern shrubs and trees, some of which were used as pharmaceutical ingredients. They came to be known as *bĕdōlaḥ* because they resembled in color the gemstone, whatever it was. Since gold and *šōham* both are minerals, probably *bĕdōlaḥ* is as well. *Šōham* often is rendered **onyx**; Speiser proposed lapis lazuli (1964, 17). Both identifications must remain tentative.

■ **13** The name of the second river, **Gihon**, means "bubbler." Its identity, too, is unknown today. There is nothing in the language of the text that would disallow the possibility that either of these two rivers, Pishon and/or **Gihon,** could have been one or two of the eastern tributaries of the Tigris that still flow into it today, though that must remain only a suggestion. One thing is certain; this is not the Gihon spring, one of the two main water sources of ancient Jerusalem. For the same reasons noted above regarding the Pishon (v 11), **it winds through** is a good translation of Hebrew *sōbēb* here also. As Hamilton notes, "Rivers more often twist and turn than encircle" (1990, 166). Because in both places (vv 11, 13) the Hebrew text actually is *hūʾ hassōbēb*, the independent/demonstrative pronoun followed by the participle with definite article, we could translate both a bit more accurately as independent, verbless clauses, *This [is] the one that winds through all the land of Havilah* (v 11)/ *Cush* (v 13).

In the Bible, **Cush** often means "Ethiopia," which included areas of what today is Sudan. However, at least three different regions are referred to as Cush, and two of these also have a Havilah nearby. If our understanding of Mesopotamia for the setting of Eden is correct, we should understand Cush here as the region of the people called the Kassites in Akkadian and Greek sources. Throughout the OT periods, Kassite groups were located both east of the Tigris and in the middle Euphrates region. If we could identify this **Gihon** today, it probably would be located east of the Tigris; the Kerkha is a possibility (Hamilton 1990, 170, n. 13, referencing Tigay).

■ **14** The third and the fourth rivers, **the Tigris** and the **Euphrates**, bear the same names today. They rise in the mountains of Armenia above the northern borders of Mesopotamia. The English name Tigris transliterates Greek *Tigris*, derived from Hebrew *ḥiddeqel*, itself a rendering of Babylonian (Akkadian) *Idaglat.* From its source southwest of Mount Ararat, the Tigris flows about 1,150 miles in a fairly straight southeasterly course, as rivers flow, until it joins the Euphrates below the site of ancient Babylon. The combined stream, called today the Shatt al-Arab, flows about another one hundred miles southeastward until it empties into the Persian Gulf. Since the Tigris did not form the eastern border of ancient Assyria, the note that it *flows east of Ashur,* may refer to the city of Asshur, west of the Tigris, for which the people, land, and empire of Assyria were named.

The Euphrates actually has its farthest source northeast of the source of the Tigris, between Mount Ararat and the Black Sea. However, it flows west, then southwestward, then south, looping around the headwaters region of the Tigris, and reaching within about ninety miles of the Mediterranean. Finally, it turns toward the southeast, completing its "Great Bend," and flows through most of western Mesopotamia; the total length of the Euphrates is nearly 1,700 miles. In Sumerian times, and perhaps through most of the several OT periods, the Tigris and the Euphrates flowed into the Persian Gulf separately, but in more recent times, according to the geological evidence, they have filled in the head of the Persian Gulf, and now empty into it as the Shatt al-Arab. If this description of Eden's rivers reflects a geology earlier than that of early Sumer, the Edenic confluence of the four rivers was disrupted somehow—later than the expulsion of the first pair from the garden, but before the appearance of the earliest Sumerian cities of Ur, Uruk, Nippur, and the rest. It is not a question for which we are likely to find an answer.

It would not be fair to move on without mentioning other interpretations proffered over the years. A suggestion found in the rabbis and the church fathers is that these are the four classical rivers of ancient Near Eastern/North African civilization, namely, the Nile, the Euphrates, the Tigris, and the Indus. The Indus, to be sure, is on the southeastern horizon of the ancient Near East, but the upper reaches of the Nile are at its southern horizon also. Some in antiquity posited a single river in Eden that went underground to emerge as these major rivers. Albright suggested that the Pishon and the Gihon are the Blue Nile and the White Nile, whose confluence is at Khartoum, Sudan. Thus, both Egypt to the southwest of Israel and Mesopotamia to the northeast and east, the two major cultural and political influences on ancient Israel, are represented here in the rivers of Eden (1922, 15-31). Many modern scholars do not think even the mention of the Tigris and the Euphrates is enough to give this account credence as a historical document from which we could learn anything of value for our understanding of Mesopotamian geography, ancient or modern. Cassuto states flatly, "Our text . . . describes a state of affairs that no longer exists. . . . The garden of Eden according to the Torah was not situated in our world" (1961, 118). As a side note on this point, it would seem that those who understand the present shapes and positioning of the earth's land masses to be one result of the flood would not expect to be able to locate Eden in lower Mesopotamia or anywhere else in today's earthly geography, but some try.

FROM THE TEXT

Whether we may rightly speak of a collective human "racial memory" of the lost paradise of Eden may be debated. The Bible itself, however, refers to Eden a number of times, directly and indirectly. Already in Gen 13:10, the author reports, "Lot . . . saw that the whole plain of the Jordan was well watered, like the garden of the Lord," i.e., like Eden's garden. Psalm 46:4, Ezek 47:1-12, Joel 3:18, Zech 14:8, and Rev 22:1-5 are examples of later biblical passages depicting God's throne in Jerusalem in the eschatological age as the source of an abundant river bringing life like the rivers of Eden. Almost the entire oracle of Ezek 28:11-19 depicts God's judgment of the king of Tyre in language that renders him a metaphor for the "guardian cherub" (v 14) whose "perfection" placed him in God's service "in Eden, the garden of God" (vv 12-13), but who lost his exalted estate by succumbing to pride (v 17). The lost paradise held a prominent place in the theology of the biblical authors. The theme of its eschatological restoration is an important element of the poignant hope they offer with great vividness in many passages, to believers of every age and every circumstance.

3. Profession, Provision, Prohibition (2:15-17)

BEHIND THE TEXT

This short paragraph demonstrates a skilled narrative pacing of the kind still admired in writers at the top of their craft today. Following immediately upon the leisurely "scenic tour" of the river and its tributaries in the preceding five verses, the narrative here accelerates to breakneck speed. These three short verses, almost bullet points in their comparative brevity, lay out in a staccato succession a profession, a provision, and a prohibition for the as-yet-solitary ʾādām. Immediately after, we will find the narrator slowing the pace again, but not all the way back to the ambling gait of the preceding paragraph.

IN THE TEXT

■ **15** This brief, straightforward report of the next of the successive activities of *Yahweh Elohim* in the longer narrative of ch 2 reveals the profession/vocation for which God had formed the ʾādām. **Then Yahweh Elohim took the ʾādām and put him in the Garden of Eden to work it and to guard it.** God had formed the first human and infused him with the breath of life; God had planted the garden and made it ready for human habitation. Now God placed the first human there. What God had in mind for human life on this earth now would begin, even though the human community itself was not yet established.

What God intended for the relationship between the 'ādām and the garden was, first, that the 'ādām would **work it** ('ābad; see the same verb in 2:5); we even could translate **to serve it.** The narrative thus clearly links this human profession/vocation with 2:5; the vocation of the 'ādām was to engage in work God already had begun. God had planted the garden; through his labor/service, the 'ādām was to keep it productive.

Symeon the New Theologian on Gen 2:15

In the beginning man was created with a nature inclined to work, for in paradise Adam was enjoined to till the ground and care for it, and there is in us a natural bent for work, the movement toward the good. Those who yield themselves to idleness and apathy, even though they may be spiritual and holy, hurl themselves into unnatural subjection to passions. (Louth 2001, 61)

The human profession/vocation also included watching over the garden. The Hebrew verb šāmar means "to guard, watch over, keep, protect, defend, secure." We cannot know now whether physical dangers lurked in the garden, dangers to the garden itself, to its plant life, or to its animals. But God's appointing the 'ādām to guard and protect the garden certainly included protecting it from exploitation, devaluation, and destruction—through misuse, abuse, and/or overuse. The twin tasks of protecting (šāmar) the garden and working ('ābad) its ground meant the primary responsibility of the 'ādām was to maintain the garden's productivity and preserve it as a place of enjoyment for future generations. Fretheim rightly finds in this verse human "responsibility . . . for intra-creational development, bringing the world along toward its fullest possible potential" (1994, 349).

John Wesley on the Garden of Eden

The place appointed for *Adam's* residence was a *garden*; . . . The heaven was the roof of *Adam's* house, and never was any roof so curiously *cieled* [sic] and *painted*: the earth was his floor, and never was any floor so richly *inlaid*: the shadow of the trees was his retirement, and never were any rooms so finely hung: *Solomon's* in all their glory *were not arrayed* like them. (Wesley 1975, 11)

■ **16-17** The passage, Gen 1:28-30, contains God's mandate and blessing to the 'ādām. Here we find another speech in which God spoke more specifically about how the 'ādām was to live in the garden. Because these two verses together constitute a single speech from the mouth of God, we will discuss them together. Conceptually they constitute, first, a provision (v 16) and, second, a prohibition (v 17)—together, the first detailed instruction for human life upon the earth.

This speech is introduced by the verb **commanded** (*ṣāvâ*), but the first part of the command is in reality an invitation to eat freely, the necessary provision for human life. For reasons that will become apparent, we will translate, *From every tree of the garden, eating you may eat*. This syntax—*eating you may eat*—is a common construction in Hebrew Scripture to indicate a superlative degree; we could translate, "You *certainly* may eat!" This "command," then, is to eat freely: eat whatever you wish, whenever you wish.

In the context of this superabundant provision, then, we are justified in translating the singular prohibition, *However, from the tree of the knowledge of good and evil you may not eat from it, for on the day of your eating from it, dying you shall die* [i.e., *you certainly shall die*]. The initial Hebrew conjunction *vav* we have translated **however,** because it is intended to introduce a sharp contrast between this prohibition and the provision that immediately precedes it. The repetition *from it* at the end of the first clause was to ensure there could be no mistake or excuse about which tree was intended as the subject of the prohibition.

The two verbal constructions are identical in their syntax: *eating you may eat* (v 16) and *dying you shall die* (v 17). (Here we backtrack a bit to bring the provision and the prohibition together in our discussion, because *all* of it bears emphatic repetition in face of the incredulous Gnosticism now rooted deep within the human psyche.) As noted, this is a very strong, emphatic way in biblical Hebrew of commanding/urging, forbidding, or stating that something was or was not done. The encouragement to eat from any and every tree in the garden was very intense, even passionate. The emphasis is on the *abundance* of the provision: the fruit of all the trees (but one) was available for human consumption.

But God did pronounce one—and *only* one—prohibition along with the multifaceted provision. First, then, we may ask what **the knowledge of good and evil** entails. The text itself does not expand on the expression. Some understand it as referring to moral good and evil or to sinlessness and sinfulness. Others, both ancients and moderns, have associated the knowledge of evil with sexual knowledge and experience.

Still others understand the phrase as referring to the omniscient knowledge usually ascribed to God, interpreting **good and evil** as a *hendiadys*, a way of saying "everything" by listing the polar opposites. However, this reading does not seem to stand up to God's statement, "The [*ʾādām*] has now become like one of us, knowing good and evil" (3:22). God certainly did not mean the humans had come to possess omniscient knowledge.

John Wesley on the Tree of Knowledge

There was *the tree of the knowledge of good and evil*—So called, not because it had any virtue to beget useful knowledge, but because there was an express revelation of the will of God concerning this tree, so that by it he might *know good* and *evil*. What is *good*? It is good not to eat of *this tree*: what is evil? To eat of *this tree*. The distinction between all other moral good and evil was written in the heart of man; but this, which resulted from a *positive law*, was written *upon this tree*. And in the event it proved to give *Adam* an experimental knowledge of *good* by the loss of [good], and of *evil* by the sense of [evil]. (Wesley 1975, 12)

What we do find in 3:7 is that after they had eaten of the forbidden fruit, the first pair knew they were naked. One may argue that what the text presents as "evil" is their sinfulness, shame, and guilt. Their nakedness was not evil, and their sudden knowledge of it did not make it evil. This new knowledge of their state, however, opened to them all kinds of knowledge, some of which would be good, some evil.

Finally, God knows both good and evil, but God does not know moral evil experientially, that is, from having committed moral evil. In God's frame of reference, "knowing good and evil" probably does mean "knowing all that can be known," that is, all that exists.

It is important to remember the context here in ch 2. God had assigned the ʾādām a profession; God had made lavish provision both for sustenance and for enjoyment within the garden; now God placed upon the ʾādām a single prohibition. With respect to positive action, faithfulness meant busying himself with stewardship of the garden. Faithfulness also has a "negative" aspect, however, the willingness to trust even when understanding is incomplete. If, indeed, the central issue was not understanding, but trust, how was the ʾādām (how are we?) to demonstrate faithfulness, except by complying with a prohibition without fully knowing why?

Fretheim on Gen 2:16-17

This command . . . indicates that, for all the creative power God entrusts to human beings, the human relationship to God provides an indispensable matrix for the proper exercise of that power. To obey the command regarding the tree is to recognize that human creativity is derivative, that human beings are not freed from all limitations in its exercise or from God's good intentions for creaturely life. The tree is a concrete metaphor for the limits of creatureliness. (2005, 59)

As the narrative continues, it is obvious neither the man nor the woman stopped breathing upon their first bite of the forbidden fruit (3:6-7); Gen 5:5 records the man's age at death as nine hundred thirty years. What, then, is the meaning of God's pronouncement, ***for on the day of your eating from it, dying you shall die*** [i.e., ***you certainly shall die***]? A traditional understanding among Christians is that the first pair died *spiritually* on the day of their transgression. This interpretation may carry an element of truth, in that their alienation from God began that day, and alienation from God ultimately is death.

Another direct action, however, did follow the first couple's direct action of eating of the forbidden fruit. God expelled them from the garden to prevent them from taking also of the fruit of the tree of life, in order to "live forever" (3:22-24). Some have understood the key to the couple's life and health in the garden to have been regular access to the fruit of the tree of life. Since the text does not mention this directly, others have taken their expulsion from the garden as preventing their first and only eating from that tree, thus denying them the immortality they did not yet possess, because they had not yet eaten of that fruit. Whether a first eating from the tree of life, or continuing access to it, is the point of the text here, it is clear that prevention of access to the tree of life is the narrative key to the certainty of death, of which God here was warning the ʾādām. As Hamilton succinctly puts it, "The verse is underscoring the certainty of death, not its chronology" (1990, 172).

FROM THE TEXT

This paragraph's teachings, and their implications, are of immense significance to our understanding of life, vocation, and relationship with God. First is its report that God assigned work to the first human person—and, by extension, to the human race as a whole—when God placed the ʾādām in the garden **to serve it and to guard it.** These two verbs suggest that some work may have been strenuous and difficult, even in the garden. However, work itself is neither a curse nor a punishment, as some have asserted. Rather, it is one of the ways we partake of and reflect the image of God. God works; God's human sons and daughters work. Appropriate work, done wisely and well, glorifies God. It also benefits ourselves, our brothers and sisters, and the world we are assigned to serve and to guard.

A corollary observation is that the immoral taking of the just fruits of another's labors is a sin against God, as well as against the person made in God's image. God granted work as a benison; stealing its rewards from another is an insult to God. This is true whether the theft is accomplished at the point of a knife or a firearm, by fraud, by the duping of the innocent and the naive, or by the unchecked force of the state.

Even so-called menial labor is not punishment, since the work of serving the garden certainly would have included some of what we now usually define as menial labor. This is confirmed in the fact that Jesus himself taught and demonstrated menial service to and for his disciples, by performing for them the lowest slave's task of washing the feet of those who came into the house as guests (John 13:5-17). Wesley ratified the principle in his covenant service, affirming, "Christ has many services to be done; some are more easy and honorable, others more difficult and menial" (The Joint Hymnal Commission, *Hymns of Faith and Life* [Winona Lake, Ind.: Light and Life Press, 1976], 501).

Forms from the root ʿābad ("to work," "to serve," etc.) are used later in the Bible to denote the service of Israel to God, of citizen-subjects to their kings and, very often, of servants or slaves to their masters. Depending often on to whom it is rendered, service may be deemed honorable or dishonorable, but work or service, in and of itself, is not dishonorable, nor beneath the human station. This is shown in the fact that often "agent" would be a more accurate and precise translation of both Hebrew ʿebed in the OT and Greek doulos in the NT, though both are usually translated, "servant," "slave," or the like. Work and service are a significant part of the dominion God ordained in and from the beginning that humankind would exercise over the earth (1:28). This also is part of what it means to be created in the image of the God who worked to bring the creation itself into being.

Work did become more onerous, sometimes more dangerous, and often less rewarding, as a result of the disturbances set in motion by the first human rebellion. But even these now-less-than-ideal conditions are not, in and of themselves, the result of God's decree. As we shall see, God's statement to the man in 3:17-19 was not a judicial sentence but an announcement of some of the natural consequences of the rebellion. Especially in light of the redemption already accomplished in Christ, we need to experience work as an important aspect of our living in the image of God. Thus it is not sinful to look for or invent ways to make our work easier, faster, or more efficient.

Though work is mandated in this text, we must exercise wisdom in choosing the kind of work we do. Work that degrades the earth and its other inhabitants, or that defaces the image of God in ourselves or in our fellow humans, diminishes both us and them and is to be avoided.

On another matter, God's provision of abundant food from the trees of the garden, coupled with the prohibition of only one, highlights God's intentions in apportioning blessing: the good, the beneficial, and the allowed vastly outweigh the forbidden, and even the forbidding is only for good reason, that we may avoid hurting ourselves and others. The multiplication of laws began with the six hundred thirteen laws of the Torah (the traditional count), and continues with the millions of laws and regulations to which every citizen is subject in the eyes of the various legal systems of the world today. The need for these is proportional, as well, but proportional now to the relative depravity or spiritual enlightenment of cultures and of their individual members. Where God's creation intentions are understood and practiced—even if only imperfectly because of the brokenness imposed upon the creation by human rebellion—justice, mercy, grace, and loving-kindness are much in evidence. Where lawlessness—or the fake lawfulness of a hypocritically religious legalism—holds sway, the layering of law upon law, of oppressive interpretation upon oppressive interpretation, breeds only more of human wickedness, and yields only more and more of human misery. God's creation and redemption intention for all is to live free of the bondage of sin and death, as Jesus declared: "So if the Son sets you free, you will be free indeed" (John 8:36).

God's command to the ʾādām in v 16 is but the first of many of God's typical commands. We could say even that it demonstrates the central character of *all* God's commands, from every time and every context: God wills absolutely the absolute good and delight of God's creatures. As parents take great pleasure in the joys and pleasures of their children, so God takes great pleasure in *our* pleasures and joys, including the physical joys God has formed us for and has created for us.

God's permission in the garden came with a prohibition and that also was for the good, for it, too, contributed to the establishment of proper Creator-creature relationship. Later, the number of prohibitions was multiplied because of human obtuseness, but the essential character of every command, whether a mandate or a prohibition, remains the same as this one: what is *mandated* is for the ultimate good and joy of all persons and all things, and what is *forbidden* also is for the ultimate good and joy of all persons and all things.

The existence of the tree of the knowledge of good and evil, here at the beginning of the human story, is a reminder that wisdom and discernment are essential to our wellbeing and to our work and that these come only in and through our relationship with God. This is a primary focus, also, of the later biblical wisdom tradition, as summed up in what we may call the "thesis statement" of Proverbs, ***The reverential fear of the Lord is the beginning of knowledge*** (Prov 1:7*a*). The knowledge the first pair acquired in eating of the fruit of the tree without permission is the ultimately destructive knowledge of the claim to autonomy from God, to self-sovereignty. Proverbs 1:7*b* assesses this approach with equal directness, ***Wisdom and discipline, fools despise.***

4. The Preparation of the Lone ʾādām (2:18-20)

■ **18** The narrator now notes God's assessment of the state of the ʾādām, **It is not good for the ʾādām to be *by himself.*** Literally, this "not good" follows on the heels of the six evaluations of "good," and the climactic seventh, the "very good" of Gen 1. Moreover, each assessment, including this one, is attributed to God. Such a jarring contradiction cannot have been accidental; it was not passed over by an editor without notice. Rather, the narrator/editor intended the reader to perceive this "not good" as belonging theologically, if not also chronologically, before the final "very good" of Gen 1:31. So long as it was **not good** for the ʾādām, neither was it yet "very good" for the whole of the earthly creation. Cassuto observes that the Hebrew *lōʾ-ṭôb* is an emphatic and categorical denial of any possibility of goodness in the situation God was evaluating, much stronger than other possible ways of expressing the evaluation. That the lone ʾādām should remain alone was not, and never could be, **good** (1961, 126-27). The evaluation **not good** anticipates the divine plan for *the ʾādām* to live in community and not in isolation from other creatures or in solitude. Just as God enjoys the fellowship of community within the triune Godhead, God intends humans to live in relational community, as an important part of our

101

identity in the image of God. The prior statement, "Male and female [God] created them" (1:27), already has alerted the reader that human life in community is an integral part of the divine plan of creation. The salient point here is that the first human needed to discover and to experience solitude, to enjoy fully the presence of another *ʾādām*.

The second part of v 18 announces God's plan to change what was **not good,** to make it "good." We translate, ***I will make for him a power/strength corresponding/equal to him*** (*ʿēzer kĕnegdô*); this is significantly different from the traditional translation (**a helper suitable for him**). A departure of this magnitude requires explanation.

Scholarly discoveries now nearly thirty years old (see Freedman 1983, 56-58) have established that the noun *ʿēzer*, occurring twenty-one times in the Hebrew Bible, is a homonym that may convey either of two different meanings. Eight times, including six times in the Psalms, *ʿēzer* does convey the well-known meaning of "help/helper." In every one of these eight occurrences, that help/Helper is God.

In its other eleven occurrences outside Gen 2, *ʿēzer* means "a strength" or "a power," in the sense of possessing the right to decide and/or to act on its own volition. If this is the meaning of *ʿēzer* here (vv 18, 20), then with respect to all but God, both the "original" human and the *ʿēzer* God now proposed to **make** would be autonomous powers.

This leaves the question of which of these two *is* the meaning of *ʿēzer* in Gen 2:18, 20. One consideration is that since the one who became the *ʿēzer* here was not God, but the woman (Gen 2:21-23), *ʿēzer* cannot mean "help/ helper." If we argue that it does, because humans can and do "help," even "save," one another, the text then would mean the female is superior to the male. But matriarchy is no more God's creation plan than is patriarchy. (In English, "help" or "helper" may designate an equal or even a subordinate, but this usage does not occur in the Hebrew Bible.) Moreover, to try to dress it up by saying the woman "rescued" the man from his loneliness is, in the end, only condescension toward both the man and the woman. This text does not address the issue of "loneliness," but of "aloneness"; the two are not the same.

A much stronger evidence for "a strength/power," as the correct understanding and translation of *ʿēzer* here, is the word *kĕnegdô* that follows *ʿēzer* in our text. The word *kĕnegdô* actually is two prepositions and a pronoun suffix, written together as one word. The preposition *kĕ* means "like, as, according to, corresponding to, of the same kind." Here it means that what God purposed to create, and what the solitary *ʾādām* could not find among the other living creatures (v 20), would be another "strength/power" of the same kind, or species, as the "original" *ʾādām*.

The second preposition, *neged* means "in front of, facing." With *kĕ* attached to it as a prefix (an inseparable preposition) it means "facing as an equal." This is confirmed for our case in postbiblical Hebrew, where these two prepositions together regularly mean "equal." The final letter of *kĕnegdô* is a suffix pronoun, third masculine singular, meaning "him." Altogether, then (and expanding slightly for clarity), we may translate *ʿēzer kĕnegdô*, **a power/ strength like him, corresponding to him, of the same kind or species, facing** [or: **opposite**] **him as [an] equal**.

As it turned out, the *ʿēzer kĕnegdô* would be the woman. Thus, this phrase, along with the text as a whole, affirms the equality and mutuality of the genders—male and female, female and male. This theological (and anthropological) principle is crucial to understanding ourselves as created in the image of God.

This statement anticipates God's next (and final) creative work. God resolved to remove the solitude of the *ʾādām* by making for him, just as God had made the *ʾādām*, **a power/strength corresponding/equal to him.** God proposed nothing less than another *ʾādām*. However, the *ʾādām* had as yet no way of knowing that, nor of knowing what it would mean. For him to discover this, most vividly and effectively, the *ʾādām* first needed to learn what could *not* be *ʿēzer kĕnegdô* in relation to him, or with respect to him.

■ **19** A few commentators have viewed v 19 as evidence of editorial carelessness in bringing together the two originally separate accounts of Gen 1 and Gen 2. They find the narrative of v 19 contradictory to the account of God's work on the sixth day, where the sequence is animals first, then humans (1:24-27). Others view the apparent change in the sequence of God's creative work as original to this narrative tradition (ch 2), which has its own origin and transmission history.

Cassuto speculated that God performed a second special creation of animals for this specific purpose (1961, 128-30; see also Hamilton for a similar view; 1990, 176). Many commentators, and most English translations—many without comment—render the first verb as a perfect; an example is NRSV, "So . . . the LORD God formed."

The NIV rendering, however, is, **Now the LORD God had formed.** Translating the verb as a past perfect implies that this account refers to God's previous creation of animal life (1:20-22, 24-25). The fact that biblical Hebrew does not have a separate form to indicate the past perfect supports this translation. When associated grammar and syntax allow, and when context calls for it, Hebraists do not hesitate to translate the Hebrew "perfect" (perfective) as a past perfect in English. When options exist, context should be the determining factor in translation. This commentator regards the past perfect rendering as the most appropriate option for this verb in this context.

Moreover, translating this verb as a past perfect (**had formed**) brings literary and theological clarity. We shall come out aright, if we bear in mind: (1) God's purpose here was to prepare the as-yet-solitary *ʾādām* for God's next and final creation ("I will make for him"); (2) This preparation would be most effective if the ʾādām could see that the creatures he may have thought could be suitable, in fact were not suitable.

How better to accomplish this preparatory objective than to bring the creatures for the ʾādām to observe and study closely enough, and long enough, to give to each its appropriate name? Seen thus in light of its real purpose, this exercise was neither a forgetful digression on God's part, nor a series of unsuccessful experiments in finding the ʾādām its proper counterpart. Nor was the woman a flash of inspiration following upon a string of failures. Before speaking (v 18), God knew the ʿēzer kĕnegdô; before the first ʾādām could recognize her, though, he had to learn from his own work of naming the beasts and birds that none could be ʿēzer kĕnegdô to him (nor he to it).

It is important to note that both here in v 19 and also in 2:7, the report of the creation of the ʾādām, the narrator used the verb **formed** (yāṣar, meaning "form," "shape," "fashion"). Moreover, in both texts, **the ground** (ʾădāmâ) was the material resource for God's creative work. These parallel usages emphasize that humans and animals share a common sensate life; physically, we are fellow creatures. We may go further and affirm that God made the rest of the animal kingdom with the same care, concern, and attention God showed in making the ʾādām. Verse 19 indicates the categories of potential candidates as broadly as possible, *** all the living creatures of the field*** (kol-ḥayyāt haśśādeh) and *** all the flying creatures of the skies*** (kol-ʿôp haśśāmayim).

Fred Bush has shown that in biblical Hebrew a formal naming requires three elements: (1) the verb qārāʾ; (2) the common noun šēm, "name"; (3) a proper noun, the personal name actually bestowed (1996, 7-9). Here God brought the larger land animals and birds to the ʾādām for the ʾādām to name— the formal naming of each. In vv 19-20, two of these three elements are clearly present (the verb qārāʾ three times and the noun šēm twice. The third element (proper noun/personal name) is present by implication: "So the ʾādām gave names to all" (v 20). Obviously, not every name could be included in such a brief account; the narrator's report that the ʾādām did bestow the various names was sufficient.

To name is to claim and to exercise authority over the thing or person named. This is the first exercise of the human stewardship hegemony conferred upon the ʾādām. It is also important here to see God's continuing invitation to participation in the creative process, the invitation we have noted previously. What God formed, the ʾādām named, becoming a partner with God in the development of "intra-creaturely relationships" (Fretheim 2005, 58).

Verse 19 concludes with the report that **whatever the ʾādām called each living creature, that was its name.** We note here yet another parallel between vv 7 and 19. Verse 7 depicts *the ʾādām* as a "living creature" (nepeš ḥayyâ). In v 19, this "living creature," named **each living creature** (nepeš ḥayyâ). The ʾādām was the name-giver, with authority over the other animals, yet both belonged together as "living creatures" (nepeš ḥayyâ), sharing the same sensate life. Their differences lay largely in two aspects: (1) only the ʾādām was/is the image of God (1:27); (2) only the ʾādām received the breath of God directly into his nostrils (2:7). These two special endowments separate the world of humans from the world of our animal "cousins."

■ **20** Verse 20 reiterates the human task of naming the animals. **So the ʾādām gave names to all the livestock,** *and to the flying creatures of the skies, and to all the [wild] creatures of the field.* Here we see again the narrative strategy of noting first the proposal/instruction (v 19), then the report of its completion (v 20). To emphasize this common narrative approach here, we even could translate the end of v 19 and beginning of v 20: *that would be its name; so the* ʾādām *gave . . .* Here, the list is expanded by one category from the two-group list of v 19. If the ʾādām already was familiar with the **livestock,** it would be natural that this initial task of naming would start with them. Alternatively, if the category of **livestock** was *established* only at the time of the naming, and as a result of the naming, that would account for its *introduction* here. One further note; the translation of Hebrew bĕhēmâ as "cattle" (KJV, NASB, and others) is much too restrictive and therefore emphatically misleading. English "cattle" refers properly only to bovines, and not even to all of them. **Livestock** (with NIV), meaning all domesticated creatures known to early Israel, is suitably inclusive.

In any case, it is natural that the category of **livestock** should be mentioned first. Ancient Israel's first readers and hearers of this account would have had daily contact with these creatures, and both human stewardship and human hegemony over them were givens. Having named the **livestock,** the ʾādām moved on to naming the *flying creatures* and the *creatures of the field,* listed here in reverse (chiastic) order from that of v 19, for purposes of literary variation, and for the artistic touch of placing creatures of the skies between the two groups of land creatures.

The name the ʾādām gave each creature was appropriate to its nature. We see here on the part of the ʾādām the first exercise of knowledge and discernment, enabled by his life of faithful, untainted intimacy with God.

Verse 20 concludes with a report: *But for the* ʾādām, *he did not find a power/strength corresponding/equal to him* (ʿēzer kĕnegdô). Some emend the verb to read, "There *was not found* for the ʾādām" (e.g., NIV, **But for Adam no suitable helper was found;** NRSV, "but for the man there was not found . . ."). However, this verb form (māṣāʾ) is active, not passive.

Less clear is whether the subject of māṣāʾ ("find") is God or the ʾādām. Without emending the active verb form to a passive, one may take the ʾādām as the intended subject, as we have done here. Alternatively, one may take God as the subject and translate, *But for the* ʾādām, *he* [Yahweh Elohim] *did not find a power like/corresponding and equal to him* [i.e., to the ʾādām]. Both translations make for awkward English but preserve the verb form as in the MT. We prefer to take the ʾādām as the subject primarily because God assigned this work of naming to allow *the ʾādām* to discover for himself that none of the other creatures could be the ***power/strength corresponding/equal to him*** (*ʿēzer kĕnegdô*) whom God intended. The ʾādām named the other animals but did not find that one among them. A secondary consideration, but important both in Hebrew and in English syntax, is that the last-mentioned subject—at the beginning of this verse, no less—is the ʾādām. In that situation, one would expect that if God were the subject of this verb, God would be named as the subject.

Those who read this paragraph as an exercise in discovery for God, as well as for the ʾādām, take a somewhat different approach. Taking *the ʾādām* as the subject of this verb means that the next action God undertook (v 21) was in response to the creaturely freedom of *the ʾādām* not to accept the option God presented to him. If God is the subject, then the decision to move on to the next action was solely based on God's discovery that the first option he had presented to the human was not adequate to resolve the issue of human aloneness. In this reading, the single task had a twofold purpose: (1) to name the other creatures; (2) to ascertain whether any of them may have been for the ʾādām the ***power like him.***

Sometimes it is possible to get to the same conclusion by different routes. We strongly prefer the understanding we have presented above, that God knew what God was about, from the beginning. Yet also in the increasingly popular understanding that God was engaged in discovery throughout this exercise, along with the *ʾādām*, this sentence is simple and clear as it stands. It reports the uneven success of the task in its two purposes: (1) the ʾādām did succeed in naming the other creatures; (2) ***but for the*** ʾādām himself, he ***did not find*** among them one like himself.

FROM THE TEXT

This short paragraph advances the reader two or three more steps on the way to understanding God's provision for the interconnectedness of God's earthly creation. We have seen already the beginning of our relationship with God (1:26-28); we have seen our connection to the earth itself (2:7, 15). Now we are reminded that God also had made the other land creatures ***from the ground*** (1:24; 2:19). In God's assignment of the task of naming them, we see that suitable human interaction with animals also is a key part of God's design for relationship among the earth's inhabitants.

Most Christians today know we should be engaged in the care of creation. We also understand, however, that much of today's thinking and action on these fronts is not informed by biblical ways of thinking. This short paragraph (along with numerous other passages) informs a healthy biblical, Christian approach. God formed our first human parent from the ground; God formed the other land creatures from that same ground. We really are related, physically. We can be comfortable with—we even can take joy in—that relatedness.

The next step (ignored or denied by some) is that God really did appoint us as stewards, caretakers, overseers of God's earthly creation. Despite the turning away in the garden, God did not take that responsibility from us. Christians know we shall, in the end, account for our stewardship, including our treatment of our fellow creatures. We know God loves and cares for all God's creation. Created in God's image, and acting as God's stewards, we do well to measure our attitudes and actions by that same measure—erring (when we err) on the side of loving-kindness, of humane care and oversight.

The first human now was well begun in healthy relationships with God, with the earth, and with his fellow creatures. Yet, this short paragraph also leads us to conclude that all these together were/are not enough. Humans also need relationship with other humans. To underscore that point is one important reason for this chapter's relatively detailed account of the human creation. The disappointment echoed in this report, **but for the ʾādām he did not find . . .** , is not the last word here, nor is it the last word for God's family of faith today.

5. God's Creation of the ʾādām: Stage Two (2:21-25)

BEHIND THE TEXT

The immediate context is the preceding report that the ʾādām **did not find a power corresponding/equal to him** among the animals God formed and brought to him for naming (v 20b). This paragraph reports God's dramatic action to remedy the lack the ʾādām now was aware of. With this "second stage," the human species was complete; for the first time, humans could live in community.

This account of God's creation of the woman expands and completes the narrative of the human creation as male and female (see 1:27). This separate report of the woman's creation also highlights her status as an equal member of the human community. Hamilton's observation that other Near Eastern creation accounts do not include reports of the creation of woman, specifically, is a timely reminder of the higher, and corrective, theology of *this* account (1990, 177).

IN THE TEXT

■ **21** This section begins with the report of the first of a series of four actions that God undertook to create a power like and equal to the ʾādām. **So Yahweh Elohim caused a deep sleep to fall upon the ʾādām, and he slept.** The object of the first verb is the **deep sleep,** not the ʾādām. A similar deep sleep is recorded as coming over Abraham (Abram) in his covenant encounter with God (Gen 15:12 ff.). Commenting on God's action here, von Rad reminds us, "Man cannot perceive God 'in the act,' cannot observe his miracles in their genesis; he can revere God's creativity only as an actually accomplished fact" (1961, 81).

Chrysostom on Gen 2:21

"God caused drowsiness to come upon Adam," the text says, "and he slept." It wasn't simply drowsiness that came upon him nor normal sleep; instead the wise and skillful creator of our nature was about to remove one of Adam's ribs. Lest the experience cause Adam afterward to be badly disposed toward the creature formed from his rib and through memory of the pain bear a grudge against this being at its formation, God induced in him this kind of sleep. God caused a drowsiness to come upon him and bid him be weighed down as though by some heavy weight. (Louth 2001, 67)

The second half of v 21 narrates the second divine action. **Then he [Yahweh Elohim] took one of his sides** [or, **one part from his sides**] **and [God] closed up the flesh in its place.** Of the forty occurrences of the noun *ṣēlāʿ* in the Hebrew Scripture, this passage is the only place it is translated **rib** by the majority of English versions. Exegetical prudence, then, dictates that we look again at this occurrence in its context. Indeed, many commentators have noted that most often this noun refers to the walls or sides: of the tabernacle in the wilderness (Exod 26:20, 26-27; 36:25, 31-32); of the ark of the covenant (Exod 25:12, 14; 37:3, 5); of Solomon's temple in Jerusalem (1 Kgs 6—7); and of the rebuilt temple of Ezekiel's vision, where most understand Ezekiel to be speaking of "side chambers" built against the main walls of the new temple (Ezek 41). In 2 Sam 16:13, *ṣēlāʿ* refers to the "side" or slope of a hill.

The LXX reinforces this understanding, translating about half these occurrences, including our two here in Gen 2:21-22, using *pleuron/pleura*, "side." Considering also that the man would recognize the woman not only as "bone of my bones" but also as "flesh of my flesh" (v 23), we should conclude that "side" is a better rendering here, as well. God took a sizable portion of bone, flesh, and perhaps other bodily tissue to make another human. It even may be that we should visualize God dividing the one human into two more or less equal parts; the meaning of the noun *ṣēlāʿ* would admit of that understanding.

The second divine activity concluded with another simple motion of mercy, **And [God] closed up the flesh in its place.** An alternative is possible: **and the flesh closed up in its place.** Given that God still was very much the active agent in this final creative act, the first understanding is preferable. God's closing up the side tells the reader that the first human was not left "half a man," or less than human. God's final creative act resulted in a whole man as well as a whole woman.

■ **22** Verse 22 begins with the report of the third divine activity in this narrative. This verse reads, literally, **Then Yahweh Elohim built the side which he had taken from the ʾādām into a woman, and brought her to the ʾādām.**

The verb **built** (*bānâ*) here is striking, since in this account the narrator previously had used "formed" to report God's making of the first ʾādām

GENESIS

2:21-22

(v 7) and of the animals (v 19). Commentators and English versions often miss (soften?) this point by translating **made,** rather than *built.* The narrator's deliberate choice of this verb here indicates the same attentive, loving care in fashioning **a woman** (ʾiššâ) as God had exercised in forming the first ʾādām. God not only forms human beings like a potter but also builds them as the divine builder. That the author intended this emphasis is clear from the parallel structure of the two statements of God's forming and building:

> v 7 ***And formed/Yahweh Elohim/the ʾādām/[of] dust/from the ground***
> v 22 ***And built/Yahweh Elohim/the side/from the ʾādām/into a woman***
> (ʾiššâ)

The only variation in the order of the two sentences is that *into a woman* occurs last in the second sentence, probably for climactic emphasis.

The man was formed from the ground; the woman was formed from the man. Because she was built from the "side" of the man, the woman also was connected with the ground. Neither the man nor the woman could claim the supposed independence of self-generation. All humans are of the same species, because of our common origin in the one flesh become two—then become one again in each of us, through the act of procreation.

The final statement of v 22, **He brought her to the man,** reports God's culminating creative work of the paragraph. Von Rad states it with a romantic flair, "Now God himself, like a father of the bride, leads the woman to the man" (1961, 82). In so doing, God brought each the gift of the other, the gift of human companionship and physical intimacy for the sake of which God created us male and female. Even God's pleasure in giving them (and us) these gifts shows through in this simple statement.

■ **23** The response of the ʾādām is the first human speech recorded in the Bible. He just had observed many creatures closely enough to understand they could not be the "power" God had in mind. As implied in the passion of his first two (Hebrew) words, *This one, this time!* [i.e., finally!], the first ʾādām was in a position to discern quite readily that God's final creation was not just another creature for him to name. She was, indeed, the ʿēzer kĕnegdô God had promised. To emphasize what the Hebrew text emphasizes, we may translate:

> *"This one, finally, is bone of my bones, and flesh of my flesh!*
> *"As for this one, she shall be called 'woman,' for from man was taken*
> *this one."*

An important note, not easily seen in many English renderings, is that the Hebrew feminine singular demonstrative pronoun zōʾt, translated here, *this one,* occurs three times: once at the beginning and once at the end of this two-line poem, and once at the beginning of the second line, that is, in the middle of the poem. All three times, it refers to the woman. The man's threefold repetition, his strategic, symmetrical placement, and his bold, emphatic, unconventional syntactical harnessing of this simple one-syllable pronoun combine to reveal him as a consummate poet. In a single syllable exquisitely

2:22-23

employed, the man declared his exuberance and joy that God now had ended the search for an equal partner, the partner he had not found through all the thought-intensive process of naming the other creatures. What God had declared, "not good," God now had rectified.

There is more in this short poem to astonish and delight the reader. The man's exclamation, **bone of my bones and flesh of my flesh,** constitutes his recognition that the woman, this new creature, was physically related to him. In other texts, one or both phrases are used in recognition of physical kinship (e.g., Gen 29:14; Judg 9:2; 2 Sam 5:1). The woman's physical identity from and with the man made her the "power/strength like [him], corresponding to [him], of the same kind or species, equal to him," whom God had promised (v 18). As Fretheim has put it, the phrase **bone of my bones and flesh of my flesh,** "literally highlights mutuality and equality" (1994, 353).

Hebrew scholars long have known that 'iš **(man)** and 'iššâ **(woman)** are from two different roots. Nevertheless, they do sound quite close, so they can be associated in the way the man did it in this declaration. It is important to note, too, that the man's statement here is not a formal naming of the woman, such as the man had done with the other creatures (v 20), and which would have signaled his assumption of authority over her. The common noun *shem* ("name"), necessary in and for a formal naming, does not occur here. "Woman" ('iššâ) is not a proper name applied to this one woman, but a common noun designating any and every woman.

Finally, the statement, ***She shall be called "woman"*** ['iššâ], ***for from man*** ['iš] ***was taken this one,*** conveys both the likenesses and the differences of human gender. "Man" and "woman" here parallel "male" and "female" in 1:27.

■ **24** This verse is not the man's statement. Rather, it is a later editorial comment of the author emphasizing the one man-one woman relationship, and *only* that relationship, as the sine qua non of the God-ordained family unit. Given the patriarchal society in which this text was produced, we probably should translate it more forcefully than we usually do: ***For this reason, a man shall abandon his father and his mother, and shall cleave to his wife, and they shall become one flesh.*** The first words, ***for this reason,*** refer to the man's exclamation of discovery that the woman was "bone of [his] bones, and flesh of [his] flesh," that she was human, just as he was. If we are justified in extending the reach of this phrase (***for this reason***) to the whole of the man's pronouncement, we could say that it means also, "because a man and a woman are of the same species, and because they are two sexually distinct individuals." When a man and a woman make the decision to marry, this phrase teaches, their marriage becomes the most important fact of their new life together. Also, ***for this reason,*** the physical and social union of a man and a woman, a woman and a man, is God's intention from the beginning of creation. When agreed to and undertaken, it is to supersede all previous, and all other, relationships.

In ancient Israel, a son usually lived as a subordinate member of his father's household, under his father's authority, until the father died. When a son married, his wife became part of his father's household, under the authority of his mother, and perhaps of his father's other wives, also. Moreover, **abandon** (ʿāzab) is a very strong verb, in Hebrew as in English. Later, the prophets often used it when they charged Israel and Judah with unfaithfulness to God, with abandoning Yahweh for the worship of other gods (e.g., Jer 1:16; Hos 4:10). This text calls on men to leave their parents' authority in every way and to establish their own households with their own wives. **Cleave** (dābaq) also is a very forceful verb. In the context of a rebellion by the northern tribes, the men of Judah cleaved to David their king (2 Sam 20:2), even at risk of their lives; Deut 11:22 includes an exhortation for Israel to cleave to Yahweh.

We may see a modern metaphor for these two extremes in the reactions of two bar magnets when brought near to each other. The strong repulsion when the same poles, positive to positive or negative to negative, are brought together illustrates the instruction to **abandon** one's parents. The strong attraction between the two if one magnet is turned around so their opposite poles come together illustrates the instruction to **cleave** to one's spouse. Given the overwhelming cultural pressures in the world of the ancient Near East for a son to cleave to his *father* until his father's death, this call for a man to cleave to his *wife*, instead, was amazingly countercultural. In much of the world, it is countercultural still.

One further note: in later passages (as we have noted), these two verbs often possess strong covenantal associations. **Abandon** signals covenant unfaithfulness, while **cleave** signifies covenant faithfulness. In light of this usage, the editor here is emphasizing the covenantal aspect of marriage, both expecting and rewarding the absolute loyalty (faithfulness) of each to the other.

This editorial comment in v 24 concludes with the note, ***they shall become one flesh.*** The first meaning of this phrase is the obvious one. When a man and a woman come together in sexual union, they are—in a very real sense, even if only for the moment—one flesh. Other meanings also are important, however. The sexual union is important, in and of itself, but it also lays a foundation for, and symbolizes, the many other profound and complex ways a woman and a man become a unit over a lifetime together, even while remaining at the same time two individuals. One of these ways we have noted, but it bears repeating; the man and the woman belong to each other in covenant relationship. Brueggemann says it succinctly, "They are *one!* That is, in covenant" (1982, 47).

One flesh also is another way of emphasizing the equality between the genders that God intended from the beginning of our creation. Finally, two parents become, in another sense entirely, **one flesh** as they produce children with essentially an equal gifting of genetic heritage from each of them. Of course, this does not mean childless couples (whether or not by their own choice) are *less* than **one flesh.** Similarly, the phrase, the verse, and the passage as a whole, do *not* state (or imply) that marriage is essential to either a man or a woman being truly and fully human.

■ **25** *Now they were, the two of them, naked, the man and his wife, but they were not ashamed.* Shame at being naked in public is a nearly universal trait among adults since the expulsion from Eden. Even though no other humans yet existed, this state of our first parents was "public" nakedness; they met with God daily (3:8). We may credit their lack of shame to their Edenic state of innocence or to their state of "childlike" innocence—perhaps to both.

However, this statement also means more than that. Shame involves the desire, felt as the urgent "need," to hide from others—to hide attitudes, desires, thoughts, and acts, among other things. Not yet having experienced sin with its resulting estrangement from God and between each other, our first parents still were transparent with God and with each other. They had no reasons *not* to be transparent, no need, as yet, for shame. Integrity and transparency once were the pattern of human relationship and community life. This verse also is the hermeneutical key to understanding Gen 3:7, where the word **naked** next occurs. Having tasted the forbidden fruit, our first parents knew immediately that they were **naked.** Their innocence fled, replaced by shame, guilt, and pitiful attempts at cover-up and blame-shifting.

FROM THE TEXT

The most important teaching of this paragraph is that God values both woman and man; we could say God values both almost infinitely. God "built" the woman with the same care, skill, and loving attention God employed when God "formed" the first human. When the one had been divided into two, the man acknowledged the woman as human, equally with himself. This is God's creation intention, clearly and unequivocally expressed in practically every detail regarding humans in these two chapters recounting the creation. Even the author/editor provided a comment that woman is not a commodity, bought and sold for the convenience and advantage of privileged sons, but a female human with and for whom a man leaves his previous loyalties to establish a new social unit, a new human unity.

The summary notice of human creation in 1:26-27 already had established, in terms of the teaching of the Jewish/Christian canon, that God intended humans to be equal—male and female, female and male, alike. This chapter still reflects God's *creation* intentions; it cannot be made to serve the ends of male-dominant understandings (or of female-dominant understandings, for that matter) based in the rebellion that had not yet occurred.

Subsequent scriptural teachings include: (1) God's ultimate *redemption* intention is to restore this earth to (and perhaps even beyond) its original *creation* perfection; (2) the promised redemption already is accomplished in Christ. If both these are true, we must not make the mistake of setting aside

God's intention of human gender equality as though it were meant only for the primeval world of the past, or even as only for the perfected world of the future following Christ's return. We have redemption now; we are to learn kingdom living now, as much as possible. For men to treat women as equals, and vice versa, is possible in this present world, even if not perfectly. It is the calling of the church to lead the way, to demonstrate redemption visibly in its most important arenas, the Christian home and the Christian assembly of believers. This is Paul's message—firmly, loudly, clearly—in Gal 3:28, the single most important NT text bearing on this issue.

Some commentators, both ancient and modern, have read male superiority over women into these creation texts and thereby attempted to see it as divinely purposed and ordained from the beginning. Some even argue that since woman was created second, she must be secondary to man, by God's design and intention. Some quote Paul and interpret his words out of context (1 Tim 2:13). If this final paragraph *were* teaching a hierarchy of human creation, the simplest logic demands that it would be the superiority of woman over man. No one would argue that man is inferior to the other living creatures because man was created after them. Yet that is what one *must* accept, if one wishes to be consistent while arguing that woman is inferior to man because *she* was created after *him*. If creation order is the determining factor, and if man, created after the other living creatures, is superior to them, then woman, created after man, also must be superior to man. To the blessing of all, male and female alike, gender hierarchy is no part of this text, nor of any other text of Gen 1—2.

Genesis 1 and 2 portray an amazing, delightful, supremely pleasurable, and joyful portrait of God's creation intentions for human life, beginning with our relationships as male and female together. But the full extent of God's bounteous intentions for and in our sexual natures and expressions can be realized only with total commitment to one spouse, as long as both spouses live. Even a lifetime together is not enough to discover all God's good gifts in this relationship. For this, and for many other reasons, as well, polygamy, serial monogamy, and other multiple partnerships are much less than God's best, cheating all involved, selling diamonds for lumps of coal. Exclusive one-to-one commitment, and all the time God may grace them with, are required for a man and a woman to become the "one flesh" God intends, in all the ways God intends. In the purity of God's creation/redemption intentions, any couple united before God and community in exclusive loyalty to each other, can be naked before each other, literally and figuratively, and not be ashamed.

As elsewhere, we could say much more, but one final note must suffice. When as yet only two humans lived, still they formed a human community of covenantal, other-centered relationship. Before their expulsion from the garden, our first parents lived according to God's original pattern. The narrative of Gen 2 introduces them, preserving a profound theology of human life and relationship in its portrait of their community of two. In our own world—vastly different, yet longing for the lost innocence and intimacy of Eden—a "relational theology of Eden" from Gen 2 is well worth articulating, embracing, and practicing.

C. Catastrophe in the Garden (3:1-24)

BEHIND THE TEXT

Genesis 3 essentially is an answer to the question, If God created everything "good," what happened? What happened was the human decision not to abide in the environment and fellowship in and for which God created us—with God, with each other, with our own selves, and with the rest of God's creation on this earth.

One interesting and significant literary feature of this chapter is its arrangement in what we may call a "double chiasm," progressing as follows:

A—The serpent tempts the woman (vv 1-5)

B—The woman eats (v 6*a*)

C—The man eats (v 6*b*)

D—The humans realize they are naked (v 7)

E—The humans hear God walking in the garden (v 8)

E'—God speaks to the humans in the garden (v 9)

D'—The man confesses he knows he is naked (v 10)

C'—The man confesses he ate (vv 11-12)

B'—The woman confesses she ate (v 13)

A'/A''—God condemns the serpent (vv 14-15)

B''—God announces consequences to the woman (v 16)

C''—God announces consequences to the man (vv 17-19)

D''—God clothes the human pair (vv 20-21)

E''—God banishes the humans from (walking with God in) the garden (vv 22-24)

Thus, the author has given us the order of events at the tree of knowledge (A, B, C, D, E), then the reverse order in the discovery at the tribunal (E', D', C', B', A'), and then, again, the original order in God's pronouncements upon the three transgressors (A'', B'', C'', D'', E'').

There is another literary arrangement that runs through this section. We saw that Gen 1:1 is a very short introductory paragraph, ending with reference to the *earth*. The *earth* then became the subject of a longer paragraph (1:2—2:3), which culminates (in terms of acts of creation) with a summary report of the creation of the *ʾādām*. Creation of the *ʾādām* then became the focus of the third paragraph (2:4-25), which ends with the note that the two humans were both naked but were not ashamed. By the count of this common literary technique, then, Gen 3 is the fourth paragraph. The adjective "naked" (*ʿărûmmîm* in 2:25) and the adjective "crafty" (*ʿārûm* in 3:1) are not related etymologically, but they do sound alike (the *-im* of *ʿărûmmîm* marks it as plural). Using a pun, the narrator achieved the same effect as in the earlier paragraph transitions. The first human couple's interaction with, and listening to the voice of the serpent (*nāḥāš*), a *crafty* creature (*ʿārûm*), resulted in their disobedient act, which further resulted in the knowledge that they were *naked* (*ʿêrummim*; 3:7); this is the subject of Gen 3.

Though the linkages are not all of this same kind, the narrative of Gen 3 does of course exhibit close continuity with that of ch 4, ch 4 with ch 5, and so on. Through the rest of the OT, however, only Ezekiel referenced Gen 3, in his lament over the fall of the king of Tyre (Ezek 28). There, Ezekiel drew on Gen 3 in comparing the fallen ruler with the fallen angel Lucifer. At several points in the NT, however, Gen 3 became a source for significant theological reflection (e.g., Rom 5:12-21; 1 Cor 15:21-22; Rev 22:1-5).

Perhaps prompted by Ezekiel's use of this narrative, some later traditions attempted to link the entrance of sin and death into this world either to the devil (e.g., Wis 2:23-24) or to the woman (e.g., Sir 25:24). Clearly, the narrator of Gen 3 did intend to report the beginning of the human turning from God, so it is not strange that Gen 3 should have become important for the development of the Christian doctrine of original sin. However, exegetical care and integrity require us to keep in mind that no word for "sin" occurs in Gen 3. Moreover, contrary to what many think or assume, this narrative does not mention "Satan," or "the devil," either. Genesis 3 refers to the nonhuman creature as *nāḥāš*, usually translated "serpent." Popular theologies linking the "fall of Satan" with Gen 3 do not arise from the narrative; they are speculations not really grounded in, and going well beyond, the text itself.

IN THE TEXT

1. Conversation: Enticed and Ensnared (3:1-7)

■ 1 The narrative begins with a description of **the serpent,** a key player in this story. Virtually all translators and commentators, beginning with the Septuagint, have identified Hebrew *nāḥāš* as a **serpent,** or snake; this probably was the common understanding even before the end of the OT period. The NT authors used the Septuagint predominantly; they appear to have viewed this creature as a snake also.

Modern Theories on the Serpent

Some modern scholars have classified this story partly as an etiology, an explanation of: (1) why the snake is regarded as clever; or (2) why it is regarded as immortal: it sheds its old too-tight skin; or (3) why it crawls on its belly and appears to eat dust and dirt; or (4) why many humans detest and often fear snakes. Some point to the role of the serpent, in the religions of several of ancient Israel's neighbors, as a bringer of prosperity or of wisdom or even of fertility, and see this account as a theological corrective. Some see in the serpent a mythological creature or symbol, with no existential reality in this world, early or late. Some argue that the *nāḥāš* represents the woman's own mental wrestlings with whether or not to observe God's proscription.

Adam Clarke on Hebrew *nāḥāš*

Adam Clarke took a remarkable approach in suggesting the identity of the *nāḥāš*, usually translated "serpent." Clarke believed the text portrays a real, live creature. Clarke also noted that some biblical references are to creatures that, in those contexts, almost certainly could not have been snakes. According to Clarke, the letters *nḥš* comprise four different roots in Hebrew. In some places the reference is to bronze, brass, and/or copper; in others, to divination or to some other aspect of religious worship; one form even can mean "lust" or "harlotry." Clarke also attached importance to a muttering, shy, and sly furtiveness he discerned in or attached to one of the roots. Arguing that none of these can be reconciled with the appearance or behavior of the snake, Clarke contended the understanding of "snake" or "serpent" was taken over with little thought from the Greek of the Septuagint, whose translators did not examine the matter very closely, either. Based partly, also, on a possible etymological connection with an Arabic noun signifying "ape," Clarke argued in some detail for identification of the *nāḥāš* with the orangutan, the higher primate closest to human beings. That the premier exegete of early Methodism could advance this proposal, so far removed from the usual, perhaps demonstrates how little evidence we have, even how little it matters in the end whether we can identify this creature with any animal known today (n.d., 47-50).

The narrator described this creature only as *ʿārûm, **more than all [other] creatures of the field which Yahweh Elohim had made.*** Since only one category is named (***creatures of the field,** ḥayyat haśśādeh*), we probably should understand this assessment as including, rather than excluding, the domestic animals. The narrative of 2:19-20 also gave the same label to the animals God formed and brought to the *ʾādām* for him to name. The NIV's **wild animals** thus may introduce a meaning not intended by the narrator. In its pronunciation, this adjective, *ʿārûm*, differs only slightly from the description of the humans as *ʿārûmmîm* (2:25). The narrator clearly intended to tie the two chapters together by the use of this punning play on words. **More crafty** (so also NRSV, NASB), "shrewdest" (NLT), and more "cunning" (Cassuto 1961, 138; Hamilton 1990, 186) are common translations of this adjective, reflecting the negative connotations intended here. In some biblical contexts, primarily in the Wisdom Literature, *ʿārûm* means "astute, perceptive" and reflects well on the one so described. In and of itself, *ʿārûm* is a neutral term; this is probably why the author used it, instead of the more commonly used *ḥākam*, which often denotes moral and ethical, as well as mental, wisdom. Here, the author readily granted this creature's intelligence, astuteness, and perceptivity but went on to narrate its perversion of this special gift.

Severian of Gabala on Gen 3:1

Since it was a creature who held such great closeness to humanity, the snake was a convenient tool for the devil. . . . So the devil spoke through the snake in order to deceive Adam. . . . Before the fall, Adam was filled with wisdom, discernment and prophecy. . . . When the devil noticed the snake's intelligence and Adam's high opinion of it (Adam considered the snake very wise), the devil spoke through the snake so that Adam would think that the snake, being intelligent, was able to imitate even human speech. (Louth 2001, 75)

The author was careful, however, to exclude any hint of dualism from this account. This creature was not supernatural; it was not an equal antagonist of independent origin; it was not even demonic in and of itself. It was only one of the many creatures *whom Yahweh Elohim had made.* This scenario suggests the possibility that God had granted at least one other species the power of speech—to be able to converse with the humans without arousing either surprise or suspicion—and perhaps even the freedom to choose to play the role of tempter, in the first place.

A common assumption, partly based on a similar perspective in the reading of later biblical texts, is that Satan, the devil, "entered into" this individual creature, with or without its consent, and used its gifts to approach the humans. While this understanding may be defensible, we must be careful not to say *this* text teaches that; it does not. It simply leaves the question unanswered, as an issue that would distract from, rather than illuminate, the narrative the author was presenting.

The second part of v 1 introduces the serpent's initial words **to the woman.** (We will use "serpent" for convenience, while leaving open the issue of this creature's identity.) **Woman** here is not a proper name; rather, it is the common noun denoting the female of the human species (2:23). (The narrative introduces the proper names of the human pair later: "Adam" perhaps in 3:17, "Eve" certainly in 3:20.) Most reasons adduced for the serpent's choice of the woman for this conversation, rather than the man, are neither biblical nor plausible. Many, such as the common charge that she was weaker of mind or of will, and thus an easier target than the man, denigrate both the woman and God who made her.

We will say more on this, but it is important to remember that the man was not absent, as many mistakenly have asserted. He was present, but silent, throughout this exchange, as the serpent's use of the plural verb form, *you* [pl.] *may not eat,* implies, and v 6 confirms. Thus, the report that the serpent spoke **to the woman** may reflect only that the woman answered, while the man did not. Some think this was the last of several conversations between the serpent and the woman, so she was neither surprised nor alarmed when it addressed her this time. Though the text is silent on that point, the suggestion may be plausible.

The serpent's opening speech usually is translated as a question. However, nowhere else do the Hebrew particles ʾap kî occur together serving an interrogative function. It seems best to treat ʾap as an interjection, **Behold!** or **Really!** followed by kî either as an interrogative (Cassuto 1961, 144) or, better, in one of its regular uses, **That.** The entire statement, then, would read, **Really! That God should have said you may not eat from any tree of the garden!** It is a subtle opening, "a feigned expression of surprise" (Hamilton 1990, 186) intended to elicit a response. It is not for nothing the serpent is described as **crafty;** its subtlety accomplished its vile purpose. Ironically, the serpent—pretending to know God better than did the humans created in God's image—initiated this first-recorded theological conversation in the Bible.

The serpent ignored everything—vocation, freedom, holiness in multiple relationships, and especially the beneficence of God's provision—to focus on the sole prohibition, and set the *nature* of human freedom as the agenda. His opening statement, however, is a travesty of God and God's character, in its false assertion that God had forbidden the humans to eat of **any tree *of* the garden**.

As all of them (and the reader) well knew, God had forbidden the fruit of only *one* tree, "the tree of the knowledge of good and evil" (2:17). The serpent intended the treacherous suggestion of *every* tree, instead of only *one*, to beguile the humans into dwelling on the minimal prohibition, rather than on the lavish provision. He wanted them to think of it as an imposition, and thus to begin thinking of God as less than benevolent. This could (he knew) lead them to distrust God, then to desire autonomy from God. The final steps of pondering, then of acting on the thought and willfully turning from the divine instruction, could be considered almost inevitable.

■ **2-3** Verses 2-3 report the woman's response. Her conduct as the dialogue began was exemplary; she directly contradicted the serpent's fraudulent misquotation. Remembering that "tree" (ʿes) is a collective noun, we may translate, **Of the fruits of the trees of the garden we may eat.** In this context, these words are the expected paraphrase of 2:16. The woman's next statement, **But of the fruit of the tree that is in the midst of the garden, God said, you shall not eat from it,** combines elements of 2:9 and 2:17. She showed full knowledge of both the permission and the prohibition. Also, her use of plural suffixes—**we may eat; you** [pl.] **shall not eat; nor must you** [pl.] **touch; lest you** [pl.] **die,** vv 2-3—shows she knew the instruction was for them both, though the verbs of permission and prohibition are singular in 2:16-17 (see Fretheim 1994, 360).

Some commentators have taken the woman's words, **and you must not touch it,** as either a misstatement or an overstatement of the prohibition. It is possible it was her own (or hers and the man's, together) expansion of the prohibition, parallel to the many expansions of the Mosaic law in Israel's later traditions.

A closer look at the verb will prove helpful. In Hebrew usage, **touch** (*nāgaʿ*) can mean much more than bringing one's fingers into contact with an object or a person. In Gen 20:6 and 26:11, the same verb is used, in contexts where the offense obviously would have been much more serious than brief skin-to-skin contact. Later, in the context of warfare, it can mean to strike a person so as to injure or even kill. The verb thus implies a forceful act. Here, it could mean to grasp in order to possess, i.e., to pluck and eat. Thus, the woman may have intended the line, not as an "addition," but as a parallel restatement of the prohibition; parallelism is the hallmark of Hebrew poetry and is quite common in prose as well. If this were her intention, it would be clearer if we were to translate, **You** [pl.] **may not eat of it; again, you** [pl.] **may not reach out and take it, to eat it.** We may wish the woman had not spoken these "extra" three (Heb.) words, but without more evidence than we possess, we cannot say she was following the serpent's lead and misrepresenting God by her words also.

The woman's response to the serpent ends with the words, **lest you die** (*pen-těmutûn*), a summary of the divine warning that accompanied the prohibition in 2:17 (**for on the day of your eating from it, dying you shall die** [i.e., **you certainly shall die**]). In a similar fashion, some have charged the woman with softening the certainty of the penalty with these words, rather than quoting God exactly, "You will surely die" (*môt tāmût*, 2:17). However, use of the particle *pen* is not a softening of a categorical statement in Hebrew, as "lest" often is in English. Rather, *pen* carries an aversive force; something must be done, or else avoided, to avert an undesired consequence.

In this context, the man and the woman were to refrain from eating of the one forbidden fruit; refraining would avert the undesirable consequence of death. Given the range of nuancing of English "lest," we perhaps would convey the idea of Hebrew *pen* more clearly by translating, **in order that you will not die.** The woman was stating the penalty negatively, rather than positively as God had stated it originally, but she was *not* softening it from a sure consequence to only a possibility, as English "lest" could imply.

The serpent picked up immediately on God's warning of death as the consequence in his reply to the woman (v 4). Whether we read the woman's response here as an overstatement, a misstatement, a legal expansion, or a literary parallelism (our own preferred conclusion), both the man and the woman had taken God seriously. Brueggemann concludes that the serpent succeeded in what he set out to do, transforming the *"boundary"* God had established into a *"threat"* in the minds of the human pair (1982, 48, emphases original).

■ **4** The serpent's response, ***you shall not surely die,*** suggests he, at least, took the woman's recital of God's words to be a faithful representation of what God actually had said. But now, instead of smarmy and insulting insinuation, he flatly contradicted God's word on the matter of death. Moreover, the serpent's perceptive wit shows in his immediate response to the woman's expressed concern. The serpent quoted God *almost* exactly. Given the context here, the switch from singular (2:17) to plural (3:4) **you** is unexceptional, as noted above (vv 2-3). The critical change was the serpent's introduction of the negative particle, **not** (*lō'*). In the Hebrew text, the particle comes first in the serpent's short declaration, heightening its emphatic denial of God's statement, ***You shall not surely die.***

The serpent's intent was not only to relieve the human pair of their anxiety about death but also to establish himself in their eyes as more trustworthy than God. The woman and the man would face a choice, whether to believe God who had created them, or this stranger who now confronted them, impugning God's character by denying God's truthfulness. The serpent's challenge also represented an attempt to subvert the order of creation. God had made the humans responsible for superintending the earthly creation (1:28; 2:19-20). Now the serpent put himself in the position of advising and instructing the humans. The reader begins to wonder, Would they perceive and resist this seditious claim, or would they succumb to its persuasions?

■ **5** The serpent's speech continues with the conjunctive particle, **for** (*kî*). Claiming insight into what **God knows,** and that God was withholding from the humans the whole truth, the serpent presented itself as the "truth-teller" (Fretheim 1994, 361). Beginning innocuously, it did reveal a fact God had not revealed. The Hebrew text reads, ***on the day you eat of it,*** again an exact quotation of God's words in 2:17 (except for the change of singular "you" to plural). The claim, **your eyes will be opened,** was true.

In a very limited sense, the second claim also was true. Eating of the forbidden fruit, they did become **like God, knowing good and evil.** But the serpent failed to tell the whole truth, in its turn, and its dreadful distortion turned this new "truth" into a lie. God knows **good** inside (experientially) and out ("objectively"). The first pair knew **good** experientially; succumbing, they came to know it objectively, also, in its newly revealed contrast with evil. God knows **evil** outside objectively, but not experientially. Eating of this fruit, the human pair came to know **evil** experientially, yet even there with woeful inadequacy, and far less than God knows it "objectively," from the outside. The promised opening of their eyes was the polar opposite of what they had imagined.

The serpent succeeded in its aim of replacing concern over death with the promise of becoming **like God.** Yet becoming **like God** has no bearing at all on whether or not humans die. The only way that could not be true would be for (a) human(s) to become God, or fully equal to God in every respect.

The desire for some such possibility was exactly what the serpent hoped to engender. The woman failed to notice this illogical connection, and the one that follows: a finite created being, by definition, never can be the equal of its creator, no matter how much or what kind of knowledge it may obtain. That being true, the only reliable and safe knowledge is gained in relationship with the Creator, rather than in ignoring and trying to bypass the Creator, as the serpent urged.

The serpent's dialogue with the woman, its recorded speech, and its independent role all end here. It appears in this text again only in the woman's response to God's inquiry (v 13) and in God's judgment upon it (vv 14-15).

Ambrose on Gen 3:1-5

The cause of envy was the happiness of man placed in paradise, because the devil could not brook the favors received by man. His envy was aroused because man, though formed in slime, was chosen to be an inhabitant of paradise. The devil began to reflect that man was an inferior creature yet had hopes of eternal life, whereas he, a creature of superior nature, had fallen and had become part of this mundane existence. (Louth 2001, 76)

■ 6 Verse 6 reports, not the woman's further response to the serpent, but both humans' action in eating of the forbidden fruit. The reader is justified in concluding they took the serpent's words as truth, actively doubting God. The woman and, we may assume, the man standing beside her, **saw that the fruit of the tree was good for food** ["physically appealing"], ***a thing desirable to the eyes*** ["aesthetically pleasing"], and ***the tree was to be desired to make [one] prudent*** ("sapientially transforming," Trible 1978, 112).

3:5-6

The first two qualities would have characterized the fruits of most of the fruit trees in the garden; they commended the fruit of this tree to the woman "merely" as not being inferior, but as (at least) the equal of all the trees. We may note also that one aspect of this tree's attraction as ***a delight to the eyes*** was the serpent's promise (v 5) that their eyes would be "opened" by eating of this fruit. The third quality is described using what we may consider a "stronger," or more forceful, root for ***desired*** (*ḥāmad*) than the second, ***desirable*** or **pleasing** (*ʾāwâ*); the knowledge of good and evil (or, as they thought, wisdom) was what the human pair really wanted. The root translated here ***prudent*** (*śākal*) is not the usual biblical root used to denote godly wisdom (*ḥākam*). In the biblical tradition, reverential "fear of the LORD" is the beginning of—the only way of gaining—godly wisdom (Prov 1:7, passim). Even the narrator's choice of ***prudent,*** rather than "wise," indicates an ungodly desire or (at least) an ungodly means of attempting to acquire what may have been a legitimate desire. Already, the reader understands their desire had killed the wisdom they hitherto had possessed; they would not get what they thought they were bargaining for.

The last part of v 6, as often when a Hebrew narrative is intended to present a very strong emphasis on an action in order to presage its gravity, comprises a series of very short clauses—in this case, four—each beginning with a finite form of a verb. Here, we should translate, **Then she took from its fruit, and she ate, and she gave also to her husband with her, and he ate;** all this in only eight Hebrew words, four of which are verbs. Once the woman had made up her mind, the author/editor allows no room for ambiguity, indecisiveness, or possibility of success in blame-shifting—which, of course, the guilty pair would try. The four verbs overwhelm all such defenses and excuses: **she took; she ate; she gave; he ate.**

Nor does the text allow us to speculate that the man somehow was an "innocent" victim. He stood by silently, **with her,** while the conversation proceeded. He did not speak up for God or resist the serpent's claims or try to dissuade the woman when she took of the fruit and ate. When she offered it to him, he ate without demur. The serpent tempted them by presenting options or possibilities, but the woman and the man together ultimately were responsible for this first transgression. With Brueggemann, we may say they "neglected" their vocation, "perverted" the permission, and "violated" the prohibition (1982, 48).

Augustine on Gen 3:6

I do not think that a [person] would deserve great praise if he [or she] had been able to live a good life for the simple reason that nobody tempted him [or her] to live a bad one. (Louth 2001, 80)

The Fruit

There is no cogent reason to assume the fruit this first couple ate was an apple, especially as the only fruit tree named is the fig (v 7). What this fruit was, and whether it still exists in the world today, would be impossible to determine. A probable reason the apple emerged as the favored candidate is that for more than one thousand years Jerome's Latin translation (the Vulgate) was the Bible in the Western church. Latin malus, "evil," and malum, "apple," are only one letter apart in their spellings, and that in a language where final letters often function as case markers, and thus are changeable. The assumption that malum is the fruit that introduced humanity to malus is understandable, if not acceptable. (Hamilton 1990, 191)

■ **7** **Then the eyes of *the two* of them were opened;** this was exactly what the serpent had promised, and yet it wasn't, either. The promise was they would come to know "good and evil," and now, in a way, they did. What this opening of two innocent sets of eyes really accomplished, however, was the altering of *how* they saw the world. No longer did they see through the lens of a faithful relationship with the God they loved, whose instruction they trusted. Now they saw "entirely through their own eyes" (Fretheim 1994, 361).

This new "knowledge of good and evil" is defined by the narrator in the statement, **they *knew* they were naked.** Their nakedness included, but now was not limited to, physical nakedness. The theological link with 2:25 is intentional and clear. There, they were not ashamed of the nakedness they "saw" every day but did not associate with shame or evil. Now, their new way of seeing gave their physical nakedness a deeper, nonphysical, and negative theological dimension. Now they knew evil; as a result, what before had been only good, now brought them shame.

Verse 7 also reports the action of the man and the woman to remedy their nakedness. **They sewed fig leaves together and made *girdles* [or, *aprons*] for themselves.** They used **fig leaves,** probably because these are among the larger leaves, and yet still are pliable. Such aprons would have covered them, and even may have been semi-comfortable, though of course their former unselfconscious splendor and beauty were gone. A fact both practical and theological in its implications is that they would have had to make new aprons every few days; this solution to their "problem" could not be permanent. Of equal theological import is that this "solution" was of their own making; the subsequent narrative is at pains to show that the remedy was—and only could be—God's doing (v 21). Moreover, even with aprons, the newly shamed pair now lived in fear and attempted to hide from God (vv 8, 10).

FROM THE TEXT

Ezekiel 28:11-19 pictures the king of Tyre as figuring another, a more ancient and a greater being, who was "in Eden, the garden of God" (v 13) "as a guardian cherub" (v 14); God "threw [him] to the earth" because of his overweening pride (v 17). Jesus told the seventy-two returning from their mission, "I saw Satan fall like lightning from heaven" (Luke 10:18). Revelation 12:9 and 20:2 both refer to "the great dragon," and name him as "the devil, or Satan." From these and other references, many Christians (and others) have inferred that the serpent that tempted the pair in Eden was Satan himself, disguised as a serpent. Others believe Satan possessed the serpent for a short time to pursue his purpose of deceiving the human pair. The first inference, that the serpent *was* Satan, is ruled out by the author's description of it in 3:1 as one of the ***creatures of the field* which *Yahweh Elohim had made.*** Both Jewish and Christian doctrine traditionally have taught that Satan *is* one of God's creatures, fallen through his pride from his original perfect state, though this view has no direct biblical evidence. However, he never was a "creature of the field." That he "entered into" and took possession of the serpent for a time may be plausible. We even may believe we can establish that scenario as factual, based on the indirect linkage of Gen 3 with later biblical texts, including those cited above (though actually, the OT itself does not make any direct reference to the

123

narrative of Gen 3). What we may not do in good faith, exegetically, is insist that Gen 3, *by itself*, teaches that the serpent and Satan are one and the same.

Many interpreters across the centuries, by following the method of allegorical interpretation, have asserted that the eating of the fruit of the tree actually was the first act of sexual congress. The obvious conclusion of this line of interpretation is that the sexual act of the first human pair was the primal sin. Though no recent interpreters of standing take this approach, the number of those who have done so, historically, is quite large, and this understanding continues today as the "official" interpretation of several Christian groups, both large and small.

An important objection to this understanding is the logical necessity it then would demand of identifying all sexual congress as sinful. Yet God both commanded and blessed appropriate sexual union already in the first blessing/command of Gen 1:28, "Be fruitful and multiply, and fill the earth" (NRSV). Moreover, the narrative of ch 2 reports that God brought the woman and the man together for the purpose of living in community. For them, and for all rightfully joined couples since, a significant part of that community is the intimate, holy, and joyful act of sexual union. This is implied in the man's joyous response of Gen 2:23; it is explicit in the editorial comment/instruction of 2:24, "a man . . . shall *cleave* unto his wife; and they shall be one flesh" (KJV, emphasis added). What God explicitly provided for, commanded, and blessed in chs 1 and 2 cannot be condemned as sinful in ch 3. Of course, we humans have made a major mess of many things sexual since our first parents ate that first fruit, but whatever it may have been, that fruit was *not* a code word for "sex." In and of itself, appropriately expressed and experienced, the act of sex between a woman and a man is one of God's precious gifts, perhaps most precious of all those we depict as "physical," though it is of course also much more than physical.

Having no existential reality, evil only can taint, tarnish, pollute, and sometimes destroy what is good. As nakedness is not intrinsically evil, the evil the first pair came to know was not their nakedness. However, evil embraced can pervert almost any good. Experiencing this is a kind of knowledge of good and evil but, left unredeemed, it does not truly enlighten. In the end, in the eyes of those who pervert their understanding of good and evil through lives steeped in sin, good becomes "evil," and evil becomes "good" (see Isa 5:20).

If space allowed, we would address a number of other issues, but we must be content with a brief statement of each. Many are obvious, but obvious does not mean trivial.

1. It is possible to distort God's words, and God's Word. Believers are to guard against distortion for many reasons—perhaps most importantly, that distortion can lead to mistrust of God.

2. The creaturely desire to become like the Creator remains as a powerful temptation; we ignore it to our peril.

3. Trusting fellow creatures, in *place* of God, also is a dangerous habit, no less today than in the garden.

4. It is crucial that we know the source of anything presented as truth, and whether it really originates with the Source of truth, God's own self.

5. In its essence, the first transgression was breaking relationship—with God, with each other, and with the rest of creation. Whatever the specific "act," sin *always* damages or breaks relationship(s).

6. "Shame" and "guilt" both are important issues, but they are not the same state or condition.

7. God really has granted humans the freedom to follow or to turn from God. We have the room to use, misuse, or abuse that freedom, as we decide.

8. Even with only two persons as parties to the first transgression, their actions are examples of the reality and the importance of both individual and corporate responsibility for human decisions and actions.

9. As coercion is not temptation, the serpent did not coerce the primal couple. To be genuine temptation, and not something else, every tempting involves misrepresentation, enticement, and persuasion, but *not* coercion.

10. Actions reported in this text are taken in Christian theology as having affected human existence as/in the image of God: Was the image of God in humans lost, distorted, marred, bent, as a result of this first transgression? Do humans need to be restored to the image of God? Is that possible? If so, how, and what would it look like? If not, why not, and how is the image of God still present within us? These questions (with several others, also) are of particular significance in Wesleyan theology.

2. Confrontation and Pseudo-Confession (3:8-13)

IN THE TEXT

■ **8** Ignoring the issue of how much time had elapsed, the narrator launched the new scene directly, with the report that the man and the woman heard **the sound of the LORD God as he was walking.** Though Hebrew *qôl* usually is translated "voice," it sometimes refers to other sounds, such as thunder or the sound of movement along the surface of the ground (see, e.g., 2 Sam 5:24; 1 Kgs 14:6; 2 Kgs 6:32). However, we should note that in these passages the references are to "the sound of marching," or "the sound of [someone's] feet," while here we do not read "the sound of God's feet" but, rather, **the sound of *Yahweh Elohim* [the LORD God] walking.** Cassuto comments that the author was subtly refraining from an overanthropomorphic depiction of God by avoiding reference to "God's" feet (1961, 151-52). This is a small point, but worth noticing, as an example of the reverence with which the author depicts all God's actions in these early chapters.

We translate the reflexive participle *mithallēk* (Hithpa'el of *hālak*, meaning "to walk"), ***was walking to and fro.*** This Hebrew verbal form can (and

125

seems here to) emphasize both the iterative (repeated or habitual) aspect of the action, and the action as done by, to, and for oneself. In other words, God was in the habit of walking in the garden, suggesting a regular, ongoing relationship between God and the human pair. We probably could not stress too much that God's appearance after the human pair's transgression means God did not abandon them or the relationship they had enjoyed together. Neither did God abandon the garden, its other inhabitants, or the rest of the earthly creation. All still belonged to God; God would not allow the new state of alienation to last forever.

The narrative includes the detail that God was walking **in the cool of the day** (*lĕrûaḥ hayyôm*); Hebrew *rûaḥ* usually is taken as a substantive, meaning here, "wind," or "breeze." The phrase, "at the wind/the breeze of the day," then, indicates midafternoon or a bit later, when the sun's heat upon the earth had begun to abate and a pleasant breeze had sprung up.

When they heard the sound of God's walking, the man and the woman **hid from the Lord God among the trees of the garden**. The forbidden tree was "in the midst of the garden" (2:9), and now they hid themselves **among the trees of the garden**; "in the midst" and "among" translate the same Hebrew preposition. In the "wisdom" the human pair thought they had attained, they imagined they could hide from divine scrutiny. The reader knows why they now were fearful of meeting God; we, too, have experienced shame and the consequent fear of being found out. The narrator draws the reader into this scene by respecting that knowledge and waiting for the man to express it directly in his response to God's first query (v 10). Desperately as the shamed pair wished it, the trees that had sheltered, nourished, and given them joy could not hide them from God, any more than their fig leaf aprons truly could cover them.

■**9** The humans having hidden from God, ***then Yahweh Elohim called out to the ʾādām, and said to him,*** "Where are you?" God directed the question to the man; both pronouns (***him*** and **you**) are singular. However, we know from the subsequent conversation God did not exclude the woman. The reason for God's directing the question to the man alone may have been simply the divine intention to elicit speech from the man, who had been silent until then.

God's question, **Where are you?** (Heb. *ʾayyekkâ*), does not necessarily imply God's ignorance of their location. This text really does not address the issue of what God knows or does not know. Rather, this question is the cry of a broken heart. It would be impossible to overstate the emotion expressed in this single Hebrew word in this context. God loved the human pair; God had delighted in their daily trysts. God was disappointed, grief-stricken, brokenhearted at this, their first failure to appear. The implications of God's grief and the measureless pathos of its expression here are of profound importance for a Christian (especially a Wesleyan) theology of relationship (see From the Text, below).

We may see God's pathos here from another perspective also. God's question was the lament of a disappointed parent who knew very well where the delinquent children had tried to hide themselves, and why. We are not amazed when a human parent knows the details of a child's transgression and confronts him or her with questions designed to elicit confession, comprehension of the gravity of the misdeed, and repentance. Just so, God used a series of questions here to bring these "children" to understand the import and the consequences of what they had done, with restoration of relationships as the ultimate goal.

Chrysostom on Gen 3:9

> You see, since he was not unaware of the truth when he asked them but rather knew, and knew very well, he shows consideration for their limitations so as to demonstrate his own lovingkindness, and he invites them to make admission of their faults. (Louth 2001, 85)

■ **10** The man neither admitted the human pair's transgression of God's prohibition, nor joined the divine pathos in expressing their own sorrow over it. Rather, his four first person singular references all suggest exclusive concern for himself, possibly even to the exclusion of any thought for the woman: **I heard; I was afraid; I was naked; I hid.**

The first part of the man's answer, ***the sound of you I heard in the garden,*** acknowledged that the pair had been aware of God's presence in the garden *before* they heard God's grief-laden question. That the opening phrase, ***the sound of you,*** is first (for emphasis) tends to support this understanding.

The second part of the response also is significant. **I was afraid** is the first biblical occurrence of the verb "to be afraid." Whereas joy, delight, and anticipation had been their normal responses to God's keeping of their daily appointments, now for the first time they experienced fear and dread at the prospect of being in God's presence. We may wonder whether the irony of their situation dawned upon the miscreants; their craven fear was a far cry from the equality with God they had thought they were acquiring in tasting of the forbidden fruit.

The man specifically ascribed their fear to their newly discovered state: **Because I was naked.** In the Hebrew text, the first person subject pronoun **I** is not necessary, grammatically; it is present only for emphasis. Remembering the fig leaves, the reader is justified in reading this emphatic admission as the man's realization—now that God had confronted them—that the leaves had not solved their problem. Previously, integrity and transparency had allowed the human pair to be naked but unashamed (2:25). Now their loss of integrity and transparency exposed an "inner" nakedness that could not be covered with physical clothing. Faced with the reality of God's grief, and the penetrating question revealing also God's purpose to bring them to account, the man's

3:9-10

confession of his nakedness still was not borne of contrition, but of resignation, as his next statement confirms.

The man's last declaration, **so I hid** *myself,* strikes the reader in its turn as another statement of fact carefully phrased to avoid admission of guilt or acceptance of responsibility. Found out in their hiding place, given opportunity to admit their transgression without coercion, the man demurred. The narrative is emphatic; they hoped only for an easy escape. If God were serious about confession, reconciliation, and restoration, God would have to try again.

It is possible to interpret the first person singular verbs in this verse—**I heard; I was afraid; I was naked; I hid**—as the man's initial impulse to protect the woman and to take responsibility for their transgression upon himself. If so, this was his first and only chivalrous act in the entire account. Hamilton says, "He does not incriminate her with 'we hid ourselves'" (1990, 193). The staccato brevity of his response, four short clauses in only nine words (Heb.), parallels the initial narrative of the woman's taking of the fruit (v 6) and indicates his desire to conclude the interview and escape as quickly as possible. His answer, in the final analysis, was not a confession, but an evasion.

■ **11** God's response to the man was a twofold question. The first, **Who told you that you were naked?** went to the heart of the matter, leaving unaddressed the fear the man had expressed. As God knew the humans had discovered their nakedness for themselves, this question is of a piece with God's original question, "Where are you?" This one, too, was designed to confront the pair with their transgression. This one, too, was designed to elicit voluntary confession. The text does not say God paused before asking the man the second question, but the reader understands that God would have listened had the man responded.

God provided a third opportunity for the man to confess voluntarily. Objectively, God knew the answers to all these questions, but God's grace, mercy, and love always impel God to make possible what is best, and "best" for the humans in this situation would have been their own admission of guilt, even though God was prompting it.

It is difficult to convey in English all the pathos of God expressed in the second question of this verse, *From the tree which I commanded you not to eat of it, have you eaten?!* The verb placed at the very end of the clause adds a climactic emphasis to the question. The *emotional* impact of their deed upon God included genuine and disappointed "surprise," even if, as many Christians believe, God knew beforehand that they would eat of the fruit of this tree. Moreover, God's "disappointed surprise" points up in vivid contrast the "feigned surprise" of the serpent's question over the nature of the prohibition (v 1).

■ **12** The man's answer, *The woman whom you gave [to be] with me, she gave me of the fruit, and I ate,* while an admission that he had eaten, essentially was an attempt to shift the blame to the woman, and even onto God. The boldness—the insolence, even—of this attempt is clear from the fact that his first word (Hebrew text) was **the woman**. The man accused her and even implicated God—***whom <u>you</u> gave [to be] with me***—before admitting his own act with a single verb, **I ate**. Placing this minimal admission at the very end of the sentence, as though hoping God would not notice, he tried to exempt himself from direct involvement and, thus, from responsibility for their act. The only mitigating feature of his answer is that this climactic ordering does parallel the placement of the same verb in God's question, ***have you eaten?*** (v 11).

■ **13** At first glance, it appears the man's strategy worked; God did turn to the woman next. But again, the narrator displays consummate artistic skill, keeping the reader in suspense for a bit. God's question to the woman was much shorter, as was her answer; both are only three words in the Hebrew text. The man already had accused the woman, truthfully; God did not need to ask whether she had eaten. The facts of the case were very near to being established.

God's question to the woman, **What is this you have done?** conveyed, rather, God's disappointed astonishment at her readiness to believe the stranger (the serpent) and disbelieve God, whom by now they should have trusted implicitly. (We continue to observe, also, the distinction between God's foreknowledge and the impact of their betrayal upon God, both cognitively and emotionally.)

Even today, in Israel, one can hear this question exactly as God put it to the woman, in tones of astonishment and disbelief that anyone could act so recklessly and foolishly. An analogous expression in colloquial English is, "*What* were you thinking?" Though this scene does not correspond quite with the later judicial setting many have seen it to be, it does bear some resemblances. In that setting, God's question is analogous to the judge's query of the defendant, "How do you plead?" What distinguishes God's question here is that a judge is supposed to be dispassionate, and God decidedly was *not* dispassionate in addressing this question to the woman.

The woman's brief answer, **The serpent deceived me, and I ate,** was neither an admission of guilt nor yet a claim of innocence. Like the man, she attempted to shift the blame—this time, to the serpent. She did not refer to God, as had the man. However, given the identification of the serpent as one of the ***creatures of the field which Yahweh Elohim had made*** (v 1), we could read her admission, also, as an indirect attempt to place the blame for their sin upon God.

It may not be possible to discern all that the woman meant in her statement, **The serpent deceived me.** Deception is not always an outright lie, though the serpent did lie in saying they would not die (v 4). The more powerful attraction of the serpent's line, and of the fruit itself, lay in his statement that they would become like God, "knowing good and evil" (v 5). True, they did come to know good and evil, but in a disastrous and deadly way, not at all in the way(s) God knows evil, then or ever. If the woman spoke truly—we have no reason to doubt her in this—she really did allow herself to believe the serpent's lies and deceptive partial truths, probably because she wanted as desperately as her husband to have an excuse to eat of the forbidden fruit. Moreover, her answer clearly was an attempt to evade responsibility for her own actions. No longer do we see the outwardly "friendly" scene of vv 1-3; the woman's answer reveals the disruption of relationship not only between her and God but also between her and the serpent. She had not yet grasped the enormity of the rift between her and the man.

Dorotheus of Gaza on Gen 3:12-13

So it is, my brethren, when a man has not the guts to accuse himself, he does not scruple to accuse God himself. . . . Neither the one nor the other stooped to self-accusation, no trace of humility was found in either of them. And now look and consider how this was only an anticipation of our own state! See how many and great the evils it has brought on us—this self-justification, this holding fast to our own will, this obstinacy in being our own guide. (Louth 2001, 87)

FROM THE TEXT

First and foremost, if we are to hope at all, we must register the fact that God entered the garden again, even *after* the first human transgression. God did not abandon either the garden or those who called it home. Rather than walking away from them, God walked toward them, sought them out. To put it most directly, in theological terms, this is the first biblical expression of God's grace in the face of sin. Our ongoing hope lies in the knowledge that it is not the last.

God's grace in this scene is revealed further as we understand that God came to prompt a healing confession from the human pair. The first words they heard from God were not indictment or judgment, but the divine pathos yearning to restore the newly broken relationships.

On another issue, some have regarded this and other theophanies (appearances of God to humans, in human form or semblance) in the OT accounts as preincarnate appearances of the Second Person of the Trinity. Others regard them as appearances of God, or of God's messengers (angels), through the temporary assumption of physical substance, or through appearance only, without physical reality, as in a vision. The text here certainly indicates God did not send an angelic agent but met with the human pair personally. More than that, this text does not allow us to assert with confidence.

Connected with this is the fact that in many biblical accounts, when humans were afraid at God's (or God's representative's) appearance, they were encouraged, "Do *not* fear!" (see, e.g., Gen 15:1; Judg 6:23; Dan 10:12; Matt 28:5, 10; Rev 1:17). Because of our sin, humans naturally fear God's judgment, but this kind of fear is not God's permanent desire for us. God always desires, and has provided, restoration of the lost intimate relationship.

Human fear of God, in the sense of seeing God as irreconcilably angry with us, stems from the estrangement precipitated here in the garden by our first parents. At this point they, who had been created in the image of God, began to live in fear of God's wrath upon them. In 1 John 4:16-21, John addressed this unhealthy fear of God, naming its remedy as the "perfect love" (1 John 4:18) of God within us.

As noted above (Gen 3:9), the clear and consistent testimony of Scripture, too often unacknowledged or underemphasized in our theology, is that God really does experience emotion and emotions—without effecting change in God's *character*; emotion, too, is one of the ways we are created in God's image. The very syntax of God's questions—**Where are you?** (v 9) and **Have you eaten?** (v 11)—reflects the biblical truth that God is love.

The question naturally may arise, if God knew they (or we) were going to disregard God's loving instruction, how could God be disappointed, even grief-stricken, as we have claimed God was (and is)? Much in the classical traditions both of Judaism and Christianity asserts that God is *impassive*, i.e., does *not* experience emotion of any kind, ever. The common theological word is "immutable." We should note in passing that this idea is part of our philosophical heritage from classical Greece. Neither the OT nor the NT, read with exegetical care and integrity, ever makes such an assertion. On the contrary, Scripture has a great deal to say about God's joy, God's pleasure, God's disappointment, God's anger, and other emotional responses to human faithfulness and human waywardness, both.

The analogy of God as divine Parent is helpful yet again. Intelligent human parents who are paying attention usually know what young children have done, together with much of the when, where, why, and how of it. If it is a forbidden activity, such parents often can tell when a child is about to do it, anyway. That they know the small rebellion is coming does not lessen their regret over the child's poor decision. Anger, disappointment, grief—all may be appropriate responses, without diminishing or making less effective the parents' love for the child or their active looking out for his or her well-being. All these may be present even when the parents knew the forbidden act was inevitable. If finite humans can know this about their children, and experience such trials along with the joys of parenting, how much more could God, with our first parents and with us? Merely knowing ahead of time that someone dearly loved would make a poor decision does not render disappointment and grief impossible, or lessen their impact, even upon God.

Another issue, really, but increasing God's grief and disappointment, was the newly acquired human capacity for evading culpability, passing blame, and avoiding genuine confession even with the bare admission of guilt. The desperate human need for self-justification blossomed instantaneously and never has left us, except with divine treatment. Perhaps more than any other perverse human "need," this one splinters relationships, often rendering them—absent divine grace—beyond the possibility of repair.

Moreover, this defective trait can characterize not only individuals and families but also whole communities and cultures. Making self-justification and self-preservation into societal virtues poisons all relationships, communally as well as individually. The culture's views of reality become permanently distorted; truth-telling becomes rare, sometimes virtually impossible. A polity, a society, or a culture caught in this vise of self-justification-above-all-else is headed for breakdown on every level—social, political, religious, even economic. As in the garden with our first parents, it begins with the disappearance of truth-telling and the rejection of personal and communal responsibility.

Scripture is filled with narratives, with wisdom and other poetic utterances, with parables and other didactic admonitions, concerning this grievous human failing, and how God's disciplines of grace make possible its cure. We list but a few: numerous cries of the psalmist (e.g., Ps 12:2); David's response to Nathan (2 Sam 12:13); the prodigal's proposed confession to his father (Luke 15:18); Paul's admonition to put away falsehood (Eph 4:25). The power to speak needed truth in love, with grace and humility, is essential both to individuals and communities of integrity.

On another vital issue, the woman's statement, **The serpent deceived me,** is viewed by some as proof that she alone was responsible for the present mortality of the human race. First Timothy 2:14 often is cited as further evidence that the man bore no culpability. Additionally, this verse is viewed by those taking this position as *the* Pauline doctrine of the first human transgression.

However, one cannot read our text with integrity and conclude that the woman was solely responsible. One point we have noted already; the man was present with the woman throughout her conversation with the serpent (v 6), yet said nothing. God spoke first to the man, and one may argue that the consequences God pronounced upon the man were more severe than those pronounced upon the woman (see vv 16-19, below).

To discern Paul's theology of the first transgression, for important reasons we begin, not with 1 Tim 2:11-15, but with Rom 5:12-21. Here, Paul spent a lengthy paragraph contrasting the death brought by the first man, Adam, with the life offered as God's gift by the sacrifice of Jesus Christ, whom many have called the second Adam. It is barely possible Paul had in mind both the man and the woman, using "Adam" here (Rom 5:14) in the collective sense it has in most of its occurrences in Gen 1—3. However, that is unlikely; it would be difficult to find an NT commentator who reads Paul that way here. Given the tenor of the passage, Paul almost certainly was contrasting the man we have come to know as Adam with the man, Jesus.

132

What is *not* possible is that Paul was referring to the woman as the agent through whom death came into the world. Yet, that is what he would *have* to be saying in Rom 5:14, if we were to read him as blaming the woman exclusively in 1 Tim 2:14. Moreover, we would have to ask how the woman could be assigned greater or exclusive blame, since she *was* deceived (as she said, and Paul accepted) and the man was *not* deceived, but sinned anyway. Unless we want to argue that Paul, the superbly logical thinker, was hopelessly illogical here, we must look for another understanding of 1 Tim 2:11-15.

Catherine Clark Kroeger, in *I Suffer Not a Woman*, her seminal work on this passage, has shown that Paul was combating a specific heresy in the churches of Ephesus and the surrounding regions of Roman Asia. Some women were teaching a mixed gnostic/pagan reinterpretation of the Genesis creation narratives, to the effect that the woman and the serpent were responsible for the generation of human offspring; the man was not part of the picture in any way. Paul was not instructing all women everywhere and for all time to keep quiet in church. He was telling *these* women to stop teaching *this* heresy as Christian doctrine. Far from being the "earth goddess" responsible, without the man, for all subsequent human life, Eve was the one who was deceived. Paul did not shift the blame entirely to the woman, absolving the man; neither may we (Kroeger 1992).

3. God's Curse upon the Culprit (3:14-15)

IN THE TEXT

■ **14** We treat vv 14-15 as a unit separate from vv 9-13 primarily because God did not engage in conversation with the serpent, as God had done with the woman and the man in vv 9-13. God simply pronounced God's curse upon the serpent, without allowing it to respond. The narrator introduced God's speech to the serpent in the usual order of Hebrew syntax: **Then Yahweh Elohim said to the serpent.** By contrast, when God spoke to the woman and to the man, respectively, the order is, **To the woman he said** (v 16) then, **And to the man he said** (v 17). **The woman** and **the man** come first in their respective sentences for emphasis. Put the other way, this is a small but effective narrative signal of God's dismissive approach toward the serpent, as compared with God's continuing solicitude for the human pair.

As noted, God did not allow the serpent to speak again. God did not need to question it. It had no defense, since the woman's reply had established its role as the tempter/deceiver. An equally important inference is that the serpent had forfeited its powers of speech through its gross misuse of them. Given all this, God's speech to the serpent begins with a word of general indictment, **Because you have done this,** i.e., you have deceived the woman.

God's pronouncement upon the serpent begins with a passive participle, **Cursed are you.** Since God's curse was only upon the serpent, we should not translate the entire sentence, **Cursed are you <u>above</u> all the livestock and . . . animals!** (emphasis added). None of the other creatures was cursed, either on this occasion or later. The preposition *min* cannot carry here a comparative force, as it often does elsewhere. Here it is partitive, the "from" of separation, exclusion, alienation. We should translate, with Hamilton, "Banned shall you be from all cattle and from every creature of the field" (1990, 194). The serpent had been ʿ*ārûm*, cunning/crafty, *above* the other creatures; now it was ʾ*ārûr*, cursed, diminished to a status *beneath*, and separated from, the other creatures.

Both categories of the larger creatures are mentioned here, **all the livestock and all the wild animals,** rather than the single, all-inclusive category, as we have taken *the creatures of the field* to be above (v 1). This doubling of the categories emphasizes the totality of the serpent's exclusion from all its former or potential associations. As v 15 indicates, its exclusion extended also to banishment from the company of the humans with whom it just had been holding converse, virtually as an equal.

The second part of the curse (diminishment) of the serpent was its perpetual humiliation. Having persuaded the humans to eat of the forbidden fruit, it now would **crawl on [its] belly** and **eat dust,** forever. Losing its power of speech, its privilege of association with God's other creatures, and now its ability to walk upright, consigned to move about forever in the dust, was a mortifying degradation for an intelligent creature, whether snake, orangutan, or something else.

You will eat dust does not mean the creature's diet henceforth would be, literally, the soil of the ground, as is the earthworm's, for example. The focus of God's curse was/is the serpent's humiliation (see Ps 72:9; Isa 49:23; Mic 7:17). However, with its head always near the ground (if it was the snake), it would "eat" plenty of dust every day, though its diet was primarily rodents and other small creatures. (On this point and the orangutan, see Clarke n.d., 49.) This is yet another example of the narrator's phenomenological approach throughout Gen 1—3. He told it as we *experience* it, or as it *seems* upon casual observation, not as we know it to be scientifically (when those two approaches do not agree). This is not primitive ignorance, but a way of speaking to all humans through the ages, whatever their level of "scientific" knowledge.

■ **15** God's speech to the serpent continues, announcing a further action on God's part, and its consequences for the serpent in its relations with humanity:

> *Moreover,* I will *place* enmity between you and the woman,
> and between your *seed and her seed.*
> *As for him, he will strike your head,*
> *and as for you,* you will strike his heel.

Those who see primarily an etiological explanation in v 15 note the usual animosity of humans for snakes, and the ease with which snakes may strike unsuspecting humans when they come too close. They note also that humans usually kill snakes by striking them on the head, or by severing the head from the body; snakes usually strike humans on the heel or the lower leg. This story then is interpreted as an attempt to explain why humans and snakes act toward each other as they usually do. Others, seeing a morality tale instead of or in addition to an etiology, find instruction in resisting temptation. Be alert for the "snake" of temptation; strike it quickly and surely by moral resistance, and it will die—lose its power to tempt you. Walk carelessly into temptation, and it will strike without warning; you may die. Neither of these explanations is necessarily wrong; however, neither is adequate by itself, nor are both, together.

We should notice, first, that *I will place* is one of only two first person verb forms from here to the end of the chapter; the second is *I will multiply* in God's announcement to the woman (v 16). Only in these two places did God pronounce a sentence that God personally would carry out, an action that God personally would do. This first one was a God-ordained change in the relationship between the serpent and the human race, from the seeming cordiality of the chapter's first scene to **enmity**. **Enmity** is a feminine noun from the same root (*ʾāyab*, "be hostile") as the participial form often translated "enemy." The word **seed** or **offspring** (*zeraʿ*) is singular in form but may be either singular or plural (collective) in meaning. God would see to it that the serpent and the offspring of the woman would be enemies. This strongly suggests more than the antipathy of all or most humans to an animal they find distasteful, one they even may fear. This was God's doing, by God's own declaration. While this is only the beginning of the story, and we cannot see from here the story's end, we are justified in understanding already, from God's action announced in this beginning, something much more than a mere etiology. That "something" will be revealed, though still cryptically, in God's climactic statement to the serpent, the next and final line of this pronouncement.

In this final line, *As for <u>him</u>, <u>he</u> will strike <u>your</u> head, and as for <u>you</u>, <u>you</u> will strike <u>his</u> heel,* all the pronouns are singular, *not* plural. Though the two subject pronouns (**he** and **you**) are not grammatically necessary, the author used them precisely for the purpose of giving this statement considerable extra emphasis. The plain meaning of the text suggests the usual antipathy between humans and snakes. However, throughout Christian history, some interpreters have taken this word as being also a prediction or a declaration of God's redemptive purpose.

The two verbs in the last line are from the same root, *šûp*, often translated "bruise." Many render the first clause, **he will crush your head.** For a variety of reasons, few translate the second clause, "You will crush his heel." Many render it, with the NIV, **You will strike his heel** or, "You will bruise his heel."

We have followed Hamilton in translating this verb *strike* in both clauses, because it allows for the "normal" actions of the human and the serpent, but also does not close out the possibilities realized in the ultimate fulfillment of God's threat to the serpent, which was, at the same time, a promise to the woman (1990, 195, 197-98). When we read v 15 in light of God's redemption fulfilled in the life and work of Jesus the Messiah, we are justified in seeing in this verse God's promise of ultimate victory over the source of temptation.

FROM THE TEXT

Genesis 3:15 has become so important in Christian theology as to have its own name. It is called the *proto-euangelion* in Greek, the *proto-evangelium* in Latin—the proto-gospel, or the first good news of the redemption God would work in Christ. According to the traditional Christian reading of this text, the divine Offspring of the woman, Jesus Christ, would crush the serpent's head, ultimately reversing the effects of sin for any and all who believe. This great work would cost him, though. The serpent would strike at his heel, and venomous serpents can kill. Jesus died, but death could not hold him. The traditional reading sees all this presaged in this verse, the *proto-euangelion.*

Several issues require attention. First, this understanding identifies the serpent as Satan, or as Satan's agent. An objection often made is that—whether this text is early, as traditionalists argue, or later, as many others think—Israel did not have a developed doctrine of "Satan" at the time this text was written. That is true. However, neither does anything in this text contradict later understandings of Satan, even those in the NT. Also, several NT writers echo this verse in their own treatments of the serpent as Satan (see Rom 16:20; Rev 20:1-3).

Furthermore, even if the serpent was only Satan's agent, and not Satan himself, in the ancient world (as today) a person's agent fully represented that person in the transaction for which the agent was sent. In other words, God's threat could have been directed both at the serpent, as agent, and at Satan, as provocateur, even though the author of Genesis did not have a developed theological perspective on Satan, but only knew him as the Adversary who sometimes came into God's presence (Job 1:6).

In that regard, it is true we must give first priority to the intentions of the human author of any text, if we are to place our understanding of that text on a sound footing. Taking that as his only canon of interpretation for this verse, Speiser quotes Driver approvingly, "We must not read into the words more than they contain" (1964, 24, n. 15). This is a valuable dictum, but who decides what the words contain? The approach often called intertextual interpretation involves investigating whether, how, and why later biblical texts appropriate earlier biblical texts. Even within the pages of the OT itself, earlier texts often are quoted or referred to and given expanded meanings within the new contexts (*sitzen im leben*) of the biblical authors who appropriated the older material. Investigation of these intertextual usages is a valuable and respected part of biblical studies today.

Notice we said "expanded meanings" above, not new or contradictory meanings; therein lies the key to relating v 15 to the Christian faith. Christians acknowledge that these words of hope were opaque words to the woman who heard them firsthand, but we are not obliged to deny they were the first promise of God's deliverance. That she could not know so much then does not require us to forget it now. We may debate whether this text speaks directly or indirectly of Christ's victory over Satan, through his death on the cross. That redemptive work, however, is the hope for all who struggle against the power of temptation.

4. Consequences for the Woman and the Man (3:16-19)

IN THE TEXT

■ **16** As with the serpent, most of God's pronouncements upon the woman and then the man were not arbitrary sentences imposed by a judge who had several to choose from in the law. Rather, they were God's revelation of some (not all) of the natural consequences of their actions. Essentially, they had tried to sever their relationship with God by their attempted declaration of independence. Now they would find all their heretofore harmonious relationships fractured: with God, with themselves individually and internally, with each other, and with the earth and its other inhabitants, their fellow creatures. At the same time, they would find their dependencies increased—in unhealthy rather than healthy ways—because of the new realities they themselves had introduced into the world.

The introduction of God's second speech is emphatic, with the addressee first in the Hebrew word order, **to the woman he said.** To her, God did not state a reason for the consequences announced, as he had to the serpent (v 14) and would to the man (v 17). This may be because she already had admitted she had been deceived, an admission of greater integrity than the man's had been.

God announced three consequences upon the woman for her part in the transgression. The first, God would cause to happen; **I will greatly *multiply.*** Most translators and commentators have treated the pairing of the two direct object nouns (ʿiṣṣābôn and ḥērôn) as a hendiadys, translating the first clause similarly to NIV's **your pains in childbearing.** As the masculine noun ʿiṣṣābôn occurs only twice more in the Hebrew Bible—in the next verse, and in Gen 5:29—this is worth checking further. Both in 3:17 and in 5:29, ʿiṣṣābôn refers to arduous, anxious, even anguished, toil for much diminished or uncertain rewards. It stands in contrast to the joyous, satisfying, and rewarding work God had appointed the human pair in the garden (1:28; 2:15). The second direct object, ḥērôn, means "conception" or "pregnancy." Because conception usually is not regarded as arduous toil, the two direct objects are connected only by the fact that God was multiplying both of them. Thus, we translate the first clause of God's speech to the woman, *I will greatly multiply your toil and your conception.* (We could argue this was two separate consequences, not one.)

137

The second clause, stating the second consequence, begins with a second reference to arduous toil, using a second noun, ʿeṣeb, similar in meaning to ʿiṣṣābôn, and from the same root. The verb here, from yalad, means "you will bear" or "you will produce." Because more than just the birth process itself is in view here, it is better to translate, **With labor/toil you shall produce children.** Because labor and producing children are linked in this second clause, many commentators and translations have linked **toil** and **conception** in the first clause, also, and have read the two clauses as essentially parallel in meaning. They are *not* parallel, partly because the first clause does not carry that meaning, as we have seen, and partly because the noun of the second clause, ʿeṣeb, is not connected with conception or pregnancy, but with having and raising children, generally.

How do we put all this together? First, the woman would conceive regularly, in a normal cycle of pregnancy, birth, nursing until weaning, pregnancy. Second, the **toil** of ʿiṣṣābôn and of ʿeṣeb, both, often is characterized by anxiety, or even anguish. We could translate "onerous labor" or "anxious labor" in both clauses. Third, God had assigned the humans to work in the garden (2:15), but that work had been anything but arduous, anxious, or anguished toil. Fourth, the woman's toil termed ʿiṣṣābôn God also assigned to the man (v 17), but the woman's toil termed ʿeṣeb God did *not* assign to the man; for the woman, it was associated with bearing children, more generally, not with conception. Finally, then, for this woman, as for childbearing women since, a major focus of her arduous, anxious, sometimes anguished toil would be bearing and raising children, but it certainly would not be limited to the sphere of children. Much of her work now would be toilsome.

A final note on this; the NIV's **with pain you will give birth to children** (similar to many others) is *not* an accurate rendering of the second clause. The idea that the process of childbirth *must* be excruciatingly painful to any (or every) woman giving birth, because God "cursed" Eve, simply is not in this verse.

The third clause is not necessarily a separate consequence of the alienation brought about by the human transgression. **And to your husband shall be your desire** is not God's announcement of a new state of affairs; the woman certainly had desired her husband before they ate of the forbidden fruit, and he had desired her. **Desire** or "longing" (tĕšûqâ), per se, is neutral. Genesis 4:7 speaks of the "desire" of sin to have Cain; because sin realized that desire, with all the evil consequences that narrative reports, the word carries a negative connotation there. On the other hand, in Song 7:10 the beloved speaks of her lover's "desire" toward her; there, the connotation is positive, because honorable human love is positive. The woman's **desire** for her husband could continue to be healthy and positive, without sin.

God's statement here follows immediately upon the two lines that speak of conception and producing children. Fretheim suggests (1994, 363) that the woman would continue to desire her husband sexually, despite the increased toil and danger of childbirth and its aftermath in their new life outside the garden. Also, though the final clause of God's speech to the woman suggests otherwise, it is possible God was warning the woman against allowing her desire to be twisted into evil, i.e., into a sinful and unhealthy desire to gain control over her husband.

The third consequence for the woman God expressed in the announcement, **and he [your husband] will rule over you.** This was not God's judicial punishment of the woman; rather it was (and is) the natural consequence of human sin. A key element of sin is the desire to control. The verb **rule over** (*māšal*) means exercising dominion or authority over another person or group (usually, a king over his people). We have seen already that man's rule over woman (or vice versa) is no part of the created order. Now, however, the man would take advantage of the woman's desire (and of the usually greater physical strength of the human male) to impose his will upon her. The joint-stewardship mandate, expressed in Gen 1:26-31 and confirmed in multiple ways in the more detailed account of ch 2, now would be usurped by the man, arrogating authority and control to himself alone. Of the three consequences God announced to the woman, this one has been by far the most tragic for women across the millennia.

■ **17** God's speech to the man was longer than his words to either the serpent or the woman. We adopt the suggested reading of *BHS* (see also Westermann 1984, 183), which requires only a repointing, *wĕlāʾādām*, **and to the man** (with the definite article), rather than *ûleʾādām*, **to Adam** (without the definite article), of the MT. The narrative clearly suggests that the narrator was reporting still from "inside" the narrative, rather than stepping "outside" to a later time and introducing the personal name prematurely. (See, however, Cassuto 1961, 166-67.) ***And to the man he said*** is the same word order as "to the woman he said," in v 16, emphasizing that God directed this speech specifically to the man.

God's speech to the man began with the indictment, **Because you listened to *the voice of* your wife,** paralleling God's indictment of the serpent in v 14, "Because you have done this." This phrase emphasizes that the man knew at least as well as (perhaps better than) the woman that this fruit was forbidden. He did not have the excuse of being deceived, either, since he had taken no part in the conversation and deliberately had watched her eat before he himself did. The man's listening to his wife was not his sin, per se. His transgression was listening in intentional silence to the conversation between woman and serpent, then taking the fruit at her suggestion without a word of demur.

Three times in this verse, and once each in vv 18 and 19, God used the verb "eat." It occurs twice in God's rehearsal of what the man had done, then in three successive lines, the last line of v 17, the single line of v 18, and the first line of v 19: *Because . . . you ate . . . "you shall not eat" . . . you shall eat* (v 17)

. . . you shall eat (v 18) *. . . you shall eat* (v 19). The great transgression was an act of eating; now all eating would reflect its disruption of the natural order.

God did not direct the first statement to the man's person, as with the serpent and the woman, but to the ground: **Cursed is the ground *with respect to you*** (v 17). The verb **cursed** (*'ārar*) is the same one God had used in addressing the serpent, and it carries the same basic meaning. English usage often equates "cursed" with "damned"; we may assume the person or thing "cursed" is consigned to destruction (if the curse, or the one cursing, is powerful enough). Though the Hebrew root *'ārar* often is translated "curse" or "cursed," this is not its meaning. (Hebrew has other ways of denoting something as "damned.") Rather, God was informing the man that **the ground** no longer would be in the relationship (***with respect to you***) of producing abundant and perfectly nutritious food for the human pair with minimal, but entirely satisfying, labor on their part. Henceforth, the ground would be changed in its relationship to the human family, from what it had been in the garden. It would be "banned" from the fullness of its former relationship with the human family, prevented from exercising fully its capacity for lavish, abundant yielding of food for human consumption. The original, creational largesse of the ground would be diminished.

This diminished relationship between the ground and the humans would result in ***arduous toil*** for the man. This noun (*'iṣṣābôn*) is the same one God had used in announcing the first consequence to and upon the woman (v 16). The woman's arduous toil perhaps would focus primarily on childbearing and childrearing, but would not be exclusive to the domestic scene. The man's ***arduous toil*** would focus on the vastly increased difficulty of wresting a livelihood from the soil. Neither would be exempt, and this new order of diminished returns for increased labor would not be temporary. It was to be for **all the days of** their **life.**

■ **18** God's announcement moved to details of the impact of the disruption of relationship between the ground and the man. The ground that had become less productive of food for human consumption now would ***cause thorns and thistles to spring up.*** Just as grains are much more prolific under human cultivation, so thorns, thistles, and many other "weeds" often grow very well in cultivated fields, or where the soil has been cultivated in the past. There is the danger they will choke out the precious seed-bearing grains (see Matt 13:7), yet if the farmer pulls them out from among the grain, he easily pulls up the growing grain, as well (see Matt 13:29).

A second impact of the ground's diminished capacity with respect to the humans would be a shift in their primary diet. God had given them to eat of the fruit of all the trees of the garden, except one (2:16-17); now they would **eat the plants of the field.** They had traded the pleasant work of the garden for a hardscrabble existence scratching the soil for relatively meager harvests of less nutritious grains. Since the transition to settled agriculture, this has been the lot of most of humankind.

■ **19** A vivid word picture is the conclusion to this first part of God's announcement concerning the diminished capacity of the earth, with respect to the humans; **In the sweat of your brow you will eat your food. Brow** is, more literally, **nose** or **nostril.** Preparation of the ground, seeding, weeding, harvest, and ingathering: all are labor-intensive, sweaty tasks. All, until very recently in human history, always have meant stooped backs, faces to the ground, and sweat running off the nose. In the economies based on subsistence agriculture that have dominated most of human history, none of these is optional; all are vital. From year to year, they are a matter of life and death.

Turning from the theme of wresting food from the soil, God moved to the matter of the man's new destiny, back to the soil. All this would occupy the man, God said, **until *your* return to the ground, *for* from it you were taken.** The object of the first preposition is an infinitive, a verbal noun, which is why we translate it as a noun. God had ***taken*** the ʾādām from the **ground** (ʾădāmâ; see 2:7), had sculpted the ʾādām a noble being, created in God's own image. From such a beginning in glory, then, God's climactic declaration, **For dust you are and to dust you will return,** presaged an ignominious departure, indeed.

Most have taken this last clause as God's announcement of death as the ultimate consequence of the transgression. However, the word "death" does not occur here, and God already had revealed that death would be the consequence of eating of the forbidden fruit (2:17). Thus, it may be that God meant the arduous toil just announced (to both woman and man) would continue until their return to the ground, i.e., until their death. The emphasis here, then, is not on death but on the unremitting nature of human toil.

Brueggemann on Gen 3

Perhaps this text runs especially to Jesus' understanding of anxiety (Matt. 6:25-33). Anxiety comes from doubting God's providence, from rejecting his care and seeking to secure our own well-being. Failure to trust God with our lives is death. To trust God with our lives is to turn from the autonomous "I" to the covenanting "Thou," from our invented well-being to God's overriding purposes and gifts. (1982, 54)

FROM THE TEXT

This text is emphatic that increased and arduous toil, even in birthing and raising children, is not God's curse upon women for the woman's sin. The newly arduous nature of much of our work, its anxiety, and even its anguish, is the result of the first transgression, but it is not a curse. Perhaps more important is that, even living within the diminished relationships their transgression

141

caused, they (and we) still are empowered to fulfill the divine mandate to "be fruitful and multiply, and fill the earth" (1:28, NRSV). They would produce new life. God's good creation, though in some ways diminished by their turning their backs on God, would continue. Sin and alienation cannot stop God's plans and purposes. That is amazing grace!

This text does teach that the arduous nature of much of our work is the consequence of our first parents' shattering of the relationships they had enjoyed in the garden. This does not mean, however, that we are prevented from alleviating human toil and hardship when we can. Many scientific and technological breakthroughs ease our toil in every area of life, they save lives, and they extend life spans. Far from being forbidden, these, too, are God's gracious provision, and for them we may be grateful.

In one sense, at least, we may take God's announcement to the woman, ***And to your husband will be your desire,*** as good news. A man and a woman still may experience mutual sexual desire and sexual intimacy, still may live together as "one flesh" (2:24). This relationship is strained in ways it was not previously, but the transgression did not break the bond the man had expressed as "bone of my bones and flesh of my flesh" (2:23).

In much of modern Western society, gender domination may work in either direction. Thus, we should examine the divine announcement, **he will rule over you,** within the context of the dominant ancient patriarchy before we attempt to understand its import for our own culture(s). It is imperative that we remember this is neither a divine judgment nor the divine sanction of man's domination of woman. This is announcement, and only that—announcement that sin had fractured the ideal relationship God intended for man and woman together. The man now would assume for himself alone the mantle of human dignity, and relegate the woman to second-class citizenship, to the status and role of servant in every phase and aspect of life. God's ideal for the man-woman relationship, however, remains the inclusive narrative of Gen 1:26—2:25. God's purposes did not, do not, and never will make peace with Gen 3:16.

This text reminds us that all gender domination—ancient or modern, secular or religious, in whichever direction—is massive evidence of human sin and sinfulness. Sin shattered God's intended equality, mutuality, and harmony in human gender relationship.

Yet sin's disruption is not the end, even in our present earthly life. God's redemptive purpose in Christ was and is the restoration of creation to (or even beyond) its original glory. First and most importantly, this means the restoration of fractured relationships, including gender relationships. We who already have begun to experience this redemption in Christ are privileged to practice relational restoration and display it before the world. In the footsteps of Jesus, who treated women as human equals worthy of male respect, in the spirit of Paul as expressed in Gal 3:28, the Christian family and the Christian church are the places where the bondage and servitude of woman ends. The Christian home and the local congregation are where men and women together teach our children absolute gender equality and mutuality, teach and model what it means for woman and man together to be ʾādām.

The redeemed are to live like the redeemed in every way possible. The church will practice gender equality consistently only when it is practiced consistently in the Christian home. The Christian home will practice it when it is taught in the church. We may need to work at it because we are out of practice. We may need to work at it because it is countercultural, both within and outside the church. In God's grace, though, it is both necessary and possible. Our daughters and our sons will benefit; our daughters and our sons will call us blessed.

It is possible to understand God's pronouncement, **Dust you are . . . to dust you will return,** as meaning humans are not immortal by creation. If that is true, their access to the tree of life may have been the vital sustenance of the first pair in the garden. Eating of the forbidden fruit, they forfeited access to the tree of life, and death began to work upon them. Being intrinsically mortal, they returned, finally, to the ground from which they had been taken. This, of course, must remain speculation, as the text is not explicit. What is not speculation, however, is the blessed hope of the resurrection of every mortal who believes in God's resurrection of Christ, the "firstfruits" (1 Cor 15:20-23).

5. Provisional Closure: Evicted and Exiled (3:20-24)

IN THE TEXT

■ **20** Verses 20 and 21 are two separate, short reports of the narrator, inserted between the end of God's pronouncement to the man and God's deliberation before the expulsion from the garden. We translate v 20, **Then the ʾādām called the name of his wife,** ḥavvâ **[Eve],** **because she was the mother of all living [humans].** Some commentators see a connection between the name ḥavvâ and the word **living** (ḥay). Hamilton suggests that the name reflects "a primitive form of the Hebrew verb 'to live' with medial w instead of y" (see Hamilton 1990, 205-6, for a detailed analysis of the name Eve). Some view this verse as a later editorial insertion, because at this time the woman was not yet a mother; that is possible. Others see the second verb as a "prophetic perfect" (a theological, not a grammatical, category), i.e., a future event presented as a certainty, as though it already had occurred. The NIV, **because she would become the mother of all the living,** appears to reflect this understanding. Von Rad interprets this verse as a pious expression of hope, "an act of faith" on the part of the man (1961, 93). Thus, many read this verse, which follows the sentence of death in v 19, as an indication of hope for the humans that life would continue, though they are under the sentence of death (see also

143

Fretheim 1994, 364). Others, including this commentator, however, find in the naming of the woman by the man the beginning of the man's subjugation of the woman to an inferior status and his "rule over" her (see v 16).

■ **21** The narrative of ch 2 portrays God as potter/sculptor (2:7, 19), as gardener (2:8), as surgeon (2:21), and as artisan (2:22). This verse presents an image of God as tailor. God made for the man and the woman *"tunics of skins"* (Cassuto 1961, 171, italics original). Genesis 2:25 notes the human pair were naked and unashamed; 3:7 reports they now knew they were naked and attempted to clothe themselves; this verse records God's solution to their problem. God's handiwork on their behalf is another grace note in a narrative filled with grace, as the divine response to human rebellion. Not only were these tunics of animal skins more durable and comfortable, physically, than were aprons of fig leaves. They also represented God's covering of the guilt and shame of their transgression, and real hope for a future in which God still cared for them.

The point often is made that this act involved the shedding of blood. Thus, God's provision of clothing can be regarded as the first sacrifice for sin. This may be a valid point, but if so, it is proleptic. The laws of sacrifice were not instituted until many centuries later.

■ **22** Verses 22-24 report God's deliberation, decision, and action as owner of the garden, following the human transgression. Verse 22 raises again the issue of the divine we/us; **Behold,** the *ʾādām* **has . . . become like one of us.** As noted in our discussion of 1:26, various commentators have taken this as the plural of divine majesty, as a reference to the divine council of (presumed) angelic ministers in the heavenly court, and/or as a prefiguring hint of the triune God. It is not impossible that all three implications were intended (or hinted) by the divine author who inspired the human author.

God's statement, **like one of us,** did not mean the human pair now really were like God in essence. Nor were they "God/gods," as the serpent had promised them. They were not even like one of the various ranks of angelic beings to whom God may have been speaking here. They now were like God and the angels *only* in **knowing good and evil,** and not even that in the ways they had imagined in listening to the serpent. Their knowledge was experiential, the paltry knowledge of alienation and negation gained through willful rebellion. Certainly it did not compare with God's creative wisdom on display in the narratives of chs 1 and 2 and celebrated, e.g., in Prov 3:13-20.

Having set forth the issue, God announced the course of divine action, **He must not be allowed to reach out his hand and take also from the tree of life and eat, and live forever.** The verb **take** (*lāqaḥ*) is the same used of the woman's first act in v 6, "she took." They had taken of the forbidden fruit; now they would not be allowed again to take of the fruit of the tree of life. If they had been allowed to continue eating of it, they would have lived **forever** in estrangement from God, from themselves individually, from each other, and

144

from the rest of creation. God's decision was an act of mercy, as well as the prerogative of the sovereign Lord of the garden.

Ephrem the Syrian on Gen 3:22

If Adam had rashly eaten from the tree of knowledge he was commanded not to eat, how much faster would he hasten to the tree of life about which he had not been so commanded? But it was now decreed that they should live in toil, in sweat, in pains and in pangs. Therefore, lest Adam and Eve, after having eaten of this tree, live forever and remain in eternal lives of suffering, God forbade them to eat, after they were clothed with a curse, that which he had been prepared to give them before they incurred the curse and when they were still clothed with glory. (Louth 2001, 101)

■ **23** Having stated the issue, God acted; **So *Yahweh Elohim sent* him** [them] **from the Garden of Eden.** *Sent* is the same verb (*šalah*) as in v 22: **Lest he** [they] ***send forth his*** [their] ***hand and take* . . . ,** God *sent* him [them] **from the Garden.** The play on words is intentional and powerful.

The last half of the verse is, literally, ***to serve [till] the ground which he*** [they] ***had been taken from there.*** The connection with the vocabulary of ch 2 is strong and intentional. The *ʾādām* had been taken from the ground, the *ʾădāmâ* (2:7), and placed in the garden ***to serve it and to guard it*** (2:15). The human vocation remained the same even after the human disobedience. As noted above (see on 3:16-19), the service/tilling now necessary to wrest a living from the soil outside the garden would be much more onerous than what they had been used to in the garden.

■ **24** The beginning of this verse, **So [God] *drove out the* ʾ*ādām,*** is not redundant. In this context, ***drove out*** (*gāraš*) is a much stronger verb than ***sent*** out (*šālah*, v 23). Even piling up English synonyms, "drove out/expelled/evicted," would not overstate its force. The repetition of the statement, but using the more forceful verb, is for the purpose of literary climax and also to emphasize there would be no possibility of return (Cassuto 1961, 173).

To prevent the evicted pair from attempting to return to the garden, either openly or by stealth, God stationed **cherubim and a flaming sword** to guard the entrance. ***To the east of the Garden of Eden*** suggests a single entry/exit to and from the garden. In antiquity, gardens usually were enclosed by walls or thick-set hedges.

The guards God posted, ***the cherubim and the flame of the sword flashing itself this way and that*** (i.e., "the sword of flame flashing every way") were two different entities. Artists often have rendered this scene with one of the cherubim holding the sword. This is not impossible, but the text does not actually say it, and the participial form of the verb, ***flashing itself this way and that,*** would seem to make it unlikely. In other OT passages, also, **cherubim** are depicted as guards of the divine presence, accompanying God and protecting God's sacred space, both within the tabernacle or temple (Exod 37:7-9; 1 Kgs 6:23-28) and without (Ezek 1:4-21; 10:1-22; 11:22-23). **The flame of the sword flashing itself** suggests a double protection of the garden: not only cherubim, but a sword; not only a sword, but cherubim, also.

The humans were driven from Eden where they had been placed; they were bereft of their previously happy home. What of the garden they had been appointed to serve and to guard (2:15)? Cassuto astutely observes that God did not leave the garden without protection. The humans having failed in fulfilling their mandate, God gave the mandate to others, to the cherubim (1961, 174). We may add that, on the scale of eternity, God intended the new arrangement to be temporary.

Bede the Venerable on Gen 3:24

The second Adam, Jesus Christ, points out that through the water of the bath of rebirth, the flickering flame—by which the cherubim guardian blocked the entry into paradise when the first Adam was expelled—would be extinguished. Where the one went out with his wife, having been conquered by his enemy, there the other might return with his spouse (namely, the church of the saints), as a conqueror over his enemy. (Louth 2001, 102)

FROM THE TEXT

The expulsion of the pair from the garden, to prevent them from eating of the tree of life, hardly was a decision of jealousy on God's part. If we take seriously at all the theology of the transcendent God, we must know God neither had nor has anything to fear from humans, or any other of God's creatures, whether "natural" or "supernatural."

Rather, that provision was in mercy. The first pair, just leaving the garden, had no idea of the depths of shame, degradation, and suffering their simple act of eating forbidden fruit would plunge their offspring into. The average citizen of the industrialized nations today cannot comprehend the miseries that ancient decision visits upon untold millions, on a daily basis, as the corruption bred by selfishness mars, maims, and kills innocents. Were such evil allowed to multiply unchecked by the death of perpetrators and victims alike, we would not need to wonder what hell is like. But death, together with the veiled promise to the woman in God's word to the serpent, gives us hope of redemption, of the reversal of the reign of death inaugurated by our first father and mother.

In v 24 is the last reference to the tree of life in Genesis. However, it is mentioned again in Ezekiel, and finally reintroduced in the last chapter of Revelation, where not one, but many specimens of the tree line the banks of the river of life flowing out from under the throne of God. There, the trees bear

146

twelve fruits on a monthly rotation, and are easily accessible to the citizens of the heavenly city.

Christians would do well to take cognizance of the great yearning, the *sehnsucht*, that gnaws at the heart of every human. In these verses, the culmination of the tragic story of the garden of Eden, lies its origin, and it haunts every son of Adam and daughter of Eve, whether or not we recognize it. We were made for better, and we know it. We have lost our birthright as human beings, Eden with its tree of life, and we know it. At least, when we will ourselves to stillness, to listening, and to reflection, we know it.

That is just the problem, however. This is such a great, visceral, and primeval sorrow that most of us will do anything to drown out the memory of Eden. We do not want to acknowledge that if we had been there, we would have made the same decision as our first father and mother. We resist confessing that we *have* made the same decision, many times, to be gods in our own right. We do not want to feel the pain of our loss, whether we don't know the way back, or whether, knowing, we continue to turn from him.

Yet, just here, too, can be a God-formed opportunity for genuine evangelism. Our Elder Brother has opened a way back; he has *become* the way back. It takes time and genuine caring to know people well enough to hear their experiences of this universal human yearning. If we will invest that time and that caring, many will discuss Jesus with us. Our ancient eviction from the garden need not be the end of the story, for anyone!

As we have noted at many points in this chapter, God's grace is infinitely greater than the alienation our first parents introduced into the world. God came to the garden again, even knowing what they had done. God persisted, to elicit even flawed confessions as a starting point for the renewal of relationship. Even in cursing the serpent, God had words of grace for the woman. Even in revealing that getting food now would be much harder, grace assured them they would eat. Even the reminder of death was a note of grace, partly because of the assurance that arduous toil would end someday, partly in the promise that the bringer of death would be done to death, himself. In that promise lay at least an intimation of death's eventual reversal. God's personal care to clothe the forlorn pair adequately was a mark of grace, of mercy, of tender loving-kindness. Finally, even the expulsion from the garden was an act of grace. Living forever without hope of redemption and restoration would not be paradise, but its opposite.

Deliberately, we have avoided using the term "the fall" in our discussion. Primarily, this is because no term or phrase for "fall" occurs in the chapter itself. A helpful principle of biblical theology is that we should avoid nonbiblical terms, unless we have good reason for introducing them. (We are not addressing here the practices of systematic theology.) Second, the term and concept of the fall has become so variously defined and applied in Christian thinking as to have become almost *un*helpful in many contexts. Finally, a fall too easily

3:20-24

147

is pictured as accidental, as "not our fault." From that perspective, our first parents did not fall. They rebelled and turned away from God willfully.

Augustine, Pelagius, and Wesley on Original Sin

Most Western Christians today follow Augustine's interpretation of Gen 3. Adam and Eve's eating of the forbidden fruit was the "original sin," in the sense of its being the first human sin. But that sin also infected all their descendants, and this infection also is called original sin. Every human being is born into, or born with, original sin and is incapable even of willing to follow God and choose righteousness.

Pelagius did not find Augustine's doctrine of original sin in the Bible. Moreover, he thought it led to the moral laxity he observed in fourth-century Western Christendom. Pelagius taught that the sin of our first parents was *not* passed on to their descendants. Each new human is born a tabula rasa, a blank tablet, able to choose good or evil individually. We all *do* choose evil, so God's grace still is necessary, from beginning to end, for our salvation.

John Wesley followed Augustine in his doctrine of original sin, though many of his opponents accused him of being Pelagian. Wesley, however, introduced (or perhaps revived) the doctrine of prevenient grace. In an age when many followed Calvin in thinking God's grace was only for the elect, those God had chosen beforehand, Wesley taught that God's grace works in *every* person. Prevenient grace awakens the sinner, freeing the will to respond (or not—it is each person's free-will choice) to God's saving grace.

3:20-24   As we have said of other issues in these chapters, the doctrine of original sin is not a clear teaching of Gen 3, taken by itself. The Western church, at least, has used other scriptures, notably Paul's interpretation in Rom 5, to find the doctrine in Gen 3. Judaism does not teach a doctrine of original sin, and the Eastern churches at least do not emphasize it as strongly as most in Western Christendom have done. (This is not to deny a doctrine of original sin, only to say that it would not have arisen from the narrative of Gen 3, taken by itself.)

II. LIFE BETWEEN THE GARDEN AND THE FLOOD (GENESIS 4:1—6:8)

Overview

The first three chapters of Genesis present three distinct but related accounts: ch 1, creation of the earth; ch 2, a more detailed picture of the creation of the first humans and their placement in the garden; ch 3, the first human sin and expulsion from the garden.

Chapter 4 directs our attention to life outside the garden of Eden. More specifically, it introduces the death of which God had warned the first pair, if they turned away from relationship with their maker and sustainer. The first pair were not the first to experience death, however. They were obliged to stand by as the sin they had passed on to their elder son motivated him to kill his brother, their second son. Adam and Eve (as we may call them now, but see comment on v 1) were the first to experience the *reality* of many parents' worst fear, the death of a child before their own passing.

Genesis 5 is the genealogy of Adam's descendants through the line of Seth, recorded through ten generations. Genesis 6:1-8 is a brief but vivid report that human life outside the garden became wicked, oppressive, and violent. Both the idyllic life of the garden and this grim and fearsome life outside the garden belong to the ancient past. The crisis of human sin brought upon the world the judgment of God in the form of the deluge; the world that God re-created after the deluge is the world that continues even today. These early chapters of Genesis teach several significant truths about the human condition, from the perspective of life between the expulsion from the garden and the judgment of the great flood.

Numerous links exist between these and the previous chapters. One obvious example we have alluded to already. In Gen 2:17, God warned against introducing death by eating of the forbidden fruit; in 3:19, God stated that death now had become an inescapable reality; in 4:8, the first physical death occurred in a most horrifying way, the murder of the younger son at the hand of his elder brother.

Adam and his son Cain both tilled, or "served," the soil; the Hebrew word is the same (ʿābad) in Gen 2:15; 3:23; 4:2; and 4:12. Both the first parents (3:6) and their son Cain (4:8) transgressed God's instruction and prior warnings. God confronted both the parents (3:8-13) and the son (4:9-10) about their transgressions, and announced to both serious consequences (3:16-19; 4:11-12, respectively). In 3:16, God promised the woman conception; 4:1-2 records the births of her first two sons. God evicted the first human pair from the garden (3:23) and exiled Cain to a life of wandering (4:12).

God's promise to Cain to avenge his death *fourteen*-fold, should someone murder him as he had murdered Abel (see on 4:15, below), and Lamech's boast that he would be avenged *seventy-seven* times (4:24), emphasize the symmetry of numerical repetition, especially of the number seven and its multiples, much as we have noted in the previous chapters. The personal names recorded in Cain's line, counting his parents, total *fourteen* (4:1, 17-22). Lamech was the *seventh* from Adam; in many ways he epitomized the arrogant wickedness that doomed the generation of the flood. In Seth's line, Enoch was the *seventh* from Adam (5:18); he epitomized righteousness in the generations before Noah. We could list many others. The Mesopotamian sexagesimal system (based on the number six and its multiples) also is well represented; and multiples of both sixes and sevens with ten also occur several times.

A. Murder, Civilization, and Polygamy (4:1-26)

I. Cain and Abel (4:1-16)

BEHIND THE TEXT

For a time, it was almost customary for commentators to explain this chapter in terms of the supposed rivalry between the settled agriculturalists and the nomadic herders of the ancient Near East. Cain, the farmer, killing Abel, the shepherd, represented the usual supremacy of the town-dwelling tillers of the soil. We must remember that virtually all who tilled the soil lived in "cities" (walled towns—all of them small, even tiny, by modern standards) or in unwalled villages (which many today would be unlikely to notice even as hamlets). This narrative becomes, then, an etiological tale to explain the normal hostility between "the desert and the sown," to use the classic phrase from a previous century.

It is true the settled populations usually exercised greater or lesser control over the pastoral nomads of western Asia, depending on the strength of a city-state or mini-empire at any given time. However, transgression of the peace and/or the spilling of blood were more likely to be initiated by the nomads, if they thought they could profit by it, and escape the retribution of the king in whose territory they committed the offenses. Yet here, Cain the farmer killed his brother Abel the shepherd without provocation, the reverse of the patterns this story is supposed to typify.

A more important objection to reading this story as an etiology is that the relationship between the farmer and the shepherd, historically in western Asia, has been one of symbiosis. Etiologies are supposed to explain "the way things are, and why they are." In western Asia throughout its history, the farmer and the shepherd have lived mostly in a state of mutual dislike and distrust, yes, but of mutual benefit, nevertheless, rather than of active hostility and aggression. If this were an etiology, it would be mostly false, and therefore useless.

On a "smaller" literary matter, we may note again the narrator's use of chiasm. (In literature, as in other arts, symmetry often contributes to the beauty of a composition, and chiasm is one kind of symmetry.) A particularly elegant example occurs in vv 2-5, with its three chiastic sentences (see Hamilton 1990, 219, though this translation and presentation are mine):

v 2   Now **became Abel** a herdsman of the flock,
       While **Cain became** a tiller of the ground.
v 3   . . . that **brought Cain** from the fruit of the ground . . .
v 4   and **Abel brought** . . . from the firstborn . . . and from . . .
       and Yahweh **showed regard for Abel and for his offering**
v 5   but **for Cain and for his offering** he **did not show regard.**

IN THE TEXT

■ **I**   This tragic narrative begins with a scene of domestic tranquillity and joy, the first human birth, ever. We may translate, ***Now the ʾādām knew* [lay with] *Eve, his wife, and she conceived, and gave birth to Cain. And she said, "I have fashioned a man[child] together with Yahweh."***

Here, the narrator used the generic noun, *the ʾādām*, rather than the personal name "Adam." This may be to remind the reader that this story of the first humans is also the story of human beings as a whole, both past and present.

The verb ***knew*** (*yādaʿ*) here refers to sexual intimacy. This verb occurs nine hundred fifty-six times in the Hebrew Bible, but in only about 8 percent of these does it refer to sexual intercourse. English translation cannot be satisfied with "knew," alone, without comment.

The report that Eve ***conceived, and gave birth*** replicates God's word to her in 3:16. God had promised that human sin would not bring about the end of the human species; the man would engender and the woman would bear children. This is the report, using the same two verbs, of the first instance of this promise being fulfilled. As the first, it became also the model, the formulaic expression of conception and birth (see, e.g., 4:17; 21:2; 29:32).

The narrator did not record a formal naming of the child but did report Eve's explanation. A noun *qayin*, spelled as **Cain** is spelled here, occurs in 2 Sam 21:16; it probably means "spear" (as something forged). Most scholars take the name **Cain** (*qayin*) to be derived from the root *qin*, and see in *qin* a cognate of Arabic *qyn*, to forge (a) metal, e.g., bronze or iron. Support for this derivation may occur in the name of one of Cain's descendants, Tubal-Cain; 4:22 lists Tubal-Cain as the teacher of those who work in bronze and iron (see Hamilton 1990, 220).

The verb in Eve's explanation of the name, *I have fashioned,* is from the root *qnh* (meaning "get," "acquire"). Most exegetes and translators take this as an example of popular etymology, and render Eve's words, "I have acquired [or: brought forth] a man from Yahweh." However, the preposition *ʾet* is difficult to understand as "from." Normally, it would have another preposition, *me*, as a prefix (lit., "from with"), though Hamilton does adduce one Hebrew example of *ʾet* without prefixed *me* (Gen 49:25), and an Akkadian phrase, *shamu itti* ("to buy from"), to support translating "from" (1990, 221). He translates this phrase, "I have acquired a man from Yahweh" (218).

4:1-2

Cassuto took both the roots *qin* and *qnh* as deriving from "one archaic root." Both have an original, underlying meaning of "fashion," "shape"; the name Cain and Eve's explanation of it make sense together (1961, 201-2). Thus, we render Eve's words, *I have fashioned a man[child] together with Yahweh.* If we are inclined to empathize with Eve, we may hear in her words a humble gratitude that God had kept God's promise of progeny, despite their rebellion in the garden. Eve's use of **man** (*ʾis*]) is unusual in referring to a child; Fretheim takes it as an echo of the man's joyful exclamation in 2:23 (1994, 372). There, the man said the woman had been taken out of the man; here, the woman (the same person, now called Eve) rejoiced that she had fashioned a man.

■ **2** The name of the second son, **Abel,** is given without reference to which parent gave him the name, and without explanation of its meaning, perhaps because none is needed. **Abel** is the noun *hebel*, used often in Ecclesiastes, and usually translated "vanity." (NIV translates "meaningless," e.g., Eccl 1:2.) Its underlying meaning, however, is "vapor," "mist," or "breath," conveying temporariness or brevity. Its metaphorical extension cannot, then, be "vanity," "meaningless[ness]"; our breath is hardly a meaningless vanity! Vapor, mist, and breath all are temporary, but not meaningless. Here, as in Ecclesiastes, we should understand *hebel* (**Abel**) as "brevity" or the like, a name perhaps suggesting parental prescience.

Inaugurating the chiastic arrangement noted above (Behind the Text), the author gave Abel's occupation first, then Cain's. Fretheim suggests this may have been to introduce the issue of primogeniture (1994, 372). Together, the brothers carried forward the Edenic mandate first given to their father (2:15). Abel was a *rō'ēh ṣō'n*, a keeper of sheep and goats. In this context, we may understand *rō'ēh* as a synonym of *šōmēr*, to watch/keep/tend/guard the earth and its nonhuman inhabitants. Fulfilling the other of the two mandates first given to their father, Cain was an *'ōbēd 'ădāmâ*, a tiller (lit., "server/servant") of the soil.

■ **3-5** Verses 3-5 report the first acts of worship in the Bible and God's responses to them. The text is quite straightforward here; to understand it, however, we must read carefully and consider these verses together. We may note, to begin, that the narrator assumes worship as a natural human act. Also, in naming Cain, Eve had mentioned Yahweh; we may take it the parents had introduced their sons to the worship of Yahweh. This occasion is pre-Mosaic, however, and the narrator said nothing about the forms or practices of worship. Anything beyond the fact that both Cain and Abel brought offerings to Yahweh would be speculation. The narrator's interest lay, not in the offerings, but in the responses the offerings evoked.

The opening phrase, **in the course of time** (v 3) (lit., ***And it happened, at the end of days***) emphasizes *in*determinacy; the length of time the two sons pursued their separate occupations before bringing these offerings is left unstated, deliberately.

Keeping to his chiastic structure, the narrator reported Cain's offering first; **Cain brought from the fruit of the ground an offering to Yahweh** (v 3), i.e., from the crops he had raised. Abel's offering was **from the first-born of his flock, even of their fat portions** (v 4a). The ongoing chiasm requires a reversal of the elements once again, and its last two lines present also an internal chiasm (AB:B'A'); **Now Yahweh showed regard for Abel and his offering, but for Cain and for his offering he [Yahweh] did not show regard** (vv 4b-5a).

The narrator did not say explicitly *why* God regarded Abel's offering favorably, but not Cain's. This has led some to suggest that Cain's problem was in bringing produce offerings, rather than animals—only animals are acceptable to God. This hardly can be the case. The brothers' worship came well before Moses' worship instructions for Israel; what was required under that system had no bearing on what Cain and Abel did or did not bring.

Moreover, the idea that the Mosaic system allowed only animal sacrifices does not arise from the Pentateuch, but from one NT text (Heb 9:22), which is not truly germane to this narrative. A sacrifice of the firstfruits was required from many of Israel's important crops. Meal offerings were prescribed, along with animal sacrifices. Furthermore, a family that could not afford to sacrifice a large animal was allowed to substitute doves; if they could not afford even

4:2-5

doves, they could bring a grain offering. *What* Cain brought was not the problem; God would have accepted Cain's produce as readily as Abel's animals.

If he did not say it outright, the narrator hinted at why God did not regard Cain's offering with favor. Cain brought *from the fruit of the ground.* Nothing is said about firstfruits, the choicest of the produce, or anything of the kind. By contrast, Abel brought, not only *from the first-born of his flock,* but *even of their fat portions.* In highlighting Abel's care in choosing the **fat portions** for his offering, and passing over the issue in silence when reporting Cain's offering, the narrator at least implied a difference. Abel's preparation was intentional and careful; Cain's was casual and lacked intentionality. Silence is not proof, but the inference is plausible.

The narrator did not say, either, how Cain discovered God's rejection of his offering, but did choose directness in reporting Cain's reaction to God's response. ***So it was very hot to Cain, and his face fell*** (v 5*b*) is a wooden but literal translation. The Hebrew verb we translate ***hot*** often records anger. However, we probably should understand the narrator here as saying Cain was depressed, rather than angry, because of the second clause, ***and his face fell.*** Certainly, Cain was disappointed in God's rejection of his offering; his disappointment may have deepened into depression. Nothing is said yet, though, of Cain being resentful toward Abel; that came later.

■ **6** In the meantime, God took the initiative and spoke to Cain; God's rejection of Cain's offering was not a rejection of Cain himself. God desired, and offered, a continuing relationship with Cain. God began with two simple rhetorical questions, ***Why did you get angry, and why did your face fall?*** These questions indicate God already knew the reason for Cain's negative reaction, and it would be easy for the reader to see them as rebuke, asked in a scolding tone. However, their true goal, indicated by God's next words (v 7), was to engage Cain, to show him God's desire to restore their relationship. We also may see in them God's concern for Cain's emotional health.

■ **7** Hamilton has described v 7 as "one of the hardest verses in Genesis to translate and to understand," largely because of several vocabulary, grammatical, and syntactical issues (1990, 225). No wonder, then, that one encounters a variety of translations. We will hope to show that the following translation (with slight expansion for clarity, indicated by brackets) accounts for the difficulties and renders the verse faithfully: ***Is it not [the case that] if you do well, [you yourself will] stand firm/be upstanding? But if you do not do well, sin is a croucher at [your] door, and to you shall be its desire [i.e., the croucher shall desire to have you], but you can/may/must master it.***

The first two clauses together are a question to Cain, of the "if . . . then" variety: Do you not see/understand that if you do well (protasis), [then] . . . ? (apodasis). The "if" is clear; the "then" is debated. There is no question that *śĕʾēt* is an infinitive from *nāśāʾ*, "to lift up"; the questions concern only its specific meaning here. Suggestions are plentiful, but the second "if . . . then" pair confirms our translation of the first.

The protases of the two pairs contrast; therefore, the two apodases contrast, also:

> *If you do well,*   *but if you do not do well,*
> *[You will] stand*   *sin is a croucher*
> *firm/be upstanding.*   *at [your] door.*

A key question, then, is what did God mean by the two protases, ***If you do well . . . if you do not do well***? We have seen already that one suggested answer is not likely, that for God to have regard for Cain, Cain needed to bring the proper offering. This conclusion is strengthened here. The narrator's contrasting of Cain's and Abel's offerings (vv 4b-5a), God's introduction of this attempted engagement with Cain by way of the two rhetorical questions, and now the alternatives introduced by these two contrasting protases—all tend toward another conclusion. Cain's problem was not his offering, but his attitude in bringing it. If Cain would accept God's words as the positive instruction they were, he could remain in control of himself (***stand firm***), and restore his strained relationship with God.

The choice was Cain's; he retained both the capacity and the freedom to respond positively to God's counsel. The second protasis, thus, was a serious warning. If Cain chose to reject God's good counsel, **sin** (*ḥaṭṭāʾt*) would continue to crouch (*rōbēṣ*) at the door of his heart and mind, a predator waiting in ambush for the split second of its prey's inattention. If Cain allowed it, sin would bring him down.

The translation issue of the second part of v 7 is twofold. First, the subject of the short clause is a feminine noun, **sin** (*ḥaṭṭāʾt*), while the participle that follows, *rōbēṣ* (translated as **crouching** in the NIV), is masculine. Second, the pronominal suffixes of v 7b, ***its desire, you must rule over it,*** both are masculine; their antecedent, then, should not be the feminine noun **sin** (*ḥaṭṭāʾt*). Reading *rōbēṣ* as a predicate nominative, ***croucher*** (as we have done), resolves both these issues. The predicate nominative need not agree with *ḥaṭṭāʾt* in gender, and the masculine noun *rōbēṣ* is the antecedent of both masculine pronoun suffixes, ***its*** [the croucher's] ***desire*** and ***you must rule over it*** [the croucher].

The narrator's use of *ḥaṭṭāʾt* here is the first biblical occurrence of any word for "sin." This noun is derived from the verb *ḥāṭāʾ*, meaning "to miss a goal or mark," "go wrong." The statement, ***sin is a croucher*** (*ḥaṭṭāʾt rōbēṣ*), images sin as a powerful predatory animal. Fretheim's observation is trenchant, "The reality of temptation is portrayed as something active, close at hand, predatory, eager to make inroads into Cain's life; it can consume his life, take over his thinking, feeling, and acting" (1994, 373).

The vocabulary and sentence structure of God's warning to Cain parallel those of God's word to the woman (Cain's mother) in Gen 3:16b: ***And to your husband shall be your desire*** [*tĕšûqâ*], ***but he shall rule*** [*māšal*] ***over*** *you* (3:16*b*); ***And to/for you shall be its*** [the *rōbēṣ,* i.e., sin's] ***desire*** [*těšûqâ*], ***but you can/may/must rule*** [*māšal*] ***over it*** (4:7*b*).

God did not sentence Eve to succumb to her husband's domination through her desire for him; rather, God informed her that "her" man would rule over her as one consequence of their sin. Here, before Cain could go further with his angry response to God's decision, God encouraged him to take stock. Cain was not too far gone. He *could* master the sin that desired to master him, if he would; to avoid the imminent disaster, he *must* master it.

In this commentator's opinion, the point is emphasized by the fact that three translations are possible here; all three are grammatically and syntactically correct: ***you may rule over [master] it; you can rule over [master] it; you must rule over [master] it.*** In such cases, it is not unusual for the Hebrew author to intend more than one meaning in the one construction. God was telling Cain it lay within the realm of possibility for him to master the sin that crouched at his door and desired to destroy him (***you may***). In addition, God was telling Cain he had the power and the resources (including a renewed relationship with God) to master the crouching sin, if he would use them (***you can***). Finally, God was telling Cain it was necessary for him to master the sin (**you must**), else it would be ready at any time to spring upon him and destroy him; it certainly would do so eventually, unless Cain acted first to destroy its power over him.

Verse 7 thus powerfully conveys God's instruction as well as God's warning to Cain, an invitation to listen to God as well as a reminder of the power of sin, God's offer of a restored relationship as well as the real possibility of further alienation and estrangement. It was now up to Cain to decide and to act. This section of the narrative ends with the haunting question present, not in the text, but in the mind of the reader, "*Would* Cain master it?"

■ **8** Given the narrator's silence, it is reasonable to conclude Cain did not respond to God's counsel, nor to the offer of renewed relationship. Moving to the next scene with the narrator, then, a natural first translation of this verse would be, ***Then Cain said to Abel his brother. And it happened while they were in the field that Cain rose up against Abel his brother and slew him***. The MT does not have NIV's, **Let's go out to the field;** it appears Cain's words have dropped from the text. Most versions, including the ancient Greek (LXX) and the (Aramaic) Targums, have inserted them, or a similar reading. One version that does not insert Cain's words is NASB, but its translation, "Cain told Abel his brother," does not solve the problem, either. What did Cain tell his brother?

Hamilton translates this first clause, "Cain was looking for Abel his brother" (1990, 228); Cassuto has it, "Cain appointed a place where to meet Abel his brother" (1961, 205). Both readings are supported by Arabic and Ethiopic usages of the root ʾmr and, as one could expect, of Akkadian *amaru,* "to see." Hamilton observes that the usual Hebrew meaning arose "through the factitive sense 'to show,' hence 'to speak'" (1990, 230). Hamilton's rendering presents Cain as looking for Abel in the field, where he naturally would have expected Abel to be looking after his flock. Cassuto understood Cain to have made an appointment with Abel in the field. If Cain originally wanted only to talk with Abel, then his jealousy overpowered him during their conversation. Alternatively, Cain may have made the appointment with the express purpose of killing Abel.

It is important to note that this scene is set, not in the place of worship, but **in the field** (*śādeh*). This was the place of Abel's vocation, though probably not of Cain's. In this and similar contexts, Hebrew *śādeh* denotes the open steppe-land, the place of pasture for domesticated stock, such as Abel's sheep and goats, and the dwelling-place of many wild creatures, both predators and prey.

Without further detail, in a matter-of-fact way, the narrative reports that while the brothers were **in the field, Cain rose up against Abel his brother and slew him.** Throughout this narrative, the narrator reports not one word of conversation between the brothers, a telling detail of omission.

The verb **rose up** (*qûm*, "to rise," "to stand") here conveys the idea of standing up as an adversary. The verb *hārāg* ("slay," "murder") is the usual verb used when referring to murder, the intentional killing of another human by a private individual without the sanction of a judicial sentence or a state of war. In this context, the author intended the reader to know Cain's act was deliberate, not accidental. By contrast, Moses may not have intended to kill the Egyptian overseer when he struck him; the verb used there is *nākâ*, which means to strike or smite, either with or without the intent to kill (Exod 2:12). In the Decalogue, the prohibition against killing is expressed with *rāṣaḥ* (Exod 20:13; Deut 5:17); it includes also accidental manslaughter.

Whether Cain went to Abel already having decided to kill him, or his hurt turned to rage as they talked, Cain did murder Abel; premeditated or not, his act was intentional. The silence of the text at this point suggests Cain merely walked away from his brother's fallen body; it hints neither at remorse over his crime, nor even at any attempt to cover it up. We should note that not only did Cain commit the first murder, but this also was the first human death. Did Cain do nothing because he did not know what to do with a corpse? We should note, too, that though God had warned of death (2:17), and had revealed death as the new destiny (3:19), human death first was introduced into the world through human violence.

■ **9** The rest of this narrative (4:9-16) focuses on the conversation between God and Cain; this time Cain deigned to answer. We should note, also, the similarities with the earlier scene of 3:8-19. Just as God had done in speaking to Cain's parents, God now initiated conversation with the offender, gave him an opportunity to confess his deed at his own volition, and announced the consequences to the defiant transgressor.

God's opening question to Cain is both direct and brief, **Where is Abel, your brother?** It also is very similar to God's earlier question to the man in 3:9, "Where are you?" The placement of the word **your brother** at the end of this question conveys emphasis; depending on the sentence, Hebrew syntax can convey emphasis by placing an element at the beginning, out of its usual order or, as in v 9, at the end of the sentence, climactically. Abel was not "just" another human; he was Cain's *brother.*

As with God's earlier questioning of Cain's parents (Gen 3:9, 11, 13), God's question was not about Abel's whereabouts; God knew that. Cain also needed to be brought face-to-face with the seriousness of what he had done. God's question was the same extension of grace to Cain as the earlier question had been to his parents, an opportunity to tell the truth and confess his sin, beginning the process of forgiveness and restoration.

Cain's response, though, was markedly different from those of either of his parents. They had acknowledged their transgression, albeit reluctantly and with disappointing attempts to shift blame onto others. In their son, their evasions now became a straight-out lie, **I do not know!** But Cain knew exactly where he had left Abel's lifeless form lying in the field; that scene never would leave his waking mind for long. Cain's defiant lie, spoken to God's face, was evidence he now had been completely mastered by sin, as God had warned him (v 7). We also may understand **I do not know!** as meaning, "I do not acknowledge my actions." Cain rejected the opportunity God had given him to confess his sin, and be restored.

Not only did Cain lie to God. He followed the lie with his own sneering counter-question, curt, rude, insulting, and in-your-face: **The watcher-of-my-brother am I?** We will understand Cain's tone if we paraphrase, "Am *I* my grown brother's babysitter?!" Von Rad also saw Cain's retort as "an impertinent witticism" and paraphrased it, "Shall I shepherd the shepherd?" (1961, 102). Since the verb is a participial form, the nominative pronoun "I" (*'ānōkî*) is necessary here; it is last in Cain's question for emphasis.

We have translated "watcher" (*šōmēr*, a participial form of *šāmar*, "keep, guard, observe") to avoid suggesting Cain had any kind of legal responsibility for Abel, as "keeper" or "guardian" could imply. In that sense, the answer to Cain's question was, "No." He was not responsible to oversee or supervise Abel, in his person or in his work.

Following on from this, though, it may be that Cain's insulting retort also was an insinuation of blame upon God. Through the rest of the OT, God often is depicted as the keeper of Israel (e.g., Num 6:24; Ps 121). If God had failed as Abel's keeper, God was responsible and could not blame Cain (see Fretheim 1994, 374).

In a broader sense, though, Cain was—or should have been—his brother's "watcher, preserver, protector." Far from murdering him, Cain should have been the first to come to Abel's aid when Abel was threatened with danger, or when he "merely" needed a helping hand. In that sense, every human is every other human's keeper, to the extent our own circumstances and abilities will allow. God was justified in asking the question; Cain's throwing it back in God's face was arrogant in the extreme.

■ **10** God was not to be put off, however, and now assumed the role of judge, as earlier God had judged the serpent (3:14-15). On that earlier occasion, too, God had asked Cain's mother, "What is this you have done?" (3:13). The question God now put to Cain was shorter by one word in Hebrew, thus a bit more direct and forceful. We may characterize it as a rhetorical question with the force of an exclamation, **What have you done?**

God's knowledge of Abel's murder is evident in the following statement, which functions as God's indictment of Cain, ***The voice of your brother's blood is crying out to me from the ground.*** Many versions and commentators translate the first word, *qôl*, as an interjection, **Listen!** This usage makes sense here, and does occur elsewhere; Isa 52:8 and Song 5:2 are clear examples. However, the image of shed blood crying out also is a biblical metaphor, as in Job 16:18 (see Hamilton 1990, 231, n. 8). This is a dramatically charged moment in the narrative.

God became directly involved because the blood spilled by a murderer cries out for justice. Moreover, God the righteous judge hears the cries of all who suffer violence, or any kind of injustice (see, e.g., Gen 18:20; Exod 3:7; 22:21-24). We may see this crying out as simultaneously a cry of accusation, a cry for help, and a cry for legal action against the murderer. No human had observed the murder; no human yet had discovered Abel's fallen body; mechanisms for bringing murderers to justice were not yet in place; despite all that, this narrative assures the reader that violence and injustice do not go unnoticed by the Creator.

The **ground** (*'ădāmâ*) out of which God had formed the first human (2:7) now had been forced to receive innocent blood, the life of the first murder victim. The ground was a victim, too, and thus a key witness; Cain hardly could have expected it to be an accessory, helping him cover up his murder of his brother. (Compare Job's plea to the "earth" not to cover his blood, Job 16:18.) The later Mosaic legislation declared that the blood of an innocent victim "pollutes" the land, and cannot be atoned except by the blood of the murderer (Num 35:33). The cry of the ground for legal action may be reflected in Heb 12:24, with its reference to the blood of Jesus "that speaks a better word than the blood of Abel."

Behind all this lies the important truth that God places incalculable value upon human life. Blood is the seat of life (Lev 17:11), and life is God's gift of grace to all. Only God possesses "property rights" over life, but God desires to preserve life, not take it. God initiated justice for the slain brother Abel, not only because no other agent was available, but because God loves, looks out for, and grieves the death of, God's human creation, individually as well as collectively.

■ **11-12** Having rendered the verdict of guilty, God passed a weighty sentence upon Cain; it begins, ***Cursed are you*** (v 11). Once again, we see an altered syntax for emphasis; this time, the participle is first in the clause. This also is the first time the divine pronouncement of curse upon a human is found in the Genesis narrative. Previously, God had decreed the serpent "cursed" from the other creatures, i.e., banned from any positive contact with them (3:14). God had pronounced the ground "cursed" for the sake of, or with respect to, the human (3:17); it would be diminished in its capacity to produce food for humans. Now, Cain himself was ***cursed,*** or banned, **from the ground,** from his means of livelihood. Cain had been a tiller of the soil; now he no longer would enjoy even its diminished post-Eden productivity. (See comments on 3:14, 17, above.)

God's sentence upon Cain established reciprocity for his crime, what some in theology and ethics call retributive justice. Cain previously had gained his livelihood from the soil. Cain now had spilled his brother's lifeblood into the soil. Henceforth, the soil no longer would yield its life-giving bounty to Cain, the life-taker. The text expresses this reciprocal change in relationship very clearly, when we translate it in its Hebrew word order, ***And now, cursed/banned are you*** from the ground, which opened its mouth to receive ***the blood of your brother*** from your hand. (NIV's **and driven from** is an anticipatory expansion; these words are not in the Hebrew text.) Once again, sentence structure makes its contribution to meaning; **from your hand** is last in the sentence for emphasis. Cain had caused the soil to drink his brother's blood; unknowingly he had, by that same act of murder, killed his own relationship with the ground.

Commentators differ on the clause, **the ground, which opened its mouth to receive *the blood of your brother* from your hand** (v 11). Some (e.g., Cassuto 1961, 219-21) regard this as one of a number of biblical narratives intended to "demythologize" the polytheism of Israel's Canaanite neighbors; this narrative is a move to deprive Mot, "Death," of divine status. Here, though, the text reflects, not Canaanite polytheism, but Israel's revealed creation theology. If we personify the ground here, as the text does invite us to, we should say, rather, that in this early time the ground was not a greedy Sheol, but a grieved, betrayed creation partner. Personified, the soil sorrowed at having to accept Abel's blood, and was relieved it no longer would have to ***give its strength*** (v 12) to Cain, Abel's brother and murderer.

God's speech to Cain concludes with another word of judgment: ***A wanderer and a fugitive shall you be upon the earth***. **Wanderer** translates Hebrew *nāʿ*, an active participle from *nûaʿ*, meaning "quiver, waver, tremble, totter," thus, by analogy, "wander, be/become a vagabond." It describes movements as small as the soundless utterances of Hannah's lips in her fervent pleas for a child (1 Sam 1:13) and as massive as the reeling of the earth (Isa 24:20). Used of the habitual wandering of a human, its focus is on the seeming aimlessness of one's journeying; the observer can discern neither purpose nor destination for the restless moving about. This differs from the movements of nomads, whose migrations have purpose and follow the rhythms of the seasons.

The second noun, **fugitive** (*nād*), is from the root *nûd* ("wander"); its semantic range is essentially the same as the first. This usage (a pair of synonyms, or two dissimilar nouns, connected by "and" that together express a meaning not conveyed by either one separately) is called hendiadys and is fairly common in many languages. Not every occurrence of two nouns connected by "and" is a hendiadys, but its occurrence in biblical Hebrew is an evidence of Hebrew's relative lack of adjectives. **A restless wanderer** reflects the meaning well, as does "a wandering fugitive" (Hamilton 1990, 229). Translations such as "a fugitive and a wanderer" (NRSV) and "a vagrant and a wanderer" (NASB; Cassuto 1961, 216) are not wrong. In not reflecting the character of the phrase as (probably) a hendiadys, though, they may leave the modern reader with a sense of unnecessary repetitiveness, a thought that would not have occurred to the ancient hearer/reader.

■ **13-14** We will understand Cain's response in one of two ways, depending on how we translate the short opening sentence (v 13). Are we to take Cain here as lodging a lament/protest or as agreeing with God?

Most versions and commentators agree in substance with the NIV, **My punishment** [*ʿāwōn* means "iniquity," "guilt," "punishment"] **is more than I can bear** (from the verb *nāśāʾ*, meaning "carry," "lift"), taking Cain as lamenting and protesting the severity of God's judgment. Beginning at least as early as the fifth century, however, some Jewish exegetes have taken these words of Cain as agreement with God's assessment, and repentance for his fratricide (*Gen. Rab.* 22.13). Whether or not he took his cue from his acquaintance with Jewish exegesis, Luther translated, "My sin is too great for me to be forgiven" (as quoted in Westermann 1984, 309). Westermann also referenced Cassuto (1961, 216) who translated, "My iniquity is too great to be forgiven" (not introducing Luther's extraneous "for me"). Westermann's objection to this translation does not seem cogent; he says only that Hebrew *ʿāwōn* refers both to "sin" and to the "punishment" of sin, which is true, but not germane. Hamilton recognized another issue, noting, "The text does not explicitly record why [Cain] felt God was overreacting" (1990, 233). Hamilton, however, does not follow up this point.

A stronger support for translating with Luther, Cassuto, and some others is a point Cassuto noted but did not develop (1961, 222). When *ʿāwōn* is used with the verb *nāśāʾ*, as here, it means the sin, the iniquity, is lifted up and carried away, i.e., is forgiven (see Exod 34:7; Num 14:18; Ps 32:5, passim).

If we accept this understanding of Cain's first statement (*gādôl ʿăwōnî minnĕśōʾ*), we may translate the two verses together, **Then Cain said to Yah-**

weh, "*My iniquity is too great for forgiveness* (v 13). *Behold, you have driven me today from the face of the ground, and from your presence I shall be hidden* [or: *I shall (seek to) hide myself*], *and I shall be a wandering fugitive on the earth. Moreover, it shall be that everyone finding me shall seek to slay me*" (v 14).

Neither this translation nor the "traditional" one reflects Cain as actually repenting of his monstrous sin. That is an inference of the ancient rabbis, not a statement of the text itself, and it may or may not be accurate. Whether Cain was sorry for what he had done to Abel, or only sorry for himself, the text simply does not allow us to say. This translation does reflect, though, what we think to be the case: Cain at least came to understand the enormity of his offense, acknowledging in his first short statement the justice of God's sentence.

Cain's next two statements (v 14) represent his understanding of how his new status as *a wandering fugitive* (the climax of God's sentence, v 12) would impact him. We should not take the first, *you have driven me today from the face of the ground,* in its most concrete sense. Unless he embarked upon the water, Cain always would be bodily upon *the face of the ground* until the day of his death. But now the ground would withhold its strength despite any and all efforts Cain might put forth. Cain had addressed himself to *the face of the ground* in his work of tilling the soil; from now on, such efforts would be futile. There would be no point in staying in one place long enough to try for a crop, for no crop would be forthcoming.

The verb of Cain's second statement is in the *Niph'al* stem, that is, it may be either a passive or a reflexive form. If we translate it as a passive, we read, *From your presence I shall be hidden.* This would represent, not a statement of existential reality, but Cain's own view that his sin had driven him from God's effective presence, as it had driven him from fruitful interaction with the soil.

Translating the statement as a reflexive yields, *From your presence I shall [seek to] hide myself.* This could indicate Cain was not truly repentant of his crime, only resigned to his punishment. However, while this statement may be suggestive, it does not constitute proof. We have yet another option; this second statement could read, "From your presence I shall hide myself." While *we* know hiding from God is not possible, we cannot know what Cain thought at this time. Cain may have imagined he really could hide from God.

As we have seen at other places in the text, we may not have to choose among these options. This is Cain's statement; it well may represent his simultaneous assumption that he would be hidden from God (passive), and his determination that he would try, and would hope to succeed, in hiding himself from God (reflexive). There is no inherent contradiction.

Cain's final statement, *Moreover, it shall be that everyone finding me shall seek to slay me* (v 14), was his voicing of a natural fear, not a reflection upon what God had told him, for it was no part of God's sentence upon Cain that he would die immediately for his crime. (This is quite an astonishing fact, given the later emphasis in Israel's law that murder is punishable by death; see further in From the Text, below.) First, we ought to note the pointed irony of the narrative here; the verb (*hārag*) is the same at both places (vv 8, 14): the murderer is terrified of being murdered! Moreover, the sentence structures climax in parallel fashion. The narrative of Cain's crime ends with the report, "and [he] slew him" (KJV); Cain's expression of his fear ends with "shall slay *me*" (KJV, emphasis added). The narrator did not want the reader to miss the point.

Many have raised the obvious question: whom did Cain fear? Did other humans exist at this time, besides Cain and Abel's parents, or was Cain's fear for the future? Intriguing as the question is, every answer must remain tentative, because every answer begins with assumptions that may or may not prove to belong to the realm of historical reality, should our knowledge increase.

Taking the text on its own terms, we may say it intends us to understand Cain as being fearful of the retribution of Abel's relatives, whoever they were, or would be. This anticipates (some say, reflects) the pentateuchal legislation regarding the responsibility of the kinsman (*goʾel*) to bring the murderer to justice, even including the right to carry out the execution himself, under certain circumstances (see, e.g., Num 35:19-21). The irony of which we spoke, above, obviously echoes here, as well. Every relative of Abel was or would be, ipso facto, Cain's relative too and would stand in exactly the same relationship to Cain as he had to Abel! (No one in that age would have envisioned a female relative seeking to kill Cain.) Cain feared he would be forever banned from making himself known to a human male, forced always to be in hiding or prepared to step into hiding instantly.

Of course, not "everyone" could kill Cain; he could die only once. But everyone Cain would meet could try. Cain feared everyone *would* try; hence, our translation, **everyone** [*kōl*] **finding me shall seek to slay me.**

■ **15** The first part of God's response is a formal pronouncement, **Therefore, anyone slaying Cain, he [Cain] shall be avenged fourteen times over.** Several points require comment. We should understand **therefore** (*lākēn*) as an elliptical expression, meaning, "Because I have not pronounced this as a part of your sentence, and to allay your fears on the matter . . ." This understanding is supported by God's next three words, **anyone slaying Cain,** i.e., "anyone who slays/murders *Cain,*" not "anyone who slays/murders *you.*" While initially addressed to Cain, this is a formal declaration ultimately intended for anyone and everyone; God expressly forbade Cain's execution by any human hand.

The next verb is passive; its subject is Cain. The Hebrew text reads **he** [meaning Cain] **shall be avenged** (not NIV's **he** [meaning Cain's killer] **will suffer vengeance**). In this context, to **be avenged** (from the root *nāqam*) is to have a suitable punishment visited upon one's murderer. Mendenhall points out that *nāqam* "refers to executive rather than judicial action, but it is always either clearly based upon some sense of legitimacy or is actually the prerogative of the divine world which of course normally is delegated to the political institution" (1974, 76-77). God was warning any and all who would contemplate **slaying Cain** that God "personally" would see to it that Cain was **avenged;** God would visit justice upon the murderer.

We come now to the word usually translated "sevenfold," or the like. Grammatically, it actually means "two sevens," obviously, **fourteen** (*šibʿātayim*). Of course, we cannot take its meaning as numerically literal; Cain's killer, should anyone be so bold, could not be executed fourteen times. In addition, even could it be possible, such a sentence would violate the principle of lex talionis, better known as "an eye for an eye." True, the first enunciation of this principle occurs later in Scripture (Exod 21:23-24), but we may expect God to have abided by God's own principles of basic justice before teaching them to Israel. (Lex talionis never *required* "an eye for an eye," and sometimes did not *require* even "a life for a life." It limited retribution to *no more* than the injury inflicted.)

So what did God mean by saying Cain would **be avenged fourteen times over**? Obviously, God did not want Cain executed for his crime of fratricide, or Cain would have been dead already. God considered sufficient the punishment already imposed: Cain's banishment from enjoying any longer the fruitfulness of the earth he had tilled; his soon-to-begin life as a wandering fugitive upon the earth. God did not want Cain's violence to beget more violence.

This suggests that the punishment of Cain's slayer, had anyone committed that further crime, would not have been immediate death, either. But God's punishment of that murderer also would have been fitting, as was Cain's. **Fourteen** is twice seven; seven is the principal biblical number of perfection. God was saying, in effect, "I am the sovereign to whom belongs the right of avenging murder. You can trust me to decide the perfect sentence (seven); in fact, you can trust me to decide the sentence with 'double perfection' (twice seven). Leave this to me; do not take it upon yourself!"

We should translate the last part of v 15, **Then Yahweh appointed for Cain a sign, that anyone finding him <u>would</u> not strike him.** Most translations and commentators have **a mark on Cain** (as in the NIV), without comment (the NASB does translate "appointed a sign for Cain," but then includes a textual note, "or *set a mark on*"). The Hebrew preposition is *le* (**for**); the sign was not necessarily "on" Cain but **for** Cain. However, in many contexts, the first verb (*sîm*) does mean "set, put, place" upon someone or something. Thus, the text does not allow us to rule out a mark upon Cain's person. But at the same time the Hebrew preposition does not permit us to *insist* the **sign** was a bodily mark of some kind.

The final verb in this clause, **strike** (*hakôt*), is from *nākâ*, meaning "strike," not "kill" or "murder," though of course when one person strikes another, the result can be the death of the one struck (see, e.g., Exod 2:12). It is an infinitive; thus, the emphasis is not outward toward any potential striker of Cain. Of course that is implied, but if that had been the focus of the clause, the verb form would have been jussive, "anyone finding Cain *should* not [may not, does not have permission to] strike him." As an infinitive, this is God's *promise* to Cain, **Anyone finding him would not strike him.** No one would murder (*hārag*) Cain, as he had murdered his brother.

Furthermore, Cain would not have to worry for the rest of his life that others would beat him (*nākâ*), but stop short of killing him. God's judgment was just—Cain already had acknowledged that—but now Cain, too, was assured (as his parents had been) that God also tempers justice with mercy, with tender concern for the sinner despite the magnitude of the sin.

■ **16** The conclusion of this narrative unit begins, **So Cain went out from the** Lord's **presence.** As the text has invited us to think of this as a face-to-face encounter between God and Cain, so this statement marks the end of the encounter. At a deeper level, Cain's new life as a wandering fugitive would be a continuous fleeing: from God; from those of his relatives who would reproach him, though they could not beat him or kill him; even from the guilt and shame that never would be absent from his own mind and heart.

In view of God's sentence that Cain would be a wandering fugitive, how can the text now say he **lived in the land of Nod?** This is a play on words; **Nod** is a place name from the same Hebrew root (*nûd*) God and Cain both had used to describe Cain's new status (the adjective *nād*, vv 12, 14). At a minimum, such a name for Cain's subsequent location(s) reflected Cain's perpetual *status* as *a wandering fugitive* with respect to his and Abel's nearer relatives. Cain the **wanderer** always lived henceforth in the Land of Wandering (the meaning of the phrase, **the land of Nod**).

In the geographical orientation of the ancient Near East, **east of Eden** meant "in front of Eden," i.e., with one's back to, and going away from, Eden. Cain not only left God's immediate presence following their interview but also continued to move away from the region where he, his parents, and his brother had known and encountered God. Cain the wanderer made himself also Cain the perpetual outsider.

In its placement here, the phrase **east of Eden** functions as another of the many connections among chs 2, 3, and 4. With small grammatical variations, it occurs first in 2:8, then in 3:24, then here in 4:16. In literary terms, it functions as another small but significant marker of the increasing human alienation from God. As the distance from their first happy home in Eden increased, so, too, did human wickedness, inhumanity, violence, suffering, and sorrow multiply exponentially.

FROM THE TEXT

Knowing "in the biblical sense" is used for the first time here (v 1). That the biblical text often uses "knew" to report sexual intercourse conveys an important truth, or set of truths, regarding God's design of human sexual attitudes and activity. An obvious point is that in sexual intercourse two people "know" each other in the most intimate and intense ways possible. Of course, this is inevitable with respect to the body. Given that God created humans indivisibly "physical" *and* "spiritual," it follows that God intends and desires sexual intercourse to be the most intimate of "spiritual" encounters between two humans, as well.

Even if those participating are not aware of it, the sexual act always involves the whole person, and always involves coming to know the other person in more than "merely" physical ways. From an all-encompassing creation-redemption point of view, this is the most basic reason why one should avoid casual sexual encounters. It also is a part of why healthy cultures do not encourage them, but advise and enable sexual knowing only in the context of lasting monogamous commitment and the continual deepening of all kinds of knowledge between the partners.

This narrative begins with a scene of domestic tranquillity, the world's first human birth. It ends in violence, murder, and homelessness. Human alienation from God ultimately destroys everything; it cannot end happily.

An early theme in this narrative is worship (vv 3-7). From Eve's invoking Yahweh's name at the birth of Cain, we are justified in assuming the brothers learned from their parents about the importance of worship. The narrator was careful not to say Cain brought the "wrong" offering. This was before the Mosaic regulation of Israel's worship and, in any case, that legislation provided for a wider variety of vegetable offerings than of animal sacrifices. A reasonable inference is that God's issue with Cain was not the offering itself, but Cain's attitude toward God, whether in bringing his offering or in something else.

Of course, we do not bring our offerings in the same way as Cain and Abel. Nevertheless, the attitude with which we come before God in worship is as important as it was for them. Worship can and should be an occasion for listening to God's instruction, for reconciliation and fellowship, rather than for spurring anger and resentment, as Cain allowed it to do. As many of us know from experience, even our personal preferences in how we worship can lead to disagreement, to devaluing our Christian brothers and sisters, even to the extent of ending in bitterness and angry separation. Jesus' instruction (Matt 5:21-26) can help us stay off Cain's road from the beginning.

We may be sure God's nonacceptance of Cain on this occasion was not arbitrary. In these chapters, every line dealing with humans either declares or intimates that God passionately longs for genuine relationship with God's human creatures. This was God's attitude toward Cain, also, even after he had killed Abel. God's protection of the murderer from being murdered was a continuing act of grace. Cain never could have wandered far enough to be out of reach of God's care for him. Moreover, this theme dominates all Scripture, exemplified perhaps most directly in God's offer to be the God of Israel (and the church), and the invitation for Israel (and the church) to be God's people (see, e.g., Exod 6:7; Hos 2:23; 1 Pet 2:9-10; Rev 21:3).

God's first speech to Cain (Gen 4:6-7) is grace-filled, evidence that God had not rejected Cain. God's warning would have rescued both Abel and Cain, had Cain taken it seriously. Sin is a powerful reality; the image of the predatory beast about to spring is accurate. Yet God told Cain to master his impulse to sin, rather than giving in to it. Too often, we allow ourselves to act like helpless victims of sin, when we do have God-given resources to help us grow up and defang it. It still is all of grace, but God wants strong, mature, grown children, not perpetually helpless infants. Taking Jude's instruction seriously (v 11), we are to avoid "the way of Cain."

Cain's question of God, **Am I my brother's keeper?** all of Scripture answers with a resounding, "Yes!" We are to keep each other in our love and caring, always. God's creation/redemption intention is that we live eternally as brothers and sisters, redeemed and brought into God's family by our Elder Brother, Jesus Christ. How we shall live hereafter, we are to begin practicing here (see an especially helpful treatment of this issue in Brueggemann 1982, 61-64).

There is no question God's curse upon Cain was a serious sentence for a serious crime. Throughout the Bible, murder is regarded and treated as an extremely grave offense. We do not take God's sentence upon Cain lightly. At the same time, we should not invest it with more meaning than it actually carries. This sentence applied to Cain; we should not speak of some generalized "curse of Cain," as though all his descendants were damned from birth. That is not how God's creation of grace works. Of course, Cain's descendants perished in the flood that came upon the earth a few generations later, but most of Seth's descendants also perished in that same flood.

On one side of the issue, some argue the OT clearly commands that intentional murder be punished by execution of the murderer. Moreover, since the NT nowhere clearly abrogates that aspect of the Mosaic law, execution for murder, at least, continues to be a valid punishment. Others argue that Christ's taking upon himself the punishment of death upon the cross makes the execution even of the murderer an act that denies grace, and ought not to be viewed in Christian theology as any longer justifiable.

Of course, this narrative of the first murder and God's judgment of Cain cannot settle the argument whether capital punishment in the present day ever is justified. What it can and should do is give the reader pause in our too-easy, too-often pitting of the OT and the NT against each other. If God did not execute Cain, the first murderer, but in fact *forbade* his execution, we cannot say the OT always and everywhere teaches the only suitable response to a murder is the execution of the murderer. The matter is not as simple as that.

The several NT allusions to Cain's murder of Abel, or to Cain's character more generally, indicate the importance with which first-century Judaism and the early church invested this narrative. These include the parallel passages Matt 23:35 and Luke 11:51; also, Heb 11:4; 12:24; 1 John 3:12; Jude 11. Even in 1 John 2:11-17, though it does not mention Cain by name, it is clear John wrote with Cain in mind. Abel's example of righteous innocence was to be emulated; Cain's violent vengefulness was to be avoided like the plague it is. In our day, too, this godly instruction remains crucial and timely as ever.

2. Cain's Descendants (4:17-24)

This pericope is the first of the many genealogies in Scripture. It is not uncommon to hear readers, even persons intending to be serious students of the Bible, wonder aloud why so many lines of Scripture are dedicated to what seem to be "only" lists of names. The first answer is that this question is its own answer. If we take seriously our belief in the reliability and importance of the biblical record, then the fact that genealogies are a part of it means they are not "only" lists of names. Their presence is evidence of their importance; if they were *not* important, the divine-human partnership responsible for their presence in the sacred text would not have included them. This is not to say that Gen 5, a genealogy, is "as important" as Deut 5, the second giving of the Decalogue, but Gen 5 and the other genealogies have their own contributions and their own importance. The one who takes time with them will be enriched—we even may say, empowered—in ways previously unknown and unknowable.

One important function of genealogical lists in Scripture is to mark the relative importance of a given line in the biblical narrative of redemption history. The genealogy of Cain in 4:17-24 accomplishes that purpose by telling us that the line of Cain does not play a significant role in the story of redemption. This list is only seven generations long, including Cain the progenitor. Seven is a number of completion; with its seventh generation, the line of Cain is finished, for redemption purposes. The text does not even tell us Cain's line continued until the flood, though we are justified in assuming it did.

This genealogy evidences the lesser redemptive importance of Cain's line in another way. The genealogies of Gen 5 and 10 are longer in the number of generations included and more detailed in the information they record. Cain's genealogy gives neither his nor his descendants' ages at the births of their first sons, nor their ages at death (as does Gen 5 for Seth's line), nor more or less complete listings of sons in each generation (as does Gen 10). Except for the sixth and the seventh, the arrogant Lamech and his children, the text records but a single male name from each generation. Yet even in Cain's line, the seventh generation made significant cultural contributions, as we shall see. The light of God's grace may seem to burn dimly in a world of great wickedness, but God never allows it to be extinguished.

Biblical genealogies also serve to link families in a common ancestry. In this one, and in the record of Adam's line through Seth (Gen 5), that common ancestry was the first human pair (though in most genealogies women's names are rare). Cain's line began in violence and may have ended in violence, yet Cain and Seth were brothers. Cain's descendants were cousins of Seth's descendants. From the perspective of these chapters, all human families are interrelated. Later in Genesis, we will see this same concern for family connectedness expressed between the descendants of the brothers Ishmael and Isaac and between the descendants of the brothers Esau and Jacob.

IN THE TEXT

■ **17** The beginning of Cain's genealogy parallels the notice of his own birth (v 1); *Then Cain knew* [lay with] *his wife, and she conceived and bore Enoch.* Except that this account does not record the name of Cain's wife, its grammar and syntax are almost identical with v 1.

The name **Enoch** (*hănôk*) probably derives from a West Semitic (Amorite) root, appearing in Hebrew as *hānak*. Its meaning is related to the idea of dedication; the festival name Hanukkah is from the same root. If, as several suggest, it has a connection with the dedication of a foundation stone at the inception of a city-building project, **Enoch** makes perfect sense as the name of both the builder and the city he built.

Perhaps the most famous question in all the Bible, without an answer in the text itself, is, Where did Cain find a wife? Only two answers seem possible. The first assumes these chapters intend to teach that Adam was the first human man and Eve, the first human woman, both formed directly and immediately by the hand of God, as Gen 2 most commonly is taken to report. If this understanding is correct, Cain lived without a wife for some years, until one of his sisters was grown, or until a daughter (or even perhaps a granddaughter) of Seth, Cain's younger brother, attained marriageable age. That the account of the birth of Seth (v 25), and the note that Adam had other sons and daughters (5:4), follow this genealogy of Cain in the text is not a hindrance to this deduction. Chronology often is not the first concern in the arrangement of biblical texts. Moreover, 5:3 gives Adam's age at the birth of Seth as 130 years. We will discuss this point below, but taken at face value it gives ample time for a sister, niece, or even grand-niece of Cain to be born to Seth or one of Cain's unnamed brothers.

Many persons of faith, including some well acquainted with these texts, follow a second approach. Keeping in mind the point we just have made, that chronology may not be the primary concern of a given biblical text, they see in these early chapters of Genesis, not only the stories of the first pair and their immediate descendants, but also other aspects of the human condition as humans began to increase upon the earth. In other words, embedded in these stories of the earliest human generations also may be events from later periods, as populations grew, men began to build cities and violence increased in the world. That sentence, we should note, is a good general description of the development of early civilization in lower Mesopotamia, where these stories originated; we may not dismiss this hypothesis out of hand.

By this interpretation, the discontinuities we discover in these stories are those inherent in the collapsing of the past and the present within a single narrative ("the present," in the sense of a later period in human history). Thus, the existence of other humans can be assumed, e.g., in 4:14-17, though the narrative at that point attests only three surviving humans, Cain and his parents. It would be difficult to argue that in v 17 the narrator did *not* assume the existence of other humans in the land of Nod, east of Eden. The lack of details in this narrative, e.g., the name or the parentage of Cain's wife, suggests only that the narrator was not concerned to give a straightforwardly chronological account. More important to this narrative is the hopeful fact that even the heinous sin of murder did not bring about the end of human history. History continued, and even Cain had a part in the growth of human population and the establishment of urban culture.

One central fact will be germane, whichever of these two approaches to the text we prefer. Many biblical narratives do have what modern thought would describe as "gaps" in the story line and/or "disjointed" chronological arrangement(s). The temptation is to close the gaps through imaginative back-filling and to add, subtract, or rearrange chronological data. If and when we do this, we ought at least to do it with a dose of humility, recognizing that our speculations and imaginative reconstructions may or may not align with an original narrator's or a later editor's intent for the text we are interpreting.

The next clause after *and she conceived and bore Enoch* we may translate one of two ways: *and he was building a city* or *and he was a city builder.* The rest of the verse is, *and he called the name of the city after the name of his son, Enoch.* The narrator begins with the report on the sexual union of Cain and his wife and the birth of Enoch; the reference to the building of the city comes next; the naming of the city is the last element in the sentence. The question then arises, who built the city, Cain or Enoch? Given the syntax of the sentence, either could have been the builder.

Most translations and commentators take the builder to have been Cain; NIV inserts **Cain,** though the subject, in the MT, is the third person masculine singular verbal suffix pronoun *he.* The narrative sequence suggests Cain as the city builder. The question then would be, What was Cain the wanderer doing, building a city? One could assume that when his son was born, Cain transitioned from his life as a wanderer to a settled life. Hamilton suggests a defiant refusal on Cain's part to live on God's terms (1990, 238). Others identify Enoch as the city builder (e.g., Cassuto 1961, 228-31; Westermann 1984, 322, 327). Cassuto noted that Cain already had been identified as a tiller of the soil. Westermann arrived at his conclusion by emending the text *kĕšēm bĕnô* ("after the name of his son, Enoch") to read **kišmô* "after his own name, (Enoch)."

Augustine on Cain and Abel

Now, it is recorded of Cain that he built a city, while Abel, as though he were merely a pilgrim on earth, built none. For the true city of the saints is in heaven, though here on earth it produces citizens in whom it wanders as on a pilgrimage through time looking for the kingdom of eternity. When that day comes, it will gather together all those who, rising in their bodies, shall have that kingdom given to them in which, along with their Prince, the King of Eternity, they shall reign forever and ever. (Louth 2001, 111)

■ **18** The middle three names in the genealogy of Cain appear together in this one verse, with no further information on any of them.

The name of Enoch's son **Irad** may be traced to a root ʿrd meaning "wild ass, onager," found in several West Semitic languages. Another plausible suggestion is that **Irad** is a Hebrew form of the Sumerian city name Eridu. If that suggestion is correct, Enoch probably founded Eridu, the earliest city of Mesopotamian tradition (Hess 2009, 40-41).

Irad (ʿirād) is probably not an alternate form of the name Jared (5:15 ff.), though the second and third consonants are the same for both (resh, dalet). However, the first letter of **Irad** (ʿayin) and the first letter of Jared (yered), which is yod, never are confused in Hebrew. The suggestion that these are the same name arises from the theory that Cain's genealogy in Gen 4, and Seth's in Gen 5, originated from a single source, which (by this theory) can be reconstructed, now that their common origin is known.

The genealogy then lists **Mehujael,** the son of Irad. The second element in **Mehujael** is ʾēl; in Hebrew, this is a title for God commonly used in personal names. **Mehujael** probably is a passive construction meaning, "enlivened by God," i.e., given life by God. If so, it is a prayer of thanksgiving for the live birth of a healthy child.

Methushael (mĕtûšāʾēl) comprises either two or three elements. Cassuto argues for methu-sha-ʾel, "man of God," from a Canaanite original (1961, 233). Hess explicitly rejects this derivation, and offers methu-shael, "man of death," that is, "man dedicated to shael/sheol," i.e., to the place of the dead personified as a deity (2009, 43-45).

The fifth and final personal name in this verse is **Lamech,** about whom the text will have more to say. The meaning of his name is not evident from Hebrew. Westermann notes, "It is usually explained from the Sumerian lumga, the title of the sky god Ea as patron of song and music" (1984, 329). That one of Lamech's sons, Jubal, is credited with musical invention (v 21) lends credence to this suggestion.

■ **19** **Lamech** was the first recorded polygamist. **Adah** and **Zillah** were the first women to experience the personal and family tragedy of never completely having a husband. Lamech was the first man never to experience the fulfillment and the joys of giving himself completely and unreservedly to one woman over a lifetime and receiving the same from her.

Adah usually is taken to mean "ornament," as Cassuto comments, "A pretty little girl is born, the *ornament* of the family, so her parents call her *'Adha*" (1961, 234, emphasis original).

Zillah may be from a root meaning "shadow" or "shade," referring to the luxurious pleasantness experienced by the traveler in the heat of the day who comes to rest in the shade of a spreading oak or terebinth. Alternatively, **Zillah** may mean "cymbal"; then, the name would refer to the musical sound of her voice. Both etymologies are plausible, but the signal accomplishments of this family across the arts, as presented in this account, suggests "cymbal" as the more likely meaning.

■ **20-21** Lamech fathered three sons and a daughter. Adah bore two of the sons; her firstborn was **Jabal** and her second, **Jubal**. Both names are from the same root, *ybl*, meaning "to bring," i.e., in, or as in, procession. **Jabal** most likely is a hypocoristicon, a name abbreviated from its full form, usually by omission of a constituent divine name. If this is the case with **Jabal,** his full name (or the name from which his name was shortened) was Jabal-El, "El (God) has brought," a name of thanksgiving to God for bringing a child, that is, for the live birth of a healthy child. If the name was not a reflection of the birth event, it could mean, simply, "God leads [the procession]."

Jubal is a passive participle from *ybl*, meaning "brought in procession." If referring to his birth, it would mean he was brought along as the second son in the procession of Lamech's children.

The phrase, **the father of,** applied to both brothers, includes, but is not limited to, their biological descendants. It means they were inventors and/or developers in their respective areas of endeavor and taught their knowledge and skills, not only to their sons (and perhaps to their daughters), but to others who came to them as apprentices or students.

Jabal's developments were in the area of **livestock** breeding and care. The reference to **tents** reflects the fact that the majority of pastoral nomads of western Asia always have lived in tents, disdaining the settled life of the city. Abel had raised sheep and goats (*ṣʾōn*); the noun here is *miqneh*; it includes all the larger domestic livestock bred in ancient western Asia: sheep, goats, cattle, and donkeys, with sheep accounting for the greatest number of animals, at least among tent dwellers. In Mesopotamia, in the earliest periods, neither horses nor camels were kept as domestic stock.

Jubal invented the first **harp** or *lyre* (*kinnôr*), and the first *pipe* or **flute** (*ʿûgāb*), i.e., the most ancient and basic stringed instrument, as well as the most ancient and basic wind instrument. (In modern Hebrew, *kinnôr* designates the violin, a stringed instrument; *ʿûgāb* is the organ, a wind instrument, though not controlled by the breath of the organist.) The participle *[everyone] who plays* (*tōpēś*) means, more precisely in this context, "one who takes up (grasps) in order to play skillfully," a reminder that playing a musical instrument is a skill usually acquired by practice.

■ **22** *As for Zillah, she also bore* two children, a son and a daughter. Her son's name was **Tubal-Cain.** The first element, **Tubal,** probably is a passive form from *ybl*; if so, his name is related to those of his half-brothers and would mean something like, "brought in procession." Alternatively, if **Tubal** is a Hurrian element, Cain would be a Hebrew gloss (explanatory word or comment), and the two elements of his name would have the same meaning, "smith" (Hess 2009, 53).

The author's description of Tubal-Cain's contributions is different from that of his brothers. The text reads, *Tubal-Cain, the sharpener* [*lōṭēš*] *of all the fashioners* [*hōrēš*] *of bronze and iron.* Beginning with one of the Aramaic Targums (a kind of paraphrasing translation), some translations have added "the father of," assuming it has dropped from the text, since both Tubal-Cain's brothers are designated "the father of . . ." However, the omission of "the father of" in the case of Tubal-Cain would be another example of the narrator's artistry; small variations as the text progresses in the development of similar themes, or the narration of similar events, add beauty to the text and avoid the monotony of exact repetition.

The phrase *sharpener* (*lōṭēš*) appears enigmatic at first glance. *The sharpener* hammered a tool, implement, or weapon on the anvil at the forge, using both heavier blows and lighter taps to sharpen the edge or the point. Cassuto regarded the use of the term here as an example in life of the proverb, "As iron sharpens iron, so one man sharpens another" (Prov 27:17). "Tubal-cain [sic] used to *sharpen* the sharpeners" (1961, 237). Tubal-Cain was the teacher of the artisans or *fashioners* (*hōrēš*) working in bronze, brass, and iron (compare NKJV, "an instructor of every craftsman in bronze and iron"), just as his brothers led in discovering, inventing, and/or developing animal husbandry and musical instruments.

Archaeological discoveries over the course of two centuries have accustomed us to think of the Bronze Age in the Near East as having spanned approximately the years 3200-1200 B.C., followed by the Iron Age, about 1200-330 B.C. Generally speaking, this is an accurate picture, yet bronze (and brass) did not fall out of use when iron came on the scene. (We still use them today.) More importantly for our purposes here, iron (mostly of meteoric origin) was discovered, known, and used in small ways long before 1200 B.C., when it began to replace bronze as the most important material for tools, implements, and weapons. There is no necessary anachronism in the mention of iron here.

Probably because of his father Lamech's bellicose statements in the following verses, some have assumed weapons were the primary focus of Tubal-Cain's energies and expertise. Yet the text is silent on what he crafted. From what we know of the earliest periods of civilization in that part of the world, early warfare was mostly localized, primitive, and inefficient. The development of the arts of civilization portrayed in these verses was largely peaceful until the lust of the battlefield became an addiction of Egyptian pharaohs and Mesopotamian kinglets (as we would call them now). By this account, Tubal-Cain *may* have developed swords and spears; he *probably* made daggers; he *certainly* made and taught others how to make plowshares (inefficient as these were by modern standards), oxgoads, pruning hooks, knives, and other tools and implements.

Naamah is not introduced as Lamech's or as Zillah's daughter. We learn of her only as **Tubal-Cain's sister.** Naamah means "pleasant" or "lovely." If Cassuto is correct in associating her name with the pleasant or lovely sound of her voice (1961, 238), then Naamah may have been an early leader in developing vocal music, as her half-brother Jubal was in the development of instrumental music.

■ **23-24** We treat these two verses together because together they comprise a short song. It is a sad commentary on the human condition that the first lines of Scripture that commentators universally agree are explicitly poetry should celebrate murder, yet that is indeed the case. Much of the preceding narrative, back to the beginning of Gen 1, we may call an exalted prose, with numerous poetic features and a poetic "feel" at numerous points. But *these* lines are the first to display the characteristic that formally divides poetry from prose in Hebrew, as in other Semitic languages. That feature is the parallel structure of the lines (not primarily rhyme and meter, as in much of Western poetry). Most modern English versions (including NIV) set out the lines in this parallel structure to make clear their poetic character and style.

Most translations and many commentators take Lamech's declaration here as his boasting of a deed newly committed. In these translations of the middle line of Lamech's poem, NIV is representative, **I have killed a man for wounding me, a young man for injuring me.** Cassuto also takes this to have been a recent event, but translates, "For a man I slew, / as soon as I wounded (him), // Yea, a young man, / as soon as I bruised (him)" (1961, 239). Cassuto understands Lamech's boast to his wives as centered in his great strength; he hadn't "meant" to kill, but he was so strong the lightest tap killed his adversary.

Alternatively, this may be Lamech's threat of what he *would* do if he found himself in the situation he depicted in his song. On this understanding, Hamilton translates, "I would kill a man for my wound, / yea, a boy for my bruise" (1990, 236). Both Cassuto and Hamilton argue effectively for a new understanding of Lamech's boast. Deciding between them is more difficult, though in this case both cannot be correct. Hamilton's approach seems the more likely.

We must leave aside a great deal in our discussion of this verse, but the immensity of Lamech's prideful boasting, and his willingness to inflict the greatest possible hurt for the smallest slight to his "honor" comes through clearly on almost any reading of these lines. That is the point; Cain's hubris (whether or not his act) against his brother was multiplied as greatly as the numbers Lamech used in the next line; and this in the man who was "only" his great-great-great-grandson. If Cain's line were to continue on this path, what could be expected in future generations?

Verse 24, the final two lines of this song, reads, ***If Cain shall be avenged fourteen times over, then Lamech, seventy and seven [times]***. Lamech referenced the memory of God's protective decree over his ancestor Cain; if anyone struck Cain (whether or not killing him), God would exact perfect justice on Cain's behalf (see v 15 and comments, above). Lamech then declared his own version of this portentous warning; this is the main point, we believe, in Lamech's utterance. As we noted in our comments on v 15 (following Mendenhall), vengeance is a divine prerogative; later in the Torah, this is expressly stated as an enduring principle (Deut 32:35). Yet Lamech either already had usurped to himself this divine prerogative or now declared to his two wives that he would not hesitate to do so, should the occasion arise. Lamech, the seventh from Adam in Cain's line, followed his first ancestor in attempting to put himself in the place of God.

More importantly, Lamech's motivations never could have been anything other than selfish, vindictive, cruel, and rebellious. He had no sense of the proportionality of justice reflected in the divine exercise of retribution (*nāqam*). He cared only to assuage his own wounded sense of "honor" by inflicting measureless shame and pain upon any opponent, for wrongs real or imagined. This is the significance of ***seventy and seven times.*** It is hyperbole so great as to be meaningless and, therefore, ludicrous. (Jesus' famous instruction to Peter in Matt 18:22 to forgive "seventy-seven times" also is hyperbole. However, it characterizes the perfect grace of forgiveness, rather than the "perfect" bloodthirsty vengeance of murder.)

Lamech's boasting did not make him the hero he thought to be in the eyes of his wives. Rather, it portrayed him as a buffoon, not to be taken seriously because he did not have the capacity to take anyone or anything seriously, beyond himself. As Jesus was later to state as one of his more famous dicta (Luke 17:33), the one who takes himself too seriously, at the expense of others, cannot, in the end, take even himself seriously. With this inordinate boast, the man fades away; this is the last we hear in Scripture of this Lamech.

"Fourteen" and "Seventy-Seven"

Numbers are not the key to everything in the Bible, but they are important. Lamech's numbers demonstrate an advanced mathematical knowledge. Fourteen is the sum of $1^2 + 2^2 + 3^2$; i.e., $1 + 4 + 9 = 14$. Moreover, seventy-seven is the sum of $4^2 + 5^2 + 6^2$; i.e., $16 + 25 + 36 = 77$. In the two numbers together, then, we have $1^2 + 2^2 + 3^2 + 4^2 + 5^2 + 6^2$, in a text whose ultimate origins lie in lower Mesopotamia, the land of the sexagesimal (base six) system, practiced alongside the decimal (base ten) system. This feature is not the reason for the existence of this text, nor is it a numerical code for understanding it. It does not negate the theological, anthropological, and other meanings and teachings of the text. It is *in* the text, however, yet another evidence of the advances of civilization in ages we are wont to call primitive.

FROM THE TEXT

We ought not dismiss or discount the cultural, even the "industrial," advances reflected in this text, just because they are attributed to the "godless" line of Cain. One of the features of God's astonishing gift of free will is that sin does not take it from us, whether for good or for ill. Sinful, prideful, and violent as some in Cain's line were, others continued to develop God's gracious gift of creativity, for good. Sin does not put an immediate end to creativity or to many other of God's good gifts. Over the course of human history, we have used some of these to good and constructive ends, some to evil and destructive ends; some to glorify God, some to exalt human pride. In any and all of our choices, though, God refuses to reverse God's original gift of free will, or to cancel our creativity—our capacity to imagine and bring into being what is not—or a myriad of other gifts we hold because created in the image of God the Creator. How great is God's confidence in the ultimate triumph of God's own goodness!

It is often noted that the author did not expressly condemn Lamech for his polygamous arrangement. This is true, but therein lies one of the great powers of narrative. Simply telling the story in its complexity of highs and lows is enough to allow and to encourage the receptive hearer/reader to understand the strengths and weaknesses, the virtues and the vices, of the characters whose stories are told. Abraham, Jacob, and David were not expressly censured for their polygamous relationships, either. But we know their stories, and these are enough to learn that polygamy forecloses any chance for domestic happiness, or even tranquillity, both for the many-wived man and for "his" fractionally husbanded women. Knowing the more famous stories, we can read Lamech's, Adah's, and Zillah's disappointments and sorrows between the lines of his dishonorable self-delusion in vv 23-24. The man who is happy at home does not take offense at every slight, real or imagined, when he ventures beyond his own door.

We have asserted that sin did not stop human use of our God-bestowed gifts of free will and creativity. The converse also is true. The use of these gifts to the advancement of civilization did not stop the cancerous growth of sin. Technology and other inventiveness, in and of themselves, are neutral. Advances in almost any area of human endeavor may have the potential to heal or to harm. How we direct and apply our creative energies is the crucial factor, and of most concern to God. In that, our embrace or rejection of hubris will be the key. As we have seen with the first human pair, with Cain, and with

Lamech, hubris is the decision to usurp the place of God, taking to ourselves the right to set the boundaries for, to craft the definitions of, moral and ethical conduct. Human hubris brought about the destruction of the ancient world. It behooves us to take care that it does not destroy ours.

In a number of respects, the opposite of hubris is forgiveness, the extension of mercy rather than the pursuit of retaliatory vengeance. The character profiles of Cain and his descendant Lamech are cautionary tales, inviting us to avoid the false promises (and premises) of vengeance undertaken in the service of hubris. Jesus held up the kingdom way of living in his response to Peter's self-congratulatory question, and the parable he related to illustrate it (Matt 18:21-35). Choose hubris and die. Walk in Jesus' footsteps, practicing forgiveness, mercy, and loving-kindness, and live. The choice is a life-defining moment, followed by daily ratifications, sometimes almost to the "seventy times seven" of Jesus' answer to Peter.

3. Seth's Line: A New Beginning (4:25-26)

IN THE TEXT

■ **25** We translate this verse, *And Adam knew* [lay with] *his wife again, and she gave birth to a son* ***and she called his name "Seth, for*** [she said] ***God has set for me another offspring*** [*zera*ʿ] ***instead of Abel, because Cain murdered him."*** We may note here, first, that the narrator did not refer to "the man," using the definite article, but used **Adam** as a proper name.

This report of Seth's birth is not identical with the report of the birth of Cain, but it is similar enough that the reader can understand the narrator viewed Seth as the "replacement" for Cain, as well as for Abel. The name **Seth** means something like "foundation." The personal name and the act of God for which Eve gave thanks are from the same root and are spelled alike, except for their vowels. In this new son, **Seth** (*šēt*, probably from *šît*, meaning "put," "set"), God had ***established*** (*šāt*, from *šît*, meaning "put," "set") for Eve a new foundation in place of the two sons she had lost: Abel, at the hand of his brother; Cain, by the act of his own hand.

Eve's focus, naturally, was on the son she had lost to death. This is clear from her words, ***another offspring, instead of Abel.*** In the name Eve gave her first son, Cain (v 1), Cassuto detected hubris (1961, 201). Be that as it may, this naming certainly was not that; it expressed humility as well as gratitude: ***God has set for me a seed.*** Eve did not claim any part of bringing about this birth but regarded it purely as God's gift. Eve also used the same verb, ***murdered*** (*hārag*), the narrator had used in describing Cain's crime and its aftermath earlier in the chapter. How bitter now had become the fruit she had desired so fiercely, so long ago in the garden!

This final speech of Eve recorded in the Bible (v 25) is the longest of her three short speeches (see 3:13; 4:1; 4:25). In this last speech, she spoke the

177

names of all three of her sons (for whom we have names preserved), but in a chiastic order from their birth. Seth, the *seed* who would be the new beginning, she named first. **Abel,** the son who was no more, she named second. **Cain,** her firstborn in whom she had fiercely exulted, who still lived but who was lost to her forever, she named last. In her final clause, the subject noun, **Cain,** follows the verb with its pronoun suffix; once again, this is for emphasis. It will be clearer if we include the preceding phrase, *instead of Abel, because murdered him* Cain. In the Hebrew text, **Cain** is the last word ever reported from the lips of Eve. Moreover, this is the last occurrence in the Hebrew Scripture both of Cain's name and of Abel's name. The story of Abel begins and ends in Gen 4. The story of Cain and his line, his descendants to the seventh generation, begins and ends in Gen 4. The narrator wanted the reader to know that the path away from God, exemplified in Gen 4 by Cain and his great-great-great-grandson Lamech, leads to a dead end.

■ **26** Though the focus of ch 4 is on a failed attempt at establishing humanity upon the earth as God had instructed (1:28), it ends on a note of hope. *In due course to Seth, also to him, was born a son, and he called his name Enosh; at that time was begun again to call upon the name Yahweh.* The pericope begins with two births (Cain and Abel; vv 1-2) and ends with two births (Seth and Enosh; vv 25-26); this is an important literary clue that vv 25-26 really do belong to this chapter.

As the birth of Seth opened once again the door of hope for the future for Adam and Eve, so the birth of a son to Seth held that door open into the next generation. Since the narrator reported the birth of Enosh as an ordinary and expected event in the life of Seth, we have translated the conjunction, *In due course.* The phrase *also to him* is not grammatically necessary to the sentence. The narrator intended it to emphasize that God's blessing/mandate, "be fruitful and increase in number" (1:28), was not just for Seth's parents. God's blessing extended to Seth and, beyond him, to succeeding generations, as well. These would be built upon the "foundation" of Seth, and the human family would continue in the world.

The name of Seth's son, **Enosh** (ʾĕnôš), essentially is a synonym for ʾādām. In this narrative, both nouns are used as personal names of individual human males, but as common nouns, both mean "human," whether male and/or female, whether individually or collectively. In naming his son **Enosh,** Seth participated in the hope of his parents, that through this third-generation "man," God would continue to bless the race begun by his father, the first-generation "man," Adam.

Against this backdrop, we now may understand the significance of the last clause, of both the verse and the chapter: *at that time was begun [again] to call upon the name, Yahweh.* Eve had referred to Yahweh (perhaps in gratitude, or in pride, perhaps even both) when naming Cain, her firstborn (v 1). Cain and Abel each had brought an offering to Yahweh (vv 3-4). In judgment upon Cain's murder of Abel, Yahweh had banished Cain from the ground (vv 11-12). Cain had gone out *from the presence of Yahweh* (v 16). A reasonable inference is that Cain no longer called upon the name of Yahweh. The narrative is silent on the worship practices of Cain's descendants but, again, a reasonable inference is that they, too, lived away from the presence of Yahweh, i.e., not in relationship with Yahweh.

With the birth of a son into Seth's family, all changed again *within this narrative.* The tragic reversal—Abel's death and Cain's banishment—had been reversed again with the birth of a son to begin the third generation. *At that time* translates the Hebrew particle ʾāz. The context, both logically and chronologically, is the birth of Enosh reported in the first half of the verse (26a).

The verb form, *it was begun,* is a *Hoph'al* (passive) perfect, third masculine singular, from the root ḥālal; in the MT, no subject noun is expressed, because none is required. Most translations supply a subject and convert the verb to an English active form; NIV's **men began to call** is a representative example. Given what we already have noted about Eve, Cain, and Abel, the narrator probably did not intend to report the absolute beginning of worship; he already had recorded that, in this narrative. At a minimum, this was a beginning again, narratively, after the just-recorded estrangement from Yahweh of Cain and (probably) his descendants. Whether Seth, his parents, all of them together, or unnamed others reestablished Yahweh worship the text does not say. More important is that with this announcement the narrative ends in hope, looking forward. The birth of Enosh represented hope for the continuation of humanity. Calling upon the name of Yahweh meant hope that humans once again might come into Yahweh's presence.

FROM THE TEXT

Eve's reference to *seed* (zeraʿ) in v 25 echoes 3:15, where God spoke of *her seed* (zeraʿ). Since this word is not used in the notice of Cain's birth, nor of Abel's (vv 1-2), we may conclude that the use of the word zeraʿ has special significance here. Though Abel had been murdered, and Cain sentenced to a life of wandering, God did not end the human race but continued to extend grace. Seth's birth rekindled hope in Eve and in Adam. From the perspective of the larger biblical story, redemption indeed did come to sinful humanity through the *seed* of the woman. Seth rightfully belongs here as the progenitor of the line of descendants culminating in Jesus the Messiah, the Redeemer of the world (Luke 3:38).

It is not uncommon for OT scholars to see the occurrences of the name Yahweh, in Genesis, as the anachronistic work of the compiler/redactor, because of God's statement to Moses in Exod 6:3 that God had not made himself known to the patriarchs by his name, "Yahweh." However, another understanding of God's statement to Moses is possible, taking into account the range of meanings encompassed within the word "know/make known." God may

179

have been saying to Moses that while the patriarchs were acquainted with the name, Yahweh, they knew almost nothing of its significance, as God now would demonstrate to Moses and, through him, to Israel, to Egypt, and to Egypt's pharaoh. The true God, Yahweh, "I Am," was about to show Pharaoh, the man who thought he was a god, who God "is." The true God, Yahweh, "I cause to be," would cause Israel to become the nation God had promised the patriarchs they would be. To "know" is more than to have a name in one's memory bank.

As noted, this short pericope is laden with hope for the continuation of the human race in the midst of sin, violence, and even death. Sin did not, sin cannot, end God's creation/redemption/restoration purposes. Amazingly, God does not withdraw grace even from sinful humanity but invites us to partnership in realizing their fulfillment.

The worship of Cain, the first person of record to bring an offering to Yahweh, culminated in violence. The resumption of worship at the birth of Enosh signaled a renewed hope for redemption and restoration. Taken as a whole, then, we may see this narrative as proposing a theology of worship, establishing worship as central to restoring our broken relationship with God. Had Cain not broken off his worship, he would not have murdered Abel. Had Cain renewed his worship even after murdering his brother, he would have found the path back to God unblocked. It is not for nothing that the final words of this chapter, "to call upon the name of the Lord," echo so frequently through the rest of Scripture (see, e.g., Ps 116:13; Joel 2:32; Acts 2:21; Rom 10:13).

B. Adam's Line, Through Seth (5:1-32)

I. God's Name for Humans (5:1-2)

BEHIND THE TEXT

This two-verse paragraph serves as a preamble to the next major segment in the primeval narratives, which focuses on the story of humankind through the line of Seth. This segment begins with the first of the three genealogical records of Adam's line through Seth (5:3-32; see also 10:1-32; 11:10-32). This genealogy (5:3-32) links Adam to Noah, thus covering the period from creation to the flood. The focus of this preamble is on God's creation of the human species, first introduced in 1:26-28, then related in greater detail in Gen 2. The developments reported in chs 3 and 4 are not mentioned in 5:1-2; this is not narrative, but an introduction to a genealogy. Unique to this preamble is the unequivocal report of God's formal naming of the human species as ʾādām—male and female, both, created in God's image. This is a theological statement of the first order, with far-reaching implications. It affirms what is clearly stated in 1:26-28, and repeated in several places in chs 2 and 3: ʾādām refers to humankind inclusively. This noun does occur secondarily as a name

180

for Adam the individual, but here the narrator is crystal clear that, originally and primarily, ʾādām is the human race God created as male and female, not an individual human being. (See also on 2:4-7, Behind the Text.)

IN THE TEXT

■ **1-2** We will translate and discuss these two verses together, since (after the first short sentence) we should separate the clauses by no more than a semicolon in English punctuation: ***This is the document of the generations of ʾādām. When Elohim created ʾādām, in the likeness of Elohim he made him; male and female he created them, and he blessed them, and he called their name ʾādām when they were created.***

On the first sentence (***This is . . . of ʾādām***), see the discussion, "These Are the *Toledot*" in the Introduction. This chapter is the genealogy of the first man and the first woman whom, together, God named ʾādām, as this short section is at very great pains to remind the reader.

After the introductory sentence, the narrator summed up the account of 1:26-28. ***When Elohim created ʾādām*** is, literally, "on the day of the creating of Elohim ʾādām." This phrase echoes the opening phrase of 1:27 ("God created ʾādām"). The clause, ***In the likeness of Elohim he made him,*** sums up the second part of 1:27 ("in the image [ṣelem] of God he created [bārāʾ] him"). We note here two slight variations from the text of 1:27. Though the word order in 1:27 is the same as in 5:1, here we have the word dĕmût ("likeness") instead of "image" (ṣelem); second, v 1 uses the verb **made** (ʿāśâ) instead of the verb "created" (bārāʾ). Genesis 1:26 mentions both "image"/ṣelem and "likeness"/ dĕmût, where they are essentially synonymous in meaning. Therefore, we may conclude that the lack of ṣelem in 5:1 does not introduce any change in meaning (see commentary on 1:26). These words reappear again in 5:3.

Another connection with Gen 1:26-28 is, of course, ***male and female he created them.*** The two occurrences are virtually identical. Here, too, it is important to note that (after the first one) the pronouns referring to the humans are plural, just as the imperative verbs of 1:28 are plural.

The statement, ***and he blessed them,*** also tracks with 1:28, but the *substance* of the blessing is radically different here. There, the blessing came in the form of a fivefold command/instruction. Here, it is God's *naming* of the human species. In a formal naming, God bestowed upon humankind the name of God's choosing. All the elements of a formal naming are here (Bush 1996, 7-8): the specific and necessary verb, ***and he called/named*** (wayyiqrāʾ); the specific and necessary common noun, "name" (šĕmām, ***their name***); the proper noun, i.e., the name itself, ***Adam*** (ʾādām). In Hebrew, *God's* name for the human race is ***Adam***; and that from ***the day of their being created.*** Precisely because ***Adam*** here is a proper name, it is not preceded by a definite article.

God had delegated the naming of the animals to the human, when there was as yet only one human (2:19). However, as we see here, God reserved the naming of the human to God's self; that fact alone indicates the high regard in which God holds the ultimate of God's creations here upon this earth. But that God's naming, and the name God bestowed, together constitute a *blessing* upon our race indicates an even higher standing in God's estimation. Moreover, this is not a blessing transmitted through a human (or angelic) intermediary, as highly valued as such blessings are throughout Scripture. This is one of a relatively few places where the blessing is directly from the mouth of God. Blessed by God in our very name from the day of our creation, we may regard ourselves as blessed indeed!

2. Adam Through Enoch: Seven Generations (5:3-24)

BEHIND THE TEXT

The ten paragraphs of this genealogy share a number of features, except that Noah's paragraph is truncated, for reasons that will become obvious when we reach Noah in the genealogy. The common features are: (1) the name of the patriarch; (2) his age at the birth of his first son; (3) the name of his first son; (4) the number of years he lived after the birth of his first son; (5) the report that he had (other) sons and daughters; (6) his age at death; (7) absence of the name of his wife; (8) absence of the names of his further sons and daughters.

Several of the ten paragraphs exhibit features that are not common to all of them. Of course, we will discuss these as we come to them.

This genealogy of Seth and the genealogy of Shem in Gen 11 also share a number of features in common. Moreover, we will understand both more completely as we consider why the numbers are as they are, and as we compare and contrast certain elements of these genealogies with similar materials from Mesopotamia. Because our discussion encompasses both Gen 5 and Gen 11, we have placed it in the Introduction (see The Literary Forms of Genesis 1—11).

IN THE TEXT

■ **3-5** We will translate this paragraph as literally as we can while allowing it to make sense in English, so the reader can see in the text a number of the points we will make about the patterns of this genealogy, as well as the departures from those patterns at several points in a few of the subsequent paragraphs.

Now Adam lived thirty and a hundred years, then he fathered in his likeness, according to his image; and he called his name Seth. Now the days of Adam after his fathering Seth were eight hundred years, and he fathered sons and daughters. So all the days of Adam which he lived were nine hundred years and thirty years; then he died.

The name **Adam** here refers to the first man (see also Behind the Text on vv 1-2, and on 2:4-7 above; 3:17, 21; 4:25). In 4:1 there was no reference to the age of the man when he became the father of Cain and Abel. However, the narrator here records the age of Adam when he became the father of Seth, because Adam's line now was to be perpetuated through Seth. In the Hebrew Bible, numbers always are written out with words, never set down in numerals. In this genealogy, the order usually is ascending, as is the first number here, ***thirty and a hundred years.*** Perhaps the most important reason for this, in this genealogy, is that twelve of its twenty-eight numbers, nearly half, begin with five or seven; putting them first emphasizes them. Eleven of the rest begin with multiples of five or seven; the reader recognizing the pattern will see it continued in these. The remaining five numbers can be related to the five-and-seven pattern, also.

The Hebrew verb ***he fathered*** here is a causative form (*Hiph'il*); we could translate, "he caused [his wife] to bear." One would have expected here a common noun ("a son") as the direct object of this verb, but it is lacking in the text. Most translations add **a son** as the direct object. It is possible that the narrator omitted it intentionally, intending to say that not only Seth, but all the children of Adam, he fathered ***in his*** [own] ***likeness, according to his*** [own] ***image.***

These two phrases also deserve comment. First, they comprise an obvious link with 1:26, where God purposed to "make *ʾādām* in our image, according to our likeness." Moreover, they comprise what we may call a long-distance chiasm:

> ***In our image, according to our likeness*** (1:26)
> ***In his likeness, according to his image*** (5:3)

The chiastic arrangement of the nouns also causes the prepositions to be reversed in their attachment to their respective nouns. This linkage, emphasized by the chiastic reversal, invites the reader to the appropriate syllogism:

First Premise: God created Adam in God's image and likeness.

Second Premise: Adam fathered Seth in his own likeness and image.

Conclusion: Seth also was in God's likeness and image.

This genealogy follows the form of genealogies in the ancient Near East in which lineage was reckoned only through the father, with but the rarest of exceptions. (Part of what makes Matthew's genealogy of Jesus, in 1:1-17, exceptional is that it includes *five* women's names.) We should note, however, that while ancient genealogies were predominantly patrilinear, this does not mean mothers were always and only passive agents in the *naming* of their children (a different matter). Beginning already with Eve (4:1, 25*a*), the text often notes the mother as the one who named her child(ren).

The naming of Seth by his mother, Eve (4:25), shows all the elements of a formal naming: the verb "she named/called the name of . . ."; the common noun "name" (*shem*); the personal name itself, "Seth." Adam's naming of Seth here (5:3*b*) also shows these same formal elements (**and he called his name Seth**). Source critical scholars explain the disparity in the name-giving by tracing 4:25-26 to the Yahwist source, and the genealogical report in ch 5 to the Priestly source. However, it is equally possible that these different reports are not contradictory; rather, they complement each other. The narrator closes the line of Cain in 4:24. Eve's naming of Seth, following immediately in 4:25, conveys the hopeful ending to the tragic narrative of ch 4. Adam's naming of Seth is very much a part of the genealogy of Adam that introduces a new line of descendants for Adam. In both cases, the naming of Seth conveys hope for the future of the human race.

This hope for a new beginning is reflected also in the quick succession of the four formal name-giving reports of 4:25—5:3. Eve named Seth; Seth named Enosh; God named the human race; Adam named Seth. This clustering of name-giving, beginning and ending with Seth, seems to emphasize that the fresh start through Seth would be successful, in contrast with the abortive beginning represented in the tragedy of Cain and Abel.

We should note also that the genealogy of Adam, presented here, actually begins with God's naming of the human race as ʾādām in 5:2. Thus, God established the principle that genealogy is to be gender inclusive ("[God] called *their* name," 5:2 KJV, emphasis added). However, most of the later OT genealogical lists exhibit a departure from this original pattern of gender inclusiveness. The gender *exclusivity* of these genealogies reflects later developments in cultural customs and practices of the ancient world. Theologically, it is not too much to say that these developments also exhibit, on this point, the divisive and destructive effects of human sinfulness.

This is a linear genealogy; it carries out the limited purposes of the linear genealogy as a literary form. This explains also the omission of the names of any of the siblings of the eldest sons who are the subjects of the genealogy, paragraph by paragraph. Siblings are subsumed under the statement, **and he fathered sons and daughters**. We will see a different purpose, and therefore a different pattern, in the genealogy of Gen 10.

The narrator reports that Adam lived **eight hundred years** after the birth of Seth, **fathered sons and daughters** and lived a total of **nine hundred years and thirty years.** This is the narrator's pattern throughout the chapter; the reasons for the exception of v 32 will be self-evident. The repetition of the word **years** when reporting larger numbers of years is the rule, rather than the exception, in Hebrew texts involving numbers. This also is one of several places in this genealogy where the larger number comes before the smaller, as opposed to the smaller number first and then the larger in other places (e.g., v 8, **twelve years and nine hundred years**).

The final statement in every paragraph but two is, **then he died.** (For Noah, the statement occurs in 9:29.) The narrator thus lends each paragraph the necessary literary conclusion and finality. A very long life span, indeed, is reported for each individual, including also the satisfaction of siring many sons and daughters. But even these long life cycles ended in death, which God had announced as the ultimate consequence of the human rebellion. Sinful humans may live long but, short of divine action, they (we) cannot be or become immortal. Death had become an inevitable—we may say even a necessary—part of human experience. (For discussion of these startlingly long life spans, see Introduction, The Literary Forms of Genesis 1—11.)

■ **6-8** The pattern of the paragraph on **Seth** is the basic pattern of the first paragraph on Adam; the few differences represent variations from the pattern in the paragraph on Adam, not found in the paragraph on Seth. For the meaning of the names **Seth** and **Enosh,** see the commentary on 4:25-26, above.

■ **9-11** The paragraph on **Enosh** follows the basic pattern of the genealogy. (Assuming the reader will look for discussion of names in the paragraphs devoted to those bearing the names, we will discuss **Kenan** in the following paragraph, and similarly through the chapter, until we reach Lamech's naming of Noah.)

■ **12-14** The name **Kenan** usually is related to the name Cain (see commentary on 4:1, above). Hess accepts the relationship and considers the second syllable (–an) to be a "hypocoristic suffix" (2009, 68, 92-94). An important literary link between the two names in the two accounts is that both Cain and **Kenan** are descended from men whose names mean "human, humankind" (Adam and Enosh). Thus, both Cain and **Kenan** demonstrate and assure (or should have done, in the case of Cain) the continuation of the human race, through the promised offspring.

■ **15-17** The name **Mahalalel** means either "praising God (El)," if its first element is a participle from *hll*, or "the praise of God (El)," if its first element is a noun from the same root. Either is possible. We may note, too, that the names and persons of Kenan the father, Mahalalel the son, and Jared the grandson are listed only here in all the Hebrew Bible.

■ **18-20** **Jared** is from the root *yrd*, meaning "to descend." Other suggested etymologies are tenuous, at best; when a valid etymology is available, it is not necessary to look further. Hess suggests, "Whether or not this is a shortened form of a name with a divine element (which would request or give thanks for a heavenly deity descending to aid at the time of birth or some other time), is uncertain" (2009, 69-70). While we cannot be sure, this seems a solid possibility.

Many have tried to link the genealogy of Cain in Gen 4 with this genealogy of Seth, starting from the fact that both begin with Adam, and both have the name Lamech in the penultimate position (in the genealogy, proper). Next, they observe that Enoch is a name common to both genealogies, though accounting for the fact that Cain's Enoch is third in the list, while Seth's Enoch is seventh, is difficult.

Where such attempts encounter greater difficulty, however, is with **Jared** and its supposed counterpart in the genealogy of Cain, Irad (see commentary on 4:18). Though both names contain *resh* and *dalet* as the second and third consonants, the two different first consonants (*ayin* for Irad; *yod* for Jared) make it impossible to equate the two names.

■ **21-24** The fact that **Enoch** occupies the seventh position in the genealogy of Seth leads the reader to expect something unusual, and we are not disappointed. On the meaning of the name, see commentary on 4:17, above.

The first departure from the pattern follows the notice of the birth of Enoch's son, Methuselah. Instead of the normal, "Then X lived . . . ," the narrator reports, ***Then Enoch walked with God, after he had fathered Methuselah, three hundred years, and he fathered sons and daughters*** (v 22). The stem of the verb, **walked**, is reflexive (*Hithpa'el*), the same verb in the same stem as the reference to God walking in the garden (3:8), after the first pair had eaten of the forbidden fruit. This is another connection between the earlier and the later narratives, and the writer used the same phrase to speak of Enoch again, just two verses later, in v 24.

Later, the narrator again used this same verb in the same stem to report that Noah "walked with God" (6:9). The imperative form of this verb in the same stem is also found in God's command to Abraham to walk before him (17:1; see also 48:15). This verb stem suggests here and elsewhere a habitual, consistent, and constant relationship with God. One may say Enoch "walked" with God each moment of each day, though he lived in a sinful world that had alienated itself from God.

The next unusual feature is the notice (5:23) that Enoch lived on the earth three hundred sixty-five years. This number corresponds, of course, to the number of days in the solar year. It is, as well, by far the shortest life span in this genealogy; the next shortest, that of Enoch's grandson Lamech, is well over twice as long (v 31).

The final verse of the paragraph (v 24) is most startling of all, ***So Enoch walked with God; then he was not, for God took him.*** The first clause repeats the first words of v 22 exactly. The second is a verbless clause in Hebrew; the particle translated ***was not*** (*'ên*) refers to nonexistence, as its opposite (*yēš*) refers to existence. In Ps 39:13, the phrase "[I] am no more" implies death (see also Gen 42:13; Job 7:8; Ps 104:35). From the perspective of those who awaited his return each day, the day came when Enoch simply ***was not,*** for on that day he did not, nor did he ever again, return.

Enoch did not just disappear, however, for someone to discover his body in some out-of-the-way place at a later date; rather, **God took** [*lāqaḥ* means "take," "receive"] **him.** In Ps 49:15, the psalmist expresses his confidence that God will "ransom" his "soul from the power of Sheol" and that God will "receive" (*lāqaḥ*) him (NRSV). The narrative of 2 Kgs 2:1 uses the verb 'ālâ (meaning "go up," "climb," "ascend") to describe the idea of God's taking of Elijah to heaven. Here (Gen 5:24), the narrator affirms that Enoch also did not traverse the usual detour-by-death through Sheol, to be reunited with God at the end of time.

Enoch in Second Temple Tradition

The mysterious glimpse of Enoch vouchsafed the reader in Gen 5:21-24 stimulated several works attributed to him in the Second Temple period (postexilic return through the first century A.D.). Three of these are the (pseudepigraphic) *1 Enoch*, an apocalypse preserved in Ethiopic; *2 Enoch*, another apocalypse preserved in Slavonic; *3 Enoch*, an apocalypse preserved in Hebrew. That *1 Enoch* is older than its Ethiopic version is clear from the fact that fragments in Aramaic were discovered among the Dead Sea Scrolls. In *1* and *2 Enoch*, Enoch purportedly received tours through the (seven) levels of heaven, guided by an angel. A later Jewish mystical tradition regarded Enoch as identical with Metatron, or "Little Yahweh," the angel seen in this tradition as closest to God.

In the NT, Jude makes a reference to Enoch and quotes from *1 En.* 1:9 (vv 14-15). Jude obviously had a high regard for Enoch and for the book attributed to him. Jude's quotation from a book later excluded from the OT canon was one reason for the fourth-century debate over whether his own letter should be included in the NT canon.

FROM THE TEXT

That Seth, born after the expulsion from Eden and begotten in the likeness and image of his father, carried also the likeness and image of God is the clear teaching of vv 1-3. In the postflood narrative, in God's speech to Noah and his descendants, the narrator returned to the theme of humankind in the image of God (9:6). These biblical texts demonstrate that the image of God in humans was not destroyed, eradicated, or taken away by, or as a result of, the event we commonly call "the fall."

Several issues are important when considering the divine-human relationship(s) before and after the first human turning away in the garden. First, the narrative of that turning away (Gen 3) clearly was/is intended to demonstrate that—in and by the nature of created existence itself—human autonomy from God simply is not possible; the only outcome of attempting to establish such autonomy is death. Part and parcel of that death, as both effect and instrumentality, is the disruption of the previously delightful intimacy and harmony of our relationships with God, with each other, and with the rest of the created order.

Because God had purposed beforehand to put into motion the work of redemption, restoration, and renewal, physical death did not take the errant pair immediately; the decay of death took time to reach its inevitable end. Thus, humans continue as creatures made in God's image, but with that image "bent" and "marred" (both biblical metaphors). Spiritual sensitivity and moral judgment are impaired; the Edenic relationship with God was broken. William Greathouse has said that the first human act of disobedience "brought a deprivation of the holiness in which man was created," which further resulted in "moral depravation for Adam's race" (1998, 43).

Because God purposed the redemption and restoration of creation—beginning with the human race, which caused the great catastrophe—we humans continue to be responsible to God to fulfill the original stewardship mandate placed upon us at our creation (Gen 1:28; 2:15). Certainly, the continuing influence of sin impairs our effectiveness in that fulfillment, but that does not absolve us of the responsibility.

That Seth was born in his father Adam's image (5:3) leads to the conclusion that Seth's descendants, because born in Seth's image, also are born in Adam's image. Thus, the reality of the human condition is that humans created in the image of God also bear the image of the fallen original father and mother. The narrator's object in bringing us to this conclusion, however, was not to drive us to despair, but to lead us to hope. That the narrator here continued to refer to humans as "in the likeness of God" (5:1) means humans continued (and continue) as the objects and potential recipients of God's measureless grace. This divine grace makes possible human presence and action as God's image and representation in the world, even in our disrupted relationships with God, with each other, and with the rest of creation. We are far from perfect in this, but we are not "nothing."

It bears repeating: That we are "something," despite our fallen estate, is due to this grace of God. This "aspect" of divine grace is so significant that Wesleyan tradition has a special term for it; we refer to it as prevenient grace. God's prevenient ("going-before") grace, permeating the world, provides the redemption-charged atmosphere (to use an imperfect metaphor) in which alienated and sinful humans are enabled—without it we would *not* be able—to respond to God's offer of the restoration of relationship, to live in reconciliation with God as God's "new creation" (2 Cor 5:17-20).

The Wesleyan doctrine of entire sanctification further emphasizes the work of God's grace in the total renewal and restoration of humanity in the image of God, into the likeness of Jesus Christ, who is the "image of the invisible God" (Col 1:15). God promises, in and through Christ, the power we need "for life and godliness," to escape "the corruption that is in the world," and to "become participants of the divine nature" (2 Pet 1:3-4, NRSV). This promise is central to the Wesleyan proclamation of the gospel of Jesus Christ.

The narrator's report twice in a three-verse span that "Enoch walked with God" is of utmost significance. Partly, this is because life as a "walk" with God is a pervasive metaphor throughout the pages of Scripture, and here we see its beginning very early, indeed. From earliest antiquity, the usual mode of human movement has been on foot. Thus, to "walk" with God is to have God as one's companion at every moment, in every place.

Moreover, walking together is an intimately relational exercise. Amos asked, rhetorically, *Do two walk together unless they have appointed [agreed upon it]?* (3:3). To characterize Enoch as having walked with God is to define him as a man of God. To emulate Enoch, and walk with God ourselves, is to walk the path of godliness, to be people of God in our day. To see and to practice life as a walk with God is not only a common metaphor but also a very helpful and satisfying way to live.

3. Methuselah Through Noah: Three Generations (5:25-32)

IN THE TEXT

■ **25-27** The first element of the name **Methuselah** is *mat/metu*, meaning "man, man of." The second element is less certain. Some take *šelaḥ* to mean spear/javelin, and understand "man of the spear" (e.g., Hamilton 1990, 258). Tsevat proposed "man of [the deity] Shalah," Shalah being the god of the "infernal river," i.e., the river of Sheol or Hades (ref., Hess 2009, 70). Either suggestion is plausible. Some scholars attempt to equate Methuselah with Methushael of Cain's line (4:18). However, neither the final letter *khet* of Methuselah, nor the penultimate letter *'aleph* of Methushael, ever will disappear (elide) in the Hebrew consonantal text, nor will either ever be substituted for the other. These two names *cannot* be made to be the same name.

Methuselah's claim to fame is, of course, his longevity. In the realm of humans, no one else has lived as long as he. Simple addition places Methuselah's death in the year of the flood. Since he was the son of righteous Enoch, and the father of righteous Lamech, most have assumed him to have been a righteous man also. It is easy to think of Methuselah's death as clearing the way for the flood, as it were. As a righteous man, he could not have been destroyed in the flood himself, but with the last righteous man gone, and the ark completed, the judgment of the flood would be unjust to no one.

Jerome on Methuselah's Longevity

By a careful reckoning it can be shown that Methuselah lived fourteen years after the flood. It appears that in this case as in many others, in the Septuagint translation of the Bible there is an error in the numbers. Among the Hebrews and the books of the Samaritans, I have found the text written thus: [vv 25-28]. Accordingly, there are 369 years from the day of Methuselah's birth to the day of Noah's birth; to these add Noah's six hundred years, since the flood occurred in the six hundredth year of his life, and so it works out that Methuselah died in the nine hundred sixty-ninth year of his life, in the same year when the flood began. (Louth 2001, 121)

■ **28-31** For a second time we find a name that has occurred already in Cain's genealogy (see Enoch in 4:17 and 5:18-24 and Lamech in 4:18-24 and in 5:25-31). Parallel names in these texts do not necessarily mean, though, that the narrator was working from a common original genealogy, as some suggest. The Lamech of 4:18-24 was a man of pride and arrogance, whereas the Lamech of these verses was a man of hope and anticipation for a better future. For the first time since Adam's naming of Seth (5:3), the narrator reports a formal naming, Lamech *fathered a son, and he called his name Noah* (vv 28-29; see commentary on vv 2, 3-5, above). We see the reason for this in the reporting of Lamech's hope or confidence invested in the name he chose.

Noah is from the root *nûah*, meaning rest, while Lamech's explanation (v 29), *this one will bring us relief*, uses the root *nāham* (comfort, bring relief). Though the name and the explanation do not have linguistic connection, they are close enough in conveying the hope of Lamech. *This one will bring us relief from our work, even from the onerous toil of our hands, from the ground which Yahweh cursed it.* Lamech defined the *work* (*ma'áseh*) from which he hoped his son would bring relief by the noun, *onerous toil* ['*iṣṣābôn*] *of our hands.* Alternatively, Hamilton may be correct in seeing here a hendiadys and translating both nouns together, "from the agonizing toil of our hands" (Hamilton 1990, 248).

This is the third occurrence of '*iṣṣābôn*; it occurs first in God's words to the woman (3:16), then in God's words to the man (3:17), as they stood before God in the garden. It is doubtful Lamech hoped for all human work to cease; what he hoped for was an easing of the onerous, irksome, anxiety-producing, "agonizing" labor required to provide food and other necessities. Hamilton suggests that perhaps "the renewed gift of the vine (9:20)," following the flood, represented the relief Lamech here expressed his longing for (1990, 259). In this connection, too, it is important to note Lamech's final words, *the ground which Yahweh cursed it.* God's curse on the ground made human work difficult; what Lamech hoped for may not have been the removal of the curse upon the ground—what basis would he have had for such an idea?—but a measure of relief that would lessen the effect of the curse.

Lamech's naming of his son shows the significant contrast between him and the Cainite Lamech. This Lamech, a man of righteousness and goodwill, voiced at the birth of his son a prayer of hope for the relief of all humankind. The Cainite line ends with the self-aggrandizing, egotistical boasting of the Cainite Lamech. Cain's line ended in the multiplication of violence. Seth's line also succumbed to the allure of violence, as we shall see, but this son did become the bringer of relief that Lamech prayed for when he named him **Noah**.

So all the days of Lamech were seven and seventy years, and seven hundred years; then he died. Seven hundred seventy-seven is both a perfect life span and a large multiple of the biblical number of perfection. Seven also is the number of God and, therefore, a reminder of God's grace. God would extend grace and relief to Seth's line, through this Lamech's aptly-named son, **Noah.**

■ **32** The genealogy ends with the report of Noah becoming a father when he was five hundred years old. The phrase, **he became the father of Shem, Ham and Japheth,** marks a departure from the literary pattern in the previous verses, where the narrator reports the birth of the first son and then a summary report of the birth of other sons and daughters. Noah's death is not reported until 9:28-29. The extended intervening narrative records the end of all life upon the land, except that of Noah and his family and the animals they took with them aboard the ark. The narrator lists the names of the three sons together, here, as a literary signal that the genealogical form would not be continued at this point. When the names of the three sons are next mentioned (6:10), it is not for genealogical purposes, but to introduce the narrative of the flood. In the flood and postflood narratives, proper (6:11—9:29), Noah and his sons appear again as the men who, together with their wives, survived the flood, and as those who would usher in a new phase in the history of the human race.

FROM THE TEXT

Many have observed that though seven of these antediluvian patriarchs (including Noah) lived more than nine hundred years, none reached the age of one thousand years, which the psalmist later was to declare is "like a day," or even only "a watch in the night," from God's perspective (Ps 90:4). Methuselah came closest, outliving his son Lamech by five years, and dying in the year of the flood (though not *in* the flood). One clear and intended teaching of this genealogy is that, far from being gods or demigods, as the Mesopotamian antediluvian kings were thought to be, these people were mortal.

In that vein, it is of interest to the lover of trivia that the years by which Methuselah failed to reach one thousand—namely, thirty-one years—represent more than the average human life expectancy from birth, through most of human history. Put another way, if we add Methuselah's age to the age of any one of most humans who ever have been born (until very recently), their combined age still will not make one thousand years!

C. Zenith of Unbridled Desire; God's Assessment (6:1-8)

BEHIND THE TEXT

The narrator digresses from the genealogy of Seth, which ends with Noah in 5:32, to insert a narrative unit that portrays the sinful condition of the human race. The story of Noah is picked up again in 6:9. Commentators usually end this unit with v 4. We consider v 8 as a better breaking point; 6:1-8 constitutes a two-paragraph unit, also, as we shall see.

The first paragraph of this unit (vv 1-4) has elicited as much discussion in translation and interpretation as almost any biblical passage, focusing primarily on the identification of those the Hebrew text designates *běnê hāʾĕlōhîm* (usually translated, **the sons of God**). Thus, it may be helpful to summarize the major interpretations of this phrase before we begin our own investigation.

One important approach has been to translate, **the sons of God,** meaning supernatural beings. Sometimes **Nephilim** is brought together with **the sons of God,** to identify them as "fallen" sons of God, i.e., as fallen angels. Therein lay their wickedness, that fallen angels—demons, really—were marrying human women and having children by them, half-demonic, half-human "monsters."

The second position is similar but relegates this episode to the realm of mythology, one of numerous stories of gods cohabiting with human women because they found them beautiful. The Hebrew Bible, especially the Torah, eliminated or demythologized most of these ancient pagan stories, but this one slipped through.

The third common approach is to translate, "sons of the mighty ones." Often in the Bible, "son of" or "sons of" denotes member(s) of a group, rather than physical descent. These, then, were human men, elite among their fellows by virtue of physical strength, intelligence, or some other giftedness or combination of gifts. Their conduct here may or may not have been sinful.

The fourth major position is that the **daughters of men** were descended from Cain. The **sons of God** were Seth's descendants, since his was the godly line. Thus, when Seth's "godly" descendants began to marry the daughters of Cain's "ungodly" descendants, it became a cause of sinfulness in the godly line, too, contributing to God's judgment in bringing the flood.

IN THE TEXT

■ **1-2** *Now it came to pass that humans began to multiply upon the ground, and daughters were born to them. Then the mighty ones saw the daughters of the humans, that they were good, so they took for themselves wives [women] from any whom they chose.*

Except for the phrase we have translated *the mighty ones,* these two verses are straightforward. That phrase, however, together with its implications for the rest of this paragraph, has caused major differences of translation and understanding as far back as the exegetical record goes. We will deal with the "easy" parts first, hoping they will help in guiding us to a correct understanding of who *the mighty ones* were.

The focus of the first part of v 1 is on the growth or multiplication of *humans* (*hāʾādām*); *hāʾādām* means here the human race, the human species, collectively, as is usual when the definite article (*ha-*) is prefixed to the noun.

Chapters 4 and 5 are two separate records of this multiplication through the lines of Cain and Seth, respectively. Humankind was doing what God had instructed (1:28). The phrase, **upon the ground,** however, instead of the expected "upon the earth," carries slightly pejorative or dismissive overtones. The use of the word **ground** (ʾādāmâ) is one of several connections between this paragraph and the genealogy of Seth. In Lamech's naming of his son, Noah (5:29), he referred to **the ground which Yahweh cursed.** The narrator may have been suggesting here that though humans were fulfilling the creational mandate, this was happening on the ground God had cursed because of the sin of the first parents. If so, the implication was that this would not end well.

The genealogies of Cain and Seth both focused on male descendants. While Seth's genealogy contains only passing references to "daughters," Cain's list does include the name of one daughter, Naamah (4:22). Here the narrator turns attention to the **daughters** who **were born** to the humans. Verse 2 describes these daughters as **good** (ṭōbōt), often translated as **beautiful,** "fair," "desirable," etc. The foundational meaning of ṭōbōt is "good." Morally and ethically, functionally, esthetically—in any and every evaluation in the world of the OT—the basic categories are "good" (ṭōb) and "bad" (raʿ). Certainly, the evaluation of these first **daughters of the humans** as ṭōbōt included perceptions of physical beauty and desirability. However, the vocabulary here suggests we should not limit this evaluation to physical beauty alone; they were **good** in many other aspects of their being also.

They took for themselves wives is a normal way of saying a man married a woman. This phrasing even is used of taking a wife for another, i.e., to arrange a marriage (e.g., Gen 21:21; 24:3-4; Judg 14:3). Thus, this is not a narrative about rape or other use of physical force, which normally would employ another verb. Similarly, the final phrase, **from any whom they chose,** is not necessarily sinister in its connotations. Any **mighty one** easily could have chosen any **daughter of the humans** without sinful intentions or acts on the part of either of them.

Yet the narrator follows this situation with a report of God taking exception to it in some way, and that report (v 3) is followed in its turn by one of the most enigmatic statements in all Scripture (v 4). This cannot be all there is to this small paragraph. We turn, then, to the *crux interpretum*, the phrase that either elucidates or clouds the whole, the Hebrew běnê hāʾĕlōhîm, which we have translated, **the mighty ones.**

We begin by noting that the root from which comes the cluster of Hebrew words, ʾel/ʾeloah/ʾelohim, does not signify deity; its basic referent is "might," understood not only as physical strength but also as occupying a place of status, influence, and/or other kinds of power. Wherever kings and priests were at the top of the social hierarchy, they, and those who aided them in keeping and using power, were **the mighty ones.** In many contexts, though not here in 6:2, this group could include women, as well.

A good example is Ps 29:1, "Ascribe to [Yahweh], O mighty ones, ascribe to [Yahweh] glory and strength." "O mighty ones" translates Hebrew *běnê ʾēlîm*. In the context of the entire psalm, this opening line is its call to worship. These ***mighty ones*** *may* have included some or all of God's spiritual and/or rational, but nonhuman, creatures; there is nothing in the psalm to prevent such an understanding. However, these ***mighty ones*** *certainly* included human persons of power, wealth, and standing, if this psalm is to make sense as a song for the *human* worship of God upon this earth—the psalm's manifest purpose. The ***mighty ones*** among humankind are called upon to lead this worship.

Moreover, here (Gen 6:2) ***mighty ones*** *cannot* refer to divine or semidivine beings, or to angels, for the simple reason that human biology does not allow for the possibility of procreation with nonhumans, whether angels or beasts. (Mary's conception of Jesus is another matter, entirely.) Nor can it refer to humans who strove to become (or were thought to have become) divine. A prominent and consistent theological theme throughout the Bible is that such attempt on the part of humans is foolish.

Here, ***mighty ones*** can refer only to human men. The most reasonable assumption, then, would be that these men had achieved greater status and power than most, by their prowess in hunting or in battle (or both), or perhaps through invention and technical skills (see 4:20-22).

The text does not state directly why God was displeased with these men taking "good" women in marriage. We will suggest that the reason is present indirectly in the statement of v 2b, ***They took for themselves wives*** [*nāšîm*] ***of any/all whom they chose.*** (As we have noted, the vocabulary of ***they took for themselves*** rules out *forcible* rape.) Hebrew *nāšîm* means "women"; it can and does refer to "wives," but it also can denote concubines or servant girls with no protection against the master's sexual advances—in short, some of these may have been women brought into any continuing sexual arrangement other than regular marriage. The phrase, ***any/all whom they chose,*** then, indicates that these mighty ones, men of wealth and status, acquired good and desirable women by the illegitimate use of their power, without love or respect for them, and without regard for their feelings and desires about entering (or not entering) into the sexual relationship. Even if some of these were marriages—as some certainly would have been—such coercive marriage relationships also would have violated the fundamental principle of marital union set out already in 2:22-24. Here, then, the narrator reported the total disregard of the most powerful men of Noah's day for God's plan for marriage and their misappropriation of God's good gifts, at the expense of the many powerless members of the opposite gender.

■ **3** Hamilton's point, with regard to the placement of God's statement just here in the narrative, is well taken, "By placing [this] verse where it is, the author is making the point that this forbidden union itself is offensive to Yahweh, rather than the fact that such a union produced (hybrid) offspring" (Hamilton

1990, 266). We differ with Hamilton on the nature of the transgressions but agree that the transgressions, not the offspring, constituted the offense.

A traditional Christian understanding is reflected in NIV's, **My Spirit will not contend with man forever.** The root form of the verb *yādôn* is not certain. Some associate it with *dîn*, which means "to judge." The Septuagint and the Vulgate both translate *yādôn* as "remain." Some commentators associate this verb with *dnn*, "to remain, to exist," which occurs in Akkadian, Arabic, Aramaic, and Syriac, as well as in Hebrew (see Cassuto 1961, 296). The best solution, on all counts, would seem to be to translate "remain." Thus, we translate the first part of the verse, *My breath will not remain in the human forever, inasmuch as he also is flesh.*

Hebrew *rûaḥ* can mean, "wind," "breath," "spirit," or "Spirit." The *rûaḥ* of God first came into the **human** (*hāʾādām*) when God breathed into the nostrils of the *ʾādām* the "breath of life" (*nišmat ḥayyîm;* 2:7). The *rûaḥ* of God is thus the animating spirit, the spirit that provides vitality and power to the humans, to continue their existence as living beings (*nepeš;* 2:7).

The phrase *inasmuch as he also is flesh* (*bĕšagam hûʾ bāśār*) also is the subject of extensive debate. Cassuto suggests translating *bĕšagam* "inasmuch . . . also" (1961, 296-97). If this reading is correct, then this phrase means that humans who are in the image of God (1:26-27) are also *flesh* (*bāśār*) like all other creatures, which also have the "breath [*rûaḥ*] of life" (see v 17).

Verse 3 ends with the statement, **Nevertheless, their [the humans'] days shall be one hundred twenty years.** In light of the longevity reported for most of the line of Seth in the genealogy of ch 5, one may see here the divine decision not to permit the humans to enjoy a long life span, but to limit it to 120 years. It took a few generations after the flood for that process to work itself out. Noah lived a total of 950 years. The genealogy of Shem in 11:10-32 also shows longer life spans, ranging from 600 (Shem) to 148 years (Nahor). We notice in this genealogy the life span gradually declining to below 200 years, which continued to be the case for Abraham (175) and Isaac (180). The number 120, here, also echoes Moses' life span of 120 years (Deut 34:7).

In view of the fact that it is rare for humans to live so long, some have preferred an alternative explanation, that the **one hundred twenty years** refers to the time between God's instruction to Noah to build the ark and God's bringing of the flood upon the earth. These years were thus the years of grace yet remaining for the wicked generation of the flood to repent, turn from their evil ways, and be spared the judgment of the flood. These two views of God's decision are not mutually exclusive; one could see in this statement both an expression of grace to the preflood human race and a limit set to human life span after the flood.

■ **4** Verse 4 is one of the most enigmatic verses in Scripture. We follow here the translation of *bĕnê hāʾĕlōhîm* (**the mighty men**) as key to our understanding of the noun *nĕpîlîm*, which is left untranslated in the NIV and in other modern translations ("giants" in the LXX; see also NLT). Numbers 13:33 is the only other place this noun form occurs in the OT. The noun comes from the root consonants *npl* ("to fall"); thus, **the fallen ones** would be the meaning of this plural noun form. Nothing in the text here *requires* us to understand the **Nephilim** as divine, semidivine, or demonic. The idea that the **Nephilim** refers to divine or semidivine beings has its origin in the interpretation of *bĕnê hā' ĕlōhîm* in vv 2 and 4 as "the sons of God." We interpret the **Nephilim,** following our interpretation of *bĕnê hā'ĕlōhîm*, as human beings; they were humans just as *bĕnê hā'ĕlōhîm* were human. Numbers 13:33 supports the view of **Nephilim** as humans. The report of the ten spies that they saw **Nephilim** in the promised land most likely conveys the idea that the land was inhabited by large humans (doughty warriors) who would have appeared gigantic to the Israelites. Lack of concrete evidence in the text does not permit us to say anything more, except to translate the term as **the fallen ones.** The author may have had in mind the "fallen" Cainites, and/or those Sethites who had "fallen away" from following Yahweh, but we cannot be certain.

Equally difficult is the relationship between this **Nephilim** reference and the rest of the verse. Hamilton treats the phrase, "The Nephilim were on the earth in those days—and later on too," as a parenthetical note of the narrator or editor, grammatically unrelated to what comes before or after it. Such parenthetical notes are a regular feature of the biblical text, though not always presented as such in translation. Hamilton calls them "frame-breaks," and lists several comparable ones from Deuteronomy (Hamilton 1990, 261, 270).

Modifying Hamilton's translation slightly, we render the parenthetical note as follows: **The Nephilim [*the fallen ones*] were on the earth in those days—and also afterward.** We also suggest that perhaps the phrase **and also afterward** constitutes a *second* note incorporated into the first. That is, the sentence (**The Nephilim were on the earth in those days**) may have been the original parenthetical note, and a later copyist may have added the phrase **and also afterward** as a second parenthetical note based on the story of Num 13. It is not possible to say how and when such notes were incorporated into the text; we only may assume here the work of later copyists. These parenthetical notes do not significantly alter the meaning of v 4.

The obvious conclusion of vv 1-4 is found in the second part of v 4: **When the mighty ones went in to the daughters of the humans, then they bore [children] to them; these [the children] became the preeminent ones of old, the men of renown.** Several points require attention. First is the implicit contrast between **the mighty ones** and **the daughters of the humans.** This line especially, with only a preposition between the two designations, often is taken as proof that the first group cannot be human, since the second group obviously comprises human women. But a different contrast is the one really intended. The small group of **the mighty ones,** human men, had access to *any* *and all* of **the daughters of the humans**—*precisely because of their privileged status*—as the narrator already had stated (v 2).

Of course, children were born to most of these unions. We have inserted **children** twice, and have translated the pronoun that actually occurs in the Hebrew text (*hēmmâ*) as **these,** only to make clear that the children referred to here were not the **Nephilim** of the parenthetical statement at the beginning of the verse. These children of **the mighty ones** attained high status as **the preeminent ones** (*hagibbōrîm*) and accomplished great things in their time, as their fathers had in theirs. The epithet *gibbôr* is more often associated with warriors and warfare than with peaceful pursuits. Some of these men may have been good—their actions constructive and beneficial—but a likely surmise is that most of them earned their notable reputations with violence, probably off the battlefield as well as on. The phrase **men of renown** is, literally, "men of the name," i.e., men with reputations. By the time of this narrative, however, they already had faded into the shadowy recesses of antiquity. Their names, their reputations, and the deeds by which they had won them—all were lost in the dustbin of history.

■ **5** What the preceding paragraph invites the reader to infer, this paragraph makes plain. The unfair advantage taken by men in positions of power, with respect to marital and other sexual arrangements, was but one symptom of the cancerous evil corrupting everyone. Some translations and commentators treat vv 5 and 6 as a single complex sentence; others as two separate sentences. Opting for the latter, we translate, **Now Yahweh saw that the evil of the ʾādām [of humankind]** *had multiplied upon the earth,* **and that every inclination of the thoughts of** *their hearts* **was only evil all the** *day.*

Now Yahweh saw does not mean that suddenly God became aware of what God had not noticed previously. The verb **saw** (*râʾâ*) here has the same sense as in 1:4, 10, 12, 18, 21, 25, 31; it conveys the idea of God considering and evaluating something or someone. The reasonable inference here is that God had been evaluating the conduct of humankind on an ongoing basis, through all the events and the generations that are the subjects of the preceding chapters. God's own work, including the creation of humankind, God consistently had evaluated as "good." Now, after several generations of opportunity, God's evaluation of humans was that they had followed the path of rebellion started in the garden by the first parents; they would not now change that direction, that inclination, of their own accord.

On the one hand, God had blessed humankind **to multiply** [from the root *rābab*] **upon the face of the ground** (v 1). On the other hand, as humans multiplied, what God saw multiplying (*rābab*) was **the evil of humankind upon the earth.** Every **thought** and every **inclination** of thought that originated in the human **heart** was **evil.** Such was God's assessment of the human condition. An **inclination** (*yēṣer*) is not merely a habitual frame of mind or thought that may or may not result in action. What God noted was constant,

6:4-5

unceasing, and active devising, planning, and carrying out of evil. We translate the second part of v 5 as follows to make clear God's evaluation of humans: *every scheme of the planning of their heart(s) was* only *evil all day long* [*and every day*]. In Hebrew thought, the heart (*lēb*) is the seat of human will, emotions, thinking, and planning; it represents the inner being. Evil had taken up residence at the very core of human existence, had taken total control of humans' inner thoughts and feelings. The phrase *all day long* characterizes the effect of this evil as systemic, permeating all human thought and action.

■ **6** Verse 5 reports God's objective evaluation of the human condition at this time. Verse 6 opens God's heart to the reader, revealing God's thoughts and feelings, both, about this state of affairs. "Feelings" and "thoughts" may be a bit too sharp a distinction, but this will be a convenient way of discussing this verse. (Also, as we have noted before, Genesis does not portray an impassive God.)

The first clause records God's thoughts about the state of humanity just reported. Given God's decision to act reported next in v 7, **The LORD was grieved** (*wayyinnāhem* from *nāham*) is too "soft" a translation, but NIV is not alone in opting for it. The Hebrew root *nāham* has quite a broad semantic range, but its grammatical form here, together with its setting in this context, narrows the choices. The stem is *Niphʾal* (a reflexive, here), indicating that whatever God thought here, the change was within and, in a sense, something God did "to" God's own self—or, better, what God's conclusion in light of this assessment "did to" God. The confirmed reality of the human condition affected God's thinking. The context requires us to understand that God not only **was grieved**—though that was true—but that God *regretted* having created humans, most of whom now had proven themselves incorrigibly evil. God changed God's mind about the wisdom of having made the human creature!

God's *emotional* response ran deeper, though, than regret and a change of mind. The final clause we may render (a bit expansively), *and it made itself an anxious, onerous, painful toiling* [*wayyitʿaṣṣēb* from *ʿāṣab*, meaning "difficult or anxious toil"] *to his heart.* This, of course, is very cumbersome, but it begins to express the excruciating weight of the burden that human wickedness put on God. Again, the verb stem is reflexive (this time, *Hitpaʾel*); God's own emotional response was having this effect on God and God's feelings about the situation. Moreover, this is the same root the narrator used in reporting God's announcements to the human pair in the garden of what life would be like as a result of their own choice and action of turning away from God (3:16, 17). God now suffered an *anxious, onerous, painful, toiling of/ to/within his heart* but not as a result of God's own actions. The humans God had formed with exquisite care, with whom God had met joyfully and lovingly each day, those years ago in the garden—*they* were the cause of the painful toiling of God's heart.

■ **7** God had evaluated (v 5); God was regretful and suffering heartache (v 6). Now, God decided on a course of action: *I will wash humankind, whom I have* *created, from upon the face of the ground—from the humans, to the domestic livestock, to the [rest of] the creatures who move about [upon the ground], even to the flying creatures of the air; for I am sorry I have made them.*

I will wash (from the root *māhâ*) comes from the world of the scribe. Water could erase words or smudges, especially fresh ones, from papyri and ostraca (potsherds written on with ink), probably in most cases by rubbing with a damp cloth (NIV: **I will wipe**). A particularly vivid and ironic example is God's instruction following Amalek's treacherous attack on Israel (Exod 17:14), *Then God said to Moses, "Write this [as] a memory in a scroll, and [also] make sure Joshua hears [it]: for I certainly will wipe* [*māhâ*] *the memory of Amalek from under the heavens."* The attack, Moses was to write down so it would not be forgotten; God would see to erasing the memory of the attackers.

This is the vivid imagery here. Humans and their evil had become a smudge upon the pristine *face of the ground.* God purposed to erase completely the blot upon that "scroll." The use of the verb *māhâ*, "wash/wipe/cleanse with water," hints already at the means God would choose, though the text has not yet mentioned a flood.

God's four-item list of the groups to be "erased" also points forward to a major theme of the coming flood. It would be God's *un*creation of (most) animal life upon the earth, and the temporary return of the earth itself to the disordered and empty state it had manifested at the beginning of God's creative filling and ordering reported in Gen 1. Thus the statement of God's resolve is in the reverse order of the creation. *The humans,* created last, are listed here first. Other land creatures of creation's day six, the *domestic livestock* and "the rest"—grouped here under the general term, [those] *who move about*—are next. Last in this list are ones earliest created, the *flying creatures of the air.* The coming flood would *un*create from the end back to the beginning, until the aspect of the earth would be the same as it had been when "darkness was upon the face of the deep" (Gen 1:2 KJV). Such is the artistry of the narrator that all this is hinted before ever the mechanism of the flood receives its first mention in the text.

The last clause records God as saying directly what the narrator had reported already at the beginning of v 6. God's own statement here is a fitting climax to this brief setting of the scene preparatory to the long narrative of the flood, which is to follow. It also is a striking crescendo, into which the coda of the next, the totally unexpected, the exceedingly brief and marvelously quiet final sentence will fall on the hearer's ear, the reader's mind, as the briefest snatch of a new melody of hope, beckoning one to follow on, for in this direction will lie the longed-for deliverance.

■ **8** The pericope ends with the sentence, **But Noah found favor in the eyes of the LORD.** We can highlight an important nuance by translating, *But as for Noah, he found grace in the eyes of Yahweh.* The narrator placed the word,

But (as for) Noah (*věnōah*), first for emphasis, which is intensified by the conjunction (*vě*) prefixed to Noah. God just had spoken the word of judgment upon humankind, **but as for Noah**—the contrast is dramatic and powerful—**he found grace in the eyes of Yahweh.**

In Hebrew, the noun *hēn* means "grace" or "favor." In the consonantal text, it is spelled *hn*. Noah also is spelled with the same two letters of the Hebrew text, but in reversed position (*nh*). The play on words perhaps is intentional, or it may be an accidence of the language. The narrator at this point does not say why Noah **found grace** in the eyes of God, though the reader finds later in the next section the narrator's description of the character of Noah (see v 9). In v 8, however, the focus is on God's grace/favor at work even in the midst of God's grief over the decision God had made to create humankind.

Chrysostom on Noah's Choice

Do you see how the Lord created our nature to enjoy free will? I mean, how did it happen, tell me, that while those people showed enthusiasm for wickedness and rendered themselves liable to punishment, this man opted for virtue, shunned association with them and thus felt no effect of punishment? Is it not crystal clear that each person chose wickedness or virtue of his own volition? You see, if that were not the case and freedom did not have its roots in our nature, those people would not have been punished, nor would others receive reward for their virtue. Since, however, everything has been allowed to remain with our choice owing to grace from on high, punishment duly awaits the sinners, and reward and recompense those who practice virtue. (Louth 2001, 129)

FROM THE TEXT

God's judgment came upon the generation of Noah because human thinking, plans, desires, and actions had become contrary to God's plans and purposes (Gen 6:5). The biblical tradition traces this condition to a corrupt and evil heart, the seat of human emotions, understanding, and will (see Jer 17:9-10). The corrupt heart has lost all sensitivity to pure thoughts and motives; it is evil through and through. Ezekiel described such a heart as a "heart of stone" (Ezek 36:26); it cannot grieve, because it is stubborn and rebellious.

God's promise to God's people is a "new heart," "a heart of flesh" that will be responsive to God's instruction (Ezek 36:26). The realization of this promise of a new heart began on the day of Pentecost; Peter described the disciples' experience on this day as the "cleansing" of their "hearts by faith" (see Acts 2:1-4; 15:8-9). In Wesleyan theology, the cleansing of the heart is the gracious promise of the Holy Spirit to all who are a new creation in Christ.

God is committed to relationship with the human beings God has created. The depth of God's caring means God sometimes gets hurt. Of course, we do not mean God is diminished in any way *as God*. We do mean, however, that the God who equipped humans with the full range of emotions and emotional responses did so because God is emotional. Not only does God experience joy, pleasure, and others of what we normally term "positive" emotions; God also experiences hurt, grief, sorrow, remorse, anger, and other emotions that we often think of as negative. By contrast with the evil human heart of Noah's generation that could not grieve, v 6 depicts God's as a grieving heart. Though sin often brings temporary pleasure to the sinner, it brings only agony and sorrow to the heart of God.

The difference between God and fallen humans at this point is that God's emotions never drive God to sinful, or even to unwise, attitudes or actions, whereas ours do with a fair degree of regularity, as each of us can testify. It is important for us to remember that God feels sorrows as well as joys, partly so we can believe God can and does empathize with us in our sorrows, as well as in our joys. The idea of the impassive God, while quite common, is neither good Bible nor good theology. For that, we all may be thankful.

In grief and sorrow, in pain and agony, God pronounced the decision to end the world God had brought into existence in joy and anticipation (6:7; see Gen 1:31). God's grief, though, did not take away the necessity of judgment. The judgment pronounced in 6:7 was sure evidence of God's uncompromising attitude toward sin.

Most have wondered at the destruction of the animal kingdom on the land. With the flood as God's chosen agency of judgment upon human evil, the other creatures could not escape. It is common to think of them as innocent victims and, of course, experience teaches that evil always brings harm upon innocent victims. But what if God had chosen another method, affecting humans only? One thinks of any number of illnesses that could have accomplished God's purpose to wipe the earth clean of its evildoers: bubonic plague, yellow fever, typhoid fever, etc. Yet God specifically included these three large groupings of the land and the flying creatures in the coming judgment. Were they implicated in human wickedness? If so, it is difficult to imagine how they could have been, at least so widely that judgment on them would be "justified" as a forensic response to their conduct.

One way to think about this theological problem is to view it in light of the wider impact of human sin on the whole creation. Hosea speaks of the mourning of the land, of the languishing of all who live in the land, and even of the destruction of the animals, the birds of the air, and the fish of the sea—all as the result of Israel's breaking of covenant (Hos 4:1-3). As we have indicated earlier, God's decision to destroy God's creation was not arbitrary; it was extremely painful to God.

From one perspective, we may ask, "What choice did God have?" The humans created in God's own image—with infinite love, care, and joy—had resisted God's purposes for the whole creation. This text serves as a strong reminder of how our sins affect not only ourselves and our human communities, but all the rest of God's good creation, as well. Not only the threatened collapse of human society, but also the increasing destruction of the nonhuman creation around us, is linked to our lack of commitment to God's creational purposes for us and for the rest of the creation. The apostle Paul anticipated the still-future time when "the creation itself will be set free from its bondage to decay and will obtain the freedom of the glory of the children of God" (Rom 8:21 NRSV).

"To find grace in the eyes of . . ." is an idiom sometimes reversed in the mind of the Western reader. Noah did not extend grace to Yahweh; Yahweh extended grace to Noah. The image is the throne room of the ancient king. Entering the room and prostrating oneself upon the floor, one looked up into the face of the seated king only when bidden. The king's welcoming expression, best read in his eyes, and his permission to rise and approach, meant one had "found grace in the eyes of" the king. Any other reception would have been chilling for almost anyone; sometimes, it could mean death (see, e.g., Esth 4:11). *Noah found grace in the eyes of Yahweh,* not the other way round.

Genesis 6:8 is a very short verse, but it conveys great hope. This succinct report of Noah finding grace shows that in the midst of God's grief, in the midst of God's decision to wipe out the earthly creation, God "already" was thinking about its future. The text introduces Noah as the sign of, and the hope for, a new humanity and a new creation to come. God was not finished with the creation that had become hostile to God's plans and purposes. Rather, God intended to *re-create* it. The grace God extended to Noah was a marker of genuine hope for the future of the whole creation. Almost routinely, it seems sometimes, one hears the view that the OT is law and judgment, while the NT is grace and salvation. *Noah found grace in the eyes of Yahweh* reminds us that nothing could be further from the truth.

In the next section (The Deluge; Overview), we will compare and contrast the Genesis flood account with (especially) the story of the "Mesopotamian Noah," as found in the Epic of Gilgamesh. For now, it is enough to note a major difference between the two. Here, we have a clear and objective statement of God's just assessment of the human condition in that age: Nearly every human was planning and practicing evil, systematically and continually. Unchecked, human evil itself would destroy God's good creation. God was "forced" to intervene, in the interests both of justice and of grace. (In the end, these are the same.) By contrast, the Mesopotamian accounts (both in Gilgamesh and in Atrahasis) do *not* attribute to human evil the gods' decision to destroy humans by bringing a flood upon the earth. Rather, the god Enlil became annoyed at humans constantly interrupting his sleep as the earth's human population increased! The theological/moral/ethical difference between the accounts is obvious.

III. THE DELUGE; ONE FAMILY SPARED (GENESIS 6:9—9:29)

Overview

One can find a variety of opinions on the proper division between the genealogy of Gen 5 and the beginning of the flood narrative. Many divide them after 6:4; as we have indicated earlier, there seems to be a theological continuity between 6:1-4 and 6:5-8. The natural place of division, by the narrator's own indication, is the title phrase of 6:9, "These are the *toledot* of Noah."

Genesis 6 sets forth God's instructions to Noah to build the ark and, in a general directive, the living beings who were to enter the ark with him. Genesis 7 adds God's instructions concerning the greater numbers of clean animals to be brought aboard, the actual entrance into the vessel, and the beginning of the flood, to its crest after one hundred fifty days.

Genesis 8 describes the gradual receding of the floodwaters, until Noah and the others could exit, and Noah could offer a sacrifice of thanksgiving for their deliverance. Genesis 9 reports the covenant God offered and entered into with Noah and his family. The last narrated episode of Noah's life does not show him in a favorable light.

"Universal" Memories of the Flood?

More than one hundred and ten flood stories from around the world have come down to the present day. Many societies and cultures possess a memory of an ancient catastrophe brought on by a devastating flood, a flood from which only a few—quite a number of these preserve the number of eight humans—were delivered by means of divine (or extra-human) warning and instruction to build a floating vessel of some kind. Many of these narratives are short and sketchy, but several are full-length stories with quite an astounding amount of detail. Some of their details parallel those of Noah, some differ from it.

The reader whose faith in God is both strong and healthy does not need extrabiblical affirmation of biblical narratives, as though the Bible is not true until we can prove it independently. Moreover, extrabiblical narratives that seem to parallel those in the Bible cannot prove we are reading the biblical narratives correctly, either. We still have that work to do. Nevertheless, when well over one hundred accounts exist, from most areas of the globe, the prudent course may be to investigate, rather than to assume they all are nonhistorical. We may not find what we thought we would find, but it seems plausible we may find *something*.

Besides the Genesis account, the most detailed flood report is the Mesopotamian story of Utnapishtim, recorded on Tablet 11 of the Epic of Gilgamesh. As with the creation narratives of Gen 1—2, comparison—here, of the Genesis story of Noah with the Utnapishtim account—will help the reader in several ways; we will mention two. First, a quite astounding number of similarities exist between Noah's story and Utnapishtim's. A plausible conclusion well could be that the two accounts are describing the same event. Second, and just as important theologically, is the significant number of differences between the two accounts. As both the similarities and the differences are instructive, this may be the place to list the more important of them. (Many other similarities and differences exist, more than we can discuss here.)

Noah's and Utnapishtim's Flood Accounts: Similarities

1. Both floods were divinely determined.
2. Both men were warned of a coming devastating flood.
3. Both men were instructed to build a floating vessel.
4. Both men were instructed on the size of the vessel.
5. Both vessels were divided into stories and rooms.
6. Both vessels were waterproofed with pitch.
7. Both men obeyed, entered their vessels, and survived.
8. Animals came to both vessels without human prompting.
9. In both stories, all life outside the vessel perished.
10. Both vessels grounded on a mountain.
11. Both men sent out a raven and a dove from the vessel.
12. On leaving the vessel, both men offered sacrifices.

Noah's and Utnapishtim's Flood Accounts: Differences

Noah	Utnapishtim
1. God caused the flood as moral judgment.	Gods caused the flood to remove annoyance of human noise.
2. Noah preached to his neighbors (2 Pet 2:5).	The god Ea told Utnapishtim to lie to his neighbors.
3. Noah built a seaworthy ark.	Utnapishtim built a cubic boat, a floating wooden box.
4. Noah's ark was about four hundred fifty feet long.	Utnapishtim's boat covered about an acre in area.
5. Noah's family of eight persons entered the ark.	Utnapishtim's family entered the boat, along with captain and crew.
6. God closed the door of the ark.	Utnapishtim closed the door of the boat.
7. God was transcendent "over" the flood.	Gods were terrified at the flood they had unleashed.
8. Rain and waters continued forty days.	Rain, only, continued seven days.
9. Noah remained aboard the ark one full year.	Utnapishtim's stay was unspecified, but briefer (weeks, not months).
10. God "smelled [the] savor" (KJV) of Noah's sacrifice.	Hungry gods "crowded like flies" around Utnapishtim's sacrifice.
11. God established a covenant with Noah and the earth.	No covenant is mentioned.
12. Noah died "normally."	Utnapishtim was made immortal, divine.

A. God's Instructions to Noah for Building the Ark (6:9-22)

BEHIND THE TEXT

We have come to the parade example (together with Gen 1—2) of the source-critical model that dominated pentateuchal studies for about a century, usually called the Documentary Hypothesis, or simply JEDP. The source-critical tradition saw the story of Noah as almost hopelessly entangled among two (or three) original sources, not very skillfully merged by redactors (editors) who tried to make them into a single narrative.

However, beginning already in the late nineteenth century, with the discovery and publication of (especially two) Akkadian flood stories, some scholars began to see that other explanations of the many repetitions throughout the narrative may make better sense of the text as its stands, rather than resorting to cutting it into a myriad of scraps and assembling it as a different "quilt," entirely. Moreover, these solutions have the advantage of placing this flood story naturally into the larger context of Israel's ancient Near Eastern history, from which it arose and to which it belongs. (This is not to dismiss source criticism entirely; it is a helpful tool, among many tools and methods available to biblical scholarship.)

Specifically, for the beginning of the story here, the source critics saw 6:5-8 as one introduction to the flood story from the hand of the Yahwist (J), and 6:9-12 as a second, duplicating introduction, from the hand of the Priestly writer, or school (P). A better explanation, partly because it is simpler, begins by identifying 6:5-8 as God's statement of the *problem* (as we have seen above) and of God's decision to do something about it, without stating what that decision was; one can identify this paragraph as an introduction (ending with a note on Noah finding favor in the sight of God, v 8).

We take the flood narrative, proper, as beginning with an introduction of Noah, the major human protagonist in this narrative (vv 9-10). This is followed by a summary description of the corruption of the earth and its population (vv 11-12) and a transition into God's direct speech to Noah (vv 13-21). When we compare the text of 6:5-7 with 6:11-12, we note more differences than similarities. The differences between these two texts suggest that the latter most likely is not a repetition of the former. Rather, 6:11-12 is a narrative introduction to God's speech to Noah, which follows immediately.

GENESIS

6:9-10

IN THE TEXT

■ **9-10** *These are the toledot of Noah.* For discussion of *toledot*, see Introduction, The Literary Forms of Genesis 1—11, "These Are the *Toledot*." This is the third occurrence of this sentence, "These are the *toledot* of X," which serves as the major indicator of the divisions within the text, from 2:4a through 37:2, at the beginning of the Joseph narrative. Noah's name was introduced in 6:8, as (among other reasons) a connector between 6:5-7 and 6:9-22. Here, the narrator begins to relate Noah's own story, introduced by this heading. We will represent the narrator's intentions if we translate *toledot*—and the phrase, *These are the toledot of Noah*—"This is Noah's history" or "These are the accounts of Noah."

This account begins with a thumbnail sketch of Noah's sterling character, probably because the problem at hand was the execrable character of his contemporaries. The translation, **Noah was a righteous man;** *he was blameless in his generations; with God walked Noah,* follows the order of the Hebrew text. This understanding comprises three clauses. The first is a somewhat general statement, **Noah was a righteous man**. **Righteous** (*saddiq*) is a definite (and intended) contrast with Noah's wicked and evil peers (v 5).

206

(Verses 11 and 13 add "violence" to the characteristics of the others of Noah's generation.)

The second clause, ***blameless in his generations,*** is linked to the first—Noah's right relationship with God shaped the way he related to those around him. **Blameless** (*tāmîm*) refers to Noah's habitual practice of integrity in all his dealings with others. Right relationship with God and integrity of conduct in relation to others were qualities totally missing ***in his generations,*** i.e., in the several generations represented among those living at the time of the flood.

The third clause, the narrator's report that ***with God walked Noah,*** shows another aspect of Noah's righteousness before God. The term **with God** before the main verb signals emphasis: it was **with God** that Noah walked, and therefore his conduct toward his fellow humans also was exemplary. Noah followed the path taken by Enoch (see 5:24) and, like Enoch, he lived in close relationship with God without any (explicitly recorded) divine directive (see Gen 17:1; Mic 6:8). The narrator portrays Noah as choosing an alternative way of life, instead of the path of the ancestor Adam followed by all his contemporaries.

Cassuto proposed another division of this short verse (1964, 48-49). Citing Job 12:4 and Num 19:2 as his guides, he took *tāmîm* as an adverb here, meaning "wholly," "perfectly." He translated, "Noah was a wholly righteous man in his generations; with God did Noah walk." The contrast with his contemporaries still is highlighted, if this is the correct grammatical understanding of the verse. Noah's righteousness, however, is defined exclusively as his walking with God. Cassuto noted that this clause is an idiomatic way of saying that Noah walked in God's *ways*, not in his own ways, while his contemporaries did walk in their own evil ways (49). Cassuto's translation merits consideration.

In v 10 the narrator introduces the names of Noah's three sons: **Shem, Ham and Japheth.** Since they do not yet enter the narrative fully, here they are only listed. Moreover, at this point in the narrative, the focus is on Noah and his exemplary character. The narrator has given the least possible introduction to Noah, but the reader will learn much more about him (and his sons) as the narrative unfolds.

■ **11-12** In his evaluation of Noah in vv 9-10, the narrator used the name Noah three times, and used three verbs to describe Noah ("Noah was") and his actions ("Noah walked"; "Noah had," or "fathered"). In vv 11-12, as a deliberate contrast with Noah, the narrator introduced **the earth** as the subject of three verbs. To highlight this, we will translate these verses as follows: ***But the earth was ruined before God, and the earth was filled up with lawlessness. Now God had seen the earth and, behold, it was ruined; for all flesh had brought to ruin its way upon the earth.*** Noah was righteous before God, but the earth was ***ruined*** before God, ***filled up with lawlessness.***

The verb ***ruined*** (*šāḥat*) occurs twice more in this section of the flood narrative (vv 13, 17). In both those places it belongs to the avowal of God's purpose to bring to ruin "all flesh" upon the earth. In effect, God's action announced in these verses is the completion of what the earth's inhabitants already had done. The narrator's report, **The earth was ruined before God,** stands in stark contrast to God's evaluation of all God had created as "good" (1:31). **The earth was ruined** conveys the idea of corruption and decay. Since God's resolve was to "wipe" or blot out humans "from the face of the earth," we may see here the idea of the total defilement or pollution of the earth (see v 7). Verse 12 traces the responsibility of this ruined condition of the earth to "all flesh."

The report, **the earth was filled up with lawlessness,** further describes the ruined condition of the earth. We have translated **lawlessness** rather than the more common **violence** only because the meaning of the latter has become restricted, in general English usage, to physical violence. Certainly, physical violence is included in the meaning of Hebrew *ḥāmās,* but *ḥāmās* is more than physical violence. The *Theological Dictionary of the Old Testament* summarizes its range well: *ḥāmās* is "cold-blooded and unscrupulous infringement of the personal rights of others, motivated by greed and hate and often making use of physical violence and brutality" (Botterweck 1977-2006, 4:482). In such a society and culture, the threat of physical violence always is present, but physical actions often are not "necessary," the threat being sufficient to gain the offender's desired ends. This ethos of violence could account for the ease with which **the mighty ones** acquired for themselves the women they desired (v 2).

Verse 12 is God's evaluation of the condition of the earth. The phrase **Now God had seen** or **God saw** (*wayyarĕ᾽ ᾽ĕlōhîm*) is often repeated in ch 1 to convey the idea of God's evaluation of what God created. The following phrase, **and behold,** does not suggest God's surprise so much as God's disappointment and grief that these generations had so quickly turned the "very good" of the earth and all its inhabitants (1:31) into the ruin it now was. The second and third occurrences of the key verb here, "ruined/corrupted/devastated" (*šāḥat*) are separated only by the particle *kî,* **for.** We may translate the verse, **Now God had seen the earth and, behold, it was ruined, for all flesh had brought to ruin its way upon the earth.** The final Hebrew clause is in its "normal" order, with the verb before the subject ("had brought to ruin all flesh its way").

To the Western mind, vv 11-12 may seem redundant; both verses may seem to be a mere repetition of the state of affairs already described in 6:1-8. However, in 6:1-8, there is only a general reference to evil (see v 5). In vv 11-12, evil is specified a bit more carefully: the earth was **ruined/corrupted,** and filled with lawlessness, a spirit of and willingness to commit violence. More important is the emphasis placed on the verb **ruined** (*šāḥat*). Not only does the evil *consist* in corruption/ruin, but the evil also *results* in corruption/ruin. With v 12, especially, the narrator wanted to charge the ruination of the earth to its proper authors, namely, **all flesh,** which had **brought to ruin its way**

upon the earth. The coming destruction of the flood merely would bring to its natural culmination the ruin this culture had been crafting for generations.

Does ***all flesh*** refer only to humans or to all animal life? Verse 17 specifically states that the floodwaters would destroy "all flesh in which is the breath of life" (ESV, NASB, NKJV, NRSV). Did animals contribute, along with humans, to the ruined condition of the earth? The NIV's **all the people** suggests that only the human race was culpable for the ruin of the earth. Verse 13 seems to support this view. However, v 17 states that animals also would suffer along with the human race (as innocents often do), when the floodwaters came.

■ **13** If the preceding verses seem repetitious, this verse seems doubly so— but again, only to the Western mind and only if we are not reflective. This verse is God's first word **to Noah.** Of course (in any ancient Eastern telling of the story), God would tell Noah the problem before telling Noah what God expected him to do about it.

This first word of God to Noah is, literally, ***The end of all flesh has come/is coming before me, because the earth is filled up with lawlessness because of them. Now, behold, I am bringing them to ruin, [together] with the earth.***

God's word to Noah begins with the announcement of ***the end*** (*qēṣ*) of ***all flesh*** (*kol bāśār*). The first verb *bāʾ* (the root verb *bôʾ* means "come," "go," etc.) is either a perfect (here, past tense, ***has come***) or a participle (***is coming***); these two forms are written the same. If it is perfect (past tense), the emphasis is on God's confirmed decision: "It's time." If it is participial, the emphasis is on the short time (***is coming***) remaining before God would initiate the judgment God now was warning Noah of. This announcement is similar to God's word to Amos (Amos 8:2) concerning Israel, "The end has come" (*bāʾ haqqēṣ*). The phrase ***before me*** emphasizes that the decision to bring an end ***to all flesh*** was God's, who alone had jurisdiction in this matter. The next clause, ***because the earth is filled up with lawlessness because of them,*** states the reason for God's decision and announcement, confirming the narrator's report that the earth was filled with ***lawlessness*** (see v 11).

We may read the final clause of v 13 in either of two ways. It is possible to take the suffixed *mem* of the verb (*mašḥîtām*) as an (untranslatable) enclitic, and read *ʾet* as the direct object marker before **the earth.** This would lead to the translation "I am bringing the earth to ruin." Another possibility is to take the suffixed *mem* as the direct object and treat *ʾet* before **the earth** as a preposition. This would lead to the translation, ***I am bringing them to ruin, [together] with the earth.***

We have adopted here the latter reading of this clause partly on the basis of God's further declaration on the matter below (v 17). Another consideration, though, is the connection between human action, and consequences directed toward the humans as a result of their action. "All flesh" had "brought ruin upon [corrupted] its way upon the earth," and the earth had been "corrupted" (a passive form, used twice in vv 11-12). Now, God's appointed **end** of the matter would be **bringing *them* to ruin, [together] with the earth,** which they had ruined. The text does not reveal here the actual agent of the coming **end;** the agent is disclosed later (v 17).

■ **14** This verse is a general, summary instruction, the details of which come in the following verses. In this verse, God was saying, in effect, "Here's the project, Noah." It is worth noting that no word of Noah is recorded throughout the entire episode of the flood itself. Only after Noah and his family had been gone from the ark for at least a year (probably three or four years; long enough for grapes to grow on the vines Noah planted) are Noah's own words recorded, at the very end of his story (9:25-27).

Make yourself an ark of cypress wood. As is commonly noted, the Hebrew word *tēbâ* (**ark**) is used only here and in the account of Moses' mother placing him in a reed-basket ark (Exod 2). Most now identify it as a loan word from Egyptian. (The ark of the covenant made for the tabernacle is Hebrew *ʾărôn.*) A more important point is that this word does not refer to a boat but to an **ark.** The Mesopotamian accounts refer to a boat; some even report sailors and a pilot on board. Here, the hearer/reader is invited to think of a rectangular box that floated, big enough that it would not capsize. No mention is made of keel, rudder, oars, or sails. The humans aboard would neither propel nor steer it. Noah would build it, but God would preserve those within it and bring them safely to ground when the deluge was over.

As *gōper* occurs only in this narrative, **cypress** is not a sure identification. However, cypress was a timber species of the ancient Near East, and it is not impossible that *gōper* and **cypress** are from the same root, or that **cypress** ultimately is a transliteration from *gōper.* Cedar is another proposal, from ancient times to the present. (As will be obvious, KJV's "gopher wood" is a transliteration, rather than a translation.)

The **rooms,** or compartments, in the ark would serve as apartments for the family and as stalls or stables for the various animals with them.

Coat it with pitch is, literally, *pitch it with pitch.* The Hebrew word here, *kōper,* is the same Semitic word as the Akkadian *kupru* of Utnapishtim's account recorded in the Epic of Gilgamesh (Tablet XI). Inner and outer coatings of pitch would render the ark's planking satisfactorily waterproof. A somewhat whimsical reminder that this vessel would be Noah's home for months on end is lodged in a literal rendering of this instruction, *And pitch it from the house[side] and from the outside with pitch.*

■ **15-16** The first clause is introductory: *This is what [how] you shall construct it.* Whereas the first verb of v 14 is an imperative ("Make [for] yourself . . ."), the verbs here and in the following verses are imperfect, not imperative. Their emphasis is on instruction and counsel, rather than on command.

The ordinary cubit of the biblical and other ancient Near Eastern records usually is thought to have been about eighteen inches (nearly forty-six centimeters, a little less than half a meter). If this ratio of conversion is correct, Noah was to make the ark about four hundred fifty feet long, about seventy-five feet wide in its beam, and about forty-five feet high. For antiquity, it was to be a very large vessel, indeed, about three-fourths of an acre in area.

Verse 16 begins with the instruction to **make a roof** for the ark. The word *ṣōhar*, often translated as **roof,** is found only here in the OT. However, it may mean here a *window* (see NASB; Cassuto 1964, 63-65). Dividing the verse differently than does the MT, Cassuto treats each half of the verse as made up of two clauses with two different instructions. The feminine suffix pronoun in the first half refers to the ark and not the *ṣōhar*, just as the feminine suffix pronoun in the second half also refers to the ark.

If Cassuto is correct, we may translate, *A window you are to make for the ark; also, to the length of* [i.e., *lacking only the length of*] *a cubit you are to finish it [the ark] above. Also, the door of the ark you are to set in its [the ark's] side; lower, second, and third [decks] you are to make.* Cassuto maintained that the roof is unnamed here because an ark (essentially a box, and *not* a boat) necessarily needs a cover; the *ṣōhar* was the window. The roof (the sixth and upper side of the box), though unnamed, needed a special instruction because it was to be different from the other sides. A sloping roof necessarily has two "sides" of its own. Noah was to finish the roof to within a cubit at its middle top; a horizontal gap, a cubit wide, would run the length of the ark at its highest point (Cassuto 1964, 65). Cassuto did not address the issue of how Noah was to keep the rain out of the ark with this gap running the length of its high point, the crown of its roof.

We may retain Cassuto's analysis and translation of the verse, while modifying his positioning of the one-cubit "gap" of the roof. Many agree with him that the one-cubit measurement here refers to the ark itself, not to the *ṣōhar* that was a part of the ark, whether it was the **roof** or the *window.* But the adverbial modifier *above* is not necessarily restricted to (Cassuto's unnamed) roof at its cap or crown. It may refer to the sides of the ark at their upper edges just below the roof, protected by the roof's overhang. In that case, as some have envisioned it, this one-cubit gap would have provided ventilation for the otherwise entirely enclosed ark.

The second half of the verse is much easier. Noah was to place a single **door** in one side of the ark. The final clause is the instruction to make three **decks** or stories in the interior part of the ark. The text simply refers to "beneath, seconds, and thirds." Most commentators consider these as references to **decks.** Depending on the combined widths of the floor/ceiling joists and the roof's rafters, the thickness of the floorings, and especially of the design of the timbered bracing between the hull sheathing and the first floor's planking, each of the ark's three stories could have been between ten and twelve feet from floor to ceiling. Of course, the text does not say they had to be of equal height.

One has only to begin to think about the questions raised by attempting to decide on and visualize details such as these, to realize God's instructions to Noah here did not represent the giving of a set of architectural blueprints. On the basis of these two verses alone, one cannot draw a picture, or build a model, of the ark. Did the hull taper into a bow and a stern, or was its width the same, fore to aft? The text does not say. Did the ark have a keel, or any kind of projection from the flat bottom? The text does not say. Was the ark flat-bottomed, or nearly so, like many of the steamboats used on nineteenth-century American rivers? The text does not say. If the one-cubit "gap" was a ventilation feature, how did Noah keep the birds from escaping? Did he have to cage them? The text does not say.

■ **17** Verse 17 reiterates and clarifies God's decision announced in v 13. ***Now as for me, behold, I am bringing the flood, water upon the earth, to ruin/ destroy all flesh which in it is the breath of life, from under the heavens. Everything which is on the earth shall perish.***

Having just instructed Noah to build an ark, God now told him why. The first word of v 17, which we have translated ***Now as for me,*** is a combination of the conjunction (*vĕ*) prefixed to the subject pronoun (*ʾănî*), emphatic by itself. This word conveys the sense of, "Now, for my part . . ." The second word, ***behold, I am,*** is a combination of the demonstrative (*hinnēh*), also prefixed to the subject pronoun (*ʾănî*). God introduced the immanent action with double emphasis. The divine decision was fixed, irrevocable. We could translate, "I am about to bring."

One more point is important here. In the syntax of the paragraph, this declaration of God's intention does not so much look *backward* to God's instruction to Noah to build the ark, as it looks *forward* to God's instruction to provision the ark in preparation for boarding (v 21). This will clarify our understanding of the intervening verses, also.

Behold, I am bringing the flood is causative; the grammar parallels that of v 13. There, God had said, "Behold, I am causing them to be ruined." Here, God said, "Behold, I am causing the flood to come." This is not needless repetition but a regular feature of much Semitic narrative, where a repetition in part always advances the information or the story line in some way. God's first statement is a general threat of "ruin," without specifying *how* God would bring ruin upon the earth. (See commentary on v 13, above.) Now, having instructed Noah to build an ark, a vessel that Noah realized would float on water, God specified the instrument of destruction.

Only here in the narrative of Noah, and later in Ps 29:10, does the term ***the flood*** (*hammabbûl* with the definite article) occur; this term refers to Noah's flood, and to nothing else. The final phrase, ***water upon the earth,*** is perhaps not a later gloss but a clarification of the meaning of *hammabbûl*, flood.

The divine purpose of the flood is made clear in the next part of God's speech: ***to ruin/destroy all flesh which in it is the breath of life.*** God's decision

212

to **ruin** (*šāḥat*) or destroy **all flesh** (*kol bāśār*) is the consequence of the earth's **ruin** (*šāḥat*) or corruption already brought about by **all flesh** (*kol bāśār*); see v 12. The phrase, **which in it is the breath of life,** reiterates the comprehensiveness of the destruction; it would include both human and animal life.

Hebrew *ʾereṣ*: Was Noah's Flood Global or Regional?

Throughout the flood story, the traditional translation and understanding of the Hebrew word *ʾereṣ* has been "earth." The flood usually has been understood as an event covering all the lands and seas of the entire globe. Another understanding, though, and almost as old, is that this was a regional event, covering only the Mesopotamian valleys of the Tigris and Euphrates or, as recently proposed, the Black Sea and some of the surrounding area. (These two currently are the most popular "regional" proposals.)

The regional understanding rests on the fact that, in most of its 2,400 occurrences in the Hebrew Bible, *ʾereṣ* does *not* mean "earth" or "globe." Usually it means "land," "region," or "district," as in "Land of Israel," "Land of Egypt," etc. Based on the word *ʾereṣ* alone, we could equally well translate 6:17, **Now as for me, behold, I am bringing the flood, water upon the land, to ruin/destroy all flesh which in it is the breath of life, from under the heavens. Everything which is on the land shall perish**—and so throughout the flood narrative. "The land," then, would designate lower Mesopotamia, or some other district or region.

Other issues remain, of course. A final decision in the matter may await some future discovery, in archaeology or in a previously unknown or unexamined text. All we are saying here is that the range of meanings for the frequently occurring Hebrew noun *ʾereṣ* includes both "earth" (in the sense of "the globe") and "land/region/district"; this noun will not decide the matter.

■ **18** Verse 18 introduces an exception to the "all flesh" mentioned in v 17. Noah and his family are listed first among those God planned to preserve when the flood destroyed **all flesh.** The disclosure of God's plan begins with the announcement of the covenant God intended to make with Noah (**But I will establish my covenant with you**). This marks the first biblical occurrence of the word **covenant** (*běrît*); the concept of covenant will be greatly developed as the entire narrative of salvation history proceeds. Here, its use is proleptic; it does not occur again until 9:9. At this point, when God just had said that "all flesh" soon would perish, Noah probably would have understood God's covenant as meaning simply that God would spare his life and the lives of those who would enter the ark with him. The contrast between the decision for judgment (v 17) and the decision for grace (v 18) is both deliberate and vivid. It bears repeating, too, that both decisions were based in justice.

However, a covenant is an agreement between two (or more than two) parties, involving specific terms, conditions, etc. Here, if these are present at all, they are implicit, rather than explicit. That God did establish with Noah and his family, following the flood, a "recognizable" covenant, leads the hearer/reader to understand that with the promise of a covenant here God intended more than their "mere" physical survival.

The contrast between the generation of evil that would perish and the righteous one who would survive is highlighted in another way, also. Remembering that God just had announced to Noah God's judgment upon the others (v 17), seven occurrences (altogether) of second person singular "you/your" forms in the thirteen words of the verse immediately following take on an added significance, that God certainly intended: **But I will establish my covenant with <u>you</u>, and <u>you</u> will *go into* the ark—<u>you</u> and <u>your</u> sons and <u>your</u> wife and <u>your</u> sons' wives with <u>you</u>.** In emphatic contrast with those who shortly would perish, Noah is the focus of God's positive attention here, and he would be God's partner in the coming covenant.

But I will establish . . . with you is the second aspect of the "But as for me . . ." or "But for my part . . ." (see v 17). Judgment and covenant both would be part of God's forthcoming action. As we shall see, the grammar and syntax of vv 19-20 make clear that they also continue the expression of God's intention to establish this covenant.

The widespread tradition (see, e.g., 1 Pet 3:20) that eight persons entered the ark is based on two reasonable assumptions. The first is that Noah's three sons followed their father's righteous example, and married only one wife each. The second assumption is that if any of Noah's sons already had fathered children, they would be mentioned here. This second assumption is borne out by the later statement that their progeny is said to have begun "after the flood" (10:1).

On the other hand, John of Damascus (who was not alone in this) went beyond the evidence of the text, saying, "When Noah was ordered to enter the ark and was entrusted with the safeguarding of the seed of earth, he was given this command, which reads: 'Come into the ark, you, your sons, your wife and your sons' wives.' He separated them from their wives, so that with the help of chastity they might escape the ocean's depths and that worldwide destruction" (Louth 2001, 133). That no children were born immediately after the flood is not evidence of marital abstinence aboard the ark. Moreover, the idea that God needed "chastity" to make it possible to save Noah and his family is not biblical faith, but antibiblical Gnosticism.

■ **19-20** Verses 19-20 make clear that God intended to bring other animal species within the circle of grace extended to Noah. *Also, from all the living [creatures], from all flesh, two of each, you will bring into the ark, to preserve [them] alive* [lit., *to cause to live*] *with you; a male and a female [of each] they will be. From the flying creature after its [respective] kind, and from the domestic livestock after its [respective] kind, from every [creature that] moves upon the ground after its [respective] kind, two of each will come to you to preserve [them] alive.*

The divine "Now as for me . . ." continues through these verses; this still is God's action at God's initiative. Together, these verses constitute a comprehensive definition of those to be included. We should note, first, that *from all flesh* is not a mere repetition of *from all the living,* but a clarifying specification; it means "from every kind of fleshly creature."

Two of each is specified more closely at the end of v 19 as *a male and a female* of each species. This, of course, emphasizes that God's intention was to preserve not just privileged individuals but the various species they represented and would propagate.

Three of the four nonmarine groupings of Gen 1 are mentioned in the list here (v 20). *The flying creature(s)* of the heavens God had created on day five. The *domestic livestock* and (lit.) *every mover of* [i.e., "belonging to" or "upon"] *the ground* belong to day six of the creation week. The "missing" category is "creatures of the field," that is, the larger wild creatures. Here, then, the intention is to include them within the final category. (Never in these early chapters of Genesis is there even a hint of anything approaching a comprehensive taxonomy.) Probably not yet able to visualize the magnitude of the impending disaster, Noah needed the nudge of God's inclusion of this final category to understand he was not to stop with allowing only the domestic livestock, the "useful" creatures, to board the ark. That Noah was to allow a considerable number of animals aboard the ark with him, also would clarify why God was directing him to build such a large vessel, rather than the tiny (by our standards) boat he otherwise would have thought sufficient for his and his family's deliverance, only.

"Allow" is the right nuance here. *You will bring* (v 19) cannot mean, "You will go out, capture, and carry in." The divine statement, *two of each [kind] will come to you* (v 20), further conveys the idea that this still is within the arena of God's action (see comments on 7:2-3 for the "sevens" of clean animals). God did not tell Noah *how* God would encourage or impel these creatures to come to him.

■ **21** The phrase, *Now as for you,* introduces Noah's task, his one area of responsibility (after building the ark) for the realization of their deliverance in and through the ark. God's instruction to Noah to take aboard the ark **every kind of food** would seem to include the range of plant-derived foods for the humans, given that God granted humans permission to eat animal flesh only *after* the flood (9:3; but see Walton 2001, 341-43). Of course, such a conclusion leaves aside the evidence accepted by many that humans always have been omnivorous, and the further question of how the carnivorous animals would have survived their months aboard the ark with only vegetable food to eat. The context of 1:29-30 before our passage, and 9:3 following it, suggests a vegetarian diet for all animal life aboard the ark, including the eight humans and the other animals we commonly think of as entirely or partly carnivorous. Whether that is the proper understanding of our passage we cannot say with certainty. If it is, we cannot in the present state of our knowledge reconcile these passages with what we know of the various carnivorous species, including our own. Much as we would like to know, we must be content to leave it at that for now.

■ **22** *So Noah did; according to all that God had instructed him, thus he did.* The verse actually begins and ends with the verb ***did*** (*ʿāśâ*). With Noah as the expressed subject of its first occurrence, then ("so did Noah"), it forms a chiasm of the simplest structure, ABA': "So did Noah . . . did." The two independent clauses for this simple affirmation, and the chiastic arrangement included within the two of them, together, both contribute to making this a very strong assertion of Noah's responsiveness to God's direction. That the narrator reported this without recording even one word out of Noah's mouth is an understatement for emphasis, reminding the reader of Noah's unadulterated righteousness—the quality that had commended him to God's favor in the first place (v 8). Noah did not need words here; his actions spoke for him.

For reasons that will become clearer in our discussion of 7:2-3, below, we take **Noah did** to mean that Noah began and completed the ark as God had directed, then proceeded to gather the required food and provender and to store it aboard the ark. It is reasonable to suppose that Noah probably had the assistance of his three sons in these large undertakings. Though God had told Noah the animals would be coming to him, this did not happen immediately upon completion of the ark. Noah would have had no place to quarter them except the ark, and nothing to feed them except the provisions he and his sons had stored. Boarding the ark, beginning the labor of feeding so many animals, and drawing down food supplies was best postponed as long as possible.

FROM THE TEXT

The contrast between a life of righteousness and a life of wickedness hardly could be drawn more sharply than it is here in these opening paragraphs of the flood narrative. Noah's contemporaries were corrupt, evil, lawless, and violent. Noah himself walked with God in righteousness, a man of integrity, blameless. From the judgment of disaster God sent upon Noah's world, God spared only Noah and his family.

Especially in the light of later biblical teaching, we must be careful not to say Noah "earned" his deliverance from death in the flood. God's grace, and the believing community's life in grace, is fundamentally relational, not transactional. Noah "walked with God" (6:9); when the time for judgment came (6:13), God delivered the one who wanted to continue to walk with God.

By way of contrast, the narrative clearly and vividly shows that moral ruin leads inevitably to material, physical ruin. When the time for judgment came, God allowed those who did not want to walk with God—who refused to walk with God—to come to the only possible end of their way, destruction.

6:21-22

God does not, in the end, force life upon those who consistently, to the end, refuse the way of life.

God's judgment is not arbitrary. We almost may say it is not "judgment," at all, but only the natural consequence of going against the grain of the world as God created it to function. Put water in the fuel tank of an automobile, and it does not matter that one's intention was honorable—to save money for "nobler" uses—the engine is ruined.

Steal honestly acquired wealth, from anyone, by any means, and it does not matter that one's (or a system's) intentions are honorable—to benefit the "disadvantaged," for example. The theft contributes to the ruination of a group, of a people, of the earth.

Play fast and loose with facts, and it does not matter that one's (or a group's) intentions are honorable—to save the planet, for example. The lessening of trustworthiness contributes to the ruination of a group, of a people, even of the planet itself, whom one ostensibly is trying to save. The ends do *not* justify the means. Rather, corrupted (ruined) means guarantee corrupted (ruined) ends.

All this means that, on one level, at least, we exaggerate if we speak of God's "raining down judgment," or use other, similarly apocalyptic imagery. The great flood only sealed the ruination with which the actions of "all flesh" already had permeated the earth. Nations, empires, and civilizations do not fall because God has decreed their fall according to some inexorable divine timeline. They fall because they have corrupted, ruined, themselves. God's judgment, then, if we want to call it that, often comes historically in the form of destruction from the outside at the very end. But the outside forces could not have penetrated, except for the internal corruption. These principles hold today, as surely as they held in Noah's day.

On the interpretive principle often referred to as the "analogy of faith" (*analogia fidei*)—Scripture interpreting Scripture—prudence would suggest that the flood's destruction of nearly all animal life was an early example of innocents suffering because of others' evildoing. On a related note, most Christians would understand those human infants and young children lost in the flood as being now in the presence of God.

B. The Deluge: Beginning and Crest (7:1-24)

1. God's Command to Enter the Ark (7:1-10)

BEHIND THE TEXT

The narrator of Genesis devoted nearly three full chapters to the story of Noah's flood. Most of ch 6 relates God's instruction to Noah, and Noah's preparations for the coming disaster. Chapter 7 recounts Noah's and his family's entrance into the ark and the actual event of the flood, to the point where it reached its crest. The resolution—God's re-creation of the world in the gradual receding of the waters—and the final act, the exit from the ark of all whom it had sheltered, are the subject of ch 8. Thus, ch 7—the chapter describing God's "de-creation" in judgment—is the one most filled with dramatic language, with the vivid scenes of catastrophic dangers, even with the pathos of small but telling details, such as the notice that God shut the door to the ark as the rains were about to begin, and the fountains of the deep about to be thrown wide open. In the classic story line of history as well as of fiction—inception, climax, resolution—the narrator now brings the reader to the climax: the flood itself.

IN THE TEXT

■ **I** God's speech to Noah, framed as an imperative, ***Go, you and all your household, into the ark,*** marks the final stage of Noah's preparations for the coming flood. By comparison with the years-long task of building the ark, what remained to do would be relatively simple.

The second half of the verse we should translate, ***for you I have seen, a righteous one before me in this generation.*** The particle *kî* (***for*** or **because**) introduces the reason for God's decision to spare Noah and his family from the flood. The narrator had already reported that Noah was a "righteous" person (6:9). Here, in 7:1, God himself speaks directly to Noah and affirms the narrator's report. God's evaluation of Noah as ***a righteous one*** is at least as strong as the narrator's in 6:9, but expressed differently, by the use of two direct objects, a pronoun and a substantive. The pronoun (*'ōtkā*) is first for emphasis. The second direct object is *ṣaddîq*, used as a substantive, and without the definite article: ***a righteous one.*** The final prepositional phrase (***in this generation***) affirms once again the contrast between Noah and the rest of his ***generation.*** Their evil character and actions had ruined the earth. By contrast, it would not distort the sense if we were to add "only" here: "for you *only*, Noah, have I seen . . . in this generation."

■ **2-3** These verses constitute an added directive from God to Noah. The following is a literal translation of these verses: ***From all the clean land creatures, take for yourself seven, seven, a male and its mate, but from the land creatures which are not clean, two, a male and its mate. Also from the flying creatures of the heavens seven, seven, male and female, to [keep] alive their seed upon the face of all the earth.***

On the face of it, these verses seem to present one of the strongest evidences in favor of discovering two (or more) sometimes contradictory sources behind the text of Genesis as we have it now. Previously (6:19-20), God had instructed Noah to take one pair of each animal and bird species with him into the ark. Here, the instruction is for seven of each animal. Which was it, two or seven? Also, in translation, where critical nuances can be muted, it is easy to read the narrative in these places as saying that Noah already had brought the pairs of animals into the ark, and now God was instructing him to bring them in again, with a few additions. How was Noah to bring the same animals into the ark twice?

Earlier source-critical methodology traced this apparent discrepancy between 6:19-20 and 7:2-3 to the narrator's use of Priestly (6:9-22) and Yahwist sources (7:1-5). By contrast, Hamilton explains the variation by translating *šěnayim* as "a collective for 'pairs'" in 6:19-20 instead of "two" or "a pair" (1990, 287). This translation has merit when we consider 7:2-3 as a further expansion of a more or less general statement of 6:19-20. Thus, *seven, seven* specifies the number of clean animals (see below), while *šěnayim* in 7:2 specifies **two** (i.e., a pair) as the number of animals Noah was to bring aboard the ark, of each of the species that *are not clean.* The only distinction that mattered in this new instruction was **clean** and *not clean.*

A number of English translations (including NIV's, **Take with you seven of every kind . . .**) can be read as God instructing Noah to take seven individual animals of each species of clean animals and of all species of birds. This does not accurately reflect the Hebrew text, which reads, *seven, seven, a male and its mate* (v 2). Of the birds, the instruction is, *seven, seven, male and female* (v 3). If only seven individual animals of each species were to be brought into the ark, obviously in every case there would be an "extra" animal or bird, either a male or a female. Moreover, given their typical mating patterns, for many species a single male would have been more than adequate to service six females.

The repetition of the number—*seven, seven*—together with the syntax of the sentences and the references to male and female, all combine to invest the repetition with the meaning, "seven pairs" of clean animals and "seven pairs" of birds, with a male and a female constituting each pair. The potential genetic diversity among seven mating pairs of each species would enhance the future viability of the clean animals. Of course, some of these individuals Noah sacrificed upon leaving the ark, but in the year aboard the ark, it certainly is possible that some of these animals, at least, would have reproduced themselves, and the species would have increased in number.

One key question here is which animals were regarded as "clean," since the Levitical sacrificial system was not instituted until the time of Moses. It would then appear that the concept of **clean** and *not clean* animals in the pre-Sinai periods was limited to differentiating among the species that either were, or were not, acceptable for sacrifice. If this is true, in this narrative, **clean** means "suitable for sacrifice"; *not clean* means "not suitable for sacrifice." We have seen already (4:2-4) that Abel was a keeper of flocks; the Hebrew term there (*ṣōʾn*) refers to sheep and goats. Since Abel brought his offering from his flock, we may assume that sheep and goats were among the clean animals, acceptable for sacrifice to Yahweh.

The command to take seven pairs of clean animals and seven pairs of birds suggests God's concern to preserve the world after the flood with a variety of clean animals suitable for sacrifice and human consumption (8:20; 9:3). The greater number of clean animals also would have enabled the various species to multiply in population and thus avoid the risk of extinction. The final clause, **to [keep] alive their seed upon the face of all the earth,** conveys the overall purpose of God's instruction. God's plan for the preservation and propagation of life includes both humans and animals. God's decision to bring the judgment of the flood did not mean an end to God's creational purposes.

■ **4** Verse 4 gives more specific details on the flood (see 6:17). We find here a chronology of events that soon would happen. God announced to Noah what he was about to do **in seven more days.** Noah had seven days to complete the last-minute preparations and get his family and all the animals aboard the ark. The statement, **I am sending rain upon the earth forty days and forty nights,** reveals for the first time in the narrative rain as the cause of the flood. The verb (*māṭar*) does not necessarily signify heavy rain, though it does not preclude it, either. This rain would be catastrophic because of its duration. Almost six weeks of continuous rainfall would saturate the ground early on; shortly afterward, the valleys would be full. With nowhere else to go, the rising waters would cover the hillsides and crest their summits. Hilltop by hilltop, the land would disappear.

The last clause is God's announcement to Noah of God's intention to wipe the earth clean of the smudge upon it that evil humanity had become. Wipe (*māḥâ*) is the same verb the narrator had used earlier in recording God's initial decision to act (6:7; see comments there).

Ephrem the Syrian on Gen 7:4

God granted one hundred years while the ark was being made to that generation, and still they did not repent. God summoned beasts that they had never seen and still they showed no remorse. He established a state of peace between the predatory animals and those who are preyed upon, and still they had no awe. God delayed yet seven more days for them, even after Noah and every creature had entered the ark, leaving the gate of the ark open to them. This is a wondrous thing that no lion remembered its jungle and no species of beast or bird visited its customary haunt! Although those of that generation saw all that went on outside and inside the ark, they were still not persuaded to renounce their evil deeds. (Louth 2001, 135)

■ **5** The instruction to bring seven pairs of clean animals aboard the ark was new. The instruction to board because the flood would begin in seven days was new information for Noah. Thus, reporting Noah's compliance here is not a duplication of the report just above (6:22; see comments there). The narrative reports two different and successive sets of God's instruction to him. At the end of each report, we find the narrator's report of Noah's obedience to God's instructions. The major difference between the wordings of these two reports is that 6:22 uses *Elohim* while this one uses *Yahweh*. (See Introduction, "The One, the Only, God" under Major Theological Themes.)

■ **6** Noah's life was divided into three unequal parts. His first son was born when he was five hundred years old (5:32). The flood came when he was **six hundred years old.** He died at the age of nine hundred fifty years (9:29). We will understand the sense of these two independent clauses if we translate, ***Now, Noah was six hundred years old, and the flood came*** [lit., ***was***], ***water upon the earth.*** (On the final phrase, see comment on 6:17, above.)

From our perspective, Noah's life span seems impossible. (See Introduction, "The Mathematics of the Patriarchal Life Spans," under The Literary Forms of Genesis 1—11.) It is worth noting, however, that the Mesopotamian version featuring Ziusudra as the hero of the flood reports he was 36,000 years old when the deluge began. By comparison, an age of six hundred years for Noah suddenly becomes more reasonable, whatever may reveal itself as the solution to the dilemma of the lower number.

■ **7** On the human side, the narrative emphasis is focused entirely on Noah, as a translation reflecting the order of the Hebrew text demonstrates, ***So Noah entered, and his sons, and his wife, and his sons' wives with him, into the ark from before the waters of the flood.*** Nowhere do the names of the women appear; in all but one place (v 13) Noah's sons are not named but are referred to collectively as **his sons.** The NIV phrase, **to escape the waters of the flood,** conveys the idea of the literal reading of the text (***from before the waters of the flood***).

■ **8-9** These lines are familiar by now. However, we must admit that even in our Western traditions, such a stupendous event as this would warrant, or even require, repetitions of various kinds along the way in the telling. Moreover, we have said that repetition in Hebrew narrative usually is not verbatim all the way through; new information is added with each return to the main lines of the report. Noah already had stabled or penned the seven mating pairs of each of the clean species God had commanded him to "take" (vv 2-3, 5). Here, we have the new information that the animals coming to Noah two by two, of their own accord, included two of each species of ***clean animal,*** as well as the two of each species of ***the animals which are not clean.***

Strengthening the probability of this conclusion is that the creatures coming to Noah are designated by another two-part division, as well. One group was ***the flying creatures;*** the other included ***all that move about upon the ground.*** Here, all the nonflying land creatures—which in other passages had been divided into two or three groups—were grouped together into a single category, all of them together contrasted with the flying creatures. Just as every species belonged to one of the two groupings, **clean** or ***not clean,*** so, too, every species belonged to one of the two groupings, ***flying*** or ***upon the***

ground, i.e., earthbound. Yet all the species came to Noah, **two, two,** i.e., a male and a female (see 6:19).

It may be that we should translate the verb here (7:9) as a past perfect; the creatures, **two [by] two, _had come_ to Noah, to the ark, male and female, just as God [Elohim] had instructed Noah [previously].** The sequence of events then would be: (1) Noah and his family had taken aboard the ark the seven pairs of clean species God had instructed them to take; (2) The single pairs of all the species had come to Noah, and Noah and his family had settled them on board; (3) Noah and his family then boarded the ark the day the rains commenced (v 13).

At the end of v 9, the narrator continued his practice of using Elohim, rather than Yahweh, when God neither spoke nor acted directly in the immediate context.

■ **10** God had told Noah the flood would begin in another seven days (v 4); v 10 reports the fulfillment of this promise. The flood did begin **after the seven days.** Moreover, this statement functions as the "theme sentence" of the paragraph. Details of the flood comprise the rest of the paragraph, a mixture of new information on the nature and timing of the flood, together with expansions upon select themes previously introduced.

FROM THE TEXT

God's word to Noah, **I have seen** (rāʾîtî), requires special consideration (7:1). This phrase conveys the sense of "I have evaluated," for two reasons. First, it preserves in English the intended, continuing contrast between God's evaluation of Noah's generation and of Noah himself. This is the verb used also in 6:5 and in 6:12. Second, and perhaps more important theologically, preserving this Hebrew distinction in English helps the reader avoid the mistaken conclusion that translations such as **I have found** may lead to. Noah's building the ark did not somehow "prove" to God Noah's righteousness, as though the narrator's report was, perhaps, a tentative one. Noah did not "earn" his deliverance in the ark by building it. On the contrary, Noah's building the ark was the response of one who consistently "walked with God" (6:9) as a habit of life. In later biblical terms, and from a Wesleyan perspective, we may say Noah was holy.

Hamilton has a detailed discussion of why several other understandings of this clause are to be rejected (1990, 286-87). One unhelpful misunderstanding would be to take God's statement here as "declaring" Noah to be "righteous" when (according to this approach) he was not, an exclusively forensic and artificial understanding of justification that is _not_ justified here, nor anywhere else in Scripture.

2. Beginning of the Deluge (7:11-16)

IN THE TEXT

▪ 11 We may understand v 11 as an expansion of vv 6 and 10, since we find here reference to a specific day for the beginning of the flood and details on the sources of the flood. We may assume the flood began **on the seventeenth day of the second month** of Noah's **six hundredth year,** as that is the year mentioned. Other dates and intervals of days will occur as the narrative progresses, so that a time frame for the entire event can be calculated. We will note these as they occur.

The dramatic intention and effect of the announcement of the flood's beginning would be difficult to overstate. Without exaggerating the tone of the Hebrew text, we may translate, ***On this self-same day, all the fountain-springs of the great deep were split wide open, and the sluicegates of the heavens were thrown open.***

This self-same day is the day just noted, **the seventeenth day of the second month.** The Hebrew word translated **deep** is *těhôm,* the name we have seen already as the designation of the primeval waters of Gen 1:2, waiting for God's creative actions upon and through them. The adjective **great** (**great deep;** *těhôm rabbâ;* see also Ps 78:15; Isa 51:10) indicates the vastness and the depth of the primeval sea that is represented by the various bodies of water, as well as by water below the earth's surface. The clause ***fountain-springs of the great deep were split wide open*** indicates the flooding of the earth by water gushing forth from every possible source. But the water also came down, as ***the sluicegates of the heavens were thrown open.*** Though many have assumed it, the text of Genesis does not actually say this was the first rain, ever; it probably was not. Still, this may have been the greatest, and it certainly was the longest, downpour yet; no one living had experienced this before, and only eight would survive it.

The Hebrew word here (*'ărubōt* in plural) is not the ordinary word for "window." This term refers to the sluices that controlled the opening and closing of the water supply to a field from an irrigation canal or ditch. In normal operations, sluicegates were opened only gradually and partially, and only one gate's opening and closing regulated the flow of water to any one field. Here, the rainfall is pictured as all the available water being released at once, with all the gates being thrown open in a single motion, not gradually and carefully. Any field so treated in the irrigation systems of ancient Mesopotamia or Egypt would have been inundated immediately, its topsoil washed away in a rush, all its plants uprooted at once.

The two sources of water God used to accomplish the task of judgment through de-creation reflect the ancient Israelites' perspective of waters above and below (see 1:6-7). God harnessed these resources as his two agents in returning the earth to the featureless vacancy from which God had caused it to emerge in the beginning. Those who have stood on a rocky shore and watched the thunderous crashing of waves and the geysering waterspouts through the holes and crevices found here and there will have an idea of the gushing forth of the fountain-springs of the great deep. Those who have marveled at a major waterfall, such as Niagara or Iguazu, will understand this scene, if they can imagine the waterfall thundering *upward*!

■ **12** The reason for the phrasing **forty days and forty nights** (rather than saying just "forty days," which would define the same period of time) is to alert the reader that the rain fell continuously, without intermission, for the entire period. It is true that "forty days" (or "forty years") can signify an extended, but indefinite, period of time (possible examples include 50:3; Exod 24:18; 34:28; Num 13:25; 14:33-34; Deut 10:10; 1 Kgs 19:8; Jonah 3:4; Matt 4:1-2; Mark 1:13; Acts 1:3). Here, however, the forty days and nights of actual rainfall also figure into the total duration of the period Noah and his family spent aboard the ark, so it is most likely that this figure is intended literally, rather than idiomatically. After the first day or two, no one on board the ark would have seen evidence of the continued gushing of the waters from the earth; thus, it is not mentioned here.

Forty Days or Seven Days?

Utnapishtim's version (Epic of Gilgamesh, Tablet XI, ll. 127-130) speaks of six days and six nights of fierce tempest, with the storm abating on the seventh day. The Sumerian version from Nippur gives a period of seven days and seven nights; in both accounts the storm abated on the seventh day. In this difference, too, the biblical record is credible, the Mesopotamian accounts are not. No storm of only a week, no matter how heavy the downpour, would suffice to flood the land completely.

■ **13-16** This section is not a superfluous repetition, either. It *is* a repetition, but here the narrator listed both Noah's family and the various groupings of the animals in greater detail than previously, adding a few new details in the process. As we have noted, also, it makes sense that this greatest event in history, to this point, *should* be the subject of artistic repetition. In excellent literature, skillfully varied repetition increases literary beauty and impact. (This is true also in music and in other artistic forms.)

Since this is what we may call an "expanded reprise," we may understand its intended effect more clearly if we translate the verbs as past perfects. To make clear also one or two other points, we will translate the whole: ***On that very day, Noah, and Shem, and Ham, and Japheth, Noah's sons—and Noah's wife, and the three wives of his sons with them—had gone into the ark, they, and every living creature after its kind: that is, every larger beast after its kind, and every smaller creature that creeps about upon the ground*** *after its kind, and every flying creature after its kind—every bird, every winged creature. For they had come to Noah, to the ark, two by two, of all flesh which in it is the breath of life. Now the ones who had come were male and female; from every [kind of] flesh they had come, just as God had instructed him [Noah]. Then Yahweh shut him in.*

All this is a flashback, as it were, pausing to take note of all who had entered the ark. The most important are listed first, though they had entered last. The narrator used another means, also, at this point, to mark this as the climactic moment, the moment from which there would be no turning back, either on God's or on Noah's part. For the first time since their introduction (6:10), and the only time in the entire narrative of the flood and the establishment of the covenant afterward, the narrator listed Noah's three sons by name. Not until the resumption of "normal" life (9:18) does the narrator name them again.

We have translated *kol habbĕhēmâ* as **every larger beast** (7:14); when it occurs without "beast(s) of the field" (*hayyat haśśādeh*), *bĕhēmâ* can include both the larger domestic and the larger wild creatures. Thus, the categories of land creatures here total two, the larger animals (*bĕhēmâ*) and the smaller creatures (*remeś*—which, in other contexts, can include *all* the creatures that move upon or above the earth), a departure from the norm in the Primeval Prologue.

At the end of v 14, **every flying creature . . . winged creature** exhibits a small expansion by the narrator. To this point, the narrator had used only the collective noun, *ʿôp*, "flying creature(s)." But here *ʿôp* is qualified by the addition of four words not used previously. **Every flying creature after its kind** (in parallel with the preceding phrases) is qualified further by the addition of **every bird, every winged creature.**

Thus, the movement of v 14 is from the whole to its smallest parts. It was not enough, in this crisis moment when all life on earth hung in the balance, to say, **every living creature after its kind.** The three broadest possible groupings of that whole are listed: **every larger beast**; **every smaller creature**; **every flying creature.** But even this level of detail is a bit too cut and dried for the drama of the moment. The third category is detailed in a way the narrator had not done previously. Because **every flying creature** includes (at least) birds, bats, and flying insects, the added detail of the last four words is not necessary, strictly speaking. But of course the three categories following **every living creature** are not "necessary," either.

What, then, we may ask, is the purpose of these first and second levels of increasing detail? In the previous paragraph the focus, with regard to the animals, had been particularly upon the clean (in this context, suitable for sacrifice), as contrasted with those that were not clean. Here the division of the nonflying creatures is between the larger and the smaller. Can it be that the intention here is to include, not just the largest of the flying creatures, the larger birds, but also even some of the smallest of the winged creatures, within the purview of God's grace and Noah's notice? Honeybees and bumblebees, butterflies and other pollinators come readily to mind, without assuming that only "useful" species were intended.

Cassuto on This Scene, This Moment

Before the door of the ark is closed (v. 16) and all that it contains disappears from our sight, the Bible passes before us, one by one, all the human beings and the various types of animal life that found refuge within it, in order that we should realize the importance and value of the living treasures entrusted to the ark's protection. (1964, 88)

After Noah, his family, and the animals all were inside the ark, in obedience to God's command, **Yahweh shut him in.** This is God's only reported action in the paragraph. Because it was a direct, immediate action undertaken on behalf of the persons and creatures within the ark, the narrator used God's name, **Yahweh** (rather than the title of divine majesty, Elohim). In the end, *God* acted to keep the ark's inhabitants safe from destruction. In the best-known Mesopotamian version, Utnapishtim had to close the door himself (Epic of Gilgamesh, XI, ll. 86-93).

FROM THE TEXT

7:11-16 In v 16 we read the fourth and final notice in just seventeen verses (also 6:22; 7:5, 9) that Noah and those who came aboard the ark with him did **just as God had instructed him [Noah].** In a corrupt, evil, and violent world, Noah remained a man of integrity and faithfulness to God across the many decades it took him (and probably his sons working with him) to complete the ark God had instructed him to build. God's instructions became for Noah and those with him the "promises of life" (Brueggemann 1982, 80). In carrying them out, Noah exercised both faith—confidence in *God's* integrity of character—and hope, hope that God indeed would fulfill the promises God had made.

At the same time, and in the same verse (v 16), the narrator's report, **Yahweh shut him in,** is another declaration of the grace first announced in 6:8. Noah, his family, and all the ark's nonrational passengers would survive because *Yahweh's* hand had shut them in. In the tragic sweep of the narrative, this is not a large detail, but even here the love and grace of God shines forth. The narrator focuses here on God's direct and personal act that kept the occupants of the ark safe from the destructive impact of the flood. Noah did his part as an act of obedience and faith in what God had said. God did his part to keep Noah, his family, and the animals safe from destruction. This statement is comforting with respect to the occupants of the ark, but it also is reassuring to all who place their life in the hands of a gracious and merciful God.

The text makes clear that Noah was delivered from the general annihilation because of Yahweh, and those with him were delivered because of Noah (see Hamilton 1990, 298). This is a common biblical theme, a theological truism. No one, ever, finds ultimate deliverance in and through self-help, self-reliance. This is not to discourage effort and responsible behavior. It *is* to affirm that, while necessary and useful to very good purposes, these are insufficient for our eternal good, whether individually or collectively. We really do need God; we really do need each other.

3. Cresting of the Deluge (7:17-24)

BEHIND THE TEXT

The focus of the paragraph is the rising of the floodwaters upon (or over) the earth. The phrase "on the earth" occurs seven times. Together, references to "the flood" (once) and "the waters" (six times) occur seven times. The verb "increased" (*rābâ*) occurs two times and "prevailed" (*gābar*) occurs four times (total six times). The first four verses detail the rising waters in terms of their effect upon the ark. The last four verses turn the reader's attention to the devastation of the earth outside the ark, reporting in vivid terms the extinguishing of all life "on the earth."

IN THE TEXT

■ **17-20** If these verses were music instead of literature, we would speak of crescendo in the repetition of a tragic theme to its thundering climax. Each repetition adds a sliver of new and crucial information, arriving in the end at the chaos of a world undone by human corruption (6:12-13; see commentary, above).

Because it rained upon the earth for forty days (v 12), **the flood continued to come upon the earth forty days** (v 17). Naturally, then, **the waters increased,** so of course **they lifted the ark, and it was raised up above the earth** (v 17).

Verse 18 begins with a new round of repetition, **So the waters prevailed, and they increased greatly upon the earth.** But even the repetition is not "merely" repetition, the waters **increased greatly.** This allowed for the next new development vis-à-vis the ark. Not only was it raised up off the surface of the earth where Noah had built it, but now **the ark floated upon the face [surface] of the waters.**

Piloted or Adrift?

Another small but important difference exists between the biblical account of the flood and those originating in Mesopotamia. Those accounts speak in terms of ships that could be steered, of sailors and pilots to man the vessel, of seeing and calculating where they were, and of some influence over where they

227

went. The biblical account implies the ark moved where the flood took it. Its seaworthiness, and the safety of its passengers, lay first in Noah's care in building it, and ultimately in God's providential oversight as it went where the winds and currents steered it. Those inside could not even observe their progress, or what lay ahead of them. By day or by night, all they could know was what the skin of their vessel might transmit to them through feeling. Every moment, their trust lay in God that the next thing they felt would *not* be the sickening crunch and rip of running aground. The biblical account emphasizes reliance on God throughout.

Verse 19 is not "mere" repetition, either: *So the waters prevailed greatly, greatly* (*mĕʾōd mĕʾōd*). In the tone of this account, the catastrophe is unrelenting; the sense of urgency increases exponentially. How greatly? *So that all the mountaintops which were under all the heavens were covered.*

Fifteen cubits upward the waters prevailed, so that the mountains were covered; v 20 adds the final bit of hard data. Though those inside the ark may not have known it then, the reader now knows the ark would not founder, even if it floated across a mountain peak below it. The draft of this thirty-cubit-high vessel would not exceed fifteen cubits. The standard cubit is thought to have been about eighteen inches; fifteen cubits, then, would be about twenty-two feet.

■ **21-22** From the conditions on the surface of the waters as they rose to their maximum height above the mountain peaks, the narrator turned to the effects of the flood on the living creatures not brought into the safety of the ark. As we have seen often, the topic is introduced by a short general statement, followed by a number of details. Here, the whole is encompassed by the first and last words of these verses, taken as a unit; both are verbs, *And [it] expired . . . they died.*

The subject of *expired* is expressed in a comprehensive phrase, *And all flesh which moves about upon the earth expired.* Within that general statement were included several groups. The first listed is *the flying creature(s),* i.e., the first of the animal life God had created (together with the creatures of the sea), that being on the fifth creation day (1:21). Next are listed the *domestic livestock* and the *wild beasts,* created on the sixth creation day. All these are commonly within the ken of human beings, especially in preindustrial ages, and in all rural settings.

The narrator included the next group, however, to emphasize the scale, the thoroughness, of this disinfection of the earth. Already at the beginning of this statement, he used Hebrew *remeś* as a general term to include all animal life (even humans) that moves above or upon the land. In this context, then, he chose a different root (*śereṣ* means "teeming" or "swarming things") to designate *all the swarming creatures which swarm upon the earth,* that is, the smallest creatures—reptiles, amphibians, small mammals, arachnids, insects, and others—whether seen by humans as beneficial or baneful. The narrator thus included all the flying creatures of the sky and all the general groupings of the land creatures in this notice of the general and complete cessation of life upon the earth.

Of course, then, the last group listed is intended to be dramatically climactic. This is doubly so, in view of the fact that among the nonhumans, the *swarming creatures* are listed last, followed immediately by (we may translate), *as well as every human*. From the smallest to the greatest, all were removed by the agency of the flood.

Verse 22, then, is a summarizing and concluding statement, but emphasizing their decease in another way, *Every [creature] which in its nostrils was the breath of the spirit of life, of all that were upon the dry land, they died.* This, too, hearkens back to the creation narrative; Gen 2:7 reports that God had breathed into the human the breath of life, and the human had become a living being, in its physicality like the rest of the animal life upon the earth. Now all of them expired together, another element of the de-creation human corruption had brought about.

It [i.e., *all flesh*] *expired . . . they died.* The text does not say "they drowned," though of course we may assume that virtually all these deaths were by drowning. This reporting of death without mentioning agency brings the reader back again to the one cautionary note in the creation accounts; if the humans were to eat of the fruit of the one tree, God had said, then "dying, you shall die." The unmaking of God's good creation, brought on by human corruption (6:12) is brought home to the reader once again.

■ **23** God had determined to wipe the earth clean, to disinfect it (6:7); God had declared that intention to Noah (7:4). This verse is the report that the flood accomplished what God had purposed. The first word of the Hebrew text is this same verb (*māḥâ* means to "wipe clean" or "blot out"), and here it is active (not passive, as NIV has it). However, it also is the verb of the second clause, and the second time it *is* a passive form.

Thus did [God] wipe clean [blot out] every living thing that was upon the surface of the ground, from the humans, to the larger [land] animals, to the [smaller] creeping animals, and to the flying creatures of the heavens; so they were wiped from the earth.

Following nine lines of unmitigated disaster reporting, the succinct reminder of the ark is dramatic and telling, indeed, *So only Noah was left, and whoever was with him in the ark.* By comparison with the vastness of the inundation, the ark was a tiny vessel, a fragile floating chip. Moreover, as we have noted, those inside had no means of moving or steering it; it went where the winds and the currents took it. By comparison with the universal loss of life outside, the handful of humans and animals inside seemed a tiny, vulnerable remnant from which to repopulate the earth. The ark with its living cargo was a pinprick of light in an ocean of darkness, the total return of the earth to the primeval night that had enveloped it in the beginning (1:2). The de-creation, the unmaking, was complete.

■ 24 The components of the first line of the paragraph (v 17*a*) are repeated, but with amplification. There, ***the flood continued,*** i.e., the downpour of rain was unabated during the period; here, though the flood/rain had stopped, **the waters** they had brought prevailed or continued to remain without receding. In both, the setting of the disaster was ***upon the earth.*** Each segment reports a total number of days, but the numbers differ. The first line reports rain (and the soon unseen fountains of the deep) continuing for forty days. Following the cessation of the inundation from above and below, still ***the waters prevailed upon the earth one hundred fifty days.*** Only in the next paragraphs will the narrator report their gradual receding.

To this point, the narrator has recorded three periods of time. The first was seven days from God's announcement to Noah that the flood would begin, to the day of its beginning (v 10). The second was the forty-day period of continuous rainfall (v 12). This period of waiting for the waters to begin receding puts the running total number of days at one hundred ninety-seven, just over six and a half months. More time segments will follow in the report of the receding of the waters. This notice marks the cresting not only of the waters (setting) but of the narrative (plot) as well. From here on, resolution will be the focus.

FROM THE TEXT

The flood is presented as a de-creation, most vividly in this chapter. Theologically, this is very important for our comprehensive understanding of God's creation from its beginning to its end. The first de-creation brought about by the flood shows that God does deal, in God's timing, with whatever threatens to destroy God's good creation. However, God did not completely destroy the earth—that is what God moved to *prevent*. Rather, God cleansed ("wiped") the earth clean of the moral (and other) pollution human rebellion had caused. By analogy, the "new creation" spoken of in the book of Revelation and elsewhere in the NT may not involve the physical destruction of the earth itself, either. The analogy of the flood, while suggestive, is not decisive, however. The canons of the NT apocalyptic genre(s), together with the vocabulary, grammar, and syntax of the pertinent NT texts, have convinced many scholars to read them, also, in terms of de-creation and re-creation. As before, God will not totally destroy God's good creation; God will renew it.

Some may wonder whether our attempts to highlight the dramatic imagery and effect of the narrative of the flood's beginning are not *too* dramatic for the sober discussion of a commentary. If anything, though, they are not dramatic *enough* to do justice to the tone of the Hebrew text here. This was the most cataclysmic event in human history to that point. Jesus himself intimated it is the most cataclysmic ever, until the skies are thrown open once again, this time for his own return at the end of this age (Matt 24:37-39).

This leads to another consideration. In December 2004 an Indonesian earthquake and tsunami killed more than 150,000 people around the perimeter of the Indian Ocean. A large earthquake in January 2010 killed at least 220,000 people in Haiti. Now, just two weeks ago, as I write (March 2011), one of the strongest earthquakes on record has staggered the nation of Japan and triggered a vast tsunami; the death toll is expected to rise much higher than the 10,000 now reported. In the aftermath of such deadly natural disasters, it is not unusual for several prominent Christian figures to announce that they are God's judgments on those affected, sometimes making a connection with the flood of Noah's day.

Are present-day natural disasters, especially the largest of them, really comparable with the flood of Noah's day? Are they to be understood as God's judgment on those who are affected by them? The short answer is, "No." Even if Noah's flood should turn out to have been what geographers and geologists would call a "localized," event, the narrator presents it as having been the cause of death of all living, breathing creatures, except those on board the ark with Noah and his family. No disaster since, however great its force or its reach, has had that kind of impact. As noted already, Jesus intimated that none ever will, until his own return at the end of this age. To compare any natural event of more recent history with the flood of Noah's day is to misunderstand the former and trivialize the latter. A universal judgment like the flood will not be experienced by some, and only reported to others. Everyone upon the earth will experience it, and all will know why it has come. Until then, we are not to judge disaster victims; we are to pray for them and help them as we are able.

C. Receding Waters; Leaving the Ark (8:1-22)

I. The Beginning of the End (8:1-5)

BEHIND THE TEXT

With the end of ch 7, the narrator has reached the climax of the flood, both literally and literarily. Through ch 8, the pace quickens (if we may use that metaphor of eight persons still unable to leave the safe haven of the ark until late in the chapter!). The narrative is straightforward and forward-looking. The past is past. Those aboard the ark await with growing eagerness their first views of the unknown new world to be revealed when God should give them the "all clear" and permission to venture out.

Theologically, ch 8 records the reversal of the reversal. With the flood, God had de-created the earth, reversing God's good creation all the way back to its earliest state of all-encompassing water and darkness (1:2). Now, with the receding of the waters, the narrator reports a second reversal. Out of the *de*-creation God *re*-created.

■ I **But God remembered Noah** follows immediately upon the last statement of the previous chapter. (The reader will recall, too, that the text originally did not have chapter and verse divisions.) We should read these two statements together to understand the full impact of the second, *So the waters prevailed upon the earth one hundred fifty days, but God remembered Noah.* This does not mean God had forgotten about Noah for a while, and then suddenly the memory of Noah and the ark came back to God. It was just the opposite. Idiomatically, **God remembered Noah** means God had not at any time forgotten Noah and the occupants of the ark. God's remembrance and concern for Noah is rooted in God's promise to establish a covenant with him (6:18). God's remembrance of Noah and his subsequent action to reverse the flood and its effects indicate God's faithfulness to his promise to Noah. (See Exod 2:24 for God's remembering of his covenant with Abraham in the context of Israel's bondage in Egypt.)

The various listings of the people and the animal groups that entered the ark occupy a significant number of lines in the narrative of its preparation and boarding. Now, as the narrative pace begins to quicken just here, such detail no longer is necessary. As head of his family in the ancient world's already-patriarchal culture, Noah represented all eight members of his family; mention of his name was enough to include them all. So, too, *all the wild creatures and all the domestic livestock* encompassed all the rest of the ark's passengers. It is well for us to note that God's remembering did not center only on Noah and his family. God's love extended, and extends, to all creation.

God caused a wind to pass over/upon the earth. Just as the flood's rising is a narrative of de-creation, in a reversal of the creation events of Gen 1, so here the narrator begins immediately to present God's reversal of the flood as a re-creation; the reversal is reversed. Hebrew *rûaḥ* (**wind** or "breath," or "spirit/Spirit") is the noun used here, echoing its use in Gen 1:2, at the very inception of the original creation narrative. The narrator intended the reader to understand the physical wind moving upon these waters as instrumental in bringing about their abatement, and as another manifestation of the moving/hovering/brooding of the Spirit of God, of a kind with the movement upon the primeval waters as creation began.

This is not to say the molecules of moving air that make up the wind, physically, "are" the Spirit of God. It *is* to say there is no place, no time, no action, and no circumstance upon the earth in which it would be accurate to say, "God is not here; God is not doing anything here." The narrator intended to remind the reader of that reassuring fact in this depiction of the climactic moment of the great flood, the moment of the beginning of its reversal. God sent the wind/breath/Spirit, *and the waters began to recede.*

■**2** *Now the fountain-springs of the deep and the sluicegates of the heavens were closed, and the rain from the heavens was brought to an end.* The narrator had reported the opening of these water sources to begin the flood (7:11). It was necessary, therefore, to report also the fact that now they had been closed. The sequence of these events is made clear in the following verses.

The most important point of this report is that both verbs are passive, just as the two verbs reporting the beginning of the flood are passive (7:11). The flood did not begin of its own volition; it did not end of its own volition. From beginning to end, it was the agent of God's judgment.

■**3** The details reported here clarify the sequence and timing of the events initiated by God's shutting off of the water sources. This happened after the first forty days (7:12, 17), and not after the subsequent one hundred fifty days (7:24); moreover, the closing of these sources ended the *rising* of the waters. The wind began at that time also, and the waters began to recede, but they continued to "prevail," i.e., to cover the earth (7:24), so that no one on the ark could know the waters had begun to recede. The one hundred fifty days are mentioned again here because the narrator wished to say very specifically that during that period the floodwaters returned to the two sources from which they had been unleashed; *Then the waters began to return from upon the earth, going [downward] and returning [upward], and the waters continued to abate to the end of one hundred fifty days.* In more precise language, we could say some of the floodwaters flowed and seeped back down into the water table and the subterranean reservoirs (*going*), while some evaporated, replenishing the normal levels of water vapor in the atmosphere (*returning*).

■**4** The significance of the one hundred fifty days (five months) was that then **the ark came to rest on the mountains of Ararat.** Whatever the passengers on the ark may have wished, hoped, or guessed before, only then could they *know* the waters of the flood were receding. No wonder they marked the date on the calendar: *in the seventh month, on the seventeenth day of the month.*

The verb in the phrase, *Then* the ark *rested/*come to rest, is from the same root (*nûaḥ*) as Noah. The ark carrying Noah, the rest-bringer (5:29), *rested.* This elegant and comforting little wordplay cannot be accidental.

The text does not say "on Mount Ararat," but **on the mountains of Ararat. Ararat** is Akkadian Urartu, the region and people north of ancient Assyria. Urartu comprised parts of today's Kurdistan (eastern Turkey and northwestern Iran) and Armenia. Interesting and tempting as is the proposed identification of the ark's resting place with today's Mount Ararat (see sidebar), this report only names the region, not a specific peak. The text itself, we may not press beyond that.

Mount Ararat/Aghri Dagh

Mount Ararat is in extreme eastern Turkey, overlooking Turkey's border with Armenia to the north-northeast, and Turkey's border with Iran to the southeast. The summit of Ararat reaches to nearly 17,000 feet above sea level. Sitting just less than thirty miles away, the mountain dominates the southern skyline of Yerevan, Armenia's capital city. On the Turkish side of the international border, as well as on the Armenian side, the population, historically, is heavily Armenian in ethnicity. Moreover, Armenian tradition holds that the nation was the first to embrace the Christian faith, as early as the first century. Thus, Armenians hold the story of Noah and the site of the ark's coming to rest on one of the upper slopes of Ararat as uniquely "their" cultural possessions.

Many stories are told of locals from a century or so ago "visiting the ark when it was not encased in ice." Aerial and even satellite photographs have been interpreted as revealing the shadowy outline of the ark, now that it is again "encased in ice." Several adventurers have mounted expeditions to find and document the ark on this site. Despite this intense interest, nothing is settled. For example, wood brought down "from the ark" has proven to be only several hundred years old. (No matter one's views on the reliability of radiocarbon dating, generally, all agree it is accurate at such a close historical range as that.) If Noah's ark truly came to rest on Mount Ararat near the modern border of Turkey and Armenia, so far it has resisted being found and paraded on public view.

■ **5** Having noted that the ark would move no more, the narrator returned to the vital subject of the receding floodwaters. *As for the waters, they* continued to recede [lit., "they were going and diminishing"; see comment on v 3, above] **until the tenth month.**

8:6-14   Of course, this does not mean the waters stopped receding after the tenth month. It only marks the date of the next important event, *In the tenth [month], on the first [day] of the month, the summits of the mountains were seen.* If the ark came to rest on the top of, or along the slope of, one mountain on the seventeenth day of the seventh month, how can this date, two-and-a-half months later, be correct? One suggestion, based on an assumption, rather than on any specific statement in the text, is that the ark rested on one of the highest elevations in the mountains of Ararat. Only by the later date did the lower surrounding peaks begin to be visible. While some discount this possibility (e.g., Hamilton 1990, 301-2), it may be that the narrator intended the passive form *were seen* to convey point of view. It was not that no other peaks, anywhere, were visible in the intervening time. Rather, from the ark in its resting place, Noah and his family could not see any of the land within their horizon until two-and-a-half months after the ark came to rest, when some of the nearby peaks emerged from the waters.

2. The Raven and the Dove (8:6-14)

BEHIND THE TEXT

The beginning of the reemergence of the land corresponds to the creation week's day three, when God had instructed the waters to be gathered together into one place (1:9). The prominence of the raven and the dove in this paragraph reprises day five of the creation week, when God had instructed the waters and the heavens to bring forth the creatures appropriate to their respective spheres (1:20-23).

IN THE TEXT

■ **6-7** Another period of **forty days** elapsed, ***and** Noah opened the window of the ark which he had made*. This presents a dilemma; it is the first mention of a "window" (*ḥallôn*) in the ark. God had instructed Noah to make a *ṣōhar* for the ark, and to finish it, apparently, to a cubit (about eighteen inches) from the top (6:16). But is this *ḥallôn* (**window**) the same architectural element as the *ṣōhar*? For our discussion of the matter, see the commentary on 6:16.

Why did Noah wait another forty days after he could see mountain summits before sending out the first bird? For that matter, how could Noah have seen the summits if he had not previously opened the window? On the second question, it may be worth noting that the text does not say this was the first time Noah had opened the window, only that he opened it, now, to release the raven. It seems unlikely that the family would have remained inside the vessel for two-and-a-half months after it had come to rest, without once looking outside.

Noah's "delay" in sending out the raven is not the most important detail of the narrative, but the reader naturally wonders about it. Not only is forty days a considerable period of time, but the ark had stopped moving more than *one hundred* days earlier. We can only speculate. One possibility is that Noah and his family easily could see for most of that time that the waters had not yet receded enough for them to exit the ark, that to send any creature outside would only endanger its life.

The names of birds and animals in the Hebrew Bible are not always limited to single species. This bird (*ʿōrēb*) probably was the **raven** proper (*Corvus corax*), but it may have been another of the Corvidae, such as a rook, a jackdaw, or another species of raven. All the members of the crow family are strong, smart, and resourceful, so it does not come as a surprise to read that this one did not return to Noah. In fact, the language of the text here does not require us to assume that he never saw this raven again, or that it never alighted anywhere to rest. The verse reads, ***And he sent forth the raven, and it went out, going out and returning, until the waters were dried up from upon the surface of the ground***.

The **raven** means one of the ravens from among the seven pairs Noah had allowed into the ark with him (7:3). ***And it went out, going out and returning*** reflects a finite verb form followed by an infinitive absolute, indicating continuous action. It describes the repetitive circling, the back and forth reconnaissance of the ground below, often seen in these species. Even if Noah saw the raven daily, this would have told him only what he already knew (v 5), that the higher elevations were suitable for it, and it was finding carrion or other food to sustain it. This was worth knowing, but the raven would not enlighten Noah about the lower elevations as they dried out. As an intelligence agent for Noah's needs, the raven was limited.

■ **8-9** **The dove,** here, also means "one of the doves," i.e., the particular dove Noah selected to send from the ark. Though the narrator had not expressed Noah's purpose in sending out the raven, he did so in reporting the sending of the dove. This may be as simple as a narrative device to demonstrate Noah's increasing awareness and engagement of the fact that the time for leaving the ark was drawing nearer.

Noah already had seen the summits of the mountains. Though the narrator did not feel constrained to state the obvious, Noah and his family had observed the gradual but continuous abating of the waters since their first sighting of the mountaintops. Noah's purpose here was something else, ***to see whether the waters had finished from upon the surface of the ground.*** Noah wanted to know whether the floodwaters had abated from the lower, arable land, from which they would have to make their livelihood, once they exited the ark.

As with the raven, **dove** (*yônâ*) could indicate any of a number of species among the doves and the pigeons. They also can fly long distances—this dove could have been what we know as a homing pigeon (Gordon 1971, 77). Doves, however, are not carrion eaters. Ranging for vegetation below the level of the ark, ***the dove did not find rest for the sole of her foot, so she returned to him, to the ark, for the waters were upon*** [i.e., still covered] ***the surface of all the land.*** **Rest** (*mānôaḥ*) is another play on the name Noah (see v 4); this form is a participle used as a substantive (noun). Not finding rest outside the ark, the dove returned to Noah, the rest-bringer (5:29), within it.

The contrast between the actions of the dove and of the raven is significant. The raven had not returned to Noah—at least, not to come again within the ark. The dove, however, came back, and Noah **stretched forth his hand and took her, and brought her to him in the ark.** It is a touching, even a tender, moment, illustrating by a small action the righteousness and integrity God had seen in Noah earlier.

■ **10-12** The emphasis of v 10 is on the *repetition* of the sending, ***So he [Noah] waited <u>again</u>, another seven days, and <u>repeated</u> his sending out the dove from the ark.*** Three different words, an adverb (*ʿôd*, **again**), an adjective (*ʾăḥērîm*, **another**), and a verb (*wayyōsep*, from *yāsap*, meaning here "to do again") combine to heighten the energy and the anticipation of the narrative: what will happen *this* time? This statement also intimates what the author had not said, that after releasing the raven Noah had waited seven days before sending the dove the first time (v 8).

***And* the dove returned to him in the evening,** i.e., when the activities of the day normally are finished for animals and for humans, and when birds normally return to their roosts. This is a homey, ordinary domestic scene, and the reader may begin to be resigned to waiting until another time. The narrator, however, is a consummate storyteller; the very next word immediately raises expectations once again, **and behold!** This survey of the landscape had been different; the dove had found, not a dead branch, but a living olive tree from which to pluck a twig. In this phrase, ʿālēh (**twig**) functions as a collective, not as a singular, noun. This was not one leaf only but a twig or small branch with freshly grown leaves along its length. This is ample reason for the narrator's **and behold!** After nearly a year of waiting and uncertainty, the dove had brought a sign of hope and renewal.

Olives do not grow on the heights, but on the lower slopes, in the valleys, and out into the plains, down to sea level. The living olive branch, with its fresh green leaves, testified to the renewal of life upon the earth in the lower elevations where human life could begin again. The dove had shown that the flood truly had receded.

Whether from an excess of caution, whether he was waiting still for God's explicit direction, or whether he simply did not know what else to do next, Noah sent out the dove again. This was now the fourth time Noah had sent a bird out from the ark. The narrator marked this occasion by the use of four notes of repetition in the account, **So he [Noah] waited <u>again</u>, <u>another</u> seven days, and sent forth the dove, but she did not <u>repeat</u> her returning to him <u>again</u>.** The same three words occur here as in v 10, but the adverb **again** (ʿôd) is both the second and the final word of the verse.

Birds in the Mesopotamian Account 8:10-13

It is both common and appropriate to note that the Mesopotamian hero of the flood, Utnapishtim, also sent out birds to check on the status of the waters after his boat (not ark) had landed on Mount Nisir (not on the mountains of Ararat). The details of his sending are different, however. Utnapishtim sent out the dove first, and she returned to him. Next, he sent a swallow, which also returned. Utnapishtim sent the raven last, but as with Noah, the raven did not return (Epic of Gilgamesh XI, ll. 145-154). As we have observed in several places above, both similarities large and small, and differences large and small, are quite numerous between the biblical account of Noah and the various Mesopotamian flood accounts. This difference does not appear to be theologically based. Utnapishtim's recitation as recorded in the Epic of Gilgamesh simply neglects to take account of the fact that it would have made more sense to send the raven before the dove, for while the raven is at home in the heights as well as the lowlands, the dove generally is found in the lower elevations.

■ **13** The narrator begins here with the date; the survivors had been in the ark nearly a full year. On the date given, **the waters had dried up from upon the earth.** The second half of the verse relates how Noah discovered this for himself; he **removed the covering of the ark** and looked out. The **covering** (miksēh) of the ark was most likely the roof, not the window (see Cassuto 1964, 64-

65). Opening the window, if it was in the roof, as often supposed, had given Noah a view of the mountaintops as they became visible (v 5), but not of the **surface of the ground** sloping away from the ark toward the lowlands beyond. Taking off the roof (or even only a part of it) would have given Noah that view, and confirmation that the **ground** below him indeed was dry. That this news, though welcome, was unexpected, is implicit in the narrator's use, once again, of the interjection, ***And behold!***

■ **14** Once again, we have not a superfluous repetition, but new information, an announcement that the episode of the flood was finished, not merely that the ground Noah could see from the ark was dry. Not only is the date given here almost two months later from that of v 13; both the noun and the verb are different, as well. The statement of v 13, ***the surface of the ground was dry,*** means that no water remained upon as much of the surface of the ground as Noah could see. Here, the statement, ***the earth/land had dried out,*** means that the land in general no longer was saturated. When they stepped out of the ark, its occupants would not be stepping into mud, but upon normally dry soil. Moreover, the verb used here (*yābšâ,* ***dried out***) is the same root as the noun of 1:9-10, when God had commanded the gathering of the primeval waters, so the "dry land" (*yabbāšâ*) would appear. The positive reversal, the re-creation after the de-creation, now was complete.

The narrator reports that the land was completely dry ***in the second month, on the twenty-seventh day of the month.*** The flood had begun on the seventeenth day of the second month in the previous year. This reckoning, however, is according to the lunar calendar, which comprises three hundred fifty-four days. Counting both the seventeenth day of the second month of Noah's six hundredth year, and the twenty-seventh day of the second month of Noah's six-hundred-first year, as this succession of dates requires, the flood lasted one solar year. Three hundred sixty-five days after entering the ark, Noah and his family left it. The season they came out into was the same season they had left behind.

3. Leaving the Ark (8:15-22)

BEHIND THE TEXT

God's re-creation of the earth from the de-creation of the flood reaches its literary and theological climax with this paragraph. God had established in their functions the land creatures, including humans, on the sixth day of the creation week. Now, all the creatures who had been sheltered by the ark emerged to begin again the exercise of their respective functions in their respective habitats. In this, they were led by the humans, who also had been the climax of the creation week itself.

■ **15-16** With respect to Noah's family, God's specific instruction to enter the ark (7:1) had been as succinct as possible, **Go, you and all your household, into the ark.** Now, the instruction to leave the ark was more detailed, **Go out from the ark, you, and your wife, and your sons, and the sons of your wives, with you.** Literarily, this simply is for the pleasing effect of variety in expression. If there is theological significance in this expansion, it reflects God's satisfaction that all who had entered the ark now would exit it; no lives God had intended to spare had been lost during the year of the flood.

This is the first of four occurrences of the verb **Go out** in these four short verses (16-19). The first two are God's instructions, **Go out** (a simple imperative), and "bring out" ("cause to go out," a causative imperative, v 17). The second two record that Noah did as God had instructed him, **So Noah went out** (v 18), and **they went out,** meaning all the creatures (v 19). On one level, this is simply a reporting of what the reader expects by this point in the narrative. Yet by using the same verb four times in this short span, the narrator emphasizes that God had intended the ark as a means, not an end. "Home" for a year, it would not be home for the rest of their lives. It was time to be about the business of repopulating the earth.

■ **17** God's instruction to Noah had been to "bring into" (**cause/allow to come in,** 6:19) two of every species; now it was to **cause/allow to exit** all the creatures in the ark with him. As we have seen before, all animal life is included, yet the wording of the instruction is not identical to any of the earlier listings. God's purpose in this instruction, as expressed here, echoes and reflects the creation blessing/mandate upon animal life to reproduce itself (1:22). Here, God specifically initiated another aspect of the re-creation that would reverse the de-creation of the flood, **that they may breed bountifully upon the earth, [that is,] that they may be fruitful and multiply upon the earth.** God's blessing/benison upon the animal kingdom was restored and reaffirmed.

■ **18-19** As we have seen, in biblical narrative—in keeping with conventional Near Eastern literary practice—the narrator must not leave the reader merely to *assume* that what had been instructed had been done. The narrator almost always must *report* that those charged with a responsibility had, in fact, successfully completed it. This is that report.

A small surprise for the reader comes at the very end, in the statement that the various animal groupings, **by their families, went out from the ark.** **Families** (*mišpĕḥōt*) is a term usually applied to humans. By no means is this the only biblical indication that God has a high and affectionate regard for God's nonhuman creatures; the attentive reader will see this theme virtually everywhere in Scripture. But this one carries greater significance than one may register at first glance, precisely because it is so magnificently understated. If

GENESIS

8:15-19

Scripture can refer to animals as comprising "families," they deserve at least our generous regard and humane care.

■ **20** Noah's first recorded act upon exiting the ark was to build **an altar to Yahweh.** His second was to offer, not one, but a number of *whole* **burnt offerings** (ʿōlōt) upon it. A *whole* **burnt offering** is the entire animal laid upon the altar and burnt there. (Whether Noah would have dressed the sacrificial animal before laying it on the altar we cannot say; this was before the Levitical instructions for sacrifice.) Noah offered at least one individual from each of the clean species; whether he offered a pair of each (or more), the text does not say. As we have noted above (see 7:2-3), these would have included at least sheep, goat(s), cattle, and a number of birds; more than that, we cannot say.

Sacrifice in the Mesopotamian Flood Accounts

Cassuto notes, "Already in the Sumerian story of the Flood . . . it is expressly stated that the hero of the Deluge offered up, after his deliverance, an ox and sheep" (1964, 75). If, as we think (with many others), the Mesopotamian flood stories reflect memories of the real event, distorted by the polytheism of their respective peoples, this reference to an ox is an accurate detail. At a minimum, then, Noah would have offered oxen (or bulls), sheep, goats, and several birds in this initial sacrifice following the exit from the ark.

8:18-21

■ **21** *So Yahweh smelled the restful aroma, and Yahweh said in his heart, "I will not anymore curse again the ground because of the* ʾādām, *however much the inclination of the heart of the* ʾādām *is evil, even from his youth; nor will I anymore again smite every living creature, as I have done."*

So Yahweh smelled is an anthropomorphism; it occurs in a few other places, as well (e.g., Lev 26:31). God is said also to see (beginning with Gen 1:4) and to hear (e.g., Exod 3:7). This language is a helpful way to affirm that God does experience the things we experience through our senses.

The phrase we have translated *the restful aroma* occurs more than thirty times (though without the definite article it has here) in the instructions for Israel's sacrificial system in Leviticus and Numbers. The adjective *restful* is from the same root (nûaḥ) as Noah, whom his father Lamech, in naming him, had predicted would be the rest-bringer (5:29). Again, as we have seen before with other uses of this root in our narrative, this cannot be accidental. Rest/ *restful* has many nuances. In this moment of Noah's and his family's worship, the narrator even could describe it as being *restful* to Yahweh.

Sacrifice and Gods in the Mesopotamian Account

When Utnapishtim told Gilgamesh of his sacrifice to the gods after the flood had subsided and he had left his boat, he said they had crowded around "like flies" (Epic of Gilgamesh XI, l. 161). In the theological system of ancient Mesopotamia, humans saw to all the needs of all the gods and goddesses, usually in their respective temples. This included feeding them. For the seven days the flood was said to have lasted in the Mesopotamian accounts, the gods and goddesses had not eaten. They had not noticed soon enough that by destroying the human population of the earth they also were guaranteeing empty plates, bowls, and cups on their own temple tables, every morning and every evening. The average Israelite may not have known Utnapishtim's version of the flood narrative, but we may be sure the educated folk who produced, preserved, and transmitted the Genesis account did know it. They certainly appreciated the delicious irony here, as much as any modern reader.

The phrase, **Yahweh said in his heart,** introduces the report of Yahweh's inner thoughts and decision. There is no direct speech to Noah here; this may have been to prevent the idea that Noah's sacrifice somehow had made God change his mind. Israel's polytheistic neighbors regularly thought their sacrifices had a magical, even sometimes a coercive, effect on their deities. Israel's God extends grace at God's own initiative, often before being asked. We are invited to pray, but God does not need to be persuaded or cajoled and cannot be bribed or threatened.

What God said **in his heart,** i.e., "to himself," is the twofold negative promise, *I will not anymore . . . nor will I anymore.* Verse 22 is its positive counterpart and sounds as though it would (or should) have been proclaimed to Noah and his family. However, a version of this promise of God's forbearance actually is part of the following covenant (9:11).

God's inner resolve centers on the future of his creation (**the ground** and *every living creature*). The English is awkward, but we have translated, *curse again . . . again smite,* to reflect the chiastic arrangement in the Hebrew text of the particle ʿôd (**again**) with the two infinitives; ʿôd follows the first one, (to) **curse,** and precedes the second, (to) *smite,* a simple AB:B'A' chiasm. The strength of God's inner resolution is emphasized also by the double use of the verb yāsap in these two clauses, *I will not anymore . . . nor will I anymore* (i.e., "do it again" or "add a second doing to this first one").

The meaning of the statement, *I will not anymore curse again the ground,* is not clear. It is unlikely that this means no more additional curses than the existing curse on the ground (3:17). Fretheim suggests this may refer to "the end of the reign of the curse"; God would not allow the curse "to control the future of humankind or the creation" (1994, 393). The creation narrative is clear that blessing is the way God relates to his creation (see 1:22, 28). The de-creation of the flood displayed the maximum destructive effect of God's curse on the ground. We may understand God's resolve here as the promise of a renewed relationship between God and the re-created world. If this is so, God's resolve means the re-created world could (and can) depend on God's blessing for its future. Once again, both theologically and literarily, this narrative is connected to the creation themes of Gen 1.

The second part of v 21 states the reasoning for God's inner resolve. The Hebrew conjunction *ki* usually means "for" or "because." However, this usual translation creates logical problems here; it would mean the reason for God's resolve to refrain from de-creation was the same as his reason for bringing on the de-creation of the flood (see 6:1-7). We have rendered the conjunction, **however much,** with a concessive force (see Hamilton 1990, 309-10). More colloquially, we could translate, "though the human heart is inclined toward evil even before they grow up." God's decision reflects the realistic recognition that to **curse again the ground** would bring only further destruction, with no real change in the human condition. Humans would (and do) continue to practice evil upon each other, upon the earth and its nonhuman inhabitants, and even upon God. The divine resolve not to **curse again the ground** rose from the recognition—deeply painful as it is to God—of the reality of sin's power over human beings.

God's motivation in making this promise (to Godself at this point) lay in God's love for and commitment to grace on behalf of God's good creation. We may say that, in a sense, God made the problem more complicated. Redemption, renewal, and re-creation are God's purposes. God determined to eschew the ready expedient of "off with their heads" and, instead, to bring the goal to reality by gentler means of grace.

■ **22** Verse 22 is a simple lyrical promise of God's commitment to the future constancy of the earth's yearly cycles; this verse amounts to an earnest of the promise that he would never again destroy the earth because of humankind. It begins with **Again** (*'ôd*), the third occurrence of this adverb in these three successive lines (vv 21-22); as usual, threefold repetition signifies strong emphasis. Its lead position in this small poem is for literary, poetic effect. In the logic of this hymnic promise, it is connected with the negated verb, which is its climax: The paired seasonal cycles (making together yearly, or daily, wholes) would not **again** cease, as they just had done in this year of the flood.

The horizon of this divine promise is **all the days of the earth.** This is not a promise that the earth will be eternal; only God is eternal. But as long as the earth does continue, God will not again interrupt or suspend these paired cycles of the seasons, either.

In ancient Mesopotamia where this narrative is set, and also in Israel where it formed part of the foundation of the national theology, **seedtime** designated primarily the time of the fall planting of wheat and/or barley in the fields. The **harvest** of these grains usually ran from mid or late March to mid or late June, the barley crop being harvested first, then the wheat. Of course, during the year of the flood, perhaps nothing had been planted and certainly nothing had been harvested.

Cold and heat and **summer and winter** almost amount to a poetic synonymous parallelism, "almost" because cold and heat are not quite the same as, but rather are the consequences of, the summer and winter seasons. We must notice, too, the other poetic and narrative device operating here; these two pairs are arranged chiastically, AB:B'A'. During the year of the flood, the usual summer heat had been mitigated by the floodwaters; likewise, the usual cold of the winter. These would not again be widely suspended, as both had been in this year.

Ephrem the Syrian on Restoring the Seasons

And because there was neither planting nor harvest during that year and the seasonal cycles had been disturbed, God restored to the earth that which had been taken away in his anger. . . . For throughout the entire year, until the earth dried up, winter, with no summer, had been upon them. (Louth 2001, 150)

Of course, day had followed night, and night had followed day, throughout the year of the flood. At first glance, this pair does not appear to belong. But those inside the ark had little or no illumination from the outside. Furthermore, much of the year of the flood would have been overcast—first with rain and clouds, then to a greater or lesser degree with fog or mistiness from the evaporation of the waters. The difference between day and night, from inside the ark, would have been very much less than normal. God would not again bring this experience widely upon the earth, either.

FROM THE TEXT

The notice at the beginning of this chapter, "But God remembered Noah," is the first occurrence of an important biblical theme, often referred to in terms of the "God who remembers." Genesis 30:22 reports, "Then God remembered Rachel; [and God] listened to her and opened her womb." The next important juncture is recorded in Exod 2:24, "And [God] remembered his covenant with Abraham, with Isaac and with Jacob." God then sent Moses as the agent of Israel's deliverance from their Egyptian bondage. The psalmist and the prophets besought God to remember (e.g., Ps 74:2; Jer 14:21) and rejoiced that God had remembered or would remember (e.g., Ps 105:8; Ezek 16:60). Though the word "remember" is not always present, they even complained that God did not seem to remember, sometimes noting (and sometimes not) that the evidence of God's remembering comes on God's timetable, not ours (e.g., Ps 73; Jer 15; 20). In these and many other permutations, the theme of "The God who remembers" is a central tenet of biblical theology.

The series of sacrifices Noah performed prefigured the offering of the firstborn and the firstfruits in the later Levitical system. Noah killed a small but significant percentage of the livestock he had brought aboard the ark, not waiting (as far as we know) until these animals had produced young to replace themselves. A more vivid and emphatic demonstration of Noah's continuing trust in God would be hard to imagine.

One more thing we can say; this was a series of *thanksgiving* offerings, thanks for God's deliverance of Noah, his family, and the animals who had shared in their year aboard the ark. They cannot have been sin offerings. It is true that God's finding Noah to be righteous, a man of integrity (6:9), did not mean Noah was without sin of any kind. Nevertheless, Noah did not need to offer sacrifices of expiation for transgression; the ark already had been (or had symbolized) their expiation. By the same token, these were not sacrifices of supplication for deliverance; they already had experienced deliverance. These were the sacrifices of hearts full of gratitude for God's complete and completed deliverance, for God's bringing them through the great de-creation to walk upon the earth once again.

Because of this narrative, the olive branch and the dove have become symbols of peace. Hebrew "peace" (*shalom*) means more than just the absence of physical conflict. It means wholeness; it means the total wellbeing of all God's creation. In ancient Israel, and over much of the Middle East to the present day, this is imaged beautifully, vividly, idyllically, by the olive grove, by the dovecote, by the promise and its sometime fulfillment in ancient Israel that every man and his family would dwell "under his own vine and fig tree" (e.g., 1 Kgs 4:25).

The simple majesty of the final poem is a solid foundation for trust, for refraining from worry. God has promised; we can depend on it. The unfailing cycles of the seasons of the year, even of the daily rhythms of day and night, are permanent reminders to all God's children of God's promise of continuing preservation. Humankind does not have to live in fear that another such great deluge may happen again at any time.

On the contrary, at least until the earth itself reaches its appointed renewal, natural cycles will not cease. Most of the seeds we plant will sprout and bear their harvest. In temperate climates, such as ancient Israel experienced, if we can't stand the heat, all we need do is wait; autumn and winter will come. If it's the cold that bothers us, again we wait; spring and summer are just around the corner, and they will come, even if March (or September, in the Southern Hemisphere) is raw and cold. The sun *will* come up tomorrow. If it doesn't, it only means either that earth's final day has come and gone, or our next awakening will be in God's presence. The believer can allow the rhythms of the earth to be a help to faith and trust in the One who keeps it so.

D. Blessing and Covenant (9:1-17)

BEHIND THE TEXT

This unit reports God's speech to Noah and his sons; it seems to be an expansion of God's inner resolve (what he "said in his heart") recorded at the end of ch 8 (see vv 21-22). It also reaffirms and expands God's promise of the covenant to Noah (see 6:18*a*). A large part of the reassurance of this speech lies in the fact that—despite having conceded the evil condition of the human heart (8:21-22)—God promised Noah that God's relationship with the post-flood world, including humanity, would continue in a covenant demonstrating God's faithfulness.

The narrator presents God's speeches in this unit in four parts. The first part, addressed to Noah and his sons (9:1-7), contains God's blessings, permissions, and prohibitions. The language of this section echoes the blessing of the first creation account (1:28-30), as well as the *you may . . . you may not* language of the second, more detailed, creation narrative (2:15-17). The word "covenant" does not appear yet, and this section is not formally a part of the covenant, though the end of this blessing is tied deliberately to the beginning of the covenant that follows. This repetition, with expansion, of the creation blessing marks the formal completion, by verbal announcement, of the re-creation God first had put into motion with the receding of the waters from their crest (8:1).

The second part of God's speech (9:8-11) contains the central feature of this covenant, the promise that God would not again destroy all life by a flood. The third part (vv 12-16) contains the formal establishment of the sign of the covenant. The fourth part (v 17) is a summary statement, speaking of this as a covenant between God and **all life on the earth.** While the women are not mentioned explicitly anywhere in the chapter, we do not have to imagine them as excluded from God's speeches in this narrative unit. This text was produced in and by a patriarchal culture, whose mind-set was to include women in the narrative only when they had what the men considered a direct part to play. The Bible does address this issue in many texts, but not explicitly in this one.

IN THE TEXT

■ **I** Verses 1 and 7 form an inclusio, indicating the beginning and the end of this paragraph. They constitute the same blessing/instruction, in virtually the same language, but with v 7 expanding it a bit, both for emphasis and for literary effect. As in Gen 1, so here also, the narrative is clear that blessing is fundamental to God's relationship with God's creation. The statement, **God blessed Noah and his sons,** certainly included the women of Noah's household, without whom God's blessing would not have become a reality. God's ultimate plan was, and is, that all the families descended from Noah and his sons would become recipients of God's blessings. Verse 1 anticipates this divine plan, which God began to reveal in his speech to Abram, a descendant of Shem (see 12:3).

The narrator used God's title here, reflecting the exclusive use of *Elohim* in Gen 1; the three verbs of the blessing in this verse are the same as the first three verbs of the blessing in 1:28. These are the same imperative plurals, a blessing in the form of a comprehensive command/instruction, "be fruitful and multiply, and fill the earth" (1:28 NRSV; see the commentary on 1:28).

In terms of the facts on the ground, it would be realistic to think of God instructing Noah and his family to "replenish the earth" (KJV, also at 1:28). Yet, in 1:28 "replenish" is a misleading translation, and here it would misplace the emphasis of God's intention in blessing Noah and his family. God already had established the re-creation by raising the earth from its watery grave, and did not intend them to restore the earth to its preflood situation, mired in wickedness. Even though "every inclination" of the human heart had become "evil from childhood" (see 8:21), God's creational purposes remained the same; this was to be a new creation. God's instruction to Noah—and, through him, to all his descendants—to produce, propagate, and nurture life was (and is) a renewed invitation to humans to take up again our stewardship assignment (see 1:28; 2:15), for the realization of God's creation mandate upon and for the earth.

■ **2** Because this postflood re-creation could not yet be a restoration to Edenic innocence—that lies still in the future even for us—the blessing/instruction here changes from what God had said to the first pair (1:28). The domination of the earth's creatures by the human family would continue, but it now would hold danger and terror for the animal kingdom at the hands of the humans, their erstwhile benefactors and protectors. Even those animals who would receive the most attentive care often would be destined for human consumption. From the animals' point of view, benevolent means would serve catastrophic ends.

Now, the fear *of you and the* dread/*dismay* of you may be the narrator's use of two synonyms together for emphasis, a common narrative device. Alternatively, this could be a hendiadys, the use of two nouns to express a single concept (where English often would use an adjective modifying a noun). If this is hendiadys, we could translate, "the fearful dread of you." Whichever syntax the narrator intended, the meaning is essentially the same; the rest of the animal kingdom would have a new fear of their human overseers. Also, translating the initial conjunction, *Now* (rather than "and," or leaving it untranslated, with NIV), emphasizes this shift from the previous, apparently more amicable, relationship between humans and the rest of the animal kingdom.

We have seen a number of variations in the listings of the animal groups; here is yet another. Most take this to be a list of four groups: the larger land creatures, the flying creatures of the skies, the smaller land creatures, and the fishes of the seas. If this was the narrator's intent, one may wonder why the shift of prepositions from the first list of two groups (ʿal) to the second list of two groups (bĕ-). Two issues here will guide our understanding of this verse. First, Hebrew sometimes uses a prepositional phrase with bĕ-, where English usage requires a noun, without a preposition, as a direct object; this may be the case here. Second, the major in-verse divider after the first two listings in the MT suggests that the Masoretes may have understood this as two groups of two listings, rather than as a single group of four.

If this understanding is correct, we may translate the verse as two separate sentences. *Now the fear of you and the dread of you will be upon all the living beings of the earth and upon all the flying creatures of the skies. Everything which moves about upon the ground, and all the fishes of the sea, into your hand are given.*

What are we suggesting? That in the world of living creatures this verse, with its two sets of two groupings, recapitulates the divisions of creation days two and three by which God originally had made the earth ready for animal habitation. The theme of re-creation is advanced by this minor echo of the original theme of creation.

The first contrast, between *all the living beings of the earth* and *all the flying creatures of the skies,* echoes the division of creation day two, between the waters above the firmament and the waters below the firmament (1:6-8). If the fear of postflood humans were to be *upon* (ʿal) all the rest of animal life, then the first phrase *living beings of the earth* (ḥayyat hāʾāreṣ) must include all the land and sea creatures. The second group of this first list, *flying creatures of the skies*, the creatures that traverse the *waters . . . above* (read here "firmament," "atmosphere," "skies") completes the mirroring here of the first major physical division upon the earth, and encompasses all life upon earth. Henceforth, all shall have reason to fear humankind.

The second contrast is between *everything which moves about upon the ground, and all the fishes of the sea.* This echoes the division of the earth's surface on the third creation day, by the gathering together of the seas so the dry land could appear (1:9-10). Since this is a second listing of two groups (evidenced, as we have noted, by the change in preposition from ʿal to bĕ-, and affirmed by the Masoretic division of the verse), the first group must designate all the land creatures including, this time, the flying creatures—most of whom, after all, spend more time at rest than in the air. The second group also is designated by a single noun, *fishes* (in the phrase, *all the fishes of the sea*). Like ḥayyat hāʾāreṣ in the first sentence, this noun also is more comprehensive than it usually is. Here, it includes all the creatures of the sea: mammals, reptiles, and others, as well as the numerous species of fish.

To be sure, the first circumstance, the fear of humans that now would be a feature of the animal psyche, would be caused largely by the second, God's giving of the animal kingdom into human hands, not now only for supervision and caretaking, but also for food. The narrator's choice of two independent sentences in v 2—by which he included all the animals, comprehensively, in *both* of his two groups of listings—perhaps was intended to highlight the dramatic change from the narrative of Gen 1. The narrator makes terribly vivid the reality of the new conditions of life for the animal kingdom everywhere.

The fear of [humans] and the dread of [humans] henceforth would be the new normal.

Walton proposes that the animals intended here are the larger wild creatures, mostly mammals, which move about primarily in herds (2001, 341-43). This verse, then, would constitute God's permission for humans to become hunters. Walton's suggestion merits serious consideration.

■ **3** We translate v 3, *Every moving thing which is alive, to you it shall be for food; just as the green plants, I [now] give you everything*; it makes explicit the reason for the new fear of humans within the animal kingdom. The comparison with the permission to eat of all the various plants that can be used for food (1:29-30) invites the reader to compare God's present generosity of provision favorably with that earlier one.

Here the narrator used a single noun, *remeś* (**moving thing**), to encompass all animal life. If we were to put it into colloquial English, we could say, "If it moves and breathes, you may eat it." In saying it that way, we would not quibble about the fact that the mussel, for example, attaches itself to a rock near the seashore and does not "move," nor that most water creatures get their oxygen by means of gills, rather than lungs. Neither does this Hebrew way of saying it intend to exclude the mussel; all animal life is permitted as food for humans.

The animals Noah had taken into the ark with him (7:2, 8) were either "clean" or "not clean" because of their suitability for sacrifice; they were not yet (explicitly) allowed as food for humans. Moreover, the dietary restrictions of the Sinai code, with their distinctions between clean animals that may be eaten, and unclean animals forbidden as food, are a later revelation, binding upon Israel as God's covenant people. The categories of "clean," "not clean," and "unclean" do not pertain to this text and its permission to eat animal flesh.

Why God now permitted the eating of flesh, when previously it had not been explicitly allowed, the text does not say. Cassuto's suggestion at least is plausible; Noah and his sons had "rescued the living creatures in their ark . . . and thus became, as it were, partners of the Creator in the creation of the life of these species" (1964, 126).

■ **4** *Only, flesh with its life, its blood, you shall not eat.* The permission to eat flesh came with a prohibition expressed strongly at its beginning and its end. The Hebrew particle *ʾak* (here we are translating, *only*) introduces a strong statement, command, or prohibition, often (as here) in emphatic contrast with what comes immediately before. The actual prohibition at the end is formed with the negative particle *lōʾ*, followed by an imperfect indicative form of the verb, *you shall not eat.* This is the strongest form of Hebrew prohibition; it is permanent, rather than temporary, and does not permit of exceptions, either by way of unusual circumstance or of temporary allowance of what usually is forbidden.

248

It now was permitted to eat flesh. It was *not* permitted to eat flesh that still had its life in it. What is the life of flesh? This verse (with others later) defines the life of the flesh as ***its blood.*** Whether or not it would be possible to falsify this idea scientifically, the taboo is not grounded, here or elsewhere, in biological science. It is, rather, a theological position: to eat blood is to eat life; therefore, out of respect for life, and for the Creator of life, humans are to eat flesh only after the blood has been drained from it.

■ **5** *And surely your blood, your own life, I will require. At the hand of every beast I will require it; and from the hand of the human being—from the hand of a man, his brother—I will require the life of the human.* This verse, too, begins with the emphatic particle *ʾak;* because this statement is construed positively rather than negatively, we have translated it here, **surely.** The emphasis of this particle here is just as strong as in the verse above. It is almost as though God were saying, "And while we're on the subject of blood, here is another instruction you are to keep without fail."

The strength of this instruction is emphasized in another way, as well. Three times in this one verse, God said, **I will require.** Shedding the blood of another human being is a serious offense, in which God takes a personal interest. Later, in the Torah delivered at Sinai, God specified for Israel the ways they were to pursue bringing to justice those guilty of murder or of manslaughter. Here, God left the means unspecified, but in the context, this instruction stands as apodictic law, the absolute prohibition of murder, for any reason, at any time, under any circumstance.

The first clause states the principle. The second and third clauses specify the extent of God's "requiring." First, even any animal that kills a human, God will call to account. Again, how this would be done is not explained here, but the later Covenant Code did provide for putting down the ox (or bull) that fatally gored a human (Exod 21:28).

Second, God would require the blood of any slain human at the hand of the human murderer. Of course, the phrasing, ***at the hand of a man, his brother,*** recalls Cain's murder of his brother Abel. But the reference here is intended to be much broader than "merely" fratricide. God intended by this way of stating the case to remind us that we all are brothers and sisters to each other. Any murderer, whether or not aware of it, truly is guilty of the murder of his or her own human brother or sister.

■ **6** This verse is not merely a restatement of the previous one. In the Hebrew text, the Masoretes arranged vv 6 and 7 as a three-line poetic unit. The first line is a chiasm:

The-one-who-sheds	*the-blood*	*of-the-human,*
By-the-human	*his-blood*	*shall-be-shed.*

This is the usual translation, rendering the Hebrew preposition *bĕ-* (beginning the second half of the line) as "by." This first line reveals the usual *agent* by whom God will require the blood of the slain human. As the murderer is human, so the agent(s) of retributive justice, too, normally will be human. Bringing the murderer to justice is the first divinely appointed function of human government. However, Hamilton's observation also is worth noting here: "The penalty for shedding blood may be exacted either by God (v. 5) or by man (v. 6)" (1990, 315).

The second line of the verse (and of the poem) restates the fact first reported in 1:26-27. Here, it serves an added purpose, presented as the fundamental reason murder is such a grave offense: ***For in the image of God [Elohim] he made the human*** (*hāʾādām*). Since this is the only reason adduced, we are constrained to view it as the most significant reason it was possible to adduce. Moreover, we should remember that the speaker here still is God. This is not human self-aggrandizement, nor even sober self-assessment; this is God's measure of human worth.

It is important to note that this is the third time this statement occurs, and that it is located in all three major settings of the Primeval Prologue: in the prefall setting of our creation (1:26-27); in the postfall/preflood setting of Adam and Seth (5:1-2); and now in the postflood setting of Noah (9:6*b*). God continues to regard and treat humans, though now marred by the evil inclination of our hearts (8:21), as what we were and still are, a being created in God's image. Neither the "fall," with its consequent expulsion from Eden, nor the judgment of the flood changed that central fact of our existence. God regards humans as creatures of value, with whom God continues to maintain a special relationship. An intentional act of murder is an offense against God, because it brings to an end the earthly existence of one who bears the image of God. This is precisely why God requires of the murderer the blood of the slain. God pays attention to the victim and holds the murderer accountable.

C. S. Lewis on the Image of God

It is a serious thing . . . to remember that the dullest and most uninteresting person you can talk to may one day be a creature which, if you saw it now, you would be strongly tempted to worship, or else a horror and a corruption such as you now meet, if at all, only in a nightmare. . . . You have never talked to a mere mortal. . . . Next to the Blessed Sacrament itself, your neighbor is the holiest object presented to your senses. If he is your Christian neighbor he is holy in almost the same way, for in him also Christ *vere latitat*—the glorifier and the glorified, Glory Himself, is truly hidden. (Lewis 1962b)

■ **7** This is the third line of the Masoretes' three-line poetic arrangement of vv 6-7. This line, ***Now as for you, be fruitful, and multiply; procreate abundantly on the earth, and multiply upon it,*** also constitutes the closing of the inclusio that begins with v 1. Two of the verbs of v 1, "be fruitful and multiply" (NRSV), are repeated here; ***multiply*** (*rĕbû*) actually occurs here twice.

The verb, *teem/procreate abundantly* (*širṣû*) corresponds to the verb "fill the earth" in v 1.

God's speech to Noah and his family, as they emerged from the ark, thus begins and ends with the blessing of the initial creation week (1:22, 28). Implied in this blessing is God's promise of faithful relationship with re-created humanity, as well as the instruction to engage again in fulfilling the creation mandate. The future depended (and depends) solely on God's promise, in the form of a blessing. Despite the great catastrophe they just had lived through, it would be no more necessary now than it had been before the flood, to bribe or cajole the "gods" to grant fertility to humans, their stock, or their crops.

The opening phrase, *Now as for you,* looks both backward and forward. What immediately precedes this verse is the serious and sober instruction and warning against murder. But that somber backdrop is not to dominate their life in the newly reborn world outside the ark. God does not intend life to be primarily about anxiously avoiding murdering or being a murder victim. They were to bring life into the world, and to do so joyfully, regularly, abundantly. It is as though God were saying, "It is necessary that I warn you about and against murder; you know it has happened before, and it will happen again. But as for *you*—*you* be about the business of life!"

This expression also looks forward. God's next words to Noah and his sons would be, *Now, as for me, behold, I am . . .* (v 9).

■ **8-10** Verse 8 introduces the second part (vv 8-11) of God's speech to Noah and his sons. This section outlines what God would do on his part (*As for me*) to bring human beings into partnership with God in the outworking of salvation history. This part of the narrative reveals God's plan to accomplish that goal through a covenant, a formal "contract" setting forth the terms of agreement for entering into a mutual relationship, offered solely at God's initiative. God already had promised this covenant to Noah (6:18); now God specifically listed the covenant partners and set the terms of the covenant.

God's speech here begins with the announcement of the establishment of the covenant (*běrît*), using the participle of the verb *qûm* ("to stand") in the causative stem, "I am causing to stand, i.e., *I am establishing.* (A more familiar—because more frequently reported—later tradition speaks of "cutting" a covenant; we will note this usage, and the reasons for it, in our comments on Gen 15:9-10, 17-18). The verb *qûm*, however, suggests the building of a relationship that did not exist before—here, a relationship between God and Noah (together with Noah's family). Based on the observation that causative forms of *qûm* mean "implementation of a previous word" in a number of OT texts, Hamilton (1990, 316) suggests this is its meaning here also, since God already had promised Noah a covenant between them (6:18). At any rate, this clearly is a unilateral covenant; that is, God established it without demands or conditions to be met by God's covenant partners.

The second part of v 9 identifies Noah and his sons (**with you,** masc. pl.) as the immediate recipients of the covenant. The prepositional phrase **with your *seed* after you** marks this as a perpetual covenant, since its termination is not part of this declaration. It also is an unconditional covenant, as no conditions are stated by which it could be abrogated or nullified. In its original ancient Near Eastern context, this covenant is of the type sometimes called a royal grant covenant.

Verse 10 extends the covenant beyond the human family God was addressing: ***and with every living creature which is with you—with the flying creatures, with the land creatures, even with every living creature of the earth with you, from all [the creatures] coming out of the ark to every living creature of the earth.***

God entered into this covenant, not only with Noah, his sons, and their descendants, but also with **every living creature.** The narrator referenced ***flying creatures*** and ***land animals,*** specifically, only because these were the groups that had survived the flood with Noah aboard the ark. Twice in this verse the narrator used the term **every living creature *of the* earth,** and once, **every living creature,** emphasizing as strongly as possible that no sensate creature was excluded from this covenant. As we have seen, here at the end of the flood narrative, when the narrator is drawing the reader's attention forward, the number of referent nouns for the animal kingdom decreases, and their individual inclusiveness increases.

The point of this verse, however, is its firm, repetitive emphasis. God made this covenant with *all* the living creatures of the earth, not just with the human family. Humans are the apex of God's creation here upon this earth, but we are not the whole of it. God's concern for all the creation is explicit and emphatic, here and in many other places in the text. God included all creatures in this first covenant, and took special care that Noah and his sons should know that. One logical conclusion is that we, too, God's appointed stewards over creation on this earth, should share God's passion for God's other creatures, demonstrated by our careful stewardship.

■ 11 Verse 11 reveals the substance of the covenant. The initiative lay with God, as the senior/superior party; thus, the wording of the actual covenant itself begins with God's declaration. The verb here is a perfect form of the causative stem of *qûm* (see v 9), ***Now I have established my covenant with you.*** This is not to say God had established this covenant at some time in the past and only now was revealing it to Noah. The perfect form emphasizes that what God was doing now (i.e., God's establishment of this covenant with Noah and all other living creatures) was, in fact, finished. Nothing more needed to be done to establish this covenant; moreover, God would not revoke or modify it.

God emphasized the reliability of this new covenant in two negative statements: **Never again will all *flesh* be cut off by the waters of *the* flood. *Moreover,* never again will there be a flood to destroy the earth.** The first statement emphasizes that *life* will not again be cut off by the waters of another great flood (*mabbûl*). The second statement, while again using the noun **flood** (*mabbûl*), is more inclusive than the first. Reference to **the earth** includes the physical earth itself, as well as all living and nonliving entities upon it (see the further comment, v 13, below). This promise of preservation is the opposite of the destruction announced in 6:13. However, the promise here does not exclude other forms of judgment, besides floodwaters, should the sovereign God once again deem judgment necessary. (See, however, 8:21.)

■ **12-13** Verse 12 introduces the third part of God's speech to Noah and his sons. God affirms in vv 12-17 the trustworthiness of his promise by freely offering to them a sign ('*ôt*) of the covenant. At the end of v 12 comes the most explicit promise that this covenant would be permanent; God was establishing it *to/for eternal generations,* i.e., **for all generations** in the future, to the end of the earth. God did not establish this covenant with a termination date in mind, and human unfaithfulness would not be able to render it null and void.

The sign would be the ***bow***; **I have set my *bow* in the *cloud*, and it will be *for a* sign of the covenant between me and the earth** (v 13). God's announcement, **I have set** (perfect tense of the verb *nātan*, "to give"), indicates that God already had acted. The action was completed, and it will not be reversed or ended until the end of the earth itself as we know it now.

The ***bow*** is the **rainbow** that appears in the sky usually during or toward the end of a rainstorm. But the ***bow*** (*qešet*) also is the bow used in the hunt and in battle for firing arrows at the prey and at the foe. In the hand of the skilled bowman, the bow was the most potent weapon in the ancient arsenal. It could fire many arrows in quick succession; it could be lethal even at a long distance; though few in antiquity used it this way, it could be fired from cover without warning. Possessing the ultimate bow and being, without question, the consummate bowman, God was the Warrior without peer (see, e.g., Exod 15:3; Hab 3:9).

The bow as the sign of the covenant, and God's action in hanging the bow in the cloud, reveal a significant shift in God's attitude and relation to the sinful world, from the monumental judgment God just had executed. Hanging one's bow signals the cessation of hunting or of war; it is an act of peace. Coming as it did immediately upon the close of the flood event, this covenant promise and its accompanying sign of the bow is a vivid reminder and reassurance, writ large in the sky, that God is neither "hunting" the earth's inhabitants, nor "at war" with us. Coming, as it often does, at the *end* of a storm, the rainbow in the cloud functions as an immediate assurance to every believing observer that, *in this storm, too*, God has kept God's covenant and God's promise.

The Sign of the Covenant

The bow as the sign of the covenant that God established with Noah and his sons is the first of three occasions where Scripture defines something as the sign (*'ôt*) of a covenant. The second is Gen 17:11, where circumcision is defined as the sign of the covenant between God and Abraham (and Abraham's descendants after him). The third is Exod 31:16-17, where God instructed Moses that the Sabbath would be the perpetual sign of the Sinaitic covenant between God and Israel. Christians may count four, understanding Jesus' institution of the Eucharist, with his declaration of the cup as his "blood of the covenant," as both the inauguration and the sign of the new covenant, in unprecedented and undreamed-of fulfillment of the ancient covenants (see, e.g., Matt 26:28; 1 Cor 11:25).

At the end of v 13, **the earth** stands for itself and all that is in it, both living and non-living. This is an example of the metaphorical figure called metonymy, in which the whole stands for all its parts, or a part stands for the whole. It also stands as the briefest possible reference to the various groups of living beings that had been together with Noah in the ark; we have noted these references becoming progressively more inclusive, until here all are encompassed (along with others, as well) in a single word.

■ **14-16** God presented the appearance of the bow in the cloud as though it were for God's prompting; *And it shall be, when(ever) I bring* [lit., "in my bringing"] *the [storm]cloud upon the earth, and the bow shall be seen in the cloud, then I will remember my covenant . . . and I shall see it to remember the everlasting covenant.*

Any ancient Israelite believer in Yahweh who thought God really needed to see the rainbow whenever God brought the rain, or else God may have forgotten the covenant promise, probably would have been hard-pressed to see any substantial difference between Israel's God and the gods and goddesses of Israel's neighbors. Yet God condescended here to allay anxieties when clouds, rain, and heavy storms should again overspread the sky: "How can we know God really means this promise? Oh, there is the rainbow God said would be the reminder. If we can see it, and remember the promise, then surely God, who rides the clouds (Ps 104:3), sees it, too, and remembers the promise."

Of course, this is an instance of anthropomorphism. Many faithful Israelites knew, as do modern believers, that God does not really need such a visible reminder. We are not in danger of God's forgetting God's promise(s). Yet, God is pleased to reassure us by such "homely" means, and many believers, both ancient and modern, have found real comfort in the midst of dark times, in these and similar reassurances. Every word of these verses is rich with tones of reassurance: Do not fear; this will not happen again.

Gregory of Nazianzus: God Keeps God's Covenant

Who "binds up the water in the clouds"? The miracle of it—that he sets something whose nature is to flow, on clouds, that he fixes it there by his word! Yet he pours out some of it on the face of the whole earth, sprinkling it to all alike in due season. He does not unleash the entire stock of water—the cleansing of

Noah's era was enough, and God most true does not forget his own covenant. (Louth 2001, 155)

Fretheim on God and the Covenant with Noah

God initiates and establishes the covenant, and remembering it becomes exclusively a divine responsibility. The covenant will be as good as God is. God establishes it in goodness and love and upholds it in eternal faithfulness. It will never need to be renewed; it stands forever, regardless of what people do. Humans can just rest in the arms of this promise. (Fretheim 1994, 400)

■ **17** This is the fourth and shortest of the speeches by which God established the covenant—together with its sign—with Noah, his family, and all other living beings on the earth. As does the third (vv 12-16), this speech begins, **This is the sign** [*'ôt*] of *my* **covenant;** these two speeches really concern the assurance of the sign, the bow in the clouds, rather than the covenant itself. As the shortest and last of the four speeches (only twelve words in the Hebrew text), this one serves to recapitulate or summarize God's self-initiated action in making this covenant, and to reassure God's human covenant partners that the bow always would be a trustworthy sign of the covenant it marked.

Another small reassurance lies in the grammar of this verse. The verb *qûm* occurs three times in vv 9-17: as a participle in v 9; as a perfect prefixed with *vav* in v 11; and again as a perfect in v 17, but without the prefixed *vav*. Translations and commentators usually translate the second occurrence (v 11) as "I establish," which is grammatically feasible (see NIV, NRSV, Hamilton 1990, 319). This interpretation implies a present action, though we have chosen to read there a perfect tense meaning (**I have established**). Whichever approach we take in v 11, however, in v 17 we can only read God as saying, **I have established**; i.e., it is done, finished, and will not be reversed or revoked. If this is the second time for God to say it this emphatically, the second time also constitutes another way of placing emphasis, besides and along with the grammatical form.

FROM THE TEXT

Those who focus on "covenant" as the organizing principle of the Hebrew/Christian Scriptures usually call this covenant the Noahic (or Noahian) covenant, because God entered into it first with Noah and his family. The major significance of the Noahic covenant is that God established it not only with these first hearers but also with all their descendants, with all living beings upon the earth and, we may say, even with the earth itself. Everyone and everything is the beneficiary of this covenant, simply by virtue of being a part of the earthly creation.

The next covenant recorded in Scripture is the one God entered into with Abram/Abraham; thus, it is called the Abrahamic covenant. As we shall see in later chapters of Genesis, God purposed through this covenantal relationship with Abraham to begin what we may call (for convenience) the "active" phase of God's plan for redemption, restoration, and re-creation of and upon this earth. God promised Abraham to bring these through his offspring, thus bringing God's blessing, also, upon all the families of the earth (12:3).

The Sinaitic covenant is so named because God entered into this covenant with Israel at Mount Sinai, having rescued them from Egyptian bondage in the Exodus. The Sinaitic covenant established God as Israel's God, and Israel as God's people. We ought not view this as a covenant of salvation; God already had delivered Israel. In accepting this covenant, Israel recognized and accepted God as their rightful sovereign. Most of the stipulations of the Sinaitic covenant were God's instructions to Israel for living in the promised land as God's people, witnessing God's desire and intention to bring salvation, through Israel, to all the earth.

God established the Davidic covenant with David, Israel's second, most famous, and most venerated king. God promised David unbroken, eternal kingship for his line. Christian theology always has understood this covenant promise to David to have found its fulfillment in Jesus, the Messiah.

In one way or another, each complementing the others, all these covenants pointed toward Jesus, both prophetically and existentially. In the person and work of Jesus, all of them have found, are finding, and will find their ultimate and perfect fulfillments.

On another issue, the narrator's use, here, of the word *mabbûl* [the flood that destroyed "every living thing on the face of the earth" (7:23)] in this covenant declaration suggests that God did not promise to prevent localized flooding with its oft-accompanying loss of life. Today, greater human caution in building on discernible flood plains and coastlands would go far to reduce that kind of tragedy. We hardly can blame God for our tendencies to forego common sense in the pursuit of convenience, or of economic gain.

As mentioned briefly, above, God also did not promise never again to bring any kind of disaster in judgment upon the earth. The NT speaks in a number of places about fire as the agent of cleansing and restoration. The most vivid example, important also because Peter linked it with the flood, is 2 Pet 3:5-13. These NT passages do seem to indicate that the coming judgment by fire will be the culmination of the present era, ushering in the next, in the same way the flood ended the primeval era and ushered in the present age.

As God hung the bow in the cloud in this earliest era, so God "in the fullness of time" planted the sword in the ground as a gesture of peace toward the earth and all its inhabitants. Jesus could have called forth limitless legions of angels, each warrior with sword in hand. Instead, he hung upon the sword-shaped, earth-planted Cross, using it as the new instrument of peace and reconciliation, replacing its previous horrendous mission of impalement unto death. The bow God has hung in the clouds; the sword God has planted in the earth. We may be sure God's intentions toward us, and toward the earth, are intentions of *shalom*, of peace, wholeness, and total wellbeing.

E. Noah, the Undressed Vinedresser (9:18-29)

BEHIND THE TEXT

What does one do for an encore, after one has survived a flood, cooped up in a floating box for three hundred sixty-five days? Noah proceeded to work the ground, planting a vineyard and promptly causing himself major embarrassment. Some (nonspecialists) have framed this as an etiological tale, told to explain the accidental human discovery of alcohol and its deleterious effects when drunk too freely. Whatever this episode is, it probably is not that.

A more plausible inference is that, insofar as ancient Israel looked with disdain upon the Canaanite peoples whom they partly displaced and partly absorbed in the process of settling into the land promised to them, this story reinforced and provided an excuse for that disdain. "Canaan" and Canaanites were not to be approached or treated with honor because of their father Ham's shameful treatment of the common ancestor, Noah.

Literarily, this episode performs several functions. Among them is to give the briefest of glimpses into what this special family did do for an "encore" upon their exit from the ark. To say nothing more about them before moving to the genealogical tables of ch 10 would have been a highly unsatisfactory narrative move—or "nonmove." Reporting this episode, unsavory as it was, at least provided a conclusion to this extended narrative interruption (chs 6—9) of the genealogical thread. Moreover, as 6:1-8 functions as a prologue to the extended narrative of the flood, so this section, 9:18-27, functions as an epilogue to the matter of the flood and its covenantal aftermath/resolution. Verses 28-29 cap the whole by returning to finish the genealogical record begun in 5:1, but interrupted at quite astonishing length—by the normal canons of genealogical form—by the flood narrative.

IN THE TEXT

■ **18-19** These two verses introduce the final episode recorded of Noah and his family, in the aftermath of the flood. The narrative unit begins with another introduction of **Shem, Ham and Japheth** as the three sons of Noah who came out of the ark after the flood. Because Canaan is mentioned later in the narrative, the narrator parenthetically introduces **Ham** as **the father of Canaan.**

In v 19 is the first note of the population of the earth through the progeny of Noah's three sons. The verb form *nāpĕṣâ* (from *nāpaṣ*, meaning "scatter," "disperse," etc.) is *Niph'al*, which can be either passive or reflexive. The NIV translators chose the passive, **were scattered**, but NIV's **came the people who** is not in the Hebrew text. ***All the earth*** actually is the subject of the verb, meaning "all the subsequent human inhabitants of the earth." Hamilton's translation, "and from these the whole earth branched out," reflects his choice of the reflexive meaning for the *Niph'al* form (1990, 319). Taking this as the first reference to the theme developed in detail in ch 10, immediately following this narrative, the reflexive understanding seems the better choice.

■ **20-21** Verse 20 introduces Noah's vocation and the first task he undertook after he and his family came out of the ark. We should note here that the narrative is very brief and does not deal with other activities of Noah after he disembarked the ark. The focus of the narrative is on the blessings and curses he pronounced on his sons. The first verb of v 20, *wayyāhel* (from *hālal*), in its *Hiph'il* stem does not mean just "to begin" (as NIV's **proceeded;** but see also the NIV alternate reading, "the first"); it means to do something for the first time. Of course, it would not do to take this verb as meaning, "Noah was the first to be a man of the soil," i.e., a farmer. That honor probably belonged to Adam; if not to him, then certainly to his son Cain. All things considered, it probably is best to translate, here, ***Now* Noah, a man of the soil** [i.e., a farmer], ***was the first*** **to plant a vineyard.** Noah was (or became) involved in fulfilling the vocation given to the first man in the garden (2:15). Noah thus functioned as a "new Adam" in this new beginning for humanity, following the flood.

At times, the biblical text can be frustrating. Many of the questions that occur to the reader in this episode, the biblical narrator ignored completely. The reader, at least, may be excused for thinking that perhaps Noah did not know about fermentation until this experience, since he is said here to be the first to grow the grape. Other questions do not seem to have any possible answers that reflect well on Noah or on his son Ham. Now, the reader may excuse the narrator for passing over them in silence. The circumspect reticence on display in the telling of this unsavory but necessary story at least shows the narrator's regard for human dignity, undignified as Noah himself appeared to his son on this, apparently his first, experience with intoxication. Speculation on many points is possible and many have speculated. Ultimately, however, speculation is fruitless, so we move on, here and at several other points.

A mild surprise comes with the notice that Noah **lay uncovered inside his tent.** A vineyard takes several years to produce a crop. Why, then, was Noah still living in a tent some years after the flood had abated, when the narrator has been careful to tell the reader Noah was a farmer, not a pastoralist? Once again, while the question is of interest, our answers must remain speculative.

■ **22-23** The narrator's point here is simple and straightforward. Ham saw his father in a state that should not be seen by a son. Even if this was inadvertent, and not intentional, Ham did nothing about it to ease his father's discomfiture; he only told his two brothers. Forewarned, Shem and Japheth took every precaution *not* to see their father as their brother had seen him, and fixed the problem the unconscious Noah did not yet even know about.

At the very least, Ham did not show the respect due a father; whether Noah deserved it or not on this occasion is beside the point here. Ham's brothers did treat their father with respect even in his undignified condition. There may have been more to this story than that; there may not have been. Most readers are tempted to think there was much more. Not a few have thought Ham took some kind of sexual advantage of his father while he lay unconscious. But from a sense of circumspection, the narrator did not say, and whatever additions we may make to the story, we must be willing to acknowledge them as our own additions—and speculative additions, at best (or worst!).

One observation we may make from other early Near Eastern literature. At least twice, the Ugaritic material references junior family members taking care of their elders after they had been too much in their cups. The legend of Aqhat indicates that a good, respectful, and attentive son helps his father walk when he cannot walk by himself, and even carries him home to bed if he is unable to walk at all. One of the stories of El, the supreme deity of the Ugaritic pantheon, records two lesser deities, both of them probably his sons, carrying him home to his palace when he had had too much to drink and could not get there by himself. Isaiah 51:17-18 is a metaphorical picture even more filled with the pathos of drunken helplessness. Isaiah pictured Jerusalem as a mother drunk on the cup of God's coming wrath, with none among her children able or available to help her get to safety.

■ **24-25** The narrator's courtesy to Noah continues, even crescendos, at this point. How much more restrainedly could one say it than this, **Then** Noah **awoke from his wine**? The narrator continues in this vein, **And he knew** what **his youngest son had done to him**. What *had* Ham done? All the reader knows is that Ham saw his father unclothed; it even may have been inadvertently, entirely without intent on Ham's part. Not even here will the narrator tell us more. The only thing we know for certain is that Ham did not treat his father with all due respect, whereas his two brothers did. But was that *doing* something to Noah?

Perhaps it was. Rather than covering his father and keeping quiet about what he had seen, Ham told his two brothers. Even if Ham took no disrespectful pleasure in seeing their father naked and helpless, nevertheless, in view of the fact that he did nothing positive to help him, Ham's report to his brothers of their father's embarrassing state amounted to malicious, disrespectful gossip. Even in a nonpatriarchal society, that would be construed as "doing" something disrespectful to one's father.

The reference to **his youngest son** has been the subject of much discussion. There really is no other way to read this phrase, though some have tried, in an effort to see the text's usual ordering of the three names as their birth order: Shem, Ham, and Japheth. With this phrase, though, we cannot assume that is intended to be their birth order. Ham definitely was the youngest of the three, so either Shem or Japheth could have been the eldest. We have concluded that Japheth was Noah's eldest son, and Shem was next, based on 11:10 (see comments there and on 10:21, below).

Here (9:25), for the first time in the entire flood and postflood narrative, Noah speaks! We have read three chapters and more of God's instruction and Noah's carrying out of God's instruction, but here, and only here, do we hear a word from Noah. It is not a pretty word, either, not the word we would have expected from this righteous man of integrity (6:9). Noah's first word is an imprecation, **Cursed be Canaan!**

And the reader's questions keep coming. Now we know why Canaan was mentioned earlier (9:18); we need that name to know what Noah was saying. But we still don't know, really. What had Canaan done? That Canaan, Ham's fourth son (10:6), even had been born yet, for Noah to speak of him, requires us to revisit our suggestion about the vineyard (9:20). Perhaps it did begin to bear in its third or fourth year, but for Ham's wife to have born him four sons (and perhaps some daughters, as well?), and for the fourth son, Canaan, to have been complicit, somehow, in his father's indiscretion against his grandfather—that would have required more like twenty or twenty-five years, rather than three or four. Did it take Noah twenty years of producing grapes before having his first encounter with their fermentation? Alternatively, did Noah and the others drink but never become drunk in those years, before this episode?

Noah's first short speech consists in only six words in the Hebrew text, **Cursed be Canaan!** *A servant of servants* [i.e., **the lowest of** servants, or slaves] *shall* [or: *may*] he be to his brothers. This curse was not magically effective simply by the force of Noah's speaking it. It was a prayer that God would render suitable judgment upon the miscreant, in the same way that Noah's next speech (vv 26-27) is a series of prayers for the blessing of Shem and Japheth—albeit still, in some measure, at Canaan's expense.

We are left still with the question, Why Canaan, and not Ham? Looking ahead to ch 10 and the lists of the descendants of Japheth, then Ham, then Shem, all observers notice that many of the names in this specialized "genealogy" are gentilics, not personal names. That is, they designate peoples, ethnic groups, thought to be descended from these eponymous ancestors, the individuals for whom they were named. The examples germane to the case here include most of the descendants of Canaan himself (10:15-18; see commentary, below): *the Jebusite, the Amorite,* etc., concluding with *the Canaanite*!

This has led many to conclude that this narrative is not really about Noah and what Ham, or Canaan, did to him. It is about the relationships between the peoples of Canaan and their near neighbors, including Israel, at the time when Israel came into the land. This has the advantage of dispensing with the unanswerable questions we have raised (and many we have not raised here). If the text is a kind of parable about Canaan and the low status it would come to occupy in the region, these questions are irrelevant.

As far as it goes, this view is correct. This story, and the relevant portions of the Table of Nations that follows, do depict a Canaan held in low regard and eventually put to the service of Israel as they settled into the promised land (see, e.g., Judg 1:28, 30, 33). After all, Noah's words were a prayer and came to function as a prophecy of the future of some of his descendants through his three sons.

On the other hand, it is possible to see in this narrative the "both/and" character of many such narratives from the ancient world. We do not have to force this narrative to be *either* about the later Canaan of Israel's entrance and settlement period, *or* about Ham's (or Canaan's?) disrespectful actions toward Noah. Ham's or Canaan's real action triggered a real response when Noah found out about it.

We are not obliged, either, to see Canaan's low status and esteem, as reflected in Israel's absorption of most of the Canaanite population, as being their unavoidable destiny because of Noah's "prophetic" prayers here. Ham and Canaan bore responsibility for their own actions, and so did their descendants. Family heritage ("nurture") certainly influences a person's and a people's character, successes, failures, etc., but it does not determine them. In the case of the ancient peoples of Canaan, God made a special point of giving them a generous portion of "extra" time in which to repent, before bringing judgment upon them (Gen 15:16). That they did not use that grace to their advantage does not mean Noah's prayer/prophecy determined that outcome.

■ **26-27** These verses are a separate speech marked by the introductory formula, ***And he said.*** It begins with an exclamation of benediction toward God, ***Blessed be Yahweh, the God*** [Elohim] ***of Shem.*** Not only does this express Noah's desire that God would be blessed, no doubt a genuine hope and prayer. It also marks all Noah's wishes/prayers expressed here as directed toward Yahweh, who alone could superintend their fulfillment. That Yahweh did so marks them also, in the end, as prophetic utterances.

The first verb of this speech is a passive participle with the thrust of a wish or prayer, "May Yahweh be blessed." The other four that follow all are jussives, third person forms expressing also a wish, an urging, or, as here, a prayer. This strengthens our contention that Noah's curse (v 25) also was not a magical incantation, but a prayer.

Another salient feature of the four jussive (wish/prayer) clauses of this speech is its chiastic arrangement:

A ***And may <u>Canaan</u> be his*** [Shem's] ***servant***

  B ***May God*** [*Elohim*] ***enlarge <u>Japheth</u>***

  B' ***And may he*** [Japheth] ***dwell in the tents of Shem***

A' ***And may <u>Canaan</u> be his*** [Shem's] ***servant.***

Though Shem is referred to in three of these four lines, Shem is not the subject of any of them. Shem's blessing, Noah already had vouchsafed in blessing **Yahweh, the God of Shem.** If Yahweh is blessed, and Yahweh is the God of Shem, it follows that Shem will be blessed. The Table of Nations that follows immediately upon this narrative will begin to demonstrate that, in giving Shem the final, climactic segment of the genealogy, though Shem was the middle brother.

May God enlarge Japheth is a pun (*yapĕt . . . leyepet*). At least in part, Japheth's enlargement, his blessing, would come through Shem, **May he** [Japheth] **dwell in the tents of Shem.** This probably is a metaphorical way of saying, "May Japheth participate in God's special blessings upon Shem."

The sober portion of this simple chiasm is, of course, its first and last lines, identical in every respect, **And may Canaan be his servant,** "his" meaning "Shem's." We do not know how, or even whether, this came to pass in the lives of Canaan, Japheth, and Shem, themselves, assuming as we have that this is a sketchy narrative of a real event in the life of Noah, his sons, and one of his grandsons. That Canaan later was put to servitude, was absorbed, and eventually disappeared into the people called Israel is abundantly clear from a comprehensive reading of the later biblical record, alongside Egyptian, Hittite, and Assyrian records, especially.

■ **28-29** These two verses comprise the return to, and the completion of, the genealogical record of Gen 5. This is vividly illustrated if we translate 5:32 and these verses together, leaving out the entire intervening flood narrative and its aftermath:

> 5:32 *Now Noah was five hundred years old, and Noah fathered Shem, Ham, and Japheth. . . .*
>
> 9:28 *Now Noah lived after the flood three hundred fifty years.*
>
> 9:29 *So all the days of Noah were nine hundred fifty years, and he died.*

Noah's life after the flood extended almost as many years as the first "wave" of his descendants; see comments on 11:12-17. As the last of the antediluvian generations, Noah also was the last of the really long-lived primeval patriarchs. The only major feature missing from the data on Noah is the notice that he "fathered [other] sons and daughters" because, of course, Noah did not do that.

FROM THE TEXT

We have noted the intense interest in the episode of Noah's drunken nakedness. We could fill volumes with the speculations generated in the attempts to fill in the details the biblical narrator deliberately omitted. One attitude we dare not adopt is that of spiritual superiority. Every serious reader of the Bible (or of any other "merely" literary work, for that matter) would delight to know the omitted details of beloved narratives. But more answers beget more questions, also. If the narrator here had answered all the questions we can raise as we ponder the story, the first result simply would be more questions.

The more important result would be that the narrative would cease to exist in its present form or, eventually, in any recognizable form. For the sake of this most important of all stories, we must be content with the fact that many of our peripheral questions will not have definitive answers. That is one evidence and one measure of our trust in the God who has given us this divine story.

One dark stain on the history of Christian interpretation is the facility with which pastors and other theologians for several centuries equated "Canaan" in this narrative with "sub-Saharan Africa." The identification was (and is) entirely specious, of course, but it was very popular for a very long time, because it purported to give a righteous biblical rationale for the enslavement of black African peoples. "Canaan" *was* "black Africa." Through Noah, God had condemned Canaan ("black Africa") to perpetual slavery. For black Africans to object, then, would be to rebel against God and God's righteous judgments. And how could others hope to live in righteousness before God, and to prosper, if they presumed to tamper with God's judgments upon a people so richly deserving of them as "Canaan" was? Moreover, did not God reinforce this judgment through Paul, Peter, and others of the NT writers as they instructed slaves to serve their masters willingly and diligently, since their service really was to God?

It is easy for us now to see the wickedness of these arguments, and to wonder how people could fall for them, let alone propound them. Yet here, too, our attitude must not be that of spiritual superiority or condescension. Rather, we ought, as Scripture repeatedly encourages, to look to ourselves, lest we fall (or have fallen) into the same trap on some other issue of interpretation. We need not be continually anxious about the central teachings of the Christian faith, but we ought to be eager, always, to enlarge, deepen, and strengthen our understanding of its various aspects, as God gives us opportunity. We, too, may have places in our thinking where God would have us shine a brighter light, see things a bit differently, see them from a different perspective.

IV. THE TABLE OF NATIONS (GENESIS 10)

Overview

This is the third of the four genealogies of the Primeval Prologue, the first eleven chapters of Genesis. The first, in ch 4, listed the abortive line of Cain through seven generations. After this, the Cainites are not mentioned again. The second genealogy, in ch 5, listed the antediluvian patriarchs from Adam through Seth's line, ten generations in all, counting to Noah, the "hero" of the flood story.

This third genealogy, after the flood, lists the descendants of Noah's three sons, but only to seven generations, and that far only in Shem's line. The fourth genealogy, at the end of ch 11, again deals with Shem's line and carries it to Abram (Abraham), again ten generations. So this third genealogy differs significantly from the others. In anthropological terms, the others are linear, usually naming only the eldest son for each generation. This one is segmented; the lines of all three of Noah's sons are included, to several generations for each. Moreover, several sons, or groups of descendants, are included in a number of the lines of each.

A quick reading is enough to show that the point of this genealogy is not to trace lineages from father to son, giving ages at the births of the firstborn, and ages at death, as do the second (Seth, ch 5) and the fourth (Shem alone, ch 11). This one, rather, sketches a word map of the nations of the eastern Mediterranean/Middle Eastern world, following the spread of Noah's descendants. For this reason, the chapter usually is titled "The Table of Nations."

Four literary features are worthy of special note. First, the opening and closing verses (vv 1, 32) form an inclusio. Verse 1 introduces the genealogy; in a similar but expanded wording, v 32 concludes it.

Second, v 1 names Noah's sons in the order they always appear, Shem, Ham, and Japheth, but the listing of the peoples descended from them is in reverse, or chiastic, order, Japheth first, then Ham, and finally, Shem.

The third feature is the similar concluding sentence for the account of the nations descended from each of Noah's three sons. Ham's (v 20) and Shem's (v 31) are nearly identical. The conclusion to Japheth's shorter segment (v 5) performs the same function but has significant variations as well as several similarities with theirs. These and other features testify to the literary skill of the author, whatever his sources.

Fourth and most important is the use here, once again, of the various significant numbers we have seen over and over again throughout the Primeval Prologue. Leaving aside Nimrod and the Philistines (the two anomalous names in the chapter), the total number of the names of Noah's sons' descendants is seventy, or seven times ten. Of course, including Nimrod and the Philistines yields seventy-two names, or six times twelve. Both multiplicands, both multipliers, and both products carried special significance, both in Israel and in its broader western Asian/eastern Mediterranean world.

The names of Japheth's sons total seven; the names of his grandsons total seven. In Ham's section of the genealogy, descendants are recorded for three of his four sons. (No descendants are listed here for Put.) The sons and grandsons of Cush, together, total seven (again, leaving out the anomalous Nimrod). Leaving out the Philistines, the sons of Mizraim (Egypt) total seven. The sons of Canaan total twelve, if we include *the clans of the Canaanite* (v 18), as we should.

Together, Shem's sons and grandsons total twelve, counting in the list as far as Peleg (v 25). Peleg's brother Joktan is another special case; all his descendants are concentrated in the Arabian Peninsula. Joktan and his sons together total fourteen persons, or twice seven.

We ought not to view, nor attempt to use, this prodigality of significant numbers throughout the Primeval Prologue as somehow reflecting or intending a kind of beneficial "magic" in biblical numbers. Neither is this phenomenon intended as some kind of numerical "code" embedded within the text, awaiting the genius of some future generation to discover its true significance, "prophetic" or otherwise. It is neither of these. It is, however, another evidence of the literary sensitivity and skill of a true author. That the author of this section (and of all of Genesis) utilized source materials—as do all authors, whether or not they acknowledge it—is beyond dispute. That this author *was* an author, and not "merely" a compositor, equally is (or should be) beyond dispute. His artful and varied use of numbers, here and elsewhere, simply helps to make that case.

While this list is constructed basically in the form of a genealogy, many of the names it contains are of nations and/or peoples, thus signifying the individual behind the name as the eponymous ancestor of the people or the nation. This is abundantly clear from the gentilic suffix (*-i*) constituting the endings of these names, identifying them as peoples of a city, a clan, a region, or an ethnicity, and not as individuals. In the commentary, we will note these as they occur.

Finally, we may affirm what often is noted about this chapter: it reflects the narrator's understanding of the geographical distribution of Noah's descendants, following their dispersion from the Tower of Babel, recorded in ch 11. Thus, the order here is not chronological, but literary. The narrator was concerned, first, to bring to a conclusion the detailed discussion of the lines of Japheth and Ham; this necessitated, also, the segmented genealogy of Shem at this point, to complete this aspect of the narrative.

Possessing this "big picture" of the geographical distribution of Noah's descendants following the flood, the reader is primed to wonder how it came about. The Tower of Babel episode is the narrator's response to that question. Placed between the two genealogies as it is, the tower narrative also prevents any confusion that would arise from having the linear genealogy of Shem's line follow immediately upon the segmented genealogy—also of Shem's line— with which ch 10 climaxes. The narrator's literary artistry, coupled with consideration for the hearer/reader, here take precedence over a strictly chronological ordering.

Several recent commentators have noted that the nations listed in this chapter reflect the geopolitical world of Iron Age Israel (e.g., Brueggemann 1982, 91; Westermann 1984, 503, 528). This genealogy includes names of individuals/peoples that belonged to the ancient past as well as those who were contemporaries of Israel. It is possible that what we have here is a later authorial/editorial "updating" of earlier source materials, a practice common in the OT canonical process.

A. The Descendants of Japheth (10:1-5)

IN THE TEXT

■ 1 Verse 1 is introductory to the entire chapter. As noted earlier (2:4; 5:1; 6:9), NIV's **account** translates Hebrew *tôlĕdōt*. For the significance of these notations, ten in all through 37:2, see the Introduction, "These Are the *Toledot*" under The Literary Forms of Genesis 1—11. **Shem, Ham and Japheth** is the invariable order in the text of the names of **Noah's sons**.

The verb of the second half of the verse is a Hebrew passive, ***Now children were born to them after the flood.*** We have translated *children*—even though only sons are named in the genealogy—since virtually all men named in biblical genealogies fathered daughters as well as sons. This fact is stated more directly in the genealogies of chs 5 and 11.

This introductory notation is important in both a positive and a negative sense. The negation by implication is that Noah and his wife had no more children after the flood. Positively, this genealogy introduces the progeny of their three sons and their sons' three wives; all the children of these three couples were born after the flood.

■ **2** The name **Japheth** was known to the Greeks, but not in so complimentary a context. Iapetos was the name of one of the Titans of Greek mythology. This connection of Japheth with the Greeks is not surprising. **Javan,** listed here as Japheth's fourth son, was the father of the Ionians; in many biblical texts "Ionians" is equivalent to "Greeks." Already well before classical times, the Ionians/Greeks were the most notable of Israel's acquaintances in the eastern and east-central Mediterranean, excepting only Israel's closest neighbors in that direction, the Phoenicians.

Gomer was the father of the Cimmerians of classical Greek antiquity; the Akkadian spelling of their name is *gi-mir-ra-a.* They appeared as enemies of the Assyrians in east central Anatolia/Asia Minor in the eighth century B.C. Speiser notes that this name is "still in use apparently for the Welsh (*Cymry*)" (1964, 66).

Magog appears together with Gog in Ezek 38—39. There Gog is king, and Magog is his land. Gog is to be identified with Gyges, king of Lydia in southwestern Anatolia/Asia Minor.

The **Madai** in the Bible are the Medes east of Asshur/Assyria, in the northwest of modern Iran. This text, then, lists **Madai** as their eponymous ancestor.

Javan, as noted above, are the Ionians, the Greeks. Eventually, they occupied not only the Greek mainland and Peloponnese, but also the Greek islands of the Ionian Sea to the west and southwest, of the Mediterranean to the south, of the Aegean to the southeast and east, and on into western Anatolia, or Asia Minor (modern western Turkey).

This genealogy lists **Tubal** as the eponymous ancestor of the Tabali, or Tabarini, and **Meshech** as ancestor of the Moschoi; the Assyrian forms of these names are Tabal and Mushki. In the Neo-Assyrian period, both were Phrygian kingdoms of east-central Anatolia.

Tiras appears to be equivalent to the Greek Tyrsenoi, another Anatolian people. If so, they (or some of them) migrated from Lydia to Italy during or just after the eighth century. There, they became known to history as the Etruscans, who preceded the Romans in central Italy (Rainey and Notley 2006, 27).

■ **3** Japheth is credited with fathering seven sons. His segment of the genealogy goes another generation deeper, naming three sons of Gomer and four sons of Javan, for a total of seven grandsons, also.

Ashkenaz usually is identified with the Scythians of the classical Greek sources. However, Jer 51:27 and Assyrian sources identify this name with Armenia, in eastern Anatolia around Mount Ararat; this could connect them with ancient Urartu, an important name otherwise missing from this chapter.

Riphath is unidentifiable. Given the locations of his brothers **Ashkenaz** and **Togarmah,** he probably was in eastern Anatolia or somewhere close to there.

Togarmah also lay in eastern Anatolia; in Assyrian documents, it was rendered as Til-garimmu. Cassuto suggested identifying it with the *Tagarma/ Tegaram(m)a* of Hittite sources and locating the district "north of the road between Haran and Carchemish" (1964, 192).

■ **4** As noted above, the sons of Javan are to be identified or associated with the Greeks. **Elishah,** the Alashiya of many cuneiform (Akkadian) texts, is the island of Cyprus.

The name **Tarshish** is a special case. A common identification is with Tartessus in Spain, a mining center whose raw materials were carried to the eastern Mediterranean by ship. Others include a location on the island of Sicily, and Tarsus in today's southern Turkey, Paul's hometown. Hoenig (and others) have connected it with *thalasses,* the common Greek word for "sea," suggesting Hebrew Tarshish may refer to the sea and, by extension, to seagoing vessels or to distant seaports (1979, 181-82). By similar reasoning, some have proposed a location along the shores of the Red Sea or the Indian Ocean. Gordon suggested a derivation from Hebrew *tirosh,* "wine," "the wine-dark [sea]," i.e., the darker hues of the sea depths plied by oceangoing vessels, and suggested the Atlantic shoreline of Spain or Portugal, or even across the Atlantic along Mexico's Gulf Coast (1978, 51-52). (This author knows of no one who has followed Gordon in accepting this proposed location, though the suggested derivation of the name could be plausible.) In light of the identifications of **the Kittim and the Rodanim,** Speiser suggested Tarshish could have been located on the island of Rhodes (1964, 66). Despite the romantic images conjured by some of these suggestions, the southern Spanish mining town of Tartessus seems most likely.

Kittim is Greek *Kition,* modern Larnaka on the east coast of Cyprus. **Rodanim** is the island of Rhodes. Speiser's suggestion is that since Elishah's descendants were located on the island of Cyprus (Alashiya), and the Kittim were associated with them there, perhaps Tarshish is connected with Rhodes, the Rodanim, in the same way (1964, 66). Not many scholars have accepted Speiser's suggestion, nor does this writer. However, even if Speiser were proven correct, this would not by any means mark the end of the expansion of Japheth's descendants, whether through Javan or through his other sons.

The Hebrew text reads "Dodanim," here, not **Rodanim**, but no place named "Dodan," or something similar, is known. Moreover, the difference between Hebrew *resh* and Hebrew *daleth* is the smallest possible difference between two letters—the tiny extension, present on the *daleth* but absent on the *resh*, called a "tittle." Needless to say, the tiniest misprint of one scribe, or the tiniest misreading of another, could account for the change in the first letter of this name from one copy of the text to the next.

■ **5** We understand this verse (*contra* Westermann 1984, 508) to be a programmatic summary of this segment of the genealogy belonging to Japheth, referring to all his descendants, not just to those of the line of Javan. We translate, *From these were dispersed the coastland peoples, by their territories, each one with its own language, by their families/clans, in their nations.*

The verb form *niprĕdû* (from *pārad*; *were dispersed*) is a Hebrew passive/reflexive (*Niph'al*), but it does not require us to think of clans or peoples moved or moving by force, against their will. The point of the recurrence of the verb (*pārad*) through this section is to advise the reader that after the flood the earth was populated by the dispersal of the peoples in the general pattern outlined here, as God intended. True, the first push for this dispersal was at God's initiative; we may assume it was against the will of the generation of Babel. But the generations that followed them *were dispersed* (or "dispersed themselves," if we read this verb as a reflexive) to a multitude of places by a multitude of promptings, some at their own volition, some in response to various kinds of threats, some fleeing force directly applied. The student of history will recognize this as a millennia-long process that continues to a greater or lesser extent in various regions of the world even today.

We have translated the subject of the verb in v 5 as *the coastland peoples,* following Cassuto (1964, 190). From Israel's later point of view, the "coastlands" (often also translated "islands") were the near points, geographically, of their neighbors' dispersions across and to the horizon of the world they knew. This chapter is not intended as a complete ethnographic catalog of the world or even of the world ancient Israel knew. Placed and framed as an anticipation of the Babel event, it is a beginning, not an end.

The terms **their territories, language***(s),* ***their families/***clans,* and **their nations** occur in the concluding statements for each of Noah's sons, though Ham's (v 20) and Shem's (v 31) are in a different order than this one of Japheth. That all these are included indicates that this list was compiled using geographical (**territories**), linguistic (**language**), kinship (*families*), and political or quasi-political (**nations**) categories, combined or ordered in ways we no longer have the data to understand fully. Thus, some of the positioning and relating of names is obscure, to us.

We can say that the sons/descendants of Japheth were located mostly to the north-northeast, north, and northwest of Israel, for whom this Table of Nations originally was intended. Japheth's descendants eventually could be found around much of the Mediterranean, around and beyond the Black Sea, through most of Asia Minor (most of today's Turkey), and beyond these regions in several directions. All those listed here belong to the larger ethnolinguistic grouping now called traditionally Indo-European.

The phrase **each *one* with its own language** anticipates the narrative of the Tower of Babel reported in the next chapter, when God confused the languages of that original small group huddled together in Shinar in southern Mesopotamia. It is repeated in a slightly different form ("by their . . . languages") both for Ham (v 20) and for Shem (v 31). This chapter, then, reports that differentiation of languages and dialects was one of the markers of the dispersal; the Babel narrative relates how and why that happened, initially.

B. The Descendants of Ham (10:6-20)

IN THE TEXT

■**6** Ham is listed as having four sons. Ham's **Cush** is different from the Cush of 2:13. The **Cush** descended from Ham usually is identified with Ethiopia, or more precisely, the region up the Nile and south from Egypt, much of which is contained within the borders of today's Sudan. The Greeks called this region Nubia.

Mizraim is Egypt. **Put** may be Libya, west of Egypt. If it corresponds to the Egyptian name Punt, it would have been south of Cush and should be identified with today's Somalia or possibly with a region even further south.

Canaan is the Mediterranean coastal region of western Asia, from Gaza in the south all the way up the coast almost as far as ancient Ugarit. Rainey (1996) has shown that Ugarit is not to be considered Canaanite, despite the close affinity between the Ugaritic language and what we may call here (for convenience) the Canaanite language. Canaan did not extend far inland from the coast, but it did include the northern half of today's Israel, all the territory included under the current political designation Palestine, and all of modern Lebanon, as well as a portion of today's northwestern Syria.

Placing this Cush together with Mizraim and Put (or Punt) makes sense geographically, linguistically, and, at least to a degree, in terms of ethnic relationships. The anomaly here is Canaan. The Canaanites were a group of Semitic peoples, both ethnically and linguistically. However, we have noted above that the criteria for groupings within this Table of Nations included geographical proximity and political relationships, as well as ethnicity and language kinships. By all the criteria of geopolitics throughout the biblical period, Canaan was closely related to Egypt, and through Egypt but to a lesser extent, to the southern Cush and to Put, as well.

271

■ **7 Cush** is credited with fathering five sons; two grandsons also are named in this verse, for the familiar total of seven. Most of these names cannot be located with any kind of precision, but they all appear to have been situated in Arabia, some of them along or near the Red Sea and thus across from the Cush that is Nubia, or Ethiopia (modern Sudan). The intent of this grouping thus seems to be to call attention to the close relationships across the Red Sea between its western and eastern shores, from time immemorial.

The regions of **Seba** and **Havilah** cannot be located precisely. We do know this is a different **Havilah** from that of 2:11. Since the Havilah of 10:29 appears to be in the same vicinity as this Havilah, the question of their relationship must remain open, especially since this Havilah is descended from Ham, and the Havilah of v 29 is from Shem. (See further the comment below on, potentially, three duplications among the segments of this genealogy.)

Sabtah and **Sabteca** are not Arab or Arabic names. Astour (1965) suggested identifying them with Sabaka and Sabataka, two brothers of Egypt's Twenty-Fifth (Ethiopian) Dynasty. They ruled Egypt in the late eighth to early seventh centuries. If Astour was correct that these are Ethiopian names, it would be another evidence of the close ties between the peoples of the two shores of the Red Sea.

Raamah was a city in southwest Arabia. **Sheba** usually is identified with the kingdom of the famous queen who came to visit Solomon (1 Kgs 10:1-13). It lay in modern Yemen, in the southern Arabian Peninsula. **Dedan,** if this is the correct spelling of the name, was an Arab tribe in northern Arabia.

In this genealogy of Gen 10 occur two, or three, duplications; one of these may be a triplicate. Havilah occurs as a son of Cush here, and the name recurs as a son of Joktan (v 29). The same name signifying two different individuals within a family is not unusual, of course. However, the purpose of these genealogies of Genesis (and others in other places in the Bible) was not only to record individual members of the various family trees, as we think of genealogy today. They also were intended to indicate the closeness (or distance) between clans and peoples, usually geographically, and also sometimes politically. That Havilah occurs in two different lines of Noah's sons may reflect the ancient existence of two (or even three; see 2:11) persons, peoples, and/or places named Havilah. Alternatively, it may reflect one people, place, or region with ties to both the Hamitic and the Semitic peoples.

The Hebrew consonantal spelling of the two names translated "Rodanim," above (v 4), and **Dedan,** here, actually is identical, except for the plural suffix of Rodanim. However, as we noted in the commentary above, the Hebrew reading Dodanim in v 4 should be corrected to Rodanim, as we have done (with most modern versions). This raises the question whether **Dedan** also should be corrected and repointed, to read "Rodan." The answer is, probably not in this case. The Rodanim of Japheth's line are to be identified with the Aegean island of Rhodes. It is virtually impossible that **Dedan,** of the line of Ham and associated with names of an Arabian and/or East African provenance, would be identical with Rodanim/Rhodes.

Finally, we find a **Sheba** here, and also a Sheba listed among the sons of Joktan in Shem's line (v 28). (A Sheba and a Dedan are listed, also, among Abraham's sons by Keturah, 25:3.) Many scholars also see Seba, Cush's first-born, as identical with this people, though that seems unlikely, since Seba is spelled with *samech*, not with *shin*. Still, the Sabeans usually are identified with the realm of the queen of Sheba and located in the southwestern Arabian Peninsula, today's Yemen. The occurrence of a Sheba in both the line of Ham and the line of Shem may reflect the existence of two ancestors, two regions, and two peoples; Sheba also is located by some in northern-northwestern Arabia. Or it may reflect, as we said of Havilah, one people, place, or region with ties to both the Hamitic and the Semitic peoples.

■ **8-9** It is tempting to suggest this **Cush,** the father of Nimrod, was different from the Cush of vv 6-7. The names of v 7 all are presented as the eponymous ancestors of the peoples identified by their names. Now the text says, ***And Cush fathered Nimrod,*** but Nimrod was "only" a man, not the eponymous ancestor of any people, nor identified with only one city or region. If this Cush is a different person, he probably was the Kassite Cush of 2:13, since the regions of Nimrod's exploits were in and near Cassite territory (see comments on 2:11-13). If this Cush and the Cush of vv 6-7 are the same individual (also an eponymous ancestor), it is difficult to see how his son Nimrod could have ranged so far afield from his father's place(s) and how he is to be related to his five "brothers" of v 7. It is possible, of course, that "fathered" here is used in the more extended sense, "was the ancestor of," and that Nimrod was not a brother of these five, but a son (possibly even a grandson or great-grandson) of one of them. At present, we have insufficient data to be certain of any solution.

The name **Nimrod** often has been taken as a form from Hebrew *marad*, "he rebelled." However, since its origins almost certainly are not Hebrew, this is unlikely. Dahood's suggestion is more picturesque, though perhaps also improbable; he proposed, "panther of Hadd," i.e., Hadad, the proper name of the Canaanite deity, Baal (1979, 129).

Employing a bit more precise understanding of the Hebrew text, we will translate vv 8-9 as follows: ***Also, Cush was the ancestor of Nimrod; he [Nimrod] was the first to be a mighty man upon the earth. He was the foremost master of the hunt by the will of Yahweh; therefore, it is said, "Like Nimrod, the master of the hunt by the will of Yahweh."***

The significant prepositional phrase, *lipnê yhwh*, occurs twice in v 9. Most often it is translated, "before the Lord/Yahweh," but that does not reflect its full significance in this context. It was not just in Yahweh's presence, or estimation, that Nimrod was a ***master of the hunt.*** It was by God's will, even by God's grace (Speiser 1964, 51, 64; Hamilton 1990, 335; see, e.g., Num 32:20-22). This insight militates against understanding the name Nimrod as meaning "rebel." Taken seriously, it also has the potential to revise our (usually negative) opinions of Nimrod.

Chrysostom on Nimrod

> While some people say the phrase "before the Lord" means being in opposition to God, I on the contrary do not think sacred Scripture is implying this. Rather, it implies that [Nimrod] was strong and brave. But the phrase "before the Lord" means created by him, receiving from him God's blessing. Or it may mean that God was on the point of arousing our wonder through him by creating such a remarkable creature and displaying him before us on the earth. Nimrod too, however, in his turn in imitation of his forebear [Adam] did not take due advantage of his natural preeminence but hit upon another form of servitude in endeavoring to become ruler and king. (Louth 2001, 165)

From these two verses, it appears that Nimrod first established his reputation by his prowess as a hunter of wild game. So successful was he in those endeavors that his name became a byword. Yet the epithet, *a mighty man* (*gibbôr*), usually describes a military and/or political leader, or even a ranking, influential member of a given community, as when Ruth 2:1 describes Boaz as *gibbôr*, a first-rank leader in Bethlehem's village society.

■ **10** *Now, the beginning of his empire constituted Babel, and Erech, and Akkad, all of them in the land of Shinar.*

10:8-10
We should understand *beginning* (*rē'šît*) in at least two senses. First, these were the initial three cities of Nimrod's first-ever "empire" (tiny as it was by later standards). Second, they constituted the sources, or "mainstays," of Nimrod's strength in the maintenance and enlargement of his kingdom (Speiser 1964, 64).

All of them (MT *věkalnēh*; see NIV's alternate reading) reflects a re-pointing of the Hebrew consonantal text, based partly on the fact that no city in southern Mesopotamia named **Calneh** is known from any texts, nor can such a city be identified on the ground in that region. Moreover, the north Syrian Calneh cannot be the referent here. Repointing (involving only vowels, if we take the initial *vav* to be a scribal addition because of the mistaken understanding of the term as a city name) to read *all of them* (thus reflecting Heb. *kullānû*) makes sense and solves the problem of the otherwise unknown city.

Babel, Erech (Akkadian Uruk, modern Warka), and **Akkad** (Accad) all were important towns in the land of **Shinar. Shinar** can be equated linguistically with Sumer. However, at least in contexts such as this one, it is both a geographical and a political designation. It includes both Sumer, the southern portion of Babylonia, and Akkad, its northern region; in Old Babylonian texts this region can be referred to as Sumer and Akkad. Erech was in Sumer; Babylon/Babel was in the *region* of Akkad; Akkad (Agade) was the capital of Sargon I, an early Amorite ruler instrumental in establishing Akkadian rule over the region. Akkad, the *city*, would have been located north of Babylon, but it has not as yet been identified.

Nimrod's prowess as a hunter—certainly together with other gifts—made him a natural leader. Indeed, one of the major responsibilities of kings in the dawn of Mesopotamian history was hunting down and destroying wild animals that posed a threat to townsfolk every day, as they left the safety of their fortified cities to work their fields. One has only to think of the exploits of Gilgamesh, a real human king before legends accrued to him, elevating him to the status of a demigod.

Dangers came not only from four-legged predators but also from the two-legged kind sweeping (or stealing) down upon a population they hoped to catch off guard. These, too, were the king's responsibility to meet and defeat, leading his city's troops and going into battle at their head. It is possible to think of Nimrod simply as so successful in defending his own city (perhaps Babel first, since it is mentioned first?) that it was natural for him to pass from the defensive to the offensive, leading to the formation of an empire based on the small city-states listed here. At least we may be justified in inferring such a scenario, from the phrasing of v 8, "He was the first to be . . ." That a consummate hunter should become history's first emperor should not be surprising.

That Nimrod's extrabiblical identity is shrouded in mystery should not surprise us either. We know next to nothing about any of Mesopotamia's earliest rulers. If we take this text seriously as a fragment of early epic history, the Assyrian king Tukulti-Ninurta (ca. 1246-1206 B.C.) is much too late, despite Speiser's otherwise cogent argument (1964, 72-73). Egypt's Amenhotep III (ca. 1416-1379 B.C.) has been suggested (von Rad 1961, 142); he also is too late, if this is an early epic fragment. Moreover, to posit a Cushite—not from Egypt, but from the next country south of Egypt—making his way through Egypt, then through Arabia or Canaan, to land right-side up in a foreign land as history's first empire builder, is a bit too much of a stretch, just to preserve his Cushite identification. Especially is this so when the Cassites (the "other" Cush) are a large part of the history of central and lower Mesopotamia already.

No necessary contradiction exists between the mention of Babel/Babylon here as one of the main centers of Nimrod's kingdom, and the story of the building of the Tower of Babel in that city, in the following chapter. One possibility is that Nimrod was part of the generation that attempted the building of the tower. If so, he certainly was not the only—he was not even the first—human to fall victim to his own pride after experiencing the grace and favor of God. Another possibility is that Nimrod established his small empire after the tower episode. Such nonchronological arrangement is not at all uncommon in the biblical narrative. If that is the case here, it would seem to be because Nimrod's story was relatively a minor consideration for the narrator; he wanted to present it in its genealogically proper context and move on, rather than interrupt his post-tower narrative, focused on Shem's descendants, to accommodate the less-important chronological order.

■ **11-12** *From that land Asshur went forth, and he built Nineveh, and Rehoboth Ir, and Calah, and Resen, between Nineveh and Calah; that is the great city.*

Again, our translation is not the traditional one; the text requires several decisions. **He went to Assyria** is not possible as the text stands, and there is no indication of corrupt transmission. As we have translated it, the first clause has two possible meanings. We agree with Hamilton, who takes Asshur to be the ancestor of Assyria, who came from Nimrod's center in Shinar (1990, 339-40). Speiser, espousing here the traditional understanding, says that is not possible (1964, 67-68). Rather, the text means the nation and culture of Asshur/Assyria had significant Sumerian roots and that Nimrod built the Assyrian cities listed here. That seems to stretch a bit too large a gap between the last mention of Nimrod by name (v 9), and the pronoun inherent in the third masculine singular form of the verb *he went out,* here. Also, this understanding leaves Asshur unaccounted for in the Hebrew text. Asshur being the eponymous ancestor of Assyria, it would be strange for his name to appear this way in this list, if the narrator intended to name Nimrod as the only builder.

Nineveh was, of course, the city on the east side of the Tigris (opposite modern Mosul in northern Iraq) that became the capital of the Neo-Assyrian Empire. Cassuto's suggestion concerning **Rehoboth Ir** seems plausible, "This may be the Hebrew form of *Rebit Nina*, one of the suburbs of Nineveh, on the northeastern side of the city" (1964, 203).

Calah is well known from Assyrian records as Kalhu. Its site south of Nineveh is the ruin mound called Tel Nimrud; local tradition, at least, regarded Nimrod as the builder, and not Asshur! **Resen** is so far undiscovered. Given its location between Nineveh and Calah, both of which are known, it may be the name of a city that became another of the many suburbs of Greater Nineveh. If so, it is not likely to be located archaeologically.

That is the great city. The presence of the demonstrative pronoun (**that**), together with the fact that the Masoretes divided the verse (v 12) just before it, seems to this reader important. The text gives us four names, Nineveh and three other nearby cities. Famously, the reference to Nineveh as **the great city** is ascribed three times to God's own assessment in the book of Jonah (1:2; 3:2, 3). Could it be that this final clause in the epic fragment introducing both Nimrod and Asshur is intended to describe Nineveh with its daughter cities (or the three cities that became "daughter" cities, or suburbs) in this summary, concluding assessment, **That is the great city,** i.e., "Greater Nineveh"? If this understanding is correct, it is not impossible that this final clause is the marginal notation of a later copyist reflecting on Nineveh in its heyday as capital of the enormous and aggressive Neo-Assyrian Empire, a note introduced into the body of the text by a still later copyist. Such small additions occasionally were incorporated into the text by just this process.

■ **13-14** As we have seen, **Mizraim,** Egypt, was a brother of Cush (on both these names see comments on v 6, above). All the names associated here with Mizraim are gentilics, as is Mizraim itself; the genealogy presents these people as having come from Egyptian beginnings. In keeping with the intent of the chapter as a whole, they total seven, leaving aside the Philistines who are said to have *come out from there,* that is, from the *Casluhim.*

The *Ludim* almost certainly were the Lydians of western Asia Minor (Turkey). Their various associations with Egypt spanned much of the history of the eastern Mediterranean.

Of the *Anamim* we know nothing more. However, Albright suggested identifying them with the *A-na-mi,* a people of Cyrene (eastern Libya) mentioned in a cuneiform text from the eighth century B.C. (1920-21, 191). If *Lehabim* is an expanded form of "Libyans," as plausibly suggested by Cassuto (1964, 205), these two peoples would have been adjacent to each other on the west of Egypt, which makes sense in this context.

Naphtuhim probably is a Hebrew form from an Egyptian phrase meaning "the northland," i.e., Lower Egypt, or more specifically, the region around Memphis (near modern Cairo), where Upper (southern) Egypt and Lower (northern) Egypt met, just above (south of) the beginning of the Nile Delta. *Patrusim* also amounts to an Egyptian loan word; a more familiar English rendering is Pathros (e.g., Isa 11:11). This term refers to Upper Egypt, i.e., Egypt south of Memphis. Together, these two include most of Egypt. Characterizing **Mizraim** as their father reflects the fact that even Egypt was not mono-ethnic or monocultural in antiquity.

The end of v 14 has been difficult. It reads, *and Casluhim, which the Philistines came from there, and Caphtorim. Casluhim* often has been identified with Mount Casius, near the coast between Egypt and Canaan, but certainly Greek Kasion cannot be derived from Hebrew *kaslukhim,* nor from any similar Egyptian word/phrase. Cassuto suggests Scylace in Asia Minor, referencing Herodotus' statement that the Pelasgians came from Scylace, and accepting Albright's identification of the earlier Philistines with the Pelasgians (Cassuto 1964, 205-9).

Caphtor is Crete; Amos 9:7 is one of several reflections of the Israelite knowledge that the Philistines came from Crete. If Albright and Cassuto are correct, the Philistines referenced here and in the patriarchal traditions later in Genesis are from the Anatolian *Casluhim.* The Philistines who came into southern Canaan shortly after Israel had entered the central highlands were of the same ethnic stock but spent generations in Crete before being driven into western Asia with the other Sea Peoples by the Dorian invasion of Greece and the Aegean region.

■ **15-18** **Sidon** is a city on the east coast of the Mediterranean, midway between Tyre to the south and Beirut, the modern capital of Lebanon, to the north. Sidon is called here Canaan's **firstborn** because in the early periods Sidon was the principal city of the Canaanites, or Phoenicians. "Sidonian" was an early inclusive term for the peoples later called Phoenician (see, e.g., Judg 18:7).

That Sidon is listed here as Canaan's firstborn, and Tyre is missing entirely from the list, is one evidence of this text's antiquity. The decline of Sidon and the ascendency of Tyre coincided with the decline of the Philistines and the rise of Israel's monarchy (Mazar 1986, 63-82). If this text had *originated* in the first millennium, the position would be reversed; it would have listed Tyre as Canaan's firstborn, and Sidon would be secondary or even missing altogether.

On the other hand, the presence of **the Hittites** as the second name on this list shows the list either originated or was adjusted late in the second millennium, following the collapse of the Hittite Empire about 1200 B.C. That empire, with its capital at Hattusas in north-central Anatolia (modern Turkey), was Indo-Aryan and never within the sphere of Canaanite influence. The **Hittites** referenced here are some of the small city-states, clans ("families"), and others from north Syria down into Canaan, left as the heirs of the Hittite political hegemony and cultural influence when the Sea Peoples (and others) put an end to the empire. These groups, for the most part, were Semitic-speaking and Canaanite, or related in some way to Canaan.

It is worth noting that all the names in this list are singular; the first two are **Sidon** and *Khet.* All the rest are singular gentilics, i.e., with the suffix -*i* (English, "-ite"), designating one as being from a place, whether a city, a region, or a country. Beginning with v 16, we read, *and the Jebusite, and the Amorite, and the Girgashite, and the Hivite, and the Arkite, and the Sinite, and the Arvadite, and the Zemarite, and the Hamathite; then afterward, the clans of the Canaanite dispersed abroad.*

The *Jebusite* denotes the people of the city-state of Jerusalem and at least some of the surrounding area, until David conquered Jebus/Jerusalem and made it his capital. The term *Amorite* had a wide usage. From the point of view of Mesopotamia (the setting of this part of Genesis), *Amorite* first meant "Westerner" and designated the Semitic peoples from the north and northwest of Babylonia, then extending south, but more inland than the region(s) designated as Canaan/Canaanite. In the Old Babylonian period (Hammurabi of Babylon, Mari, etc.), most of the city-state dynasties and mini-empires along the Euphrates comprised Amorite ruling classes, though not all their populations were Amorite. In Israel's settlement period, it was a general term, including most (but not all) the population of the hill country where Israel first settled, and extending north of Israel into the Beqaʿ and the Anti-Lebanon mountain range. In the Transjordan opposite the Israelite hill country, Sihon was ruler of an Amorite kingdom (Num 21:21-32).

It is not possible to identify the **Girgashite** or the **Hivite** with confidence, except to say that they also occupied portions of the hill country. Based on textual evidence from each of the Synoptic Gospels' accounts of Jesus' healing of the demoniac (Matt 8:28; Mark 5:1; Luke 8:26, 37), Hamilton (1990, 341) suggests, plausibly, that the name **Girgashite** may be preserved with the NT Gergasenes, east or southeast of the Sea of Galilee, i.e., in the Transjordanian highlands.

The last five in this list of Canaan's "sons" are names of city-states. **The Arkite** designates those of the city and the region of 'Arqat or 'Irqatu, near the present-day Lebanese-Syrian border. **The Sinite** refers to the city and people of Siyannu, about forty-five miles north of 'Arqat. Arvad (**the Arvadite**) was, like Tyre, an island-and-mainland seaport town about fifteen miles north of 'Arqat, along the present southern Syrian coast. Zemar (**the Zemarite**) was a few miles south of Arvad; its name in classical sources is Simyra. Hamath (**the Hamathite**) is inland, on the Orontes River, about one hundred twenty miles north of Damascus. During much of the period of Israel's monarchy, Hamath was an important Aramean center. If the whole area of Hamath's influence (and sometime hegemony) in the valley of the Orontes is meant here, then Hamath east of the Lebanon Mountains is a bit larger region north to south than the territories of 'Arqat, Siyannu, Arvad, and Zemar together, along the Mediterranean coast on the west of the Lebanon range.

Both Mazar and Cassuto (following an earlier Hebrew version of Mazar's essay) were at pains to place the northern boundary of the Canaan later promised to Israel at the southern reach of Hamath's territory, at Lebo-Hamath ("Lebwe of Hamath") in the Beqaʿ (the valley of Lebanon), on one of the source springs of the Orontes (Mazar 1986, 189-202; Cassuto 1964, 211-12). They were correct. However, the Canaanite territories envisioned in and by this list of Canaan's "sons" extended further north than the southern border of the later kingdom of Hamath. While Ugarit was not reckoned as Canaanite, Siyannu (**the Sinite**) was, and it lay less than twenty miles south of Ugarit (Rainey 1996).

To this point, the descendants of Canaan total eleven names, most of them gentilics. This lends support for taking the phrase **the clans of the Canaanites** as the twelfth and final name intended in this list of Canaan's descendants, as such lists nearly always comprise numbers considered significant; with seven, ten, and twelve (and their multiples) being most significant of all. Moreover, the Phoenician coastal city-states, of which five are included in this list, were the earliest colonizers of much of the Mediterranean, and even beyond. From their beginnings along the Levantine coast, some of them, at least, dispersed quite widely.

■ **19** As the list of Canaan's sons begins with Sidon, so does the description of Canaan's borders. Since it does begin with Sidon, it is evident this extremely short résumé is intended as a link with the accounts of Abraham in Canaan, which begin only two chapters later, in Gen 12. The parts of Canaan lying north of Sidon will hold no further interest for the narrator.

From Sidon as you come [in your coming] to Gerar, as far as Gaza, would be confusing if we did not know the narrator's intention, shortly, to begin the accounts of Abraham's sojourn in the south of Canaan. Abraham (and Isaac too) would spend a great deal of time near Gerar, and in contact with Gerar's king(s). In light of what is to come in the narrative, to cite this city as marking the southernmost edge of Canaan makes sense. Gerar was a little more than ten miles southeast of Gaza, and inland, while Gaza was the southernmost of the Canaanite coastal cities. Going from Gaza to Egypt, the next important centers were Egyptian. Thus, it made sense also to mention Gaza in this summary of Canaan's boundaries.

The rest of the verse realizes the continuation of the southern border of Canaan eastward through the Negev, until it reached the cities of the *circle of the Jordan,* as they are described in Gen 13:10. These cities probably were located at the southern end of the Dead Sea, perhaps even beneath what, until very recently, was the shallow southern end of that famous body of water, and now is the site of chemical works both for Jordan and for Israel. Once again, their importance here is linked to Abraham's later presence in the region. **Sodom, Gomorrah, Admah and Zeboiim** were four of the five cities whose captive citizens Abraham rescued along with his nephew Lot (Gen 14). Here, they represent the southeastern extremity of that large area called Canaan. An implication, confirmed in a number of other places both within and outside the Bible, is that Transjordan, east of the Jordan Rift valley, never was considered a part of Canaan.

The syntax of this last part of the verse is the same as the first part, *as you come [in your coming] to Sodom and Gomorrah and Admah and Zeboiim, as far as Lasha.* The problem here is that **Lasha** is unidentifiable. What we do know is that, tempting as it sounds in English, ***Lasha*** *cannot* be Laish in the north, later called Dan. The two names simply cannot be confused or equated in Hebrew.

■ **20** Not counting the special cases of Nimrod and the Philistines, the descendants of Ham included in this segment were his four sons; the five sons and two grandsons of Cush, for a subtotal of *seven;* the *seven* peoples reckoned as descendants of Mizraim; and the *twelve* peoples listed as descendants of Canaan. Altogether, Ham's descendants totaled thirty, or half sixty, the central number of the sexagesimal system used extensively in the Primeval Prologue (along with the decimal system).

By their clans and languages, in their territories and nations; see the commentary on v 5, above.

C. The Descendants of Shem (10:21-32)

IN THE TEXT

■ **21** At the beginning of this verse, a dropped word (haplography) requires restoration, and the second half seems susceptible of two different meanings. It appears that "sons" (*bānîm*) was left out of the Hebrew text at some point; this may have caused the plural suffix of the verb to be dropped also. Restoring "sons," the text reads, ***And to Shem sons were born, also; he was the ancestor of all the descendants of Eber, the brother of Japheth, the elder.*** The second clause contains two statements in apposition to **Shem.** This will be clearer, perhaps, if we rearrange the verse to read as the normal arrangement of an English apposition would read, ***And to Shem—he was the ancestor of all the descendants of Eber, [and] the brother of Japheth, the elder—sons were born, also.***

The question of the second clause remains, however. Was Shem the elder brother of Japheth, or was Japheth the elder brother of Shem? (From 9:24, we know Ham was Noah's youngest son.) The English translations are divided on this issue, and most do not alert the reader that another reading is possible. Most commentators also ignore the issue. Cassuto (1964, 218) argues for Japheth being the elder, but he argues his case partly on the basis of fratriarchy, which cannot have been operating yet among Noah's sons, as Noah still was alive. The order of these three genealogical lists of their descendants does not help, either, as here Shem and his descendants are last in the chapter for emphasis; the family of Shem will be the focus of the narrative from here on.

Finally, the grammar of the clause allows for either understanding. Adjectives in Hebrew normally follow the nouns they modify. Following both ***the brother of*** (**brother** referring to **Shem**) and the name of his brother (**Japheth**), the adjective, ***the elder,*** could refer to either. It is customary to think of Shem as the eldest of the three sons of Noah, but if this were all the data available to us, we would have to be content with not being certain. However, the narrator does supply one more fact in his second, and longer, version of Shem's genealogy, following the report of the episode of the Tower of Babel. We will discuss it further there (11:10).

The narrator's mention of **Eber** in this context should catch the reader's eye. Eber was not Shem's son, nor even his grandson, but his great-grandson. This is a preliminary signal that not all Shem's descendants would be the focus of the narrative to follow, but only that branch of his line that would come through Eber.

Eber was the eponymous ancestor of the Hebrews, i.e., the ancestor from whom that people took their name; a "Hebrew" is an "Eberite." In the Bible, "Hebrew" is one term (not the only one) used by non-Israelites when referring to Israelites (e.g., 1 Sam 14:11). It also was a self-designation of Israelites when speaking with non-Israelites (e.g., Jonah 1:9), or when, among themselves, they contrasted Israelite(s) with non-Israelite(s), in speech or in writing (e.g., Jer 34:9, 14). In other contexts, the usual self-designation was "Israelite."

■ **22 Elam** was the mountainous region east of the Tigris and lower Mesopotamia that constituted much of what later was called Persia, today's southwestern Iran. Though the eponymous ancestor is listed here as **Elam,** Elamite is not a Semitic language, one indication among several that the relationships highlighted in this chapter are not based primarily on linguistic affinities.

Asshur is the eponymous ancestor of the Assyrians. The reader will recall that we have seen this name already, in the discussion of Nimrod and his exploits, yet without a definitive statement that Asshur was a Hamite (v 11). The later Assyrian theological system deified Asshur, making him the head of the Assyrian pantheon and the patron deity of the nation. Assyria was an aggressive and successful military power in several periods, spreading the name Asshur/Assyria widely. Assyria proper, however, lay north of Babylonia along both sides of the upper Tigris River, encompassing also many of its tributaries, both east and west; the region today basically comprises northern Iraq. Assyrian in its several dialects was/is a subset of Akkadian, usually classified as an east Semitic language.

Arphaxad is the son whose line is the center of attention in the ensuing narrative. His also is the name we cannot associate with any people or region of Israel's horizon, as we can with most of the names in this chapter. The only possible suggestion is to identify Arphaxad with the place name Arraphu, which occurs in a number of cuneiform sources. That suggestion, however, arises more from a desire to suggest a possibility, than from anything approaching certainty; linking the two names linguistically is next to impossible. Thus, it may be that, unlike the names of his four brothers in this verse, we are not to understand **Arphaxad** as an eponym, but only as a personal name.

Lud is the same name encountered above (v 13) as a son of Mizraim, except that here it is a singular form. Given the purposes of ancient genealogies, which were more comprehensive than is modern genealogical practice, it is not impossible that the people known as the Lydians are included in both these genealogies for reasons that now escape us. However, Elam, Asshur, and Aram essentially were next-door neighbors, from east to west. **Lud** may be included here because the Lydians were near neighbors to the west-northwest of the northern Aramean peoples, continuing the westerly direction of the listing. If that is not the correct identification of this **Lud,** then he simply may be an eponymous ancestor whose descendants no longer are identifiable, either in biblical or in extrabiblical records.

Besides Shem, Abraham's nephew Kemuel also is called "the father of Aram" (Gen 22:21). However, this **Aram,** Shem's son, is the better candidate as the ancestor of the majority of the great collection of tribes, clans, peoples, and kingdoms referred to under the name "Arameans," some of whom later were Israel's neighbors to the north and northeast. Partly, this is because the Arameans' territory extended well beyond Israel's immediate neighborhood, all the way to lower Mesopotamia. Abraham's nephew living in the first half of the second millennium was not early enough to be the ancestor after whom all of them would be called. More importantly, in a liturgy celebrating Israel's divinely appointed origins and destiny, individual worshippers were to declare, "A wandering Aramean was my father" (Deut 26:5 ESV), referring to Jacob/Israel. Jacob certainly was not a descendant of Abraham's grand-nephew Aram, but he was in the line of descent from Aram, son of Shem.

■ **23** A similar juxtaposition occurs with the name of Aram's (presumably) firstborn son, **Uz.** The firstborn son of Abraham's brother Nahor also was named Uz; a nephew of this Uz was the Aram, son of Kemuel, already mentioned (Gen 22:21). We cannot at this late date sort all this out, except to say that both the Uz named here as Aram's son, and the Uz named later as Nahor's son, were located in northern Mesopotamia, probably not far from the present-day Syrian-Turkish border.

Of **Hul,** *and* **Gether,** *and* **Mash**, we can say nothing except that they were the eponymous ancestors of Aramean tribes or clans, or the eponymous founders of Aramean cities. The NIV **Meshech** is taken from the parallel passage, 1 Chr 1:17; in copying this genealogy, the Chronicler apparently was attempting to identify a name that no longer meant anything to him as it stands in our verse here. A number of commentators have suggested identifying *Mash* with Mashu, one of the Akkadian designations of Lebanon. Another suggestion is the Mount Masius in northern Mesopotamia noted by Strabo (*Geogr.* 11.14.2).

■ **24-25** **Shelah** is otherwise unknown. The one thing we can say is a negative; he is not to be identified with the son of Judah named Shelah (Gen 38:5; 46:12). In Hebrew, the final letter of the name of Arphaxad's son is *het* (ḥ); the final letter of the name of Judah's son is *he* (h). The identical spelling of the names in English means nothing; the letters *het* and *he* absolutely are *not* interchangeable in Hebrew.

Shelah's oldest son was **Eber.** He is the only child mentioned here, but we will see (11:15) that Shelah did father other children, both sons and daughters. Shelah's son **Eber** had two sons who are named here. The first was **Peleg,** and the narrator commented on the meaning of his name.

Peleg means a "split," "division," "cleft," or "(artificial) channel," the last being an irrigation canal or ditch. Initially, his name simply may have commemorated an especially difficult birth. This was his mother's firstborn, in all likelihood, as well as his father's; she may have felt during his birth that he had "split" her apart. (It is important to state that this is a conjecture; Peleg's name may have had another significance altogether, though not another meaning.)

Whatever the original significance of his name, the narrator explained Peleg's name, "Division," with the observation, **because in his *days* the earth**

was divided. This is the only such "extra" notation in this genealogy of Shem, and it occurs only seven lines before the beginning of the Babel narrative. It follows that the narrator intended to emphasize that **Peleg** was the firstborn of the generation that experienced the "division" and scattering of the peoples following the Tower of Babel fiasco.

■ **26-30** The list of Joktan's sons is a subset of Shem's genealogy. Consistently with most of the rest of the chapter, we should view these names also as eponymous. Though some cannot be located, those we can be sure of are in the Arabian Peninsula. It follows, then, that the rest belong there, also, even if they are no longer identifiable.

In Arabic, **Almodad** means "the friend." With an "e" vowel following the aleph (as in LXX), instead of the Masoretic "a," it would mean, "God is a Friend." **Sheleph,** Arabic Salaf/Salif, is a district, and also a tribe, in Yemen, in the south of the Arabian Peninsula. **Hazarmaveth** is the Hadramaut, the mountainous district on, and inland from, the south central coast of Yemen along the Gulf of Aden.

Jerah means "moon"; the moon was perhaps the most important of pre-Islamic, pagan Arabia's gods. This does not mean, of course, that Joktan imagined his son Jerah was the moon god, only that a place or region named after Jerah almost certainly would have become a center of moon worship in early Arabia, as did the famous Jericho ("Moon Town") near the Jordan.

Hadoram probably is a sentence name; if so, it would mean "The god Hadh is exalted" (Cassuto 1964, 222). A location in Yemen, in the south of the Arabian Peninsula, is a plausible suggestion. **Uzal** is identified either as an early name of Sanaa, Yemen's capital, or with Azalla, a city near Medina that Ashurbanipal, king of Assyria, claimed to have conquered. **Diklah** means "Date Palm," i.e., a "Palm Grove"; as a tribe or a location named after this ancestor, it cannot be located. **Obal,** too, is uncertain, though a possible identification with Arabic 'Abil would place it also in Yemen.

Abimael is explained as containing an enclitic *mem*; it means, then, "My father is God," or "My father truly is God." Whether Joktan's intentions in giving his son this name reflected continuing faith in Yahweh as Father, or whether this already is a pagan name, we cannot say. The location of his descendants named for him is likewise unknown.

Sheba was the ancestor of the Sabeans. Whether a northern group is indicated here, or the more famous and more important kingdom in the southern Arabian Peninsula (also located in today's Yemen) is a subject of discussion. Another point of uncertainty arises from the inclusion of **Sheba** here in the list of Joktan's descendants, in the genealogy of Ham, above (v 7) and, finally, as the son of Abraham's son Jokshan by Keturah, following the death of Sarah (25:3).

Ophir and **Havilah** are storied names. **Havilah** we have encountered already; in Gen 2:12, it is identified as a region of fine gold. A region named

Ophir also was a source of gold (1 Kgs 9:28). However, despite the conjunction of these two names here, these gold-producing regions of Ophir and Havilah probably are *not* the two locations intended here. All the other sons of Joktan named here are to be located on the Arabian Peninsula. It follows that we must look for these two there, as well, and Arabia never has been noted for its production of gold. If this **Havilah** is not identical with the Cushite Havilah (v 7), it is another Havilah in the Arabian Peninsula. Suggestions for locating the gold-producing **Ophir** range from eastern Africa as far as the west coast of India; this, though, must be another Ophir, almost certainly on the Arabian Peninsula, but so far unidentified.

The probability of Arabian locations for Ophir and Havilah is strengthened by the presence of **Jobab** immediately following Havilah in this list of Joktan's descendants. Given this context, we probably should identify **Jobab** with Juhaibab in the western Arabian Peninsula, "in the vicinity of Mecca" (Hamilton 1990, 346).

The notation of v 30 corresponds with that of v 19 concerning the western and southern borders of Canaan, but without as much detail as we find there. Here, too, the description of territory applies only to the descendants of one son. Here it is Joktan, as indicated by the last clause of v 29, **All these were the sons of Joktan.** Both **Mesha** and **Sephar** remain unidentified. The most we can say is that probably Mesha is a point or a region on the western edge of the nomadic migrations of Joktan's descendants, as Sephar certainly is a point or a region—a mountain or a place within the mountains—of **the eastern hill country** of the Arabian Peninsula.

■ **31** But for one preposition, the concluding statement concerning the descendants of Shem is identical to that concerning the descendants of Ham (v 20), and only a little different from that concerning Japheth's descendants (v 5); see comments on v 5, above.

As we have seen in the segments of Japheth and Ham, above, the numbers of the subsets of Shem's descendants also are significant. From Elam through Peleg, the total of names is *twelve*. Shem's sons number five, leaving the number of their descendants (from three succeeding generations) listed here at *seven*. Counting Joktan the progenitor, Joktan's list (vv 26-30) contains fourteen names, two times *seven*. Throughout the genealogies of Genesis, the numbers of persons listed (as well as their ages when those are given) provide a subtext affirming God's blessing upon these early generations of humankind or, at least, God's willingness and desire to bless them. Further than this (e.g., as in looking for hidden prophecies), it is not wise to go, but if there is a "number code" in Genesis or in the rest of the Bible, this is it.

■ **32** The first half of the verse is a shorter variation on the concluding statements regarding the descendants of each of Noah's three sons (vv 5, 20, 31); see the comments on v 5, above.

285

We will translate the second clause, ***And from these were dispersed the nations throughout the earth after the flood.*** The verb is the same as that of v 5, regarding the dispersal of Japheth's descendants, but here its subject is broadened to include all the peoples of the earth. This clause functions as a final grace note on the opening statement of Noah's saga, "But as for Noah, he found favor in Yahweh's estimation" or, more familiarly, "But Noah found grace in the eyes of the LORD" (6:8 KJV). So, too, have all of us since, if only by virtue of our memberships in the various nations providentially ***dispersed . . . throughout the earth after the flood.*** How God effected that beneficent dispersal in the face of human resistance is the subject of the fascinating narrative that opens ch 11.

FROM THE TEXT

Five of Japheth's sons reappear in Ezek 38—39, often regarded as an eschatological text, associated with Magog in their planned assault on Israel at some future time. If we consider that the Medes (Madai) were subsumed under the name "Persia" in Ezekiel's prophecy (38:5), and note the presence of Gomer also in Ezekiel's roster of Gog's confederation (38:6), Ezekiel implicated five of Japheth's seven sons in the future treachery. Where Ezekiel's predictions are to be placed chronologically is another issue.

On another matter, this chapter does not conform to all the expectations of modern genealogical practice; its purposes were/are different than ours usually are. One of its purposes is to alert the reader to the multitude and variety of the people and peoples God had in mind in announcing to Abram/Abraham, just a few lines later (Gen 12:3), that in him all the families of the earth would be blessed. These many centuries later, every reader of these lines may be grateful for God's promise to Abram, for each of us now is included in that promise also.

V. THE TOWER OF BABEL (GENESIS 11:1-9)

BEHIND THE TEXT

If this event, usually titled "The Tower of Babel" or something similar, occurred during the lifetime of Peleg, Shem's great-great-grandson (see comments on 10:25, above), it belongs chronologically after the beginning of the genealogy of ch 10, but before its end. If we take the numbers of 11:11-19 at face value, Shem, Arphaxad, Shelah, and Eber all were still alive, also, no matter when in Peleg's lifetime it happened. (By these numbers, Peleg, Reu, Sereg, and Nahor all died before Eber.) The first generations following the flood did not immediately pursue the blessing/mandate God had renewed upon the human race when Noah and his family emerged into the new postdiluvian world (9:1, 7).

As in much that has gone before, we can discern a chiastic arrangement in the two paragraphs of this pericope:

A *all the earth* with **one language,** together (v 1)

 B *in the land of Shinar, they settled there* (v 2)

  C the people's decision: **Come, let us build** (vv 3-4)

   D Yahweh's investigation (v 5)

  C' Yahweh's decision: **Come, let us** [stop their building] (vv 6-7)

 B' *Yahweh dispersed them from there* [the land of Shinar] (v 8)

A' *all the earth* with many languages, dispersed (v 9)

287

IN THE TEXT

■ 1 On the issue of whether we should understand here **the whole world** or "the whole land," see the commentary and sidebar on 6:17, above.

Two of the more important characteristics distinguishing the earth's peoples from one another are a common ancestry for each and a common language (or dialect) for each. (Of course, as anthropology this is greatly oversimplified, but as a general statement it is valid.) The Table of Nations of Gen 10 presents a general kinship pattern for most of the peoples within ancient Israel's horizon and notes, without comment, that they spoke different languages (10:5, 20, 31). This narrative accounts for the acknowledged abundance of spoken languages, meaning that its purposes are partly etiological, answering the question: If this statement was true of the first few generations after the flood, what happened to bring about the multitude of human languages since that time?

Some have suggested another explanation, namely, that **one language and a common speech** signifies a single language of trade and commerce understood by all, though each group spoke also its own language or dialect (Hamilton 1990, 350-51). Sumerian has been proposed; it has no known cognates among the languages of the world, yet Akkadian in its various dialects owes Sumerian a considerable debt, both in vocabulary and in orthography (the writing system). Attractive as this proposal is at first consideration, it seems to founder on the observation introducing God's response to the building project, "[They are] one people" (v 6).

■ 2 *And it came about in their journeying in the east that they discovered a plain in the land of Shinar, and they settled there.*

The antecedent of the pronoun "their" and subject of the two verbs that follow must be "the whole world" of v 1, i.e., virtually all then-living human beings. If the numbers of the genealogy that follows this narrative are intended as real life spans, scarcely anyone born since the debarkation from the ark would have died, as yet.

The phrase *in their journeying* suggests a purposeful return to lower Mesopotamia, where it seems most likely Noah had built the ark, or an aimless "wandering," as postulated by Cassuto (1964, 240). In either case, it appears that in the first decades (or more) of the postflood era, Noah and his growing family lived in tents (see also 9:21, 27), and a significant number, at least, traveled from place to place. (This does not take into account the seemingly intractable problem of the ages listed for the prediluvian and postdiluvian patriarchal generations.)

The prepositional phrase *in the east* (*miqqedem*) reflects a later Israelite perspective of the narrative as we have it in its canonical form. The Hebrew preposition *min* usually is translated "from" or "out of," i.e., as a partitive. The ark had landed "on the mountains of Ararat" (Urartu/Armenia; 8:4), well to the north of Shinar, not to the east. While Shinar is south of Ararat, both these regions are *in the east* from the perspective of Canaan/Israel.

Shinar is the region of lower Mesopotamia known in Akkadian as Sumer (see, e.g., Rainey and Notley 2006, 114). Sumer (south) and Akkad (north) together made up the region later called Babylonia. The region of Sumer is the cradle of the earliest Mesopotamian urban civilization. This narrative purports to go back to the beginnings of Mesopotamian urban civilization. It does not provide enough detail to be helpful in archaeological identification(s) or historical reconstruction(s) pertaining to ancient Sumer, but neither is it to be set aside as (merely) fanciful theologizing. It preserves a historical memory that we cannot, with our present knowledge, locate with chronological precision in the "secular" history of lower Mesopotamia.

And they settled there is repeated exactly, as the final clause of the next-to-last verse of this chapter (v 31); there, it is reported of Terah and his family's settling in the city of Haran. In both instances, the place of settlement was not the desired final destination. Here, it was (or became) an explicit and intentional defiance of God's mandate/blessing given to Noah and his sons as they left the ark (9:1). There, Terah's settling became a temporary delay in the fulfillment of God's call upon his son Abram. This is not to say that "settling" always is wrong. It is to say that settling down is wrong if and when God has called us to journey on.

■ **3** *And they said one to another* [lit., *each man to his neighbor*], *"Come, let us brick bricks, and let us burn [them] to a burning." Now there was to them the brick for [instead of] stone, and the bitumen was to them for [instead of] mortar.* We have translated quite literally to emphasize several features of the Hebrew text.

Having found, as they thought, a suitable place to settle, the erstwhile nomads devised a plan. The idiomatic expression *each man to his neighbor* hints at participatory democracy, both in the process of decision-making, and in the joining of the agreed-upon action(s). The proposal(s) and their implementation(s) were a community vision, rather than imposed from the top down. (This observation is not necessarily in conflict with the statements about Nimrod; see comments on 10:10-12, above.)

This is the first of three occurrences of the hortatory, **Come,** in this pericope. It is an expression of encouragement and/or resolve; here and in the next verse, it is both. But what these people resolved and inspired each other to attempt to build up, God resolved to shut down (v 7), using the same expression, **Come, let us . . .** This is but one example of the narrator's effective use of irony to highlight the contrast between the effort and energy expended by the builders to accomplish their "grand" objective, and the ease with which God thwarted their plans.

Let us brick bricks means, of course, "Let us make bricks." Grammatically, this is called a cognate accusative; the object of the verb is a noun from the same root as the verb. This is not an unusual construction in Hebrew; we may compare the statement of Jonah 1:16 that the pagan sailors "sacrificed sacrifices to Yahweh and vowed vows."

Let us burn to a burning also has a noun from the same root as the verb, but it is the object of the preposition, rather than the direct object of the verb. The expression means "to fire"; they proposed to make kiln-dried bricks, rather than settle for sun-dried bricks. These would be waterproof, and last many times longer. A number of the ziggurats of southern Mesopotamia, the architecture this text reflects, feature inner cores of rubble or of sun-dried (adobe) bricks, covered with outer layers of kiln-dried bricks. These, the visible parts of the structures, not only were fired, but sometimes were highly decorated.

An etymological irony exists in the choice of phrasing here. The Hebrew root of **burn** and **burning** is *śārap*. It also is the root of the title for some of God's most intimate attendants, the seraphim, "the burning ones," i.e., "the gloriously glowing, unapproachable ones who attend the enthroned presence of the Unapproachable One" (e.g., Isa 6:2, 6). These people, though, burned (fired) bricks for the purpose of approaching God with hostile intent, of coming into God's presence uninvited (because of their hostile intent), and by unauthorized means.

Lower Mesopotamia has no stone of the kinds, quality, and quantity needed for large building projects, and these people did not have the capacity to bring stone in from a long distance. The mortar mentioned here also required limestone or other calcium-rich material as a key ingredient; they could not make mortar, either. From the perspective of Canaan/Israel—the perspective of these finished texts—bricks (even fired bricks) and tar/pitch/bitumen/asphalt were poor substitutes for stone and mortar, the good building materials so abundantly available in the central highlands. *There was to them . . .* is a common way of expressing possession, but here it conveys a kind of amused, even sarcastic, condescension: "Look, they want to build an impressive project that will force their access to the heavens, but they don't even have the best, the strongest, the most esthetically pleasing building materials! Their failure is guaranteed before they start!"

■ **4** This is the second occurrence in this pericope of the hortatory, **Come;** see the comment above (v 3).

Let us build *for* **ourselves a city.** Cities are not intrinsically evil, but the phrase *for* **ourselves** already hints that the builders of this city were not looking to fulfill God's renewed mandate to populate the earth (9:1). Even a tower as an architectural feature of a city is not necessarily an ominous portent; a tower as an element of a city wall can serve nonmilitary, as well as defensive, purposes.

However, this was to be no ordinary tower. Most translations read, "with its head/top in the heavens," or something similar, but the Hebrew syntax actually is a bit stronger, **Let us build** *for* **ourselves a city,** *and* **a tower,** *and its* *[the tower's] head shall be in the heavens.* Did they really think they could raise a structure high enough to gain access to God's dwelling place? In this early period, perhaps they did; perhaps they did not. It is possible this way of stating their grandiose intentions was merely hyperbole; Deut 1:28, for example, speaks of cities fortified *to the heavens* (*baššāmayim*, the same phrase used here), and it clearly is intended as hyperbole there. Even if, as we probably should, we read it as hyperbole, rather than as their literal goal, this statement of intention nevertheless stands as an unabashed expression of bravado, the opposite of responsiveness to and reliance upon God.

Its Head in the Heavens: The Mesopotamian Ziggurat

The text here is describing a Mesopotamian ziggurat, a stepped solid "tower" between sixty and two hundred feet on each of its four sloping sides. The remains of nearly thirty ziggurats—some larger, some smaller—still exist in southern Mesopotamia; the earliest may be from the fifth millennium B.C. The ziggurat was not itself a temple for human worship. On the small platform at the top, it had a chamber for the use of the god for whom it was built. The temple of that god, where humans worshipped him or her, was a separate structure at the base of the ziggurat.

The name of the first-millennium ziggurat of Marduk (probably together with its temple) in Nebuchadnezzar's Babylon was Etemenanki, "The House of the foundation of heaven and earth." The ziggurat at Sippar was named, "Temple of the stairway to pure heaven." These and other names reveal the function of the ziggurats as intended by their builders. The top of the ziggurat was regarded as the gateway to heaven; the ziggurat itself was the stairway from earth to heaven. It is significant that our text does not represent the builders as saying they themselves intended to climb their tower/stairway to heaven, only that its "head" would, they proposed, "be in the heavens." This is, in effect, the first biblical mention of polytheism, of humans bringing "the gods" down to their location and, in the process, fashioning gods in their (our) own image.

And let us make for ourselves a name is yet another aspect of their purpose. As the Hebrew syntax presents it, the builders intended to build a city, to build a tower, and to make a **name** (i.e., a reputation) for themselves. They did not view the **name** as a hoped-for result of their building projects. It was the third part of their three-part plan for success.

What they hoped to achieve as the *result* of their efforts is expressed as a negative, *lest we be scattered over the face of all the earth.* With this negative expression of purpose/result, the reader's intuition is affirmed. This was not the first step in carrying out God's instruction to fill the earth, but a deliberate plan to do just the opposite, to stick together permanently in resisting God's blessing/mandate.

■ **5** *But Yahweh descended to see/evaluate the city and the tower which the earthlings built* [i.e., *were building*]. This verse is the hinge, the corner, or the bridge of the narrative; the narrator turns the reader's attention from the action of the "mere" mortals (***earthlings***) to the action of God (***Yahweh***). Consistent with his practice throughout, the narrator used the divine name ***Yahweh*** "where deity is thematic in a given paragraph" (Hamilton 1990, 286), i.e., when God acted (as here) directly and immediately; for convenience, we may say "immanently."

The narrator's use of ***earthlings*** (*bĕnê hāʾādām*) here is an amused, bemused, sardonic thrust of irony (again). The children of earth were firing the very material they were made of, physically, in an attempt to build an entry into God's presence. They were boasting that their marvelous structure would have "its head in the heavens." They imagined stepping from the top of their tower unto a street, or unto the floor of the heavenly palace of God. But it didn't turn out that way; God couldn't just look out a window and see their tower at eye level. So far were they from being successful in reaching the heavens that Yahweh "had" to come down to see what they were about: ***But Yahweh descended.*** Of course, this is the broadest stroke of irony in the entire narrative!

It is a much smaller point, but even the word order in this sentence reflects the proper evaluation of the situation. Yahweh's action and Yahweh's name come first; the earthlings' action and their collective name come last.

We have seen before, especially in Gen 1, the statement, "God saw," used in the sense of, "God evaluated." Here, we may see (evaluate) God's move as an act of justice. God descended to investigate and evaluate at first hand, as it were, the activities on the earth below that had drawn the attention of heaven above. No one would be able to accuse God of acting without knowing the facts.

The sense of the narrative to this point, and the specific statement later that the building project was left unfinished (v 8), lead us to understand the last verb here as meaning the earthlings **were building.** They were in process, engaged in continuing construction even as Yahweh **came down** to see. But the verbal form actually is a perfect, which usually would be translated "built," or even "had built." The narrator's point here is that though they did not know it yet, the project actually was finished. The perfect aspect of the Hebrew verb stresses completed action, whether from the narrative point of view of past, present, or future. The builders to that moment thought the project still had a significant future. ***But Yahweh descended*** and pronounced it finished. What they *had* built now was all they *would* build. The project was in fact ***built,*** finished, even though they were forced to leave it uncompleted. The verb here anticipates that outcome; the next verses state it explicitly.

■ **6** *Then Yahweh said, "Behold, [they are] one people, and they all possess one language, and this is [but] their beginning to do. And now there will not be withheld from them anything which they propose to do."*

We have translated rather woodenly, only to show that the Hebrew syntax does not exhibit, formally, the conditional structure of protasis and apodosis ("If . . . , then . . ."), as many versions render it. However, that is the import of God's words, "If this [already an impressive city and tower] is but the beginning of what this people can do, united, then nothing they decide to do will be beyond their abilities."

Of course, God's assessment was with respect to the earth and the spheres of human activity and influence upon it. God could not be threatened in God's person, nor could the existence of the universe, or of the earth itself, be cast into question by this or any other human activity. God knew, however, that a humanity forever united in ethnicity and language, and in their (our) perpetual bent to hubris, would deny itself nothing and could be denied by no one or nothing else, if God did not intervene.

We have noted that the arrangement of Gen 10—11 is not primarily chronological. This statement of God's assessment confirms that finding. Genesis 10 summarizes the rise of the families and kindreds of the earth, but without saying how they came to be dispersed. This narrative identifies the catalyst for the dispersal, rooted in God's assessment that continued unity of kindred and language would be a detriment to humans, in much the same way as our first parents' eating of the forbidden fruit had been. Mitigation of the worst effects then had been an act of God's grace. As unchecked hubris can lead only to disaster, God's intervention here would be of grace also.

God's observation, ***And now there will not be withheld from them anything which they propose to do,*** reveals God's recognition of human ability and potential on display in this enterprise. God knows humans are capable; God created humans to be capable. But this generation used God's good gifts sinfully, motivated by hubris and the conscious intent to circumvent God's expressed blessing/mandate. They had to be stopped, for the good of all the earthly creation. That said, God's judgment of what humans would be capable of, if God did nothing, affirms that human creation-gifted ability remains amazingly potent, even in its postfall diminishment, however much or little that may have been.

■ **7** The builders had said, twice, "Come, let us . . ." Now, God said, **Come, let us go down and *let us* confuse *there* their language so they will not *hear* [i.e., understand]** *each one the speech of his neighbor.*

Many have pointed out a seeming redundancy here. God already had "come down" (v 5); why would God now say, **Let us go down**? As in many other places, it is difficult to imagine that a later compiler would have done such a clumsy job of cutting and pasting, if this were the combining of two radically different sources. The idea that God had come part of the way down from heaven to see and evaluate the situation and now proposed to come all the way down to the city and the tower to accomplish the confusion of speech among the builders is not logically impossible, but it does seem forced.

Cassuto offers a more plausible solution, citing other passages also (e.g., 26:22; Exod 2:10) where "and [he or she] said" refers not to words spoken aloud, but to thought, to "reflection that took place at the same time as the action." Cassuto renders these verses, *"But the Lord came down . . .* thinking: *Behold, they are one people* etc.; therefore, *Come, let us go down*—it is desirable that I go down" (1964, 247). If humans engage in mental self-talk, perhaps it is another way we reflect our creation in God's image!

■ **8-9 So the LORD scattered them;** in such a short narrative, the text does not report God's act of confounding human speech; the statement of purpose immediately preceding is better literary artistry here. Stating the result of that action is sufficient to show God had done it.

God had blessed Noah and his family with the instruction to spread across the earth and fill it (9:1). A part of the conclusion of the genealogical segments of each of Noah's sons is the notice that they were dispersed in their territories, families, and languages (10:5, 20, 31); 10:32 even provides a concluding statement to that effect for all three sons, together. This simple statement reveals that this great dispersal was God's doing in the end. To accomplish God's purposes, God pushed the nestlings from the nest they had begun to build for themselves. With only a tiny remnant staying in place, we may infer, too few were left to finish the project, *so they left off building the city.* Work stoppage on the tower, too, is implicit in this report.

Babel is an Akkadian word meaning "[The] Gate(way) of/to God." Verse 9 amounts to a denial (or corrective) of that pagan idea. Far from being a gateway to God, or to the gods, Babel/Babylon was the place where God confronted this kind of human hubris and scattered the builders from God's presence, as it were. The narrator made the point with the deliberate use of a pun, substituting a similar-sounding Hebrew root (*balal*), the same verb God had used when declaring God's intention to confound the language of the builders (v 7).

In v 2, the narrator had reported, "and they settled <u>there</u>" (*šām*). Now he makes a point of using the same adverb, "there," twice in v 9, *because* <u>*there*</u> *Yahweh confused the speech of all the earth, and* <u>*from there*</u> *Yahweh dispersed them across the face of all the earth.* The place that generation had refused to leave became the place to which most of them never again returned.

Commodian on the Tower

They foolishly began to build a tower that touched the stars and thought they might be able to climb the skies with it. But God, seeing that their work proceeded because they spoke the same language, intervened and caused them to speak different languages. Then he scattered them by isolating them in the islands of the earth, so that nations speaking different tongues arose. (Louth 2001, 169)

Both this city and its citizens stand as early examples of the human pride and arrogance that continues in our own day—often, still, in the urban centers of human civilization. Humans continue to engage in prideful attempts to immortalize their accomplishments through city building and other enterprises. Individually and corporately, some do it with bricks, concrete, steel, and marble. Some do it in restless and relentless efforts to move upward in an upwardly mobile society. We often forget the truth, "Unless the LORD builds the house, its builders labor in vain" (Ps 127:1).

Where there is pride and rebellion, God steps in as the heavenly Judge. Many have viewed this *only* negatively, that God's decision to confuse the language was punishment of their rebellion and resistance to God's plans, of their attitudes of self-sufficiency and autonomy in their one-celled, microcosmic, proto-urban society. However, we also find here God fulfilling his will for his creation (Gen 1:28; 9:1) through this judgment of scattering. It resulted in the separation of humanity into distinctive ethnic and language groups. We even may say God created diversity in the human community as a gift to us, to promote cooperation and mutual understanding, and to enhance our personal and communal existence. From the perspective of the gracious freedom of God, we understand the end result of this judgment as something good and willed by God, because "in all things God works for the good" of God's creation (Rom 8:28).

On a related theme, we should note that God's multiplication of languages in this narrative is not a curse, but God's solution to human intransigence, and the catalyst for doing what God had instructed Noah and his sons to do from the beginning, as they first descended from the ark. For us, many centuries removed from that event, to view the abundance of languages as curse is to read into this narrative what it does not say. Language is a marvelous gift of God; that we are privileged to speak in such an abundance of delightful keys (to borrow an image from music) can be difficult work, but it cannot be a curse. John the Revelator hinted as much in reporting that he saw people of every language standing before the Lamb in the heavenly throne room (Rev 7:9).

The rest of the biblical story informs us that the God who divides and scatters in judgment is also the God who gathers and unites God's people to experience his redemptive plan. The next chapter (ch 12) focuses on the actual beginning of the gathering activity of God. God encountered and called Abram (Abraham), a member of this scattered humanity, to obedience so that through him God may unite and bless all the families of the earth (12:1-3). This narrative also anticipates the gathering of various nationalities and language groups in Jerusalem on the day of Pentecost—a varied multitude, all of whom heard and understood in their own languages the Spirit-filled proclamation of the gospel of Jesus Christ (Acts 2). The community created on that day is now no longer confined to the city of its origin, but exists as the people of God scattered strategically throughout the world, boldly proclaiming the gospel among all nationalities, ethnicities, and language groups.

VI. SHEM TO ABRAM, THE SECOND TEN (GENESIS 11:10-32)

BEHIND THE TEXT

The nine paragraphs of this genealogy share a number of common features: (1) the name of the patriarch; (2) his age at the birth of his first son; (3) the name of his first son; (4) the number of years he lived after the birth of his first son; (5) the report that he continued to sire sons and daughters; (6) the absence of the name of his wife; (7) the absence of the names of his further sons, and of any of his daughters. (The exception is the ninth paragraph concerning Terah; the data on Terah is exceptional in several ways, for reasons that will become apparent.) As we have seen, these also are the features of Seth's genealogy, Gen 5. The major difference between the two is that the narrator does not give the total life span of any in this list (except Terah).

The portion of the genealogy of ch 10 (the Table of Nations) pertaining to Shem (10:21-31) comprises five generations, comparable to those of Shem's brothers Japheth and Ham. The intent of that genealogy, as we have seen, is to show how the various peoples on ancient Israel's horizon related to each other from the common ancestry of Noah's three sons. By comparison, this list spans ten generations, if we count Abram (Abraham) and his brothers, as we should do, since the purpose of this second genealogy of Shem is to arrive at Terah's son Abram. Structurally, the major difference between these two genealogies reflects those two differing purposes. The genealogy of Gen 10 is segmented ("horizontal," in naming several offspring in some of the generational levels), while this one is linear ("vertical"); it names only the eldest son in each of the succeeding generations.

For more on the names and the persons of the first five in this genealogy, from Shem through Peleg, see the commentary on 10:21-25.

■ **10-11** *These are the accounts of Shem;* see the Introduction, "These Are the *Toledot*" under The Literary Forms of Genesis 1—11.

Shem was one hundred years old, and he begat Arphaxad, two years after the flood. This statement appears to supply the one additional piece of information needed to solve the question of the birth order of Noah's sons. Noah first became a father at the age of five hundred years (5:32). Noah was six hundred years old when the flood came (7:6). Shem was one hundred years old when he fathered Arphaxad, two years after the flood. This would place Noah's age at Shem's birth at five hundred two years. Ham was Noah's youngest son (9:24). Japheth, then, was the son who first made Noah a father at the age of five hundred years; Shem was two years younger than Japheth.

Shem's total life span was six hundred years. As a transitional figure between the generations before the flood and those after the flood, Shem lived a shorter life than his ancestors, but a longer life than his descendants.

Shorter Life Spans After the Flood

As often noted, the life span of the preflood patriarchs was more than double that of their immediate postflood descendants. Most of those of the preflood era are recorded as living more than nine hundred years. Following Shem, the first generations after the flood lived a little more than four hundred years. The second group in this genealogy of Shem lived about two hundred years, or a bit more. Life expectancy was halved, then halved again. If we take the numbers literally, this would seem to represent a cumulative effect of sin and evil upon the human person. A nonliteral approach to the numbers still could view this as one of the didactic intentions of these genealogies, together.

■ **12-17** Shem's son Arphaxad lived altogether four hundred thirty-eight years. Shem's grandson, Shelah, lived four hundred thirty-three years. Shem's great-grandson, Eber, lived four hundred sixty-four years. These three generations reached, essentially, half the average life span of the generations before the flood, excluding Enoch and including Noah. For more on these men, see the commentary on 10:22, 24-25, above.

■ **18-25** Eber's son, Peleg, lived "only" two hundred thirty-nine years, just over half the life span of his father. The segmented genealogy of Shem (10:21-31), ending with Peleg and his brother Joktan, noted that Peleg was named "Division" because in his days the earth was divided (10:25). The primary intention of that statement almost certainly is to foreshadow the scattering of the peoples as a result of the confusion of languages at Babel, the account reported only a few short verses later (11:1-9). We may note in passing, however, that Peleg's generation marked another kind of division, also, this one between the postdiluvians of a longer life span and those of a shorter life span. The first "step down," to a little over four hundred years, ended with Peleg's father Eber; the second "step down" began with Peleg.

Peleg's son Reu also lived two hundred thirty-nine years. Reu's son Serug lived two hundred thirty years. The average life span of these three, then, was essentially half the life span of the three generations immediately preceding them. Within six generations, from Noah to Peleg, the average life span noted in these genealogies went from nine hundred years to just over two hundred years. Serug's son Nahor died after reaching only one hundred forty-eight years.

■ **26** The last paragraph in this genealogy concerns Terah, son of Nahor. We have seen already, with Noah's entry at the end of the first Genesis genealogy (5:32), this change from linear to segmented (in the naming of three sons), as a way of concluding a genealogy. It is more than an ending, however. This change of pattern also signals that in this generation, something more than "merely" the passing of the generations will occur. In the genealogy of Gen 5, from Adam to Noah is ten generations; the name, Noah, was the "goal" of that genealogy. From Shem to Abram also is ten generations, indicating that the name Abram, likewise, is the "goal" of this one. It will prove to be a different sort of salvation story, but the salvation inaugurated by God's finding of a righteous partner in Abram will have eternal ramifications at least as great as the deliverance through Noah.

This is the first occurrence in Scripture of the name Abram; as Abraham (see 17:5), he would become perhaps the most significant OT personage and certainly the most consequential OT figure for the NT explication of the meaning of faith. In both Testaments together, Abram/Abraham is mentioned about two hundred eighty times. With no evidence to suggest otherwise (as there is with the sons of Noah, for example), it is reasonable to assume the text here lists Terah's three sons in their order of birth.

■ **27-28** *Now these are the accounts of Terah.* This notice breaks up the genealogical entry for Terah, as the narrator had done with Noah's also. Here, the "insertion" is much briefer, only five verses (vv 27-31) as compared with four chapters between the initial facts of Noah's entry in Adam's genealogical line (5:32) and the notice of Noah's death (9:28-29). The repetition of the names of Terah's three sons, when they had been listed already in the verse immediately preceding, is occasioned, even required, by the introduction of this "insertion" by its title, *these are the accounts of Terah.*

On the face of it, it is unusual to list the offspring of the youngest son first. Here, the narrator did so for at least three reasons. The first is the notice, immediately following, that Haran died before Terah died, even before the family moved from Ur to Haran (v 31). Haran himself would not be part of that move. But Haran did father three children, and they would be part of the story immediately. By contrast, neither Abraham nor Nahor would father children for quite some time. Together, these facts constitute the narrator's second reason for listing Haran's children here. Finally, within a very few verses, the reader will learn this is to be the record of God's calling of Abram, of Abram's response to and adventure with God. Anything extraneous to that focus is not included in the narrative. Anything that is important, but can be dealt with early on, is dealt with early on, then set aside.

It is important to emphasize straightaway, though it is an aside here, that the city of Haran, where Terah settled with members of his family (v 31) was not named for Terah's deceased son Haran. The name of the son is spelled with Hebrew *he*; the name of the city is spelled with Hebrew *het*. In Hebrew, these two letters are not interchangeable; it is unfortunate they are spelled identically in English.

The phrase **Ur of the Chaldeans** presents a well-known problem. The name **Chaldeans** is not the problem, though the Chaldeans did not reach the region of the southern Ur until several centuries after Terah's time. Insertions of place names or gentilic designations from later times (anachronistic names) into the biblical text are quite common, for the sake of later readers who would not recognize or know the locations by their earlier names. Another example of this, only three chapters on, is Abram's retrieval of his nephew Lot; a later scribe used the place name "Dan," though in Abram's day it was known as Laish (14:14).

The issue here is whether this Ur where Haran died is the famous Sumerian Ur of southern Mesopotamia or a lesser-known Ur in northern Mesopotamia, not far from the city of Haran. (The northern city also could have been characterized as "Ur of the Chaldees/Kasdim," meaning the original Chaldean homeland before they migrated to the region of the southern Ur.) Significant arguments exist in favor of both. Hamilton provides an excellent summary, then comes down in favor of the northern Ur (1990, 363-65).

Three names in this genealogy seem to support a northern location for Terah's family. Serug was Terah's grandfather, Nahor was Terah's father (after whom Terah named his second son, also, vv 22, 24, 26). However, Terah (Tell Terah) also was a town in the valley of the Balikh River, a tributary of the Euphrates in northern Mesopotamia. Serug (Sarugi/Saroug) and Nahor (Nahur) also are nearby place names; Nahur is mentioned in the Mari letters from about the time of Abraham. Finally, all three of these towns were not far from Haran, where Terah settled with his family before he died (v 32).

One set of factors that has been used on both sides of this issue is the supposed worship of the moon god, Sin, by Terah and his family. Both Ur in southern Mesopotamia and Haran in northern Mesopotamia were centers of this god's cult (temples, etc.). Terah's own name is one of several forms meaning "moon." (Some scholars associate his name with Akkadian "ibex.") If Terah moved from one center of moon worship to another, it would lend credence to the supposition that he and his family worshiped the moon god. In the end, whether Terah's son Haran lived and died in the better-known southern Ur or in the lesser-known northern Ur is an interesting question but not a crucial one.

■ **29** **Sarai** is introduced at this point in the narrative because she soon will become one of its central characters, as the focus shifts to Abraham. **Nahor** and **Milcah** will have a small but important place, also, so it is appropriate to introduce them here, as well. **Iscah** is included as the sister of Milcah, though she will not be mentioned again.

Some have suggested that because Lot is not included here, the Haran who fathered the two sisters was a different Haran from Lot's father (e.g., Cassuto 1964, 277). It seems more likely that Lot is not mentioned here because the focus is primarily on the two wives, Sarai and Milcah, of the two surviving brothers, Abram and Nahor. Lot already had been introduced as Haran's son; it was not necessary to repeat his name here.

If this is correct, then Nahor married his niece, Milcah. It was not a common practice even then, but it was one way to provide for orphaned daughters who were not yet married at the time of their father's death. It is worth noting that even the later list of Lev 18 did not prohibit marriage to one's niece.

■ **30** Sarai's barrenness will become a central issue in the unfolding of her life with Abram; it is appropriate to give the reader that information right from the start. By implication later in the narrative (22:20), Milcah also did not bear children to Nahor for some years. Abraham did not hear of his nephews' births until after the near-sacrifice of Isaac, when Isaac was about seventeen years old. That information is not important to the narrative yet, however, so the narrator leaves it aside for the time being.

■ **31** In the patriarchal system of most of ancient western Asia, Terah was head of his entire extended household. Within that system it was appropriate for him to take with him his eldest son Abram, and Abram's wife, ***Sarai his daughter-in-law,*** as the text identifies her, when he moved from one place to another. It was appropriate for him to take his grandson Lot, son of his own deceased son Haran. The surprising development here lies in whom the text does *not* say Terah took with them, namely, his other surviving son Nahor and Nahor's wife, Milcah. (That Iscah is not mentioned here may indicate she now was married outside the family, or to a more distant relative than her sister Milcah had married, and now "belonged" to her husband's family.)

Why did not Nahor and Milcah journey with the others? The text gives no hint. This surprising omission may constitute, however, indirect evidence that the family was from the northern rather than from the southern Ur (see comments on v 28, above). Later on, Abraham sent his servant (probably Eliezer; see 15:2) to find a wife for his son Isaac, from among his brother Nahor's family, and the servant traveled to ***the city of Nahor*** (24:10) in Aram-Naharaim ("Aram of the two rivers," i.e., to the northern region between the Euphrates and the Tigris), rather than to the Ur in southern Mesopotamia. Whether ***the city of Nahor*** (Nahur) was named for Abraham's grandfather

11:27-31

Nahor, or for his brother Nahor, the family had a strong presence in northern Mesopotamia, suggesting that **Ur of the Khasdim/Chaldees** was not far away. If Abram's brother Nahor had stayed behind in the southern Ur when the rest of the family moved away, why and how would Abram's (by then, Abraham's) servant find Nahor's grandchildren in **the city of Nahor** in northern Mesopotamia (near the present-day Turkish-Syrian border)?

Cassuto asserts there was no need to list everyone who accompanied Terah on this first stage of the journey. Abram is listed as Terah's son and principal heir, and the person on whom the narrative will focus from here on out. Sarai is listed as Abram's spouse, and because she, too, will be a principal character in the succeeding narrative. Lot is listed because his father already had died, and because he would accompany Abram and Sarai on their subsequent journey to Canaan. As that journey really was the project of Abram, Sarai, and Lot (Cassuto reasons), the narrator mentioned only Terah, as head of the household, of the rest who journeyed as far as Haran. The reader may and should assume that Nahor and Milcah also journeyed to Haran with the rest of the family. Like Terah, though, they did not continue on to Canaan (Cassuto 1964, 277-82).

To go to the land of Canaan; if Terah and his family traveled from the southern Ur, they would have journeyed along or near the Euphrates in a northwesterly direction. Haran was an important crossroads city in the upper Balıkh River valley; in Akkadian, *harranu* means "road" and also "caravan" (i.e., "those who travel the road"). The Balikh is a tributary of the Euphrates, flowing into it from the north. From the southern Ur, Haran would not have been far out of the way of a direct route to Canaan ("direct" for those days, when travel straight across the Syrian Desert was not possible).

Starting from a nearby northern Ur, it also could have made sense to pass through Haran on the way to Canaan, depending on exactly where the northern Ur was located (still a matter of some conjecture). However, if Terah started from a nearby northern Ur, why did he stop (permanently, for him) in Haran, when his destination had been Canaan? This conundrum would seem to lend support to identification of **Ur of the Chaldees/Khasdim** as the southern Ur.

In Cassuto's discussion already cited, he argues for Canaan as being really Abram's destination, not Terah's (1964, 280-82). The others went as far as Haran with him, Sarai, and Lot. Because Haran, like Ur (Cassuto favored the southern Ur), was a center of worship of the moon god, Sin, and they were not the thoroughgoing Yahwists Abram had become, they settled in Haran. Abram, Sarai, and Lot, after a stay of unspecified length in Haran (12:5), continued on to their real destination of Canaan. Cassuto's line of reasoning here deserves consideration.

■ **32** Since this is the notice of Terah's death, it would be easy to assume Abram waited in Haran for his elderly father to die before resuming the journey to Canaan. The numbers do not allow for that assumption, however. Terah was seventy years old when he fathered Abram (v 26). Abram was seventy-five years old when he set out for Canaan from Haran (12:4). Therefore, Terah was one hundred forty-five years old when Abram left him (and perhaps his brother Nahor, also?) to go to Canaan. Isaac was born when his father, now Abraham, was one hundred years old (21:5), making Terah a grandfather once again at the age of one hundred seventy years. Terah lived to the age of two hundred five years; Isaac was then thirty-five. Isaac married his first cousin once removed, Rebekah, when he was forty years old (25:20). Though we are justified in assuming Isaac never met his grandfather, Terah had been dead only five years when his grandson and his great-granddaughter married.

This last verse of the Primeval Prologue also is the last entry of its genealogical information. As noted above (on v 27), this conclusion of Terah's entry follows a five-verse "insertion" that serves to introduce the characters who will become central in the next section of Genesis, and the family move to Haran that set the stage, as it were, for the world-changing events recounted there. Abram/Abraham will stand at center stage for most of the next fourteen chapters of Genesis.

FROM THE TEXT

Theologically, the last narrative snippet of the Primeval Prologue (v 32) serves as a "bridge," as the canonical link, between the primeval and the patriarchal narratives. Terah's journey from Ur to Haran is the last reported movement of the generations scattered upon the cessation of the building at Babel. But Terah's journey also represents the beginning of the patriarchal journeys, of their sojourning as resident aliens in lands not yet theirs. This is so, if only by reason of the fact that Terah took his son Abram with him when he left their ancestral home. Terah and his journey are the indispensable link, theologically and literarily, as well as geographically, between the Mesopotamian primeval world and the new "western" world of the patriarchal narratives to follow.

Terah's journey also is the earliest representation of "journey" as a theological motif. This journey stands as the very beginning of God's specific actions to create the promised community. In allowing us the exercise of divinely granted free will, God works within (as well as outside) the arena of human desires, plans, hopes, and dreams. We do not know what prompted Terah's journey from Mesopotamia, but his was the first of many journeys in the process of God's regathering of the scattered human race into a community of believers, into God's own family. So much is this the case, that "journey," "way," "progress," and many similar terms are common in our expression of our own relationships with God and with God's people, our fellows upon the way. Lest we think this "journey" characterization is an idiosyncrasy of the modern church, we may recall that it forms the opening of Stephen's defense

303

before the council that condemned him, in which Stephen not only mentioned Abraham by name but also specifically referenced Terah in the phrase, *after his father died* (Acts 7:4).

The theological history of the human species represented by the Primeval Prologue has come to an end. As portrayed by the narrator of Genesis, that history has been virtually unmitigated failure, frustration, and futility. The genealogical notice of Terah's death in Haran is its fitting conclusion. Yet God never leaves God's people without hope, even in the direst of circumstances. Already the reader has been introduced to Terah's son, Abram (Abraham). The astute reader understands—"merely" by virtue of the fact that the story continues in the persons of Abram and Sarai—that this is not a story devoid of hope. God has planned a great reversal, its beginnings to be realized in these two.

But even hopeful stories have twists and turns, and the narrator already has introduced us to a major turn in this one: Sarai was barren. Brueggemann characterizes this stark moment vividly, "This family (and with it the whole family of Genesis 1-11) has played out its future and has nowhere else to go. Barrenness is the way of human history. It is an effective metaphor for hopelessness. There is no foreseeable future. There is no human power to invent a future" (1982, 116).

But, as we have said above, this chapter ending is not only a gap but also a link. Brueggemann continues (his entire comment here, 116-17, is worth reading), "But barrenness is not only the condition of hopeless humanity. The marvel of biblical faith is that barrenness is the arena of God's life-giving action." We will find it to be so as we turn to Abraham and Sarah's story, as it has its "real" beginning in Gen 12. The rest of the biblical witness is an eloquent affirmation that all who believe, as simply and as profoundly as they believed, will experience "God's life-giving action" for themselves, will be no longer "barren."